SPY ON THE ROOF
OF THE WORLD

SPY ON THE ROOF
OF THE WORLD

Sydney Wignall

LYONS & BURFORD, PUBLISHERS

First published in Great Britain in 1996 by Canongate Books Ltd, 14 Hight Street, Edinburgh.

Printed in the United States of America

1   3   5   7   9   10   8   6   4   2

Library of Congress Cataloging-in-Publication Data

Wignall, Sydney.
Spy on the roof of the world / Sydney Wignall.
p.   cm.
Originally published: Great Britain : Canongate Books Ltd., 1996.
ISBN 1-55821-558-1 (hc)
1. Wignall, Sydney—Journeys—China—Tibet.   2. Espionage, British—China—Tibet.   I. Title.
DS786.W46   1997
915.1'50455—dc21   96-47350
CIP

THIS BOOK IS DEDICATED TO
THE TIBETAN PEOPLE
WHO HAVE SUFFERED MORE THAN FORTY YEARS
OF CHINESE COLONIALIST OPPRESSION

also to
THE INDIAN ARMY
AND TO THE MEMORY OF
THE FOLLOWING PRINCIPAL PLAYERS IN MY STORY

GENERAL K.S. THIMAYYA DSO
FORMER CHIEF OF STAFF INDIAN ARMY
whose warning that the Chinese communist military build-up in Tibet posed a threat to India's northern border was ignored by Prime Minister Nehru

LT-COLONEL B.N. 'BAIJ' MEHTA MA
INDIAN ARMY
my Case Officer, killed in action during the Chinese invasion of northern India, 1962

SUN TIAN-SUN
a soldier in the People's Liberation Army of the People's Republic of China, executed south-west Tibet, 1956

and
GIN DIN RHOU
Abbot of Jitkot lamasery, died in a Chinese slave labour camp during the Cultural Revolution

Foreword

The title of this book was suggested to me in 1969 by the late Trevor Howard. We were enjoying a quiet drink in a bar in Dingle, County Kerry, Ireland. Howard was playing in David Lean's film *Ryan's Daughter* which was being shot in the Dingle peninsula. My excavation of a flagship of the 1588 Spanish Armada off Great Blasket island was into its second year.

Trevor was a great cricketing buff, and he was fascinated by the story about my old headmaster Mr A. W. Heap who, as a fourteen-year-old boy, had bowled out the immortal W. G. Grace for a 'duck'. When I enlarged on my cricketing tale to explain how it became part of my 'acceptance credentials' for spying on the Chinese People's Liberation Army in Tibet in 1955, Howard said, 'Write the book. I've got the title for you. Call it "A Spy on the Roof of the World".'

I explained to Trevor Howard that although parts but not the whole story had been told elsewhere, I could not reveal my intelligence-gathering role in print for at least another eleven years, because I had given my word to Indian Army friends that the true story would be secret for at least twenty-five years. This to protect the careers or pensions of Indian Army officers who, motivated by patriotism and love of Mother India, had decided to disobey Prime Minister Nehru's instructions that no intelligence-gathering activities were to be targeted against Nehru's new-found 'anti-colonialist' friends Mao Tse-tung and Chou En-lai, and the rapidly expanding Chinese communist army in Tibet.

Two major figures now enter my story. The first is General K. S. Thimayya DSO, arguably the most brilliant soldier India ever produced (the only Indian national to command a brigade under the British in World War Two). Thimayya made no secret of the fact that he regarded Nehru's right-hand man Krishna Menon as a communist. Indeed, Thimayya was eventually to make that accusation in public.

It is against the above background that General Thimayya, known with affection by all ranks of the Indian Army as 'Timmy', set in motion intelligence-gathering operations to obtain proof that the Chinese were building up a huge army in Tibet and had ambitions to wrest territory from India, by force if necessary. I became one of 'Timmy's Boys', unpaid agents whose task it was to potter around the Tibetan border seeking intelligence data. It led me to a face-to-face meeting with he who had commanded the Chinese communist invasion of Tibet five years earlier, the infamous 'Butcher of Tibet' General Chang Kuo-hua, and to a freezing cold, rat-infested prison cell in south-west Tibet, accused of being an agent, not of India, but of the American CIA. I regarded that as a well-deserved promotion.

For those readers unfamiliar with China's recent history, there follows a brief summary of the major events in China relating to my story.

The demise of China's Manchu dynasty in 1911 resulted in the rise to power of Dr Sun Yat-sen's Kuomintang (KMT) nationalist party (a disparate body of liberal idealist pro-democracy groups). The new Chinese republic attempted to unify the country with a promise to end poverty, exploitation by landlords and money lenders, not to mention the oppressive warlords. It ended in acrimony and finally in civil war between Sun Yat-sen's successor General Chiang Kai-shek and the burgeoning Chinese Communist Party.

The Japanese invaded Manchuria in 1931, and thrust into northern China proper in 1937. The Japanese occupation of China lasted until 1945, during which time the KMT and the communists (led by Mao Tse-tung) formed an uneasy alliance against the Japanese invaders.

In 1946 the Chinese Civil War broke out as the two adversaries fought for control of China. The KMT, finally routed by the communists in 1949, fled to Formosa (now Taiwan), where they established their self-proclaimed Chinese Republic, which continued to occupy China's seat in the United Nations.

The Chinese mainland, now freed from Japanese occupation, was a land laid waste. During nine years of Japanese occupation, China had been drained of natural resources to feed Japan's war machine. Industrial output was low, wages unpaid and peasants died of starvation.

Mao Tse-tung, realising that revitalising China's bankrupt economy, to which he planned to add the unpopular move of nationalising all land, could lead to unrest, decided on a course of action intended to distract people's minds from their own problems by entering into 'a popular war of liberation'. The target was to be Tibet.

In 1950, the People's Liberation Army (PLA) commanded by General Chang Kuo-hua invaded the independent God-Kingdom of Tibet.

My recruitment into an espionage role led me to illegally enter Tibet in October 1955, heading for the mountain of my dreams, 25,355-foot-high Gurla Mandhata, carrying a British passport and a loaded, cocked Browning automatic pistol. It also led to me meeting three of the four individuals named in the dedication to this book – an Indian Army officer, a Chinese soldier and a Tibetan lama. All three were to die at the hands of the Chinese communists. I survived, but only just.

This then is the story of how I became a spy on the roof of the world. It is also the story of how history might have been changed by a discarded Chinese cigarette packet bearing the emblem of a flying horse.

Sydney Wignall
Gwynedd
North Wales
United Kingdom

Acknowledgements

I wish to place on record my admiration for those Indian Army officers who formed General Thimayya's clandestine intelligence-gathering band. I have to thank one of the remaining survivors with whom I have kept in touch, for assistance in setting out the details of how it all came into being. He has asked to remain anonymous and I must respect his wishes. I can only state that he was one of the survivors of the 4th Division, Indian Army which sustained 90 per cent casualties when the Chinese People's Liberation Army invaded northern India in 1962.

I must express my gratitude to the Marquess of Anglesey, whose agreement to be patron of our expedition assured us both academic and financial support. I am most grateful to Sir John Mills CBE for proof-reading and warm endorsement of this book. Similar thanks are due to Lord Alexander Rufus-Isaacs, of the Hollywood and Beverly Hills Cricket Club; and film producer Bryan Forbes for wise counsel.

For leg-work in researching recent events in India and Nepal I am indebted to my friends Chris Balmforth, Chandra Mohan and editor of the *Himalayan Journal*, Harish Kapadia. For up-to-date information on the perceived threat on Indian soil, to the life of the Dalai Lama, by Chinese communist spies, I am grateful to Guy Williams of the Tibet Support Group UK and the *World Tibet News Network*. Bereft of a photograph of my place of incarceration, Taklakot, the gap was filled by Bryan Beresford who in recent years has travelled extensively in the area. Beresford's photograph shows the Taklakot cave dwellings and traders' tented bazaar. My former prison is just fifty yards out of frame in Beresford's photograph.

I must record my appreciation to Bill Massey and Judy Moir for the patient editing of this book. And I must *take time* to thank Rolex for providing my expeditions with chronometers for the past thirty-eight years.

List of Maps and Sketches

Tibet and Neighbouring Countries   xiv
Chinese Highways   xv
Plan of the Taklakot area   78
Author's sketch of the view from his cell   118

List of Black-and-White Plates

Page 1   The author at base camp, West Nepal, 1955
Page 2   Members of the expedition at base camp
Page 3   Damodar Suwal, our official Nepalese government liaison
         officer
Page 4   Koila, the Sirdar of the expedition's Nepalese porters
Page 5   John Harrop's birthday peak
Page 6   The camp comedian does a dance for the camera
Page 7   Tibetan traders at the base camp making yak butter tea
Page 8   The author crossing a river in full monsoon flood in West
         Nepal
Page 9   Entrance to the Seti Gorge in summer
Page 10 View into Tibet from the Nepal border
Page 11 The author in the Jung Jung Khola, illegally entering Tibet
         The cave dwellings and tented traders bazaar, Taklakot
         (by kind permission of Brian Beresford, taken 1992)
Page 12 The winter return over the Himalayas from Taklakot
Page 13 Both sides of the Chinese cigarette packets
Page 14 Damodar makes use of the Chinese flag
         Descending into the Seti Gorge, 18 December 1955
Page 15 The village of Dhuli, the first habitation reached on the return
         march from Tibet
Page 16 At Chainpur: John Harrop, Major R. M. Dass, the author and
         Mr Ram Wat Awhastie, the local schoolmaster

Photographs by the author and John Harrop were taken on Kodachrome
1, emulsion speed 10 ASA.

TIBET AND NEIGHBOURING COUNTRIES

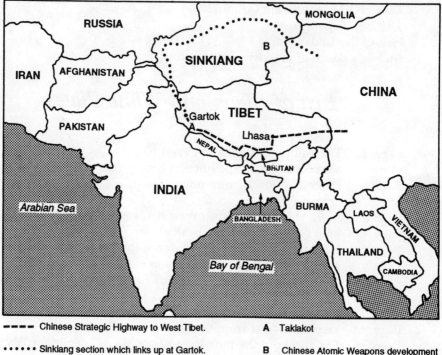

- – – – Chinese Strategic Highway to West Tibet.
- • • • • Sinkiang section which links up at Gartok.

A Taklakot

B Chinese Atomic Weapons development at Lop Nor.

CHINESE HIGHWAYS

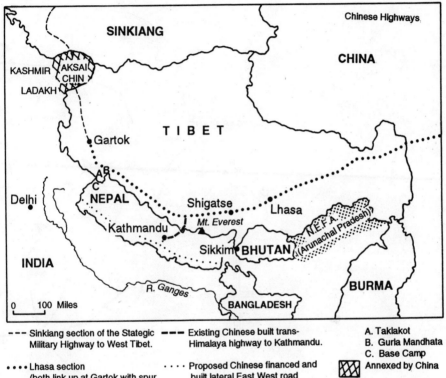

Chinese Highways

SINKIANG

CHINA

KASHMIR — AKSAI CHIN

LADAKH

TIBET

Gartok

Delhi

A
B
C

NEPAL

Shigatse   Lhasa

Kathmandu   Mt. Everest

N.E.F.A.
(Arunachal Pradesh)

Sikkim BHUTAN

INDIA

R. Ganges

BURMA

0   100 Miles

BANGLADESH

- - - Sinkiang section of the Stategic
Military Highway to West Tibet.

▪▪▪▪ Lhasa section
(both link up at Gartok with spur
road to Taklakot)

▬▬ Existing Chinese built trans-
Himalaya highway to Kathmandu.

· · · · Proposed Chinese financed and
built lateral East West road
on South side of the Himalayas.

A. Taklakot
B. Gurla Mandhata
C. Base Camp

Annexed by China

Claimed by China

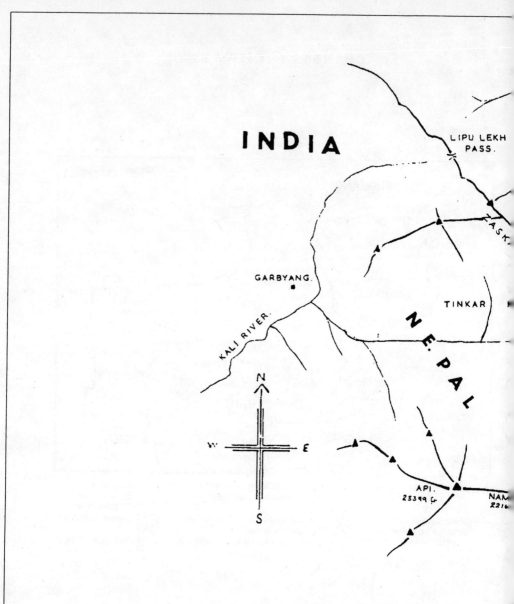

REVISED MAP OF WEST NEPAL AND SOUTH WEST TIBET
by S. Wignall and J.F. Harrop. Welsh Himalayan Expedition 1955

Scale 0 1 2 3 4 MILES

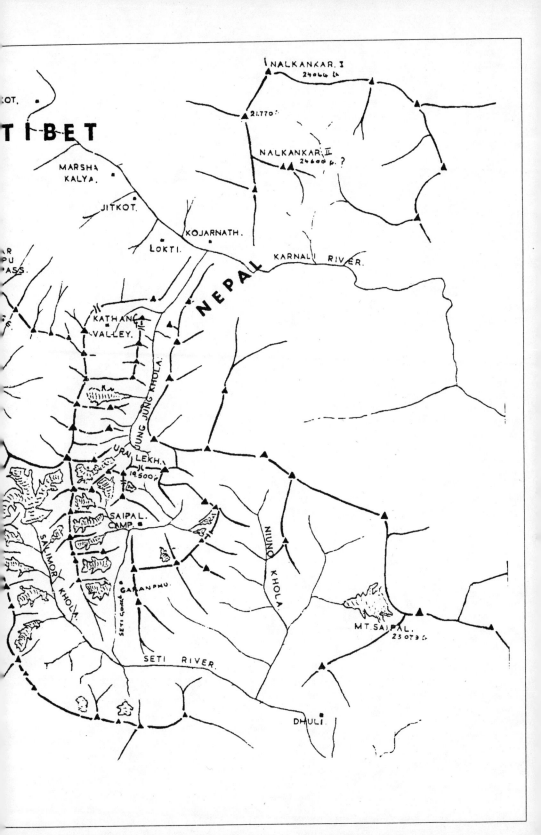

Prologue

B y the light of a flickering candle stub I wrote up my diary of the day's events, to wit the intensive interrogation I had been subjected to by my captors, the People's Liberation Army of the Republic of China, who had imprisoned me in Tibet, at Taklakot (now called Burang by the Chinese), a Tibetan provincial centre, close by the borders of both India and Nepal.

Only one of my interrogators spoke passable English. I and my companions in incarceration, John Harrop and Damodar Narayan Suwal, called him 'Smoothy' because of his oily, unctuous manner. I sat up in my quadruple-layered down-filled sleeping bag. It was identical to those used on the ascent of Mount Everest two years earlier. That bag should have kept me warm, but the temperature inside my unheated mud-walled prison cell often dropped to 20 below and rarely rose above freezing point, and most nights I shivered and slept badly. Occasionally I had to visit the lavatory in our prison yard, which consisted of a couple of deep holes dug into the hard ground. I would climb out of my bag, put on my boots, walk bent double to the cell door (because the ceiling of my cell was so low I could not stand upright), knock hard, and eventually a Chinese guard, clad in a khaki quilted jacket and trousers with a padded greatcoat on top, would open the cell door and conduct me to the prison's primitive thunder hole. At all times the guard would keep his 7.65 mm PPSh assault rifle pointed at me.

That night, I had a tale to tell to my illicit diary. The Chinese had forbidden us to make notes or write letters home. But after a 'Thought Reform' session that very day, Smoothy had granted me a concession. I had grown tired of the interminable accusations that I was a 'Western Fascist Lackey Imperialist Running Dog', and having all my truthful answers to questions being thrown back into my face with the by now familiar cry of, 'What you say is a lie. You must answer more honestly.' I had made up a fictional story of a UK-based spy ring, operating on behalf of the American Central Intelligence Agency. Smoothy took it all in, and then stated, 'You have been more honest today. As a concession you may have some writing paper. On this you will write down your life's history from the age of eight so that we can analyse the contents and find out at what age you became a Western Fascist Lackey Imperialist Running Dog.'

The writing paper proved to be very thin Indian toilet paper. Toilet paper was something of which I was in great need. I kept having a recurrence of dysentery, resulting in the passing of blood, severe dehydration, dizzy spells and occasional lapses into unconsciousness. Harrop, Damodar and I regarded toilet paper as the one facet of civilised society we greatly missed. I decided to tell Smoothy at my next Thought Reform session that I had used all the toilet paper for the abstersion of my fundament.

In the meantime, after completing my notes on the day's interrogation session, I duly rolled up a thin sheet of paper and pushed it down the inflation tube of the pillow of my inflatable mattress. The diary was written not only on toilet paper, but also on chocolate wrappers (last vestiges of our high altitude rations not confiscated by the Chinese) and also our Chinese guards' cast-away cigarette packets. I was eventually to take it with me, out of Tibet, after my release from imprisonment by those whom the Indian and Nepalese traders and the Tibetans referred to as 'The Cheenee Burra Rajah Sahibs' (The Chinese Great Royal Gentlemen).

I snuggled down in my Everest bag, and pulled my woollen balaclava helmet right down over my face. I was wearing a shirt I had not washed for more than two months. Once a week I turned it inside out, or outside in. It mattered little. The inside of my sleeping bag had long since acquired the gentle fragrance of a skunk's armpit.

I reached out of my bag to grasp the mug of Chinese tea I had taken into my cell at dusk. It was a wasted effort. The tea had frozen into a solid block of ice. There was a wind blowing outside. The two unglazed windows in my cell, each only about six inches in diameter, one looking south towards the Himalaya and Nepal, the other looking to the east, admitted a constant icy draught. My candle flame flickered. It died out. I still had my three-cell electric torch, and there was just a little life left in the batteries. I lay on my back, and gradually dozed off to sleep.

Sometime in the night, I was conscious of something warm on my forehead. I switched on my torch, and shone the beam onto my head. I could espy a ball of black wool in the mouth of Megan, a good Welsh name. Megan was a pregnant Tibetan snub-nosed tail-less rodent, and she had entered my bag while I was asleep, bitten into my woollen sweater, and retreating onto my forehead, was in the process of winding in wool, rotating it in her mouth, for the nest she was preparing for her offspring.

I reached into my bag, and with both hands snapped off the thread. Megan was at this game every night, and the hole in the chest of my sweater kept increasing in size. At this rate, I would have no sweater left by the time Megan gave birth. I shooed her away with a cry of, 'Right Mrs, that's your lot.'

I couldn't get back to sleep. The wind was getting up and we were now deep into winter. All the passes to the south, into Nepal and India, were closed until the spring. I shivered. 'Christ, if they ever let us go, how the hell will we get back over the top in winter?'

I ruminated on our plight. Harrop, my expedition surveyor and deputy leader of the first Welsh Himalayan Expedition, which I was privileged to lead, was a completely innocent party to all this, as was eighteen-year-old Damodar Narayan Suwal, our Nepalese Liaison Officer, who was a student from Kathmandu. I was not an agent of the hated CIA, as my Chinese captors would insist. But I was on a Security Penetration and Intelligence Gathering exercise for India. I avoided thinking of myself as a spy, although that in fact is what I was. I was no professional. I was not trained in espionage. I had neither been offered nor had I requested any financial remuneration.

The public at large think of spies in terms of James Bond: dashing devil-may-care fellows. The truth is far different. There is no such thing as a typical spy. Security services the world over often recruit 'stringers' either as intelligence gatherers or as couriers. The most common intelligence stringer is the foreign correspondent. A great many European and American media correspondents have in the past worked for their respective governments' intelligence services. What is not generally known is that explorers are sometimes requested to obtain intelligence data, or carry messages. I had been recruited on just that basis, earlier that same year.

'I must have been mad,' I said to myself as I shivered in my sleeping bag. 'You are a married man, with a wife and small son, and you owe nothing to those who recruited you. You are more or less on trial for your life; you could spend years in a Chinese prison, and for what? A love of India? The spirit of adventure?'

1

My visions of organising and leading a Himalayan expedition began in 1954 in the bar of the Bryn Tyrch Hotel in Capel Curig, Snowdonia. I had just come down from climbing on the Three Cliffs at Llanberis with two of the old-guard rock climbers, Scotty Dwyer and Dickie Maudsley. Alcoholic oiling of the wheels set in motion my plan for us to form the Mountaineering Club of North Wales. We clubbed together, and raised £5. I was appointed secretary by Scotty and Dickie, and we soon enlisted another fifteen enthusiasts. Within a week we had stationery printed in red and green Welsh national colours, with a dragon, climbing rope and ice-axe motif professionally drawn by our club treasurer, Fred Taylor, a retired commercial artist who owned a guest house in Capel Curig. Within three weeks I sprang my bombshell. 'Why don't we plan and organise the first ever Welsh Himalayan expedition?' I fully expected raspberries all round, but received nothing but encouragement. Who should lead the first Welsh Himalayan Expedition? My suggestion that it should be Dr Charles Evans was immediately accepted. Charles Evans and Tom Bourdillon should have been the first to reach the summit of Mt Everest in 1953. Sadly, Evans's oxygen apparatus malfunctioned just short of the summit and he and Bourdillon were forced to retreat. Descending to the South Col, they passed Hillary and Tensing, on their way to the first ascent of the highest mountain in the world. Charles Evans met our club committee and explained to us that he had been offered the leadership of the forthcoming attempt on Kangchenjunga. This expedition to Kangchenjunga was to be a complete success. As he left the meeting, he said, 'If the offer of Kangchenjunga had not come along, I would have been proud to lead the first Welsh Himalayan Expedition.' In response to my query, 'Where do we find an expedition leader now?', Evans said, 'You have done all the spade work. You should lead the expedition.' And so it came to pass. If Charles Evans had been able to lead the first Welsh Himalayan Expedition, I would not be writing this story now.

We needed acceptance – the approval of people respected in the North Wales community. I made three approaches for patronage and all three gave me their imprimatur: Lady Megan Lloyd George, daughter of the Welsh Wizard, the late David Lloyd George; Sir Michael Duff, a kinsman of Her Majesty the Queen; and the Marquess of Anglesey. I was careful to advise my patrons that I was not soliciting their money, just their formal written approval of the expedition (to be much publicised) and my plans.

Finance was the next priority, and the good names of my three patrons put to rest any doubts *Life* magazine might have had. *Life* offered some financial support and to supply still cameras on loan. The *Liverpool Daily Post*, a provincial newspaper with a reputation for responsible journalism, came up with the balance of my modest budget of £2,400, which would cover six expedition members' expenses – Wales to Nepal and back, including food and equipment. I soon realised however that I had underestimated the costs, and proceeded to approach suppliers and manufacturers of climbing and camping equipment, with considerable success. Our most prized donated acquisitions were the bright blue windproof Everest suits identical to those worn by the successful conquerors of Everest two years before.

Then the Standard Motor Company agreed to hand-build two of their Standard Vanguard Estate Cars, to be painted in Welsh colours, with the name of the expedition on the sides, for a 6,500-mile journey to India, via Belgium, Germany, Austria, Italy, Yugoslavia, Greece, Turkey, Iran, Afghanistan, Pakistan and India, and up to the border of west Nepal.

But where were we to explore and to climb? I decided on the mountain Gosainthan, in Tibet. The Chinese had been in occupation of Tibet for four years and at that time had not allowed foreigners access. One could attempt Gosainthan from the Nepal side without even notifying the Chinese. The summit lay inside Tibet, but one could approach it above the snow line, from the Nepal-Tibet border, without going down onto the Tibetan plateau proper.

I was a stickler for legal formality, so I tried a three-track approach. The first was a formal written application to the Chinese *chargé d'affaires* in London (China did not have an ambassador in the UK at that time), followed by an approach to Eric Reeve, a climbing friend whom I knew to be both a member of the Communist Party of Great Britain, and a committee member of the Marxist-controlled Anglo-Chinese Friendship Society. Eric readily agreed to assist, and in due course the Anglo-Chinese Friendship Society voted to support our application for permission to enter Tibet and climb Gosainthan. The third track was the Parliamentary Labour Party in the House of Commons. I learned that a delegation of Labour MPs was to visit Peking, and that Welsh MP Aneurin Bevan was a prominent member of that delegation. I wrote to Bevan and he readily agreed to co-operate. The parliamentary delegation took a copy of my formal application, along with a copy of the Anglo-Chinese Friendship Society's endorsement of my project. Peking responded with a flat refusal, on the grounds of 'transport difficulties'. The Chinese evidently took the attitude that an attempt on Gosainthan had to be made from the Tibetan side. None of us could fathom what the 'transport difficulties' amounted to.

Eric Reeve was as deeply disappointed as I. He explained to me that China was anxious to have full ambassadorial accreditation to the Court of St James, and he thought Chinese approval of our expedition plans could have helped Anglo-Chinese relations.

My wife and I spent a weekend at Eric's house in the East End of London. A week later, he turned up in Snowdonia, and he was very disturbed.

'Our house was broken into,' he complained.

'Par for the course if you choose to live in London,' I commented.

'This was no ordinary break-in,' Eric countered. 'You see there was this broken white wax candle in the entrance hall.'

'Everybody has candles in the house, don't they?' I responded.

'Not me,' Eric said.

'Don't tell me that burglars carry candles to light their way around when they break into houses,' I said.

'You don't understand,' Eric continued. 'It is standard procedure. When MI5 and Special Branch break into a house on an intelligence raid, they sometimes leave a broken wax candle in plain view, and that is the message to the CID when they investigate and fill in a report, that the break-in was an official counter-intelligence operation. This is what my contacts in the Communist Party told me.'

'You mean they think you are a spy, Eric?' I enquired. 'Sounds a bit far-fetched to me.'

Nothing would mollify Eric, he was concerned and his wife was very worried about the matter. 'Can't be anything to do with my project,' I suggested. 'I doubt if MI5 give a damn about which side of the Himalaya we climb Gosainthan from.'

My expedition was eventually to make waves for Eric and his political allies and result in his rejection by both the communist party and the Anglo-Chinese Friendship Society, on the grounds that he had been party to a Western imperialist plot working against peace-loving communist China.

I tried to forget about China and my plans to climb Gosainthan. After all, the Greater Himalayan chain was a couple of thousand miles in length, and there must be areas to explore and mountains to climb which offered no political problems. I do not use the word 'explore' lightly. I have never had a great regard for the peak-bagging brigade (into which category sadly most Himalayan expeditions have fallen). I preferred to leave some more indelible mark on the pages of history, or preferably on the blank areas of maps. And so I approached the Royal Geographical Society, which august body proceeded to train two members of my expedition – John Harrop, an agricultural scientist on the staff of the University College of North Wales, and Geoffrey Roberts, a North Wales school teacher. We were to conduct a cartographical survey using plane tables and a photo-microptic theodolite, a surveyor's instrument for measuring angles. The RGS also provided us with scientific sponsorship, which would be invaluable when applying to the Nepalese government for the necessary permits to enter their country.

The other three members of our expedition were Scotty Dwyer and Jack Henson, two very able professional climbing guides, and Humfrey Berkeley, an engineer and keen amateur photographer. Having written to the Himalayan Club in India for advice, I was put in touch with the late Lieutenant-Colonel H.W. (Toby) Tobin, OBE, DSO, vice president of the Himalayan Club and editor of the *Himalayan Journal*, who was to become my mentor. Tobin had served in the Indian Army. He retired to Darjeeling and with a few friends founded the Himalayan Club in 1928. Earlier, in 1920, he had joined H. Raeburn on a reconnaissance of Kangchenjunga, and he was invited to join the German expeditions of Bauer in 1929, and Dyrenfurth in 1930 as transport officer. In 1931 Tobin was back with Bauer on the second Bavarian attempt on that mountain. Tobin was on the Joint Himalayan Committee of the successful 1953 Everest expedition, and when the Mount Everest Foundation was formed, he was elected to the committee of management.

Tobin became a sort of father figure for post-war Himalayan mountaineering aspirants, and his home in Lymington, Hampshire was always open to tyros who wanted to climb on the sacred snows of Himachal. He advised me on expedition organisation and logistics and assisted me when I applied to the Indian government to enter the forbidden 'Inner Line' area which abuts the border of Tibet, for an attempt on Panch Chuli. The Indians said no. They did not want any European climbers on their frontier with Tibet, and as India had signed a treaty with China in 1954, recognising Chinese sovereignty over Tibet, China was not to be disturbed in her plans for 'freeing the Tibetan serfs from medieval slavery'. I then decided to further investigate the possibilities of climbing Panch Chuli. A correspondence ensued with Brigadier Ian H. R. Wilson, Surveyor General of the Survey of India, based in Dehra Dun, who was delighted to learn that the expedition was more interested in geographical survey than 'peak-bagging'. I was immediately offered surveyors with theodolites, accompanied by bearers – all on the staff of the Survey of India. All I had to furnish was their rations; they would bring their own tents, bedding and cooking equipment.

I regarded this as both a coup and a very great honour but my feelings of exhilaration were not to last long. The Indian political bureaucracy again quashed our joint plans. My dealings with Brigadier Wilson were to have repercussions in another quarter.

I then decided on Nalkankar. It was in west Nepal, and as far away from Mount Everest as one could get, while still climbing on Nepalese territory. When I showed Tobin the location of Nalkankar on the map of west Nepal, he said, 'You might be able to do some friends a favour. Can I set up a meeting?' I readily agreed.

Two weeks later I was back in London. I met Tobin in an Indian restaurant. His contact turned out to be from the Indian High Commission in London. After introductions, our Indian friend said, 'Colonel Tobin says that you are going to visit the extreme west of Nepal, and that you might feel disposed to do some small service for India?' I nodded my assent, not quite sure what was in the wind. At this point, Tobin got up to leave. 'You two have got a great deal to talk about. If you can help my Indian friend, Wignall, it could be a great deal of fun. Bit of cloak and dagger work. I'll get in touch with Bill Tilman, and I'll be suggesting to Tilman that he seconds your application to join the Himalayan Club.'

My Indian contact got down to business right away. 'You've just been turned down for permission to cross the Inner Line and climb a mountain called Panch Chuli. I saw the application. The British created the Inner Line many years ago to please the Tibetan authorities in Lhasa. Tibet wanted complete political isolation. When you notified Brigadier Ian Wilson in Dehra Dun that having been refused a permit for the "Inner Line" and Panch Chuli by the "politicals" in New Delhi, you were going to obtain a permit from the Nepalese to climb and survey in west Nepal, only a few miles from the Chinese military establishment at Taklakot in Tibet, Ian Wilson notified us in New Delhi. He is aware that we are interested in what the Chinese communists are up to in Tibet. By the way, forgive me if I do not use my real name. You can call me Singh. Oh, yes. I also know that the Chinese refused you permission to enter Tibet.'

Before he could continue his line of talk, I threw in a question. 'How on earth can I be of service to India? Why should India be interested in a Welsh Himalayan expedition operating in Nepal?'

Singh thought for a moment. 'I wish to make some suggestions to you. You can of course reject them. If you do, can I have your assurance that what passes between us will remain completely confidential?'

I had no hesitation in giving Singh the assurance he required. 'You have my word on it. But what is this meeting all about? How could India be harmed if I broke confidence?'

Singh gave me a smile. 'It isn't India I am thinking about. I'm talking about my own skin; my security in my job, and that of others back in India who could also be victimised if intelligence of this conversation leaked out.'

'Go on,' I said, by now completely intrigued.

Singh continued, 'Let us forget the Inner Line for the time being. Let us talk of matters strategic and of national security. How would the average Englishman feel if there was a huge Soviet army entrenched in Paris, no more than 250 miles from London, well equipped, with excellent lines of communication along which it could bring up reinforcements in quick order?'

'But such a scenario is impossible,' I countered.

'Allow me to continue,' Singh suggested, 'and you will probably be even more bewildered. You will probably think that what I am telling you is right out of your Mr George Orwell. You now have in your mind that huge Soviet Army in Paris. Imagine that your British government creates an Inner Line, which amounts to a fifteen-mile-deep area along your English Channel coast, and bans all Englishmen and foreign nationals from entering that Inner Line without formal written approval. How would you feel if you were in British intelligence and given firm instructions that you could not carry out any intelligence-gathering or surveillance of the Soviet forces in occupation of France? Furthermore, how would you feel if you were directed to turn to the West, and regard the Irish Republic as your only enemy, with all your military resources entrenched on the border between Britain and Ireland? And if you disobeyed those orders, and undertook what your government regarded as unauthorised intelligence-gathering targeted at the Russians you would be dismissed from civil government or military service, with no right of appeal. Well just how would you feel, Mr Wignall?'

I was astounded by what Singh was putting forward as official Indian government policy. 'You are telling me that your Prime Minister, Mr Nehru, regards Pakistan as India's enemy, and the Chinese occupation of Tibet as no threat to India?'

'Just so,' Singh continued. 'People are afraid to speak their minds in public. Any senior army officer or civil servant who expressed such thoughts in public would come under the ever watchful eye of that extremely vindictive man, Krishna Menon. He has destroyed the careers of several sincere patriotic men. Remember that no nation has ever recognised Chinese claims to sovereignty over Tibet. When Menon, on behalf of India, and Chou En-lai, on behalf of China, signed that infamous trade treaty on Tibet last year, we for the first time used the words "Chinese sovereignty" in Tibet. Bear in mind the independence and freedom of the Tibetan people was signed away by India and China without the Tibetan government or its people being consulted. Similar to what your Prime Minister Neville Chamberlain and Adolf Hitler did over Czechoslovakia in 1938, and we all know what that led to.

'Not only are we banned from spying on the Chinese, but our capability to do so, even were it to be permitted, is practically nil. After the end of World War Two, the British ran down the Indian Army Intelligence Service on the basis that no country posed a threat to British Imperial India. After the British got out in 1947, the Indian Army in general and our military intelligence service in particular was down-graded in national status by our government. The army is under-equipped, financed and trained. Military intelligence is deemed to be of no importance. We do not regard either Nehru or Menon as friends of the Indian Army,' Singh confided. 'They were warned about the Chinese danger in 1950. The commandant of our Defence Services Staff College, General "Joe" Lentaigne, denounced India's leaders for their passive approach to China's invasion of Tibet. He predicted that India would pay dearly if she neglected to reinforce her northern defences.'

'Do you think that China would actually attack India and seize Indian territory?' I enquired.

'Some Chinese generals have already been making bellicose statements to their troops, claiming that large areas of northern India, Nepal, Sikkim and Burma, are really Chinese territory and would soon be liberated. We obtained this information from Chinese Kuomintang agents who were deliberately left behind on the mainland. This information when presented by us to Nehru is treated as tainted because it comes from the American CIA, and Nehru will not believe any ill of the Chinese communists. He says that the Americans are trying to damage his "Hindee Cheenee Bhai Bhai" policy. It's the standard Indian Congress Party motto now. It means "Indians and Chinese are Brothers".'

'I have the picture,' I said. 'So Colonel Tobin has told you that I'm taking an expedition into Nepal and, as our mountain, Nalkankar, straddles the border between Nepal and Tibet, you would like me to pick up for you whatever information I can on a possible build-up of Chinese troops on the Tibetan side of the border.'

Singh nodded. 'With your background you would be ideal for what we have in mind. You are trained in cartography and survey.' He continued, 'When the Chinese turned you down for that proposed climb on Gosainthan, you advised Colonel Tobin that you could have crossed the Nepal/Tibet frontier, and made your ascent without going down onto the Tibetan plateau proper. Is that so?'

'True,' I said.

'Would it be possible to make an attempt on the highest mountain lying completely in Tibet, Gurla Mandhata, over 25,000 feet high, only a few miles from the border, by continuing along the ridge which connects Nalkankar in Nepal, to Gurla Mandhata in Tibet?' Singh enquired. 'The distance is less than fifteen miles.'

The suggestion caught me unawares. 'You mean illegally enter Tibet?'

'You would not be the first to attempt to climb Gurla Mandhata, and one of the earlier attempts was quite illegal,' Singh countered.

In 1905 Dr Tom G. Longstaff made an attempt on Gurla Mandhata, accompanied by two Swiss guides, the brothers Brocherel. It was strictly lightweight, no big expedition structure. They got fairly close to the summit before they were swept down by an avalanche and had to bivouac on the west face. This was an official party; the illegal attempt was by the Austrian mountaineer Herbert Tichy in 1936. He rode to India from Austria on a Puch motorcycle, and crossed the Lipu Lekh pass from India into Tibet disguised as an Indian religious mendicant. He got within 2,000 feet of the summit before he retired due to exhaustion and cold.

'I can't take a full expedition over the frontier into Tibet, can I?' I asked Singh. 'There will be porters and a Nepalese liaison officer with us.'

'Think back on both Longstaff's and Tichy's attempts on Gurla Mandhata,' Singh suggested. He was obviously very knowledgeable. 'They were the very essence of lightweight expeditions, were they not? Three men on the Longstaff ascent, and Tichy alone in 1936. They climbed alpine style.'

'So you suggest that I make a lightweight run over the border, and see if I can climb Gurla Mandhata?'

'Exactly,' Singh suggested.

'But how will that help you, how can that assist India?' I enquired.

Singh smiled. 'You would be in a position to have one of the most glorious panoramic vistas in the world, the Greater Himalayan chain to the south, the sacred lake of Manasorawar to your north-west, and just beyond its shores, Kailas, the holiest mountain in the world. If the Chinese are building a military highway to west Tibet it would pass just north of Manasorawar. Down below to your south-west, just a few short miles away, you would see the Tibetan town of Taklakot. That's where the local Chinese military are garrisoned. Or so we are told by our sole informant, an Indian trader, who visits the Taklakot tented market. He says that there are no more than two hundred Chinese in Taklakot.'

'Your man at Taklakot must also be an illegal?' I suggested.

'Yes, officially he does not exist,' Singh responded. 'Our esteemed Prime Minister Pandit Jawaharlal Nehru would be most displeased if he knew, and Krishna Menon would have apoplexy. Menon is a dangerous and extremely vindictive man. He is far from forgiving of those who disobey him or cross him in any way.'

'If there are only two hundred Chinese soldiers at Taklakot,' I countered, 'and they have to patrol several hundred square miles of surrounding territory, including the nearby Indian and Nepal borders, it should not be difficult to slip past them in the night, and get a foothold on the north-west ridge of Gurla Mandhata.'

'I would not think that it would be an insuperable problem,' Singh commented. 'How many would you take with you?'

A waiter now approached us. He wanted to clear the table. Singh glared at him, and gave him a bollocking in Urdu. The waiter bowed to Singh and retreated.

'To keep the party light, I would suggest just myself and my deputy leader, John Harrop. Harrop is a scientist and a trained observer. I would need about four porters. I would have to spin a yarn to our expedition liaison officer, a university student who will be joining us from Kathmandu. But as he will not be a mountaineer, he will probably be happy to sit in our base camp and stuff himself with European food.'

I stared at Singh. 'You want me to be a spy,' I said. 'How many others have you contacted?'

Singh looked me right in the eye. 'You don't expect me to reveal to you who our agents are?' he said with a half smile.

'Not exactly,' I said. 'I just want to know if I am the only Aunt Sally in this great game of yours.'

Singh laughed. 'The answer to that must be both yes and no. We have asked British Himalayan explorers to assist us. You happen to be the only one visiting what to us is the most sensitive area in the whole border region. We suspect that the two hundred Chinese soldiers at Taklakot could be a true figure, but as the Chinese ban all Indian and Nepalese traders from travelling to the north of Taklakot, we have no means of knowing if the Chinese People's Liberation Army have been reinforcing their Taklakot garrison by establishing a cantonment to the north-east. From a vantage point on the north-west ridge of Gurla Mandhata you would be able to see, with a telescope, any sign of a military encampment in that area, and you could look for evidence of the building of that military highway to west Tibet. At what height would you establish your observation post?'

'I would think at about 22,000 feet,' I said.

'What about cameras?' Singh enquired.

'I have been promised some newly designed German single lens 35 mm cameras with long focal length telephoto lenses, and I also have a 16 mm cine camera with telephoto lenses.'

Singh warmed to this. 'It could not be better,' he commented.

'Who do I see when I come out?' I enquired.

'Oh, you mean debriefing? I will arrange that. I suggest that we have one more meeting, and at that meeting I will hopefully have information for you on a venue for a debriefing session.'

I nodded my assent. 'I will have to bring Harrop into our little plan.'

'I don't want to offend you,' Singh said, 'but you know what a secret is; it's something you tell to just one person at a time.'

I laughed at this. 'Just Harrop and my wife at this stage. Just that I have a plan for a clandestine adventure, the ascent of the highest mountain in Tibet, Gurla Mandhata.'

'Take a pistol,' Singh said. 'You never know. Just one or two border guards might come across you. You could disarm them. No shooting. No international incidents, you understand?'

I was somewhat taken aback by this. 'Guns, I never thought of guns. Himalayan explorers and mountaineers don't carry pistols.'

'No military calibres,' Singh said. 'No .45s, no 9 mm Parabellum, no 38s are allowed in India. I will arrange your Indian permit. No permit is required in Nepal. Just pop into Cogswell and Harrison in Piccadilly, they are very fine makers of gentlemen's sporting guns. They will let you have a hunting rifle and a .32, that's a 7.65 mm calibre automatic pistol. Legal for India. Lightweight and easy to handle. I don't think that you will have to shoot anybody.'

'What if we run into your Chinese friends?' I queried.

'You are innocent Himalayan explorers travelling on your lawful occasions and you just lost your way, for, after all, the exact position of the frontier isn't all that precise, and as the Chinese themselves decline to accept the current Nepal/Tibet frontier, you will probably get off with just a good wigging.'

'As simple as that?' I suggested. 'What if they accuse us of being spies?'

'To be perfectly honest, my dear chap, we would deny all knowledge of you and your friend Harrop.'

'And that's all?' I asked, feeling more than a little apprehensive. (At that time I was unaware of the fate of two American CIA agents, John T. Downey and Richard Fecteau, who had been captured in Manchuria two years earlier; they were to serve twenty years in prison before their release in 1973.)

'Well, not quite. If you are picked up and subjected to interrogation, there are three counter-interrogation cardinal rules to be followed.'

'And they are?' I enquired, feeling even more nervous now that the uncomfortable subject of possible capture had been brought into the conversation.

'Deny everything, admit nothing, and keep the other side talking to ascertain how much they know, and to try to glean some valuable intelligence data from them.'

I was much later to reflect on this piece of sage advice from Singh, and to use it to considerable advantage.

Singh and I arranged for one further meeting. I was aware that Colonel Tobin knew of what was afoot, and I advised Singh that I proposed to bring one other person into my confidence. When I told Singh that it was the universally admired Major H. W. Tilman, leader of the 1938 Everest expedition, Singh raised no objections.

Tilman was the doyen of the lightweight school in Himalayan exploration. Not for Tilman £50,000 budgets and cases of champagne. He had organised and led the last Everest expedition before World War Two on a budget of less than £3,000. They were defeated not by under-financing, but by bad weather. In 1936 Tilman and Noel Odell made the first ascent of Nanda Devi, 25,645 feet high. That summit height record stood until the French climbed Annapurna in 1950. Tilman was said to be a hard man who, according to his boon companion on many Himalayan expeditions, Eric Shipton, would give you a boot in the back to arouse you from your sleeping bag with a gruff cry of, 'Porridge's ready'. After more than ten years climbing together, in Kenya and in the Himalaya, Shipton once asked, 'Why don't you call me Eric, and I'll call you Bill?' To which Tilman responded, 'Shipton and Tilman is good enough for me.' I took Colonel Tobin's advice, which was, 'When you meet him, don't address him as Mr Tilman, he won't like that. Just call him Tilman, and for God's sake don't call him Major, he will like that even less.'

I drove my Standard Vanguard Estate car, painted in Welsh national colours, with its dragon emblem, to Tilman's home Bod Owen, near

Barmouth in North Wales. Tilman was standing in the drive of his home when I drove up. He met me with a strong handshake. 'Come into my study, Wignall. I have some knowledge of you from Tobin. Tell me about your plans.'

Tilman was short of stature, but rugged looking. He had a shock of greying hair, and a short bushy moustache. He offered me a chair while he half sat on the edge of his desk. I prattled on about Nalkankar, and west Nepal and, remembering Colonel Tobin's advice, addressed my host as 'Tilman'.

'I will be taking six climbers in my party. Would you regard that as a light expedition?' I enquired, fully confident that Tilman would give me the assurance I was seeking.

Tilman answered directly: 'I regard two as a large expedition.'

This rather took the wind out of my sails. 'We are travelling light. All our essential foodstuffs are dehydrated stuff from the Ministry of Food Experimental Station in Aberdeen.'

'Don't take ship's biscuits, like I did on one occasion,' Tilman advised.

I had difficulty in repressing a smile. Tilman's ship's biscuits story was well known in Himalayan mountaineering circles. Tilman had the idea that by taking ship's biscuits as the expedition staple, and just adding water, a nourishing meal could be provided, and the weight would be kept to a minimum. The experiment was doomed to failure. The biscuits failed to become soggy when immersed in water, proved to be far from digestible, and to add insult to injury, while on the trek to base camp Tilman accidentally lost his only set of artificial dentures in a mountain stream. In his book on the expedition, Tilman said that the man who invented the Ship's Biscuit should have been stoned to death with his own product years ago.

The conversation eventually came round to my meetings with Colonel H. W. Tobin and Singh. Tilman thought for a moment. 'You have counted the risks?' I nodded my assent. 'You know the penalties? People taken by the Chinese communists have been held sometimes for years.' I nodded again. Tilman grunted, and thought for a moment. 'My advice to you is to work out the absolute minimum of gear you will require, and then reduce that by fifty per cent. Ration yourself to one meal a day. This will save weight. You will lose weight and get run down, and will tire easily after a week, but if you are in good condition when you cross the border, you will be able to survive on half rations. Weight is going to be your greatest problem. It will be your albatross. Travel by night when close to the border area and, for your own good, cut the cackle. People talk too much anyway, and you know how sound carries down and across valleys in the mountains. And I wouldn't bother taking a doctor. All he can do is diagnose what you died of.'

All this time, Tilman's face had not shown the slightest sign of emotion.

Tilman the private man was totally different from Tilman the author. His books gave one the impression that Tilman was a man filled with great good humour. One smiled, nay laughed out loud, at some of the passages in Tilman's books. The man himself was a different kettle of fish.

His mouth showed the faintest glimmer of a smile. 'I would like to go with you on this trip of yours,' he said. 'But my doctor says that I mustn't go high any more. That's why I took up sailing; bought myself an old Bristol Channel pilot cutter, called *Mischief*. I have sailed her up to Iceland, and later this summer I plan to sail her across the Atlantic, with some young volunteers, and try to make the first crossing of the Patagonian ice cap.'

'And no ship's biscuits, this time?' I suggested timorously. This time Tilman smiled. 'That's right. No more ship's biscuits.'

Tilman walked me out to my car. We shook hands. 'Remember my advice. Travel light. Minimum personnel, move at night, and cut the cackle.'

Tilman never climbed again. He sailed the seas in three successive Bristol Channel pilot cutters on his oceanic voyages of exploration, and vanished with all hands, somewhere between Argentina and the Falkland Islands, in a converted steam tug in 1977.

Colonel Tobin advised me that my application for membership of the Himalayan Club, proposed by him, and seconded by Tilman, had been accepted. I made one more trip to London, to collect our high-altitude tents from the makers, Benjamin Edgington. These yellow 'Windcol' windproof cotton/nylon tents were identical to those used at the high camps on the ascent of Everest in 1953.

I also had my last meeting with Singh. 'When you come out of Tibet, you will have a choice of returning the way you came, over the Urai Lekh into Nepal, or via the much lower, easier and therefore safer Lipu Lekh into India. As you will be heading into Tibet during the post-monsoon season, do bear in mind that if you are on the Tibetan side of the Himalaya in late October, the Urai Lekh and all the Nepalese passes will be closed until May the following year. You will never get back over the Urai Lekh in late October, and from what I hear, the Seti Gorge is far from safe in summer, let alone in winter. I suggest you return via the Lipu Lekh into India.'

'There are two problems there,' I countered. 'The first is that the other members of my expedition, having been advised by me that Harrop and I intend illegally entering Tibet to climb Gurla Mandhata, will expect us to return to base camp. If we return via the Lipu Lekh, they will think that we have died on the mountain. The second and more serious problem is that to get to the Lipu Lekh we would have to pass close to Taklakot, and would then risk discovery and apprehension by the Chinese.'

'Whatever happens, we will have men stationed on the Indian side of the Lipu Lekh,' Singh said, and then added, 'and we will be saying the odd prayer for the success of your mission and your safe conduct. The Nepalese are more concerned about Chinese intentions than our political masters are. There are moves afoot for India to participate in forming the foreign policy of Nepal, and the Nepalese, having literally no armed forces of their own, would like India to station detachments of the Indian Army at certain strategic places close to the Nepal/Tibet border. If those negotiations come to fruition while you are in Nepal and Tibet, we might have a patrol in the offing, with an intelligence officer ready to debrief you when you come out.'

Singh insisted that I have a code name, so on reflection I chose the name of a Welsh river close to which I had lived for many years, 'You can call me Code name Conway,' I said.

I realised the considerable risks Singh was running, taking me, a complete stranger, into his confidence, laying his career on the line, in disobeying Nehru's and Krishna Menon's orders that no intelligence operations were to be conducted against the Chinese occupiers of Tibet. Singh was not alone in his activities. There were others, and the sole motive for their highly irregular activities was their love of India. I was to some degree inspired by my favourite poem, 'Hassan', by James Elroy Flecker, and those memorable lines: 'Always a little further it may be. Beyond that last blue mountain barr'd with snow. Across that angry or that glimmering sea.' Was I going into this with both eyes open, for love of India? I found it difficult to analyse my feelings. I have a great love of India, and yes, I am proud to say, of British India, of the days of the Raj. There was also the matter of Indian Army involvement. I have yet to meet an Englishman who, having studied the history of India, does not hold the Indian Army in high esteem. I would be working with and for the Indian Army. I regarded that as an honour and a rare privilege. Perhaps also, there was the element of adventure, the challenge, and the excitement or what my Dublin friends would call 'the crack'.

I left Singh in that Indian restaurant and drove over to the headquarters of the Royal Geographical Society in Kensington Gore to collect the two plane tables and photo-theodolite the RGS was lending to my expedition. I visited the map room, and made reference notes of the maps of northern India and west Nepal that I would require. I had no need to order my maps through commercial sources. All of my requirements had been arranged in advance by Colonel Tobin, who had been pulling strings for me in the War Office in Whitehall to which I now repaired. A uniformed commissionaire showed me to a Mr Ross who advised me that I had been cleared at high level as a recipient of War Office maps. Ross conducted me down below street level into the basement, where space was at a premium.

'West Nepal,' I said. 'That's the area we will be visiting. And also south-west Tibet, the area around Taklakot.'

Ross ferreted out my requirements. 'Here, this lot will cover you across from the West into central Nepal, right up to the Annapurna range. Now what about this road trip of yours, to New Delhi, from Llandudno in North Wales. I can let you have maps of your entire route.'

'I can't quite understand how I got this clearance,' I commented.

'Churchill, old man,' Ross replied. 'Winston Churchill decreed that British expeditions proceeding overseas must be given every assistance on the grounds that you never know what useful information they might bring back.'

In due course my clutch of maps was weighing me down. 'Don't go without these,' Ross said, handing more maps to me. 'Never know when they might be useful to you.'

I looked over this latest bundle of maps and my astonishment showed on my face. They were all marked 'SAC,' the US Strategic Air Command, and stamped 'SECRET' in big letters. Ross winked at me.

2

I decided to bring the editor of the *Liverpool Daily Post* into my plans. A contract had not at that time been signed and other prospective expeditions to the Himalayas were in the process of contacting the *Daily Post* to seek financial sponsorship. I had to clinch the deal by dangling a scoop in front of the editorial board.

The plan to illegally enter Tibet and make an attempt on the highest mountain in Tibet was just the kind of story they were looking for. I made no mention of my contact with Indian intelligence. Only three people were to know of the Gurla Mandhata plan – the managing editor, the editor and the assistant editor. The latter, Norman Cook, became my anchor man with the *Liverpool Daily Post*, and we became good friends. We agreed on a code word. If Harrop and I were able to climb Gurla Mandhata, we would send a cablegram to the *Daily Post* when we reached the Indian hill station of Pithoragarh in the United Provinces, close by the western border of Nepal. The code word would be 'Conway' and would enable the *Daily Post* to be the first to announce that the Welsh Himalayan Expedition had climbed the highest mountain in Tibet.

The day of departure duly dawned. On 2 July 1955 the members of the first Welsh Himalayan Expedition assembled on Llandudno promenade with our two identical Standard Vanguard estate cars, to be given a civic send-off by Llandudno's chairman and all the city fathers. Our MP, Peter Thomas, gave a short speech wishing us well, God speed and all success.

We had 6,500 miles to travel to India, and we all looked forward to that road trip as a great adventure, through strange and exotic lands. Motoring through Europe was prosaic and unexciting, punctuated by the sheer bloody-mindedness of customs officials, particularly those in Yugoslavia who insisted not only on having us unload both estate cars, and open up every bag and box, but also unscrewed all the door panels to search for contraband.

In Persia, after a meal at a hotel owned by the Shah, I contracted dysentery, and it was to plague me for the next six months. In eastern Persia I was able to obtain sulpha drugs from an American medical dispensary, after spending three days flat on my back, feeling like death, passing blood-stained faeces. The sulpha drugs quelled but did not cure my dysentery.

Eventually we crossed the frontier from Persia into Afghanistan. We were seemingly in the middle of nowhere. No town. Very little vegetation. Mainly bare ground with occasional scrub. A solitary telegraph wire passed overhead, and quite unbelievably it was occupied by literally thousands of game birds, hawks, all sitting shoulder to shoulder, with hardly room for them to stretch their wings. The customs and immigration post consisted of a group of white-painted mud-brick buildings.

The senior customs officer gave the cars a cursory glance and made a chalk mark on front wings of both vehicles. Now we came to the guns. All three guns were entered into my passport. The customs man thumbed through my documents.

'Can I see your weapons please?'

I tore off the wrappings and displayed the Browning pistol, the rifle and the shotgun, expecting all hell to break loose, as we had been warned that it would at so many customs posts when the Afghan visas were observed in our passports.

'Now Mr Wignall. The other five members of your party: where are their guns?'

'This is all we have. We decided that it would be simpler to have the three weapons on one passport,' I answered.

He shook his head. 'You must not camp at night in open country, Mr Wignall. Bad people attack travelling strangers in open country at night. Always stay in a town. And it is very hot driving in the daytime. I would advise you to drive at night, when it is cooler.'

So there was to be no problem in Afghanistan over our guns. By Afghan standards we were under-armed. I enquired of the senior customs officer, 'There have been three wars between Britain and Afghanistan. Do you not resent us British travelling across your country?'

He grinned. 'On the contrary. You are most welcome. You see we have a great deal in common, you British are like us Afghans, you are great warriors.'

We had several days of motoring across Afghanistan to get to the Pakistan border and the famed Khyber pass. From there we were able to enjoy driving on tarmac roads past Peshawar, Lahore and Amritsar into India.

The secretary of the Himalayan Club, Bobby Hotz, invited us to stay at one of his family's chain of hotels. The Cecil Hotel in Delhi just oozed the old Raj atmosphere. White-clad turbaned bearers were constantly at our beck and call. We put up in three twin-bedroomed cottages in the Cecil's extensive grounds. I had several contacts to make. The first was at the Nepalese Embassy where I collected our permit to enter west Nepal and climb and explore in what is described as the Api-Nampa-Saipal ranges, close by the Nepal/Tibet border. There then followed an interview at one of the Indian government ministries where I was questioned about our route into Nepal. This information had already been made available and

I presumed that we were getting the old bureaucratic run-around. As I was leaving that ministry a civil servant conducted me to the door and, saying goodbye, shook my hand, pressing a piece of paper into it. I slipped it into the pocket of my blazer, and read through it in the taxi taking me back to the Cecil Hotel.

The note was from one of Singh's intelligence contacts in Delhi. It contained instructions. I ordered the taxi driver to change direction and he took me to Connaught Place. I was to look for an Indian carrying a folded copy of the *Times* of India and an umbrella with a short piece of white ribbon fastened around the handle. I located him standing alongside a street vendor selling iced water. My contact spoke first. 'I bring you greetings, Mr Wignall, from a mutual friend in London.' He had no difficulty in identifying me, with my pale skin and navy blue blazer.

'You are a friend of Singh's?' I asked.

'Indeed I am,' he responded. 'And you must be "Conway"?'

'Any news about Chinese activities at Taklakot?' I asked.

'Not really,' he answered. 'I'm instructed just to fill you in on the present state of play. Batting on a rather sticky wicket at present, old chap. You would not believe what our political masters are up to.' He waited for my response.

'You play cricket, quite obviously,' I commented. 'Not a good cricketer myself. My headmaster was Albert William Heap. We all worshipped him, and he was a stern disciplinarian and a first-class cricketer. He once told us during assembly that when he was a boy, his school was visited by the great W. G. Grace. As the school's best junior cricketer young Albert was invited to bowl at the great Grace, which he did, bowling out W.G. with his first and only ball.'

My Indian friend was most impressed with this. 'Singh said that you were just the chap for the job,' he exclaimed. 'Bowled out W.G. in one, your old head. Great stuff. Wish I was going with you into Nepal.'

'Cricket Wallah' hailed a cab. 'We can talk better in here,' he said, and instructed the driver to take us on a tour of Old Delhi. 'Now to brass tacks, old chap. We are getting some intelligence data, so called, from our one agent at Taklakot. He is posing as an Indian trader, and repeatedly crosses and re-crosses the Lipu Lekh, between India and Tibet, with loads of Indian sweetmeats, and even odd items of furniture including tubular steel chairs for the dear old Cheenee Burra Rajah Sahib. The Chinese hierarchy are deliberately not based at Taklakot, where we would be able to place them under surveillance. The Chinese military governor of south-west Tibet is in station at Gartok, that's a few days' mule ride to the west, on the old Lhasa-Ladakh track. Our man at Taklakot, who has a tented stall there, still comes up with the same numbers: about two hundred Chinese are to be counted on the south side of the Taklakot Lamasery ridge.'

'How do the Chinese get re-supplied?' I enquired.

'By mule from Lhasa. It takes the blighters weeks. That's why they have to have that confounded road.'

'No sign of apprehension on the part of Nehru?' I asked.

'No, the beggar's brainwashed our Congress Party. Right now, Nehru and Menon are pushing hard for China to have a seat in the United Nations. They will not listen to any advice which suggests that communist China could be a threat to India. And it gets worse.'

'Fill me in,' I pressed Cricket Wallah.

'You know that the holiest mountain in the world is Kailas?' he asked of me.

'I know that many Nepalese and Indians go on a pilgrimage to circumnavigate Kailas every year.'

'Not any more, old boy,' Cricket Wallah chipped in. 'A group of Indian religious mendicants have just returned over the Lipu Lekh. They got just beyond Taklakot where they were stopped by a Chinese Army patrol, and bundled off back over the border.'

'What significance do you place on that?' I enquired.

'The Lhasa to Ladakh track is where the Chinese may be working on their military highway. You have to cross it to reach the foot of the holy mountain Kailas. The information about the pilgrims was conveyed to Menon, and he tried to prevent Nehru hearing of it. He need not have worried. Nehru said that he would take it up with Chou En-lai and that it was probably just some over-zealous Chinese junior officer acting without orders. Just how naïve can you get? There can be no dialogue with a closed mind.'

'Well we'll go hell for leather for Gurla Mandhata,' I said. 'We won't be able to pose as religious wallahs heading for Kailas, as I'd planned. If they grab us, we will plead imprecise knowledge of the real frontier, and with luck they'll believe us, and bundle us back over the Urai Lekh into Nepal.'

Cricket Wallah was silent for a few moments. He sucked his teeth loudly. Then he spoke. 'Look here, old man. I have some information for you about the state of play for chaps picked up by the Chinese. I'm afraid it's not all good news. There's a British radio operator in Lhasa, who allegedly worked for the Dalai Lama. We all know that he was a British SIS or MI6 agent, whatever you like to call it. Name of Robert Ford. The Chinese had him in prison as you know. Poor beggar was in there for five years. And there's a missionary, name of Bull; they had him also. Then there are those two poor American chaps. They are both CIA. They were caught in Manchuria in 1952. The Chinese put on a show trial last year in Peking. One got life and the other twenty years. The Americans deny that those two are CIA but we have it on the grapevine that they are indeed Company agents.'

My heart sank at this news about Ford and Bull and the two American CIA agents. It was not going to be any kind of a jolly romp into Tibet. We weren't going to be shoved back over the border with a friendly cheerio from the Cheenee Burra Rajah Sahib, if we got caught. I was now thinking about John Harrop. He was keen to make the first ascent, albeit clandestinely, of the highest mountain in Tibet. But should I risk his freedom in the cause of a friendly commonwealth country, namely India, whose rulers did not even believe that their country's security was at risk?

'You can pack it all in right now,' Cricket Wallah said. 'We'll quite understand. Bloody awful risk you would be taking, old chap. You don't owe India anything. As far as I know, you are not even being paid.' Then he laughed. 'It won't affect your pension prospects if you don't go through with it.'

I pondered for a moment. Then I said, 'Well, as a cricketer you will remember that cricketing poem, it's one my old headmaster Albert William Heap hammered into all of us.'

'You mean Newbolt's "Play Up and Play the Game"?' Cricket Wallah said, with a huge grin. 'I'd almost forgotten that. Damn good poem. I learned that at school also. My Indian headmaster was also a keen cricketer.'

'Yes,' I said. 'Just about sums it up. If I back out now you will think us British a load of shits. I've painted myself into a corner and there's no backing out.'

'Just one final thing,' Cricket Wallah said. 'I'll fill you in on the latest episode of our "Great Game". You have heard that we are building a road up to our side of the Lipu Lekh pass, only a few miles from Taklakot?' I nodded. He continued. 'Well, the Chinese, having explained their transport problems between Lhasa and Taklakot, have approached our government for permission for just a few Chinese civilian personnel to travel to India and wend their way to Taklakot up through Uttar Pradesh and over the Lipu Lekh.'

'So the Chinese will be able to do all the intelligence gathering they wish, with the full co-operation of the Indian government?' I said, unbelievingly.

'Yes,' said Cricket Wallah. 'Some of them have already slipped through and I have it on good authority that one of those was a senior Chinese military officer. It's just like your *Alice in Wonderland*.' Then he added, 'Do watch your time-table. Your Urai Lekh pass is closed for the winter from late October until May the following year. Don't get trapped on the Tibetan side when the winter snows set in. You'll never make it back. Just one final bit of news. It might be a load of rubbish but I hear that we might be sending some of our own army patrols up into Nepal. With luck we might have a military post established in your area before you come out of Tibet. If we do, then that detachment will be equipped with a radio transmitter, and any intelligence you can bring out of Tibet will be sent to our HQ here in Delhi very quickly.'

Our conversation was coming to an end now. I enquired as to how I would be able to recognise the Indian trader spy if I came across him.

'I doubt if you will see him,' Cricket Wallah said. 'He is in Taklakot and you won't be going there. Do understand that we operate on the cell system. Better that he does not know of your existence in case he is captured by the Chinese and they interrogate him in an unsporting manner. Also you must bear in mind that the Chinese have some Indian communists working for them. Be careful who you talk to. You're one of "Timmy's Boys" now so put up a good show.'

'Just who the hell is Timmy?' I asked in a bewildered manner.

'Shouldn't have said that,' Cricket Wallah countered. 'Slip of the tongue. Remember to keep a straight bat old boy.' Cricket Wallah's taxi dropped me off at the Hotel Cecil.

Harrop and I left the other four members of our team in Delhi and headed off south-west to Bombay to collect all our heavy gear which was being sent out by sea. We were to meet the others at the railway junction at Bareilly.

In Bombay we were met by the local agent of Norwich Union Insurance Company who was handling our expedition insurance. We had to get our gear, packed in plywood boxes, off the ship, through the Indian customs, and onto the train to Bareilly before midday, for in India, at noon on Saturday, English customs and habits still prevailed and everything came to a standstill until Monday morning. We were greeted with the bad news that all the dock workers had just gone on strike, and nothing would move until Monday. The strike leader was informed that his strike was impeding the onward progress of a Himalayan expedition. He asked to meet me, and I was greeted with, 'No expedition to the sacred snows of Himachal can be held up by strike action and your equipment Sahib, will be totally transferred to the railway in soon moment.'

I enquired about the reason for the strike. He answered that his men were taking industrial action for more money. The sum concerned would have just about purchased a cup of coffee in London or New York. The six men who manhandled our gear ashore I tipped with five rupees each. They could not have been happier if they had won the Derby. Harrop and I boarded the train, and had an air-conditioned compartment for the overnight journey to ourselves.

We were awake early, and served with a first-class breakfast by a smiling bearer. That is what I remember most and love about India, the 'Do everything with a smile' attitude of those whom sophisticated Western society would regard as menials. Indian middle- and high-ranking civil servants in 'The Political' were a different kettle of fish. Many of those we met, or rather crossed swords with, were arrogant to the point of rudeness.

We made one change of train, and then on to the railway junction at Bareilly where we were met by Berkeley, Roberts, Henson and Scotty Dwyer.

3

The tiny narrow gauge train finally arrived at the railhead at Tanakpur. Our equipment boxes were loaded onto ox-carts and transported to the bus depot, from which we would depart the following day for the hill station of Pithoragarh. We moved into a small single-storey guest house. Our rooms were devoid of furniture other than single beds, called charpoys, consisting of hand-carved wooden frames, covered with hemp or sisal rope woven over the sides of the bed frames to form a flat, very firm base. No sooner had we sat on our charpoys than a young man entered the room shared by Harrop, Henson and myself, and introduced himself as Damodar Narayan Suwal. This was our official Nepalese government liaison officer. Damodar (as we came to call him) was a shy but personable eighteen-year-old student who was attending the University of Benares in India. He spoke good English and was more than a little nervous. Damodar explained that he had acted as liaison officer for an expedition from Kenya earlier that year and looked forward to this summer vacation task, for which the Nepal government paid him a small stipend, as a means both to supplement his pocket money and improve his English.

Damodar wore running shoes, grey European-style trousers and a short checked lumber jacket. We quickly had him wearing British ex-army khaki trousers, shirt and sweater, a balaclava hat, a bright yellow windproof hooded climbing anorak, thick woollen stockings, and a stout pair of British-made climbing boots, plus an Austrian ice axe.

'Do I have all this for the duration of the expedition, Wignall Sahib?' Damodar enquired.

'No, Damodar,' I informed him. 'It's all yours to keep, and we'll even throw in an expedition umbrella, bought in New Delhi. And don't call me Wignall, and even worse, don't call me Sahib. I'm Syd to you, and this is John, and Jack and Scotty, and Geoff and Humfrey. Got that?'

Damodar shook his head from side to side. Obviously he hadn't got it. It took some minutes for us to realise that while we English nodded our heads for an affirmative, a Nepalese would shake his head from side to side. Damodar was pale-skinned, with huge dark brown eyes and flashing white teeth. At this stage he was out of his depth, anxious to fit in, and ever willing to perform any task required.

Damodar quickly proved his worth by recruiting labour to load our boxes of equipment onto the bus the following morning. I slept the sleep of the just. We had travelled 6,500 miles by road, 1,000 or so by Indian railways, and here we were in the foothills of the Himalaya. The downside was that none of us was in fighting trim. That six-week road journey had taken it out of us. I was worse than all the others. I had lost about twenty pounds in weight due to my dysentery, which fortunately my American-donated sulpha drugs were keeping at bay. That night it rained cats and dogs. The Indian monsoon was at its height.

The bus service up through the Terai to the hill station of Pithoragarh was an adventure in itself. The road was single-track. On the right reared a steep hillside. On the left, one looked down the 'khud' into a ravine several hundred feet deep. As the buses were unable to pass each other, the road system to Pithoragarh was run like a single-track railway. There were places for the 'up line' and 'down line' buses to pass and these were called 'gates'.

The 'Morning Gate' bus from Tanakpur departed at 6 a.m. The next bus left at 2 p.m. Buses passed each other at the two gate stops of either Ghalti or Champarwat. At the gates, one could purchase hot Indian meals and tea. Although the journey to Pithoragarh was less than ninety miles, that road trip took two days, due to a combination of the gate system and the appalling state of the road which was constantly being wiped out by mud-slides precipitated by the monsoon rain. The buses occasionally stopped at roadside shrines, where one could make an offering to any one of a dozen or so Indian gods. The shrine was always at a place where a bus load of passengers had gone to their deaths 'down the khud'.

I discovered that having chosen the solitary passenger seat beside the driver, I had to pay a first-class fare. 'Why do I have to pay twice as much as the thirty-odd people in the back?' I asked the driver.

'It is not obvious, Sahib?' he replied, as he negotiated a bend, his right front wheel almost scraping the cliff face, as his left front wheel scrabbled along the edge of a two-hundred-foot drop. 'Only driver and first-class passenger can be lucky people with any chance of escaping if bus goes oh blimey over the edge. So if you feel that we are sadly leaving the road,' he bellowed in a hoarse voice, barely audible over the sound of the engine, 'then make all haste to be soonest out of that door, and try to grab hold of a tree branch or any damn thing you can, Sahib.'

It was a hair-raising first day, progress constantly impeded by huge mud-slides. At one point the road had collapsed down into the ravine. A gang of labourers from the Indian Works Department were shovelling mud, and trying to create a narrow track across the huge mud-slide. I took a look down the khud and my heart sank. A Road Works Department official approached me to tender his department's apologies for the 'unseemly delay in your onward progression to Pithoragarh, Sahib'. We were three hours at that impromptu hold-up.

We arrived at the Evening Gate, and there was the bus which had been coming the other way, heading for Tanakpur. We would spend the night here, and the following morning we would head on up to the next gate. It had been a good day according to our driver. We had covered no more than fifty miles, after being all day on the road from Tanakpur. The gate possessed the usual tea and food stalls. There were plain wooden benches to sit on, but no overnight accommodation. We were advised that we could use our inflatable air mattresses and park them under our bus, which had quite high suspension. It looked like it would be a dry night. No sign of rain. I opted to sleep out in the open. We decided that it would be too much trouble to uncrate our tents.

We were sporting our Cogswell and Harrison bolt-action hunting rifle, which was much admired by the locals. 'Good gun for killing man-eating tiger, Sahib,' was the cry. According to Indian and Nepalese hill people, all tigers were man-eaters, which I knew to be arrant nonsense.

Night fell. Some of the Indian travellers had lit wood fires and they lay around them wrapped in blankets. I was standing by our bus, hunting rifle hanging from my shoulder by its sling, talking to Damodar, when I heard the most horrendous screaming cry. It was a tiger. Damodar dived under the bus. I followed him at a rate of knots. We were not alone. It appeared that the entire population of the Indian state of Uttar Pradesh had just taken a fancy to bedding down under our bus. All the members of our expedition were there.

'You've got the rifle, Syd. Go and shoot the sodding thing,' somebody cried.

'Actually, I'm a poor shot,' I answered somewhat lamely, trying to get my exposed posterior under the bus's petrol tank. 'You can have the rifle, go and have a try.'

At 8 p.m. the following day our bus rattled its way into Pithoragarh. We camped on the lawn of the home of an American missionary lady, and spent two days repacking our gear. Then thanks to Damodar's ability as a translator cum liaison officer we were able to recruit a total of thirty porters to carry our loads. After a day's march we stood at the frontier between India and west Nepal. It amounted to a log placed across the centre of the suspension bridge which spans the Kali river. Step across that log, or trip over it if you prefer, and you have left India and entered the Kingdom of Nepal.

Henson, Damodar and I went on ahead to arrange for a campsite for the night. We trudged for about 5,000 feet up a forested hillside until we reached the small Nepalese township of Baitadi. I was at the point of collapse, not having recovered from the enervating effects of my last bout of dysentery. The three of us spent the night alone. The rest of the expedition arrived midday next day. We found that getting thirty porters to keep moving was a tiresome task.

Unlike the approaches to mountains like Everest, where one heads up towards the spine of the Himalaya in a zig-zag line, from south to north, to reach our base campsite in the upper reaches of the Seti river we had to march for twenty-five days across the grain of the country, up a ridge, down the other side, across a river, up a ridge, down the other side, across another river. On one day we crossed and recrossed the same river on no less than eight occasions, heading north-east.

It took us sixteen days to reach the small town of Chainpur. The young Rajah Oom Jung was not 'in station' and had gone to Kathmandu. The local schoolmaster, who was an Indian from Pithoragarh, introduced us to Rajah Oom Jung's uncle, who told us that when he and Oom Jung and their retinue tried to make their annual pilgrimage over the Urai Lekh into Tibet for the journey around the holy mountain of Kailas, they were turned back at gunpoint by the Chinese troops at Taklakot, with no explanation given. I was also introduced to a Nepalese by the name of Perimal who had been the Sirdar of porters for an Oxford University expedition into the Nepal/Tibet Himalaya the previous year. I offered him the post of Sirdar, but he explained that he now had a full-time task as an intelligence officer for the Nepalese government, checking on traders coming south from Tibet, to ascertain if the Chinese were infiltrating agents into west Nepal. Perimal further advised me that a group of Indian and Nepalese traders had been told by the Chinese authorities that China would eventually 'liberate' them from the threat of 'foreign imperialist intervention'. This had caused concern in Kathmandu. From this conversation I understood the reasons why Indian military intelligence detachments were being sent into the Nepal/Tibet border area at the request of the Kathmandu government. Perimal unnerved me with the estimate from his Nepalese trader contacts in Taklakot that there were now about 2,000 Chinese at Taklakot. He further advised me that as the Oxford University expedition was packing up to leave Saipal campsite the previous year, a Tibetan trader coming over the Urai Lekh from Tibet told the Oxford climbers that the Chinese at Taklakot knew of their presence and were about to dispatch a patrol of soldiers over the Urai Lekh to capture them. The Oxford group expedited their departure from Saipal. Ian Davidson of the Oxford expedition confirmed this item in the *Himalayan Journal* the following year. I decided not to impart this information to the other members of my expedition.

Young nobleman Oom Jung did not fit into the English image of a rajah. When I jokingly asked the rajah's uncle where they kept the Rolls Royce, he smiled, 'What use would such a conveyance be here, sir? There are no roads in Chainpur. There are no roads to Chainpur. The only way across west Nepal is on foot, or on a pony. We much prefer our tranquil way of life. We have no longing for the appurtenances of civilisation. My nephew had to visit his father in Kathmandu and make a report to our king about the Chinese activities at Taklakot. The Chinese treat the Tibetans as if they are serfs. The Chinese preach equality but they came to west Tibet as armed conquerors. We are afraid of them. That is why Oom Jung is petitioning Kathmandu for armed troops here in the west of our country. India now has a great say in the foreign policy of Nepal. Perhaps India will protect us? Who knows? My nephew has no liking for the flesh pots of either Kathmandu or India. He will return here to continue administering this area, and to give an education to the local children.'

We were now on the last leg of our journey. All the earlier porters were paid off, and we set out for the upper reaches of the Seti valley using thirty porters hired for us by Perimal. Perimal recommended a young hill farmer by the name of Koila to act as our Sirdar. Koila, who had been with Perimal as a load carrier on the Oxford University expedition, turned out to be a sterling chap.

At the end of the next day's march we camped on a broad flat ridge where there was ample sweet mountain-spring water. Up to that time we had seen no sign of the Nepal Himalaya, it had all been shrouded in cloud. That night, all changed. There was a tremendous monsoon cloudburst, followed by thunder and lightning. We left our tents to witness it. The flashes lasted only split seconds, and yet all was revealed to us. We saw a panorama of great Himalayan peaks which stretched from west to east for nearly a hundred miles. It was grand, it was breathtaking, it was outstandingly beautiful.

The next morning those great mountain ranges were buried in cloud again. On the advice of both Colonel Tobin and H. W. Tilman, I had chosen to climb during the post-monsoon season. This meant that we would have to endure the monsoon rain in our march to base camp, but once it had expended itself, we should enjoy clear cloudless skies, but very cold weather. The post-monsoon season had two advantages – it would provide optimum conditions for our theodolite survey of the peaks of the Saipal/Nalkankar area and I would have an opportunity to photograph the Chinese military build-up in the Taklakot area.

The last habitation one encounters when heading up the Seti river is the tiny village of Dhuli. The houses were quaint, and very small, with doors so low one had to crouch to enter them. The Dhuli people were tiny. I doubt if any of the men was taller than about five feet two inches. They sat smoking pipes, watching the women work in tiny terraced fields. We saw only one ox, and by Dhuli standards the owner must have been regarded as a wealthy man. Here we re-sorted our loads, and discharged a few porters.

From now on it was all uninhabited territory, apart from a camp called Saipal where Tibetan traders who crossed the Urai Lekh pass, four to five days' march to the north, grazed their herds of sheep and goats on west Nepal's rich and lush mountain pastures, and awaited the arrival of Nepalese traders. They conducted barter transactions of Tibetan rock salt and borax for Indian and Nepalese ata and tsampa flour. The former is a coarse-ground wholewheat flour. The latter is parched barley, baked in an oven and then ground.

Ata was the staple food of the hill people of both India and Nepal. They made their flapjack-cum-pancake chapatis from it. The chapati is unleavened and a great deal of pounding and pummelling of the dough takes place before it is put in its concave pan on a wood fire. We were averaging about three to four thousand calories a day by supplementing native bread and potatoes with our dehydrated beef slivers and pemmican blocks. I doubt if our porters ever consumed two thousand calories a day, which I thought was too little when one thought of their 82-pound loads, which they carried suspended from a head-band. I enquired of one of our porters, whom I saw consume no less than fifteen chapatis after a day's march, 'What would like to eat if you were rich?'

To this he made the surprising comment, 'Chapatis, Sahib.'

'But what if you were very rich, like a maharajah and you had lakhs and lakhs of rupees.'

'Oh, many more chapatis, Sahib.'

'There,' I thought to myself, 'sits a contented man.'

The tsampa parched barley flour is the staple diet of the Tibetans. They mix it with tea and fashion it into a ball or a sausage which they munch at meal times. I thought that tsampa would provide a perfectly lousy meal until I mixed a bowlful with some of our expedition powdered milk. I was amazed by the taste. 'Try this,' I suggested to the other members of the expedition, 'and tell me what it reminds you of.' We were all of the same opinion. Tsampa with milk was almost indistinguishable from Weetabix.

Harrop and I set out one day ahead of the others. We planned to reconnoitre the dreaded Seti Gorge, after hearing that part of the track had finished down the khud, and would be dangerous for our heavily laden porters. It took us three days from leaving the village of Dhuli to reach the entrance to the gorge. Due to some past seismic upheaval, the mouth of the gorge had lifted for a hundred feet or so, creating a fine waterfall. The track threaded its way through a glacial moraine of huge, house-size boulders, until finally we passed on the right-hand side of the waterfall and into the face of the gorge proper.

There was no natural track through the Seti Gorge, which was only a few hundred feet wide at its narrowest, hard by the waterfall, but it widened out to the north. As one marched and scrambled along that highly dangerous track on the right-hand face, one gained height until reaching a maximum of about 1,500 feet above the fast-flowing white ribbon of the Seti river.

The very entrance to the Seti Gorge fills one with foreboding. The initial track is entirely man-made. Tree saplings were jammed into crevices and cracks in the cliff face, and flat stones laid onto them. This man-made staircase, only about three feet wide, wended its way for several hundred feet up the side of the gorge. Place a foot wrong and you would vanish down the khud. Not the sort of place for those who have no head for heights, or lack a steady nerve. Eventually the angle of the vertical face eased off, and in grassy areas one tramped along a track just as narrow. I wondered at the ingenuity, courage and craftsmanship of the Nepalese people from Dhuli, whose annual task it was to repair the man-made parts of the track each spring, after the winter snows had melted and the Urai Lekh pass to the north was open once again.

There were some quite horrible places where the grass track had fallen into the gorge, and one had to scramble along slippery boiler-plate slabs of rock, which leaned down into the void below. At one place, the man-made track descended down to the river's edge. The monsoon was in full force, and the Seti was in spate. There was just room to edge along the cliff face, with the fast raging river lapping one's feet. Then round a corner, and zig-zag up a huge wide scree-filled gully until one reached a rock face on the left. A portion of track had long since fallen into the gorge, and the bare face lacked the cracks and crevices for the insertion of wood saplings. It was a rock climb, and I feared for the safety of our bare-footed porters, carrying their 82-pound loads on a single head-band.

Eventually the track became easier and on a flat escarpment, beneath a cliff face, we came across the traders' camping site of Garanphu. To provide shelter from icy winds the Nepalese had dug large circular pits, which were lined with stone, with flat floors and a raised fire hearth. There was a single entrance and the floor was about three feet below it. The iron-age-style dry-stone-walled dwellings were about ten feet in diameter and roofless. I was unable to ascertain when the Garanphu huts were built, but I was later to be informed that they had stood for several centuries, providing shelter for both Nepalese and Tibetan traders. There were several such stone circle huts at Garanphu.

The following morning, still ahead of the rest of the expedition, Harrop and I marched the last few miles from Garanphu to the place where our expedition would be based, the trading site of Saipal (not to be confused with the mountain of the same name, which lay to the east). We crossed the river up to our knees in ice-cold water, trudged for fifty feet up the face of an escarpment, and ended our march on Saipal camp's flat plateau. We were completely surrounded by mountains now, and black rock walls rose all around us, vanishing into thick cloud, for sight of the snows of Himachal was still denied us.

We were not alone at Saipal. There were at least a score of Tibetan traders with their sheep, goats, yaks and jiboos. The latter are a cross between a yak and a cow. Stone-built dwellings dotted the plateau, and canvas and yak-skin covers protected their Tibetan occupants. Each hut was surrounded by stacks of hand-woven bags, made from sheep wool or the thick hair of the yak. The bags contained rock salt or borax, which the Tibetans would trade with the expected influx of Nepalese for ata or tsampa flour, which they purchased to supplement their inadequate annual crops of wheat and barley.

Smoke spiralled up from each of the huts. Our four porters dumped their loads, and the six of us wandered around Saipal campsite seeking suitable lodgings for the night. We eventually located two unoccupied stone huts, and proceeded to make them as comfortable as we could. We pumped up the pressure of our paraffin stoves and made tea, then cooked a dinner of pemmican and dehydrated potato, with dehydrated Brussels sprouts and diced carrots. This was followed by reconstituted dried raspberries and evaporated milk. We had three varieties of canned food – milk, jam and cheese. We finished off a can of cheese opened the night before and threw the can away, only to see it pounced upon by a gaggle of struggling giggling Tibetans. That open-ended can, a throwaway item in Western society, was a highly prized and valuable container for our new-found neighbours.

Our Tibetan fellow occupants of Saipal were a rum lot. They dressed in sheepskin coats, called Shubas, and if the weather was mild, they withdrew their arms from the sleeves of their voluminous overcoats, and let the sleeves and top half of the coat hang from a piece of hand-woven rope which they wore around their waists. They all wore the ubiquitous Tibetan rope-soled boots with felt uppers. One Tibetan with a face like a cross between Methuselah and Rameses II (after he had been mummified) told our porters that he was about twenty-five years of age. He looked more than ninety to me. He had a bad odour about him. They all did. None of them ever washed. They stank to high heaven. But one could forgive them their lack of cleanliness when one considered the climate on the Tibetan plateau. At a mean height of 14,000 feet, almost as high as the summit of the Matterhorn in Switzerland, with limited fuel for their fires, and no over-abundance of water, which often had to be carried for half a mile from stream to dwelling place, they had a licence to smell.

The most endearing thing about the Tibetans is their sense of humour. They are always playing schoolboy practical jokes on each other, and fall over laughing at the least provocation. They were all thieves at Saipal, but in the nicest, friendliest way. There was none of the Paris Metro or London Underground professional pickpocket finesse about them. They would crowd round you, and quite ostentatiously plunge their hands into whichever of your pockets took their fancy. Harrop and I were constantly snatching back items which the Tibetans repeatedly purloined.

Rather than wait for the next relay of Sahibs and porters to arrive, Harrop and I took three porters the following day on a reconnaissance and dry-run to the summit of the Urai Lekh pass. It was 17 September and only one day away from Harrop's twenty-ninth birthday. I was determined that he should enjoy a snow and ice climb on that important occasion. The route from Saipal up to the Urai Lekh was grass-covered with no sign of snow.

We trudged for four hours from our base camp and pitched our tents on a flat piece of ground close by a rivulet of sweet fresh mountain water. The water glistened when one let it run through one's fingers.

It was full of mica scoured from the mica schist rock through which it ran. That mica water was to have a drastic effect on our insides. It acted as a high-velocity laxative. We knew that our three-week gradual cross-country ascent had allowed us to acclimatise slowly and thoroughly, but I was still in poor physical shape. Our porters were a sorry bunch. They were not high altitude sherpas and they whinged and whined, and hid behind a rock, and would not even make the effort to pitch their own high altitude Meade tent or even cook their own meal. We had rigged them out in European heavy-duty warm trousers, sweaters and windproof Everest anorak jackets, in bright orange in contrast with our climber's blue Everest suits. Harrop cooked our meal while I wrote up my diary. Then he got a chapati pan hot, and browbeat one of the porters to make chapatis for themselves. Our efforts to persuade them to eat our very sustaining and nutritious pemmican blocks had been without avail. They quite rightly were convinced that our pemmican was made from the flesh of the cow, a creature treated with reverence by followers of the Hindu religion.

After our meal, Harrop and I set off alone for the summit of the Urai Lekh. We reached it in less than an hour, to find the top of the pass at nearly 20,000 feet completely free of snow. We could see snow on nearby peaks and mountain slopes all of which were at a lower altitude than the Urai Lekh. The Lekh was free of snow due to the ever present strong biting cold wind which blew up the Jung Jung Khola, the valley on the Tibetan side of the pass.

On the western side of the pass a great rock and snow peak more than 21,000 feet high towered over us. On the eastern side of the pass stood a huge rock spire, 20,000 feet high, like some huge granite sentinel. Harrop and I trotted down the northern, Tibetan side of the Urai Lekh.

'Are we in Nepal or Tibet?' Harrop called back to me after we had descended about a thousand feet into the Jung Jung Khola.

'I'm not at all sure,' I responded. 'My Survey of India maps of 1927 show the border as lying on top of the Lekh. The Nepalese governor in Baitadi is of the opinion that the real frontier lies down there at the far end of the Jung Jung Khola, around that corner to the right, a good day or two's march away, close to the Karnali river.'

There was little point in proceeding down the Jung Jung Khola, so we turned back and plodded uphill. Both Harrop and I were elated by the fact that there was no snow on the Urai Lekh and none in the Jung Jung Khola. The trip to climb Gurla Mandhata was going to be a 'piece of cake', or so we thought.

Back at our temporary campsite our porters were huddled in their Meade tent, moaning about their lot. Harrop and I cooked our evening meal and bullied the porters into making themselves chapatis on our paraffin pressure stove. The next day we were awake at 5 a.m. and cooking breakfast at 6 a.m. I decided that as it was Harrop's birthday we would find a peak, on the summit of which he would celebrate his success in reaching the ripe old age of twenty-nine. Over to the west lay a col, a depression between two summits. I reckoned the height of the col at about 21,000 feet. There was a summit of about 22,500 feet to the north of that col. We headed in that direction. The scale of the territory was so vast, what looked like a twenty-minute walk to the snout of a glacier took two hours. We donned crampons and climbing rope and, using our ice axes, chipped steps over the glacier snout. Our glacier was short and steep, with only one narrow and harmless crevasse to cross.

We reached the foot of the slope that led to the col and Harrop and I took turns cutting steps in the snow face with our ice axes. Eventually we breasted the col. By now we realised that the 22,500-foot summit was out of our reach in a one-day dash. We really should have moved our campsite to the foot of the glacier snout. We settled for a subsidiary summit on the ridge at a height of about 21,500 feet. Sitting down in the snow, with our cramponed boots dangling over a 2,000-foot drop on the western side we had a lunch of sweet biscuits, chocolate bars and a vacuum flask of coffee laced with dreadful rot-gut cheap brandy we had purchased in Greece. Looking to the north, along the flanks of the as yet unclimbed 22,500-footer, I espied Gurla Mandhata. 'GM' is a huge mass of a mountain, rather reminiscent of a crouching lion, with the summit lying at the lion's head. Beyond Gurla Mandhata, on the far horizon, we could see a sliver of white stretching across the field of view. This could only be what Sven Hedin called the 'Trans-Himalaya', later renamed the 'Kailas Range'. There in the centre of that silver line I saw a snow-white pyramid of almost perfect proportions. This was Kailas, the holiest mountain in the world to Hindus. I was mindful when looking out across that magic vista at the most sacred of all the peaks of the Himalaya of a verse from the Indian holy book, the *Bhagavad Gita* or 'Song of the Blessed One': 'And he who dies on the sacred snows of Himachal, so shall his soul be cleansed of all sin. In a hundred ages of the gods I could not tell thee of all the glories that are Himachal, where Shiva lived, and the Ganges falls from the foot of Vishnu like the slender threads of the lotus flower.'

But we were in no danger of dying on the sacred snows of Himachal, were we? It was a wonderful feeling to be up there on that icy throne of the gods. Peak on peak abounded around us. I felt exultation and exhilaration.

Harrop brought me to earth. 'Time to be getting back. We can't risk a bivouac here when the rest of the party have no knowledge of our whereabouts. A dose of frostbite now would destroy our chances of going for Gurla Mandhata.'

I nodded my agreement, and we romped down to the col and on down the glacier snout onto the terminal moraine. When we got back to our temporary campsite we were greeted by Scotty Dwyer and Geoff Roberts. They had marched into Saipal campsite fo find Harrop and me off climbing, so they dumped their loads and left Jack Henson and Humfrey

Berkeley to establish our main camp and hurried on up the Lekh to greet us. Dwyer and Roberts had not brought a tent with them, so the four of us spent a far from comfortable night crammed in a tent seven feet long by five feet high by five feet wide.

Our porters were still bleating. They didn't like being this high up for two nights in succession, even though each of them had carried loads to Taklakot for Nepalese traders, or had carried gear for the young Rajah Oom Jung to the holy mountain Kailas. I told them that all they had to do was move the two tents to the snout of the glacier that day, so that Roberts and Dwyer could make an alpine-style ascent of the 22,500-foot peak from the glacial moraine to the summit and back in one day. So that is exactly what they did. Dwyer and Roberts climbed that hitherto virgin peak at speed, getting down to their campsite well before dusk and, in a burst of energy, struck the tents, packed the porters' loads, and marched into Saipal in triumph just as light faded. It was a real *tour de force* by my two expedition colleagues.

I was amazed on their return to see the porters, who were well provided for with expedition gear, walking barefoot, their mountaineering boots hanging off the rear of their loads. They had collectively decided that the boots given to them by the Sahibs were too valuable for expedition work, and once back in Chainpur they would be able to sell them for the equivalent of a month's farming income.

The following morning Harrop and Roberts were away at first light equipped with the photo-theodolite from the Royal Geographical Society. This is what the expedition was really about as far as I was concerned. The survey duo were going to examine a peak and valley system to the west of the mountain which Roberts and Dwyer had claimed. This area, which I named 'The Hidden Valley' was not shown on the Indian survey maps of west Nepal.

We formed the opinion that when the Indian surveyors had accurately fixed the positions of all the major peaks, they completed the 'fill in' areas by guesswork, seated in a comfortable bar in New Delhi, pencil in hand over a pint of beer.

4

We now settled into a daily routine of surveying and exploration, during which time Harrop and I revised our plans for our attempt on Gurla Mandhata. The Tibetans split up into two groups. The main body left a handful of men to take care of their herds of sheep and goats, while the larger party trudged off down the Seti Gorge to the camping site at Garanphu. They were awaiting the arrival of Nepalese traders who would be back-packing their loads of ata and tsampa from Dhuli.

Of those who stayed behind at Saipal, there was one Tibetan who was better dressed than the others. He was clad in a dull red Shuba adorned with white lambswool cuffs and hem. He wore a dark green felt hat, also decked out in lambswool edging. Damodar observed, 'He doesn't appear to have any sheep to look after.' He spent a great deal of his time asking questions of Damodar. Where had we come from? Were they any more Sahibs coming up behind? What were our plans, in which direction did we intend to explore? A few days later our inquisitive friend had departed. As I had not at that time acquainted Damodar with the fact that Harrop and I intended illegally entering Tibet to attempt Gurla Mandhata, I felt secure in the knowledge that, if the red-coated Tibetan was a spy in the pay of the Chinese, which in the event he was, Damodar could not have passed on any intelligence which could provide useful to the Chinese at Taklakot.

We were to learn later that the Tibetan spy had repaired immediately to Taklakot where he had informed the Cheenee Burra Rajah Sahib that six Europeans were encamped at Saipal, just over the frontier; that they possessed surveying equipment, cameras with very long lenses, and that the leader of the expedition would take out a bolt action rifle and an automatic pistol and proceed to shoot at cardboard targets. His information that our porters and our Nepalese liaison officer were all clad in what looked like army trousers and sweaters (which they were, ex-army, bought cheaply at a surplus store) must have set the alarm bells ringing at Taklakot.

We possessed a radio with nine wavebands and this luxury allowed us the privilege one evening of hearing a cello concerto played by the late Pablo Casals, and on another occasion, to hear Stirling Moss win the Mille Miglia road race in Italy. Then it snowed. Our radio gave us daily weather forecasts from Delhi. They were addressed specifically to the Welsh Himalayan Expedition in west Nepal. Each evening we sat and listened to the forecast of more snow. 'What the hell has happened to the post-monsoon season?' Jack Henson roared when we had snow forecast five nights in succession. Ten Tibetans from Garanphu returned to Saipal with sheep loaded with saddle bags of ata and tsampa. Then they were gone back over the Urai Lekh to Tibet. Those Tibetans had read the weather much more expertly than either we or the meteorologists in Delhi. There was to be no post-monsoon season that year. The monsoon had arrived later than usual, and down on the plains India was experiencing one of the worst periods of flooding in meteorological history. Soon we were waist-deep in snow. The Urai Lekh would be impassable if the heavy precipitation of snow continued. I called the kind of conference the British SAS quite appropriately term a 'Chinese Parliament'. Everybody had their say, and let their hair down. The consensus was that we had no chance of climbing Nalkankar, and as for Wignall's plan for an illegal foray into forbidden Tibet to attempt Gurla Mandhata, well he must be 'out of his tiny Chinese mind' to contemplate the idea.

Kept in camp by continuous snow falls, we were consuming rations, and achieving little in the way of surveying and nil in the way of climbing mountains.

I sent our Sirdar of porters, Koila, back to Dhuli to obtain further rations in the form of ata flour and potatoes. When Koila returned two weeks later, complaining that huge avalanches had wiped out some of the most difficult passages on the face of the Seti Gorge, I began to worry. As Humfrey Berkeley had not enjoyed good health since we arrived, I decided that he should head back to Chainpur with one porter to help carry his load. Berkeley's task was to hire twenty porters to march up to Saipal and carry our equipment out. I worked out that given no undue difficulty, Berkeley's porters would be with us in about three weeks' time. Berkeley could then head off back to India and apprise *Life* magazine that we were snowed in, short on food, and planning to get the hell out of there.

Our one hope was that the snows would cease, and after a few nights of hard frost, consolidate, providing us with a hard surface for the proposed attack on Gurla Mandhata, if I decided to go ahead with the plan. I talked the matter over with both Harrop and Damodar. Damodar was of the opinion that with no command of Urdu, Harrop and I stood no chance of shepherding four unhappy porters over the Urai Lekh, across Tibet, and onto Gurla Mandhata. So it was decided that if we went for GM, Damodar would accompany us. Damodar beamed at this news. He regarded the plan as the opportunity for the greatest adventure of his life. Koila agreed that he and the other three porters would carry our loads. But there was a fly in the ointment. Being snowed in had reduced our high-altitude rations to the extent that we would be hard pushed to get to GM, ascend the mountain and get back without spending several days with nothing in our bellies.

On 16 October, my birthday, Harrop and Roberts set out to complete a survey, and lost our Royal Geographical Society theodolite when a huge avalanche almost engulfed them. On 17 October it did not snow. Neither did it snow on the 18th. Without that theodolite our survey programme could not be completed. What the hell else was there to do but go for Tibet and GM and a 'look see' at the military build-up of the forces of Comrade Mao Tse-tung, and perhaps get some still and cine long-range shots of activity resembling road construction on the Lhasa to Ladakh track.

We rose early on 19 October, packed our gear, and Harrop, Damodar and I with Koila and three other porters, set off on The Great Adventure. Dwyer, Roberts and Henson accompanied us and volunteered to blaze a trail through the soft snow up to the first day's camp, which we over-optimistically hoped would be just short of the summit of the Urai Lekh pass. Under normal conditions one should be able to leave Saipal, cross the Urai Lekh and reach the far end of the Jung Jung Khola in two days. In the event it was to take us five.

The going was perfectly bloody. The soft snow had a hard crust on top. One took two or three steps on hard snow and then the crust collapsed and one went through thigh-deep, or occasionally was engulfed in wet soft snow up to one's waist. Dwyer, Henson and Roberts did sterling work, changing position, soaked in both wet snow and perspiration, forcing a route for us towards the summit of the Urai Lekh. We covered no more than six miles in a solid day's march. The time had come for Henson, Dwyer and Roberts to turn back. We carried only two Meade high-altitude tents, one for Harrop, Damodar and me and one for the four porters. It was going to be cramped living. We camped for the night, and enjoyed a good meal. The next day it fell to Harrop and me to force the way through the soft snow. I cannot recall anything so arduous in the whole of my life. Take a step. OK. Take another, and through the hard crust you went, up to your waist in wet snow. I was still in poor shape due to recurring bouts of dysentery, and felt like I had been put through a wringer.

After eight hours, the summit of Urai Lekh pass was in sight. We pitched camp. I got out the map, and looked behind me. It was unbelievable. I could see our last campsite, seemingly close by. We had slogged and plodded for eight hours and only covered about 800 yards. At half a mile a day it would take forever to reach the north-west ridge of Gurla Mandhata. The porters were now complaining to Damodar. They had never been this high and this close to the frontier before so late in the season. 'The passes are closed from late October for the whole of the winter,' they kept hammering at Damodar. 'We will be trapped in Tibet and we will die of starvation.' The outlook was grim.

The following morning the sun shone. The going was not as bad as the day before. One only went through the snow crust every ten or twelve steps. Harrop and Damodar stayed behind to chivvy Koila and the other three porters. I was feeling a bit chipper that morning. No dysentery, a good bowl of hot tsampa Weetabix and some digestive biscuits, followed by a mug of tea, had set me up for what lay ahead. I reached the summit of the pass about ten minutes before the others. My optimism was dashed when I looked down the Tibetan side of the Urai Lekh. Where the ground had been snow-free a month earlier, it was now carpeted with fresh snow. I took a step downhill. The crust held. I took another. The crust broke, but I only sank in about a foot before my climbing boot struck hard snow again.

I trudged a few steps back up to the top of the Lekh. Harrop was panting up towards me. I turned and looked back into Tibet. Gurla Mandhata and Nalkankar were wreathed in snow cloud. There was not a puff of wind. The air was still. I ruminated on our situation. Until that expedition my wife and small son and I had never been separated for longer than one of my occasional rock climbing weekends. I missed them both dearly. 'Christ, we could die on that bloody stupid mountain,' I said to myself. 'We could be boxed in and have to give ourselves up to the Cheenee Burra Rajah Sahib, and have to face the winter in their officers' mess, stuffing ourselves with chop suey. The Chinese might be unpleasant and dispatch us to a hard regime prison in China proper. Why are we here? Is it all that important to climb the highest mountain in Tibet? Why risk your life for Mother India when her Burra Rajah Sahib Pandit Bloody Nehru doesn't even believe that the Chinese communists pose a threat to India?'

I went on like this for several minutes, sometimes talking aloud to myself. I was well and truly in a state of blue funk and beginning to talk myself out of taking any further steps in the direction of Gurla Mandhata. 'So that's it,' I said to myself. 'Nothing to be ashamed of. The weather has scuppered your plans. You are on the edge of the Tibetan and Himalayan winter. The passes will be closed behind you. You will be into November when you head back for the Urai Lekh. Honourable defeat and all that. You've had a go and lost. OK, then it's agreed. Here comes John Harrop. Tell him it's all off.'

Harrop plodded up onto the top of the pass, and without looking back or ahead, turned to me and gave me a thumping great slap on the back. 'Sorry for the delay. Porters went on strike. Damodar, Koila and I talked them out of it. No problem.' With that he was gone, gambolling in his usual very long strides down the Tibetan side of the Himalayan watershed.

I called after him. 'Are you sure you want to do this?'

Without looking back he called over his shoulder, 'I haven't anything else planned for this afternoon, have you?'

My friend and climbing companion John Harrop had made the decision for me. Damodar and the four porters trudged past and I watched them plod down the northern side of the pass. The clouds parted and the sun shone brilliantly. There beyond us lay the great massif of Nalkankar. It was good to be alive. I felt at peace with myself as I sauntered down the Lekh into the Jung Jung Khola. We were off on the greatest adventure of our lives totally unaware that a few miles to the north, a heavily-armed patrol of Chinese soldiers was moving south, on the lookout for Western Fascist Imperialist Running Dogs of the American CIA.

As we progressed down into the Jung Jung Khola, so the going improved. As the Tibetan side of the Urai Lekh pass received the full force of the icy cold winds blowing south from the Tibetan plateau, the snow at this point was rock hard. The steep track which had been snow-free when Harrop and I ambled down it was now a steep ice slope, and we spent several hours wearily cutting steps down it for our four porters. Koila was magnificent, but the other three, Ungya, Ratti and Giddy, were not made of such stern stuff, and they repeatedly complained about the dangers they faced if they fell. Harrop, in despair, shouldered Giddy's 80-pound load and carried it over one difficult stretch. That solved the problem. The other two followed Harrop and Koila down the ice slope to where Damodar and I were waiting.

Harrop and I showed the others how to glissade, sliding on one's backside down the now gently sloping ice sheet. Damodar and the porters joined in the fun, and we all ended up in a rag tag bundle at the bottom of the face, the previously dour and apprehensive porters now laughing their heads off. Once away from the shadowed confines of the head of the pass, the sun softened the snow and we were back on the soul-destroying routine of breaking trail for several miles. At 4 p.m. Harrop, Damodar and I halted in the shadow of a low stone wall that had been built by Tibetan traders as a shelter from the northerly wind. I donned a sweater and a down-filled jacket, but still that ice-cold wind chilled me to my bones. The porters arrived half an hour later, and Harrop and I unpacked our two Meade tents from their loads. Handicapped by frozen fingers we cursed and struggled with tent guys, and because we had to melt snow for our evening meal, cooking proved to be a slow and tedious business. It was 7 p.m. when we crawled into our sleeping bags.

The next morning we limited ourselves to tea, intending to cook a better meal once we got below the snow line. We set off at 7 a.m. to discover to our dismay that the deep snow here was almost as bad as on the southern side of the Urai Lekh. This was because we had to traverse a section of completely flat valley bottom where, for some three-quarters of a mile, the snow lay in drifts. Harrop and I took the lead, taking it in turns to trail-blaze, sinking up to our thighs with almost every step. We reached the far side of the snow drifts in a state of exhaustion, and soaked to the skin with perspiration.

Here the valley narrowed and turned slightly north-east through a narrow neck, then it widened and to our delight we saw running water. Koila unpacked one of our aluminium billy cans and filled it. Then we all retired to the leeward side of a house-sized boulder and set up our primus pressure stove for a welcome brew of tea. We had covered less than a mile in three hours. Then, we wearily plodded on through deep snow until we passed two lakes, neither of which was marked on the India Survey maps.

On our left soared majestic ice-covered peaks, all more than 20,000 feet in height which, Harrop drily observed, must be a mirage as according to the map we should have been standing on a bleak stone-covered plateau with an uninterrupted view of Tibetan villages, the Karnali river, and the great lamasery of Kojarnath lying on its far bank. I commented to Harrop that the errors displayed in the India Survey maps of Nepal were not going to make our journey to Gurla Mandhata easier. As the terrain did not fit the map description, we would have to route-find on an empirical basis. This could add a day or two to our timetable, and throw our ration allowance further out of kilter.

At 3 p.m. the snow started to thin out and patches of bare ground appeared. The wearying part of the journey lay behind us. Henceforth the going would be much easier. We turned a corner of the track to find the ground completely free of snow. Koila pointed to a circle of stones lying lower down on the left-hand side of the track. 'Tharedunga, Sahib.' These were standing stones.

A few yards further on we found a flat piece of ground on which we pitched our tents for the night. Here we were able to conserve our precious paraffin supplies, our porters cooking dinner on a brushwood and yak-dung fire. The next day's march would be a short one, to a place called Kalapani (black water). To the west of Kalapani lay the Tibetan village of Khatang, and straight ahead at the foot of the narrow northern end of the Jung Jung Khola lay the Karnali river. Once we were across the Karnali we should be able to see the whole of the hitherto totally unexplored Nalkankar group and at the foot of Nalkankar, Kojarnath lamasery. This was to be our last day of daylight travel on the route to Gurla Mandhata. From Kalapani onwards, we would have to travel by night. Our biggest headache was the Survey of India maps, they were so inaccurate.

The following morning, 23 October, took us under and past a great 3,000-foot-high limestone cliff resembling the Marmolata in the Dolomites. Its red and orange buttresses and gullies soared above us. We hurried past that great rock face. It was not a good place to loiter, as newly shattered rock debris on the track testified. After an hour's pleasant meandering along a fine level path we dropped down to the edge of a river. Higher up in the Jung Jung Khola, this river had been a mere trickle of water. Here it was about twenty feet wide and too deep to ford. Ahead we espied a small Tibetan-built wooden cantilever bridge across the Jung Jung river. We crossed it, and Koila, pointing up a scree slope which lay ahead, shouted 'Kalapani, Sahib.'

Kalapani did not live up to its name. There was no black water. A small spring issued from a rock gully, at the foot of which grew a small solitary tree. The water was clear, sparkling and mineralised, it was like drinking champagne. We dropped our loads and set up our tents. We could see right down the Jung Jung Khola now. By climbing a couple of hundred feet above our new campsite we saw the great Nalkankar complex of ice-covered peaks and, using binoculars, were able to identify Kojarnath lamasery. There were now only two escape routes into Tibet out of the Jung Jung Khola. One could either ascend the Khatang pass which towered above us to the west, or continue down the Jung Jung Khola towards the Karnali.

Koila further dashed my plans. He explained through Damodar that my maps which showed comparatively easy going down the western side of the Jung Jung Khola to Kojarnath were hopelessly inaccurate. There was no route down the remaining five miles of the Jung Jung Khola. There was no track, other than a narrow one used by wild goats, which Koila said petered out after a mile or so, and the walls of the Jung Jung Khola were too difficult for porters carrying heavy loads. If we wanted to illegally enter Tibet and try to climb Gurla Mandhata we would have to cross the Khatang pass and enter the Khatang valley, and leave it over a small low pass to the north which led down to the Tibetan lamasery at Jitkot. My plans were bring thrown further adrift.

'Can we get past Khatang village at night, without being observed?' I enquired of Koila.

'Perhaps, Sahib. But the headman, old Phrupa, he may have only one eye, but he does have Tibetan mastiff dogs, and they have ears and a sense of smell. If we get past Khatang without being detected, we could cross the small pass which leads down onto the Tibetan plain, and follow the track down towards Jitkot Gompa. Then we would have to cross the Karnali river. The river is fordable in places, but I don't know if there is a ford in that area. If there is not, then we would have to march almost into Taklakot to reach a ford that I know of.'

The only good news from Koila was that the Chinese did not station any troops either in Khatang or on the north side of the small pass which led down to Jitkot. According to Koila, the Chinese garrison stayed in Taklakot nearly all the time, and the only troops stationed on the border itself were on the Tibetan side of the Lipu Lekh pass which led into India.

Koila might have been right about the movements of the Chinese in the past, when he passed that way as a porter for the young Rajah Oom Jung, on his annual pilgrimage to the holy mountain Kailas. But things had changed. News that Europeans were on the Nepal side of the Himalaya had been taken by Chinese army couriers on mules to the west Tibet headquarters of the People's Liberation Army of the Republic of China at Gartok, 120 miles to the north-west of Taklakot. At that time the Chinese in west Tibet only had one short-wave radio capable of communicating with Lhasa, and that radio was at Gartok. Chinese HQ at Lhasa instructed the military governor of west Tibet to apprehend the 'Foreign Devils' even if that entailed crossing over into Nepal.

As a consequence of those instructions, a Chinese patrol, with Tibetan interpreters, including the man who spied on our base camp at Saipal, was now visiting each of the three passes which led down in the direction of Taklakot. The first of these, the Lipu Lekh, on the Indian border, was an easy day's mule ride or march on foot. The second pass, closer to Taklakot and to the east of the Lipu Lekh is the Tinkar Lipu, which leads into an area of north-west Nepal separated from our base camp by a range of mountains most of them at that time unclimbed, including Api and Nampa. The Chinese ignorance of the terrain on the southern side of the Himalayan watershed was such that they thought that the 'Foreign Devils' could wander about and cross any one of those three passes to spy on the PLA at Taklakot.

By now the Chinese patrol had visited their border post on the Tibetan side of the Lipu Lekh to be advised by their border guards that no Europeans had come into view. From the Lipu Lekh, the Chinese patrol had headed back down the pass, and once on the Tibetan plateau had turned east until they reached the approaches of the Tinkar Lipu pass. The Tinkar Lipu was not at that time guarded by the PLA, and the Chinese patrol had perforce to ascend to the summit of the pass and then descend illegally into the Tinkar Khola in west Nepal, which they duly did. Still no sign of the Western Fascist Lackey Imperialist Running Dogs.

Returning down from the Tinkar Lipu, the Chinese, seeing no sign of tracks in the virgin snow, had one last pass to examine, and that was the Urai Lekh. Now running short of rations, for there were no villages in the Tinkar area from which they could commandeer supplies, the Chinese intended seizing whatever requirements they needed from the Tibetan village of Khatang. Our paths were soon to cross.

The news that we would not be able to proceed further down the Jung Jung Khola, and would have to pass by night through inhabited areas where the local populace kept ferocious mastiff dogs made the outlook far from promising. It had taken us five days to cover a bare seventeen miles. At this rate, our daily rations of no more than 2,000 calories, quite insufficient for hard work at high altitude, would be totally inadequate for the remainder of our march to Gurla Mandhata and an exhausting climb to 22,000 feet for that proposed observation camp.

Harrop and I went over the route, the timing and the ration scale again and again, and just when things looked really bad, we received the death blow to our Gurla Mandhata plans. Koila had been talking in a heated manner with Damodar, who delivered the *coup de grâce*. 'Koila says that the sheep meat pemmican bars you have been boiling for our main meal at night are not really sheep meat, and he and the other three porters believe that the pemmican bars are made from the flesh of the cow. The cow is a holy creature in the eyes of the Hindu religion. There can be no persuasion, Syd Sahib. They will not eat any more of the pemmican.'

'On that basis,' Harrop interjected, 'there will be just about enough food for the three of us, that is if you will eat our cow meat pemmican, Damodar? But no rations for our porters.'

Damodar replied, 'I tried to fool Koila and the others into believing that the pemmican was sheep and not beef meat, Syd Sahib, but they no longer believe me. I will eat the beef, if it gets us up that mountain, but what to do about the porters? We have too little tsampa, which they do not like, and very little more ata for making their chapatis. They cannot survive unless we can get about a hundred pounds of ata and tsampa to supplement what we have got.'

'That's it then,' I commented. 'All our plans are shot. Goodbye Gurla Mandhata.'

'Oh, it's not as bad as that, Syd Sahib,' Damodar said. 'Koila says that he could go into Khatang and say that he was with a party of Nepalese pilgrims on their way to Kailas, and that they were short of food, and he could buy some native flour from old Phrupa.'

'Too risky,' I countered. 'Phrupa may only have one eye, but the old blighter must surely have more than half a brain, and wonder why all the Nepalese pilgrims don't just walk in with Koila.'

'We could tell Koila to say that the going was so bad, the Nepal party have thought better of it, and are going to return back over the Urai Lekh and are short of food,' Damodar suggested.

'It's worth a try,' Harrop interjected. 'It would be a damned shame to have travelled all this way for nothing, when a hundred pounds of flour could solve all our problems.'

'Let's put it to the vote,' I suggested. 'No more dictates by me as leader of the expedition. We will be running the risk of death by starvation, exposure, and possible incarceration in some damn bamboo pagoda in China. Hands up all those who say that Koila should go into Khatang and try to pull the yak wool over old Phrupa's one remaining eye.'

Three hands shot up. It was a fateful decision. We were going into Tibet, come what may, and to hell with the Cheenee Burra Rajah Sahib. Reassured by our unanimous decision I handed Koila a bundle of rupee notes and at noon he and Ratti departed on the four-mile journey to Khatang over the nearby pass. Koila was to try to purchase fifty pounds of tsampa and the same quantity of ata, and he promised to return the following afternoon. Harrop and I decided that we would spend the day sorting and repacking our porters' loads, so that we could set forth the following morning on a reconnaissance survey. We would ascend the Khatang pass, and from a rock bluff on the northern side of the pass, should have a splendid viewpoint for our photographic record of Gurla Mandhata and the whole of the Nalkankar massif. Furthermore, we would be able to examine through binoculars and telephoto lenses the ridges which connect Nalkankar with Gurla Mandhata, in order to work out our approach route to the latter mountain. Our completion of that task would coincide with Koila's return over the Khatang pass, and

Harrop, Damodar and I, being lightly laden, would be able to take spells with Koila and Ratti in sharing their load carrying. But, as His Grace the Duke of Wellington was reputed to have said, 'No plan of battle survives contact with the enemy.'

Sleep proved difficult as our Meade tent was pitched on a slope and, being on the outside, I suffered the combined weight of Damodar and Harrop rolling onto me. On the morning 24 October Harrop, Damodar and I, accompanied by tiny bow-legged porter Ungya, headed for the summit of the snow-free Khatang pass. It was a dreadful track, covered with sharp angular stones. Higher up, the angle eased and we traversed a pleasant little hollow filled with tiny whinberries. The rock track gave way to pleasant grass slopes interspersed with patches of bare soil. To the left rose a great rock peak, its upper reaches sheathed in ice. This was part of the mountain barrier which stretched all the way back to the Urai Lekh. On our right, on the northern side of the pass, rose a light brown limestone peak and it offered a good viewpoint for our photo survey of Tibet. Ungya called out. Damodar beckoned us back.

'Look what Ungya has spotted,' he cried.

I looked down on pug marks in the soil, and could make no sense of them.

'There has been a thin layer of snow,' Damodar said, 'and after it melted, it moistened the earth just slightly, sufficient for these pug marks. Look, here are the marks of an ibex. Now look at the distance between this patch of marks, and those further on. Ungya says that some time this morning, an ibex came up here, tracked by a snow leopard. This is the spot where the leopard leaped onto the ibex. Look how the leopard pug marks are deeper now, as it carried off the ibex.'

I looked around. Somewhere up there in the rocks, the snow leopard would be lying with its kill, in all probability looking down on us. We continued our scramble up onto the summit of the limestone peak. As a viewpoint it lacked nothing, all we had come to see was there. Down on the far left lay the Khatang valley and, even with the naked eye we could see the four seemingly miniature houses which made up Phrupa's village. The landscape ahead was dominated by the majestic massif of Gurla Mandhata, 25,350 feet high, its great south precipice looking most forbidding. The other, easier route, via the north-west ridge, ran at right angles to our line of vision.

'Looks like a piece of cake,' Harrop said. 'You don't even have to set foot on a glacier to get onto the west ridge, and it's just a long plod to the summit.'

An intervening ridge hid Taklakot from our gaze. The sacred lake of Manasorawar was also out of view, hidden behind a ridge which ran up to GM. On the far horizon there was no mistaking that beautiful pyramid-shaped peak of the holy mountain, Kailas.

'If you want Nalkankar there it is,' Harrop said.

I looked to the north-east. There were far more peaks on the Nalkankar massif than are suggested by the Indian Survey map. The peak shown on the map as being 24,062 feet in height was by no means the highest. The highest summit was nearer to us and could not have been far short of 25,000 feet. While Harrop took down compass bearings I filmed and photographed the panorama of peaks and passes surrounding us with three 35 mm still cameras and a 16 mm cine camera. Our limestone peak vantage point at about 17,000 feet also commanded a fine view of the final five miles or so of the Jung Jung Khola. Straight ahead lay the Tibetan village of Kojarnath, distinguished by its trinity of great red lamaseries. I turned and focused my binoculars on the tiny village of Khatang. Someone was discernible in a small field near to the largest house, it was a Tibetan driving half a dozen yaks.

The track over the Khatang pass ran steeply down the Tibetan side, levelling off by the banks of a small river. There was a cantilever wooden bridge, and then the track vanished into a shallow gully, to reappear on a small plateau, threading through a few small fields until it reached the houses. The brown and purple hillside behind the houses was cut by long straight horizontal lines, denoting channels dug into the hard ground to funnel glacier water off the snow peaks down to the fields. We sat until late afternoon, but there was no sign of Koila. I took a last look at Khatang through my binoculars. I saw what appeared to be horses tethered outside the largest of the four houses. The Cheenee Burra Rajah Sahibs had arrived at Khatang, although we did not know it, and poor Koila and Ratti were tied hand and foot and being beaten and kicked into confessing that they were conducting two Europeans and a Nepalese into Tibet.

Disheartened, we returned to our camp at Kalapani, Damodar and our other two porters expressing the opinion that perhaps Phrupa did not have sufficient flour for our needs and that he would probably have to send someone down to Jitkot for further supplies. Back at camp we sorted out some fossils Harrop had collected near to the summit of the pass. We were happily ignorant of the fact that those harmless-looking pieces of stone were to cause us a great deal of trouble and heartache in the very near future.

The author at base camp, West Nepal, 1955.

Base camp, West Nepal: (left to right, back row) Geoff Roberts, John Harrop, "Scotty" Dwyer, (front) Humphrey Berkeley, the author, Jack Henson.

(Opposite, top) Damodar Suwal, eighteen years old, our official Nepalese government liaison officer. (Opposite, bottom) Koila, the Sirdar of the expedition's Nepalese porters.

Tibetan traders at the base camp making yak butter tea.
The man on the extreme left was the Tibetan who spied for the Chinese.

(Opposite) The camp comedian does a dance for the camera. The Tibetans camped inside stone circles which are hundreds of years old.

John Harrop's birthday peak.

View into Tibet from the Nepal border. (A) West ridge of Gurla Mandhata. (B) Taklakot lies on the lower slopes

The author crossing a river in full monsoon flood in West Nepal.

The author in the Jung Jung Khola, illegally entering Tibet, October 1955.

The morning of December 18th, 1955, the author, feeling physically incapable of forcing the Seti Gorge (suffering from malnutrition, dysentery and frostbite), scribbled intelligence data on the Chinese Peoples' Liberation Army on the back of a discarded Chinese cigarette packet, and secreted it, along with a list of final instruction for it to be conveyed to the Indian Army, inside Harrop's rucksack.

(Opposite) Entrance to Seti Gorge in summer. In winter the stone track is swept away by avalanches.

The winter return over the Himalayas from Taklakot. The Urai Lekh pass lies on the skyline. (Photo of the author by John Harrop.)

(Opposite, top) The cave dwellings and tented traders bazaar, Taklakot. A new Chinese PLA barracks is situated in the lower left corner. (Photo taken in 1992, reproduced by kind permission of Brian Beresford.)

(Opposite, bottom) Damodar makes use of the Chinese flag.

18 December 1955. Looking down into the Seti Gorge.

The descent of the Seti Gorge; Damodar on the left, Harrop on the right.

The village of Dhuli, first habitation reached on return march from Tibet.

At Chainpur: (left to right) John Harrop, Major R. M. Dass, Indian Army Intelligence, the author, Mr Ram Wat Awhastie, local schoolmaster.

5

I spent most of that night being squeezed against the side of the tent by Harrop and Damodar, and morning came none too soon. Little by little the sunlight crept across the valley and stole along the cliff face above until it bathed our tiny Meade tent in its resplendent glow.

Already fully dressed, I struggled through the tunnel entrance of our tent and donned my climbing boots. Ungya and Giddy were still asleep and I roused them to go and find dead dwarf juniper wood for our fire, and water from the nearby spring. Our fireplace was at the foot of the solitary tiny tree which grew at the cliff face hard by the track. I busied myself with a few twigs and some dried yak dung, using our rubber bellows-style air mattress inflator to provide forced draught for the fire which soon roared into life. The porters supplied more wood and yak dung and I brewed up a large billy-can of tea.

My thoughts strayed to the relative luxury of our base camp at Saipal, where to hand were soup, dehydrated meat, potatoes, cabbage, gooseberries and apples. In comparison with our monotonous diet of pemmican and chapatis those at base camp fared well. How I hated chapatis. They may be filling, but being unleavened and not completely cooked (a well cooked chapati is like plywood) they produce strange effects on one's digestive system, resulting in the almost uncontrollable passing of great draughts of wind. So much so that our porters on the march would give vent to noises that for all the world sounded like a ruptured rhinoceros calling to its young. Some disrespectful mountaineers refer to this most unsocial phenomenon as 'Sherpa oxygen'.

Damodar pushed his face through the tent entrance and asked for some unexplained reason what day it was. Some mental reckoning led me to suggest that it was 25 October. After breakfast I sat outside the entrance to our tent writing up my diary. Harrop was using up the last of our native flour in an effort to make oatmeal cakes, and Damodar was assisting him to the extent of eating every other one, after plastering it with the contents of one of our three remaining tins of strawberry jam.

Ungya and Giddy made their own fire on which to cook chapatis, diminishing their own stock of ata flour. Ungya kept looking up the track seeking signs of Koila and Ratti. Without Koila to mother him, Ungya was a pretty miserable character. After about a dozen or so partly cooked chapatis each, Ungya and Giddy relieved our boredom and their bowels with great feats of the art of venting Sherpa oxygen, each seeking to outdo the other with the acoustic effects attained. I returned to scribbling in my diary, only to be distracted by Ungya, who drew my attention to the track leading down from the Khatang Pass.

'Koila, Sahib, Koila, Sahib,' he kept repeating, while patting his stomach to signify that another dozen chapati 'wind breakers' would not go amiss. I took up my binoculars and focused them on the higher reaches of the track. I could detect figures hopping from boulder to boulder. They were Tibetans. There were four of them and, without speaking to us, ignoring Damodar and Ungya's greetings in Urdu, they sat down on the track, as it were cutting us off from access to the route back to the Urai Lekh. I recognised one of the four. It was the short Tibetan in the red cloak who had been at our campsite at Saipal. The Tibetan spy was back.

I heard more clattering on the track and focused my binoculars on the tiny figures. They were clad in brown quilted cotton trousers and jackets. Some wore army boots, others smart-looking rubber and canvas basketball boots, brown or blue in colour. As they descended I could identify their fur-trimmed caps, each with an enamelled metal red star on the front. I saw weapons, and they were ubiquitous Soviet-style PPSh 7.62 mm assault rifles. Harrop and Damodar kept asking, 'Who is it? Can you see? Is it Koila?'

I spotted bandoliers and stick grenades. Harrop and Damodar's vision was obstructed by the small tree under which they sat. 'It's only the People's Liberation Army of the Republic of China,' I replied.

Damodar, his mouth full of oatcake, his fingers sticky with strawberry jam, was unable to speak.

'They've chosen a most inconvenient time to call,' Harrop commented without looking up or even raising an eyebrow. 'We haven't enough of these oatcakes to go round as it is, let alone feed visitors.'

I felt helpless. It was impossible to make a run for it. We could only sit it out and play dumb. 'Took the wrong turning just after we left Leicester Square, Cheenee Burra Rajah Sahib. Promise we won't let it happen again, officer.' Perhaps they were customs and immigration, just checking up on unauthorised intrusions by people who should have applied for a visa? But why here? The Governor of Baitadi in west Nepal had looked over our maps and advised me that the Jung Jung Khola was inside the frontier of Nepal, and had been regarded as such for centuries. My thoughts were interrupted by the arrival of the Chinese.

The first infantryman ran straight past us and halted about twenty feet along the track, between us and the Urai Lekh. He cocked his PPSh and aimed it at us. Number two ran past and dropped down into a gully leading down to the river bank, presumably to deny us an exit in that direction. He also aimed his rifle at us. Number three climbed some broken rocks on to a ledge projecting from the cliff face above and sat, legs dangling, his assault rifle aimed at my head.

These armed men, or youths, for none looked older than twenty-one or so, adopted a routine which had obviously been worked out beforehand. Our escape route was cut off and we were well and truly in the bag. The last two came down the track at an easier pace. Both wore long great-coats, lined with sheepskin, and fur-trimmed hats with an enamelled red star on the front. They were armed with pistols. I recognised the wooden combined holster and shoulder stock of the 1896 German 'Broom Handled' 7.63 mm Mauser automatic pistol. The two men were obviously officers. One was short and the other tall. The tall one gave us a big smile and held out his hand, which I shook.

'We're off to a good start,' Harrop commented.

'No problem. A few hours from now we'll be having chicken chop suey in the officers' mess, and after a toast or two to Chairman Mao, we'll be on our way home.'

I was due for a shock. I was to come across only two Chinese communists whom I would regard as 'decent chaps' and this tall fellow was one of them. The other I was yet to meet. The tall one spoke in Mandarin, and when we signified that we did not understand, he broke into fluent Tibetan. One of the Tibetans translated into Urdu for Damodar's benefit.

'This is Jungpah. Jungpah says that you are illegally in occupation of the territory of the People's Republic of China. He says that he must see your documents, he must search your equipment. We must all be searched.'

By now the small weedy officer had drawn his Mauser pistol. It looked like a cannon in his tiny hands. He and Jungpah wore plain khaki drill trousers and tunics under their great-coats, and they also wore black leather hobnailed footgear reminiscent of the British Army 'ammunition boot'. The infantrymen armed with PPSh assault rifles wore rubber and canvas basketball boots of flimsy appearance, totally unsuited to Himalayan mountain terrain.

A crowd of Tibetans came down the track to join the increasing throng. There was the usual ragbag of sheepskin-clad, felt-booted individuals followed by two who, because of their bearing and the cut of their clothes, stood out from the rest. As the latter two entered into conversation with the tall Chinese officer, the newly arrived Tibetans started to go through our kit, taking all the porter loads apart, including our three rucksacks. The sight of them upending a kit bag which contained hundreds of pounds' worth of valuable cameras and telephoto lenses was too much for Harrop and me. As I yanked one Tibetan out of our food box, another dived into the entrance of our Meade tent. I pulled him out by his boots, becoming aware that his feet smelt like dead rats. I was tripped up by another Tibetan who made for Harrop's rucksack. Damodar, wise in Tibetan ways, decided that it was all in the hands of the gods and took the opportunity to scoff the remaining oatcakes that Harrop had just cooked. Harrop picked up one small Tibetan, and placing the man under his arm, spanked his bottom as if he were a naughty child.

At this the tall Chinese officer laughed, as did the two better dressed and more dignified Tibetans. When it was all over the Tibetans, by weight of numbers had won the day, and our possessions were strewn all over the track. Then they sat about in little groups examining everything, item by item. The binoculars interested them most and they fought for turns to look through the wrong end, falling about in paroxysms of laughter when they observed tiny images of their friends. A word of command from the older of the two better-dressed Tibetans brought the depredations to an end. The hilarity ceased. I took a good look at the old boy who had so effectively exercised discipline over his compatriots. His cloak was made of good quality purple Indian cloth, trimmed with silver and gold thread with a high fur collar. Around his waist was a belt of linked silver plates. His high felt hat was trimmed with fox fur and his leather riding boots were far superior to the rope-soled footwear worn by his compatriots.

This patrician-looking Tibetan came over to me and tried to engage me in conversation, as Damodar had volunteered the information that I was the leader of the party. The old gentleman spoke Urdu fluently and introduced himself as Gin Din Rhou, Abbot or High Lama of Jitkot lamasery. His companion, he said, was a high-ranking Tibetan official who was satrap of the Chinese at Taklakot. As the Chinese and other Tibetans were at work going through our equipment, we were able to engage in a short conversation with Gin Din Rhou. From the tone of the conversation, he was hinting to me through Damodar that one of the Tibetans present could not be trusted. It became obvious that Gin Din Rhou did not have too much liking for the Chinese. The Tibetan who was not to be trusted was the tall one dressed entirely in black, who wore a saturnine expression on his face. He then told Damodar that the tall Chinese called Jungpah was in fact the Dzongpon of Taklakot.

By now the two Chinese officers had examined our gear and were writing down a list of our possessions. I turned to Harrop. 'The Dzongpon is always a Tibetan, a sort of magistrate. It looks as though the Chinese have replaced the Tibetan Dzongpon with their own man, a Chinese officer. The Tibetan civil administration has been taken over by the Chinese military.'

'Gin Din Rhou says,' Damodar continued, 'that the Chinese patrol came into Khatang just after Koila arrived, and they were commanded by that small officer, who had Koila tied up, and that he beat Koila and kicked him with his boots to make him tell about us. Then a soldier was sent back to Taklakot and the Chinese in command at Taklakot sent the Dzongpon, and he called at Jitkot lamasery on his way here, to collect Gin Din Rhou to act as interpreter, because the Dzongpon does not trust the ordinary Tibetans to tell the truth.'

Harrop said to Damodar, 'Ask the old boy what the Chinese propose to do with us.'

Gin Din Rhou obliged. 'The tall one, the Dzongpon, is the highest-ranking Chinese civil official at Taklakot. He says that he wishes you well and would willingly allow you to return over the Urai Lekh, but he fears that his superior, the Chinese military governor at Gartok, might be annoyed if you were not brought in for questioning. He also humbly apologises for searching your equipment and for any inconvenience you might suffer.'

It was put so nicely, how could we possibly be offended? I asked Damodar, through Gin Din Rhou, to convey my greetings to the Dzongpon, and also to advise him that we came from a country where people did not point guns at one another. Dzongpon took this ever so well. He gave me a big toothy smile and, turning to the PLA soldiers, ordered them to lower their weapons. Things were beginning to look up. Then Harrop put the damper on my improved spirits.

'Where have you hidden that damned pistol of yours? I didn't see it being emptied out of our bags.'

I patted the kangaroo-pouch pocket on the front of my anorak. 'By a coincidence, I happen to have it right here. It's fully loaded, with one round in the breech and the safety is off. As the Chinese have lowered their weapons, how would you view the following scenario? I pull my pistol, and shout HANDS UP. Yes? . . . No?'

There was a violent shaking of heads on the part of both Harrop and Damodar.

'Not a chance,' Harrop retorted. 'I've seen you shoot. You couldn't hit a barn door at twenty feet. Take on five of them, three with tommy guns and two with pistols. My God, I don't want to play this game any more. I just want to go home.' That settled it. 'Go on,' Harrop said. 'Give them the bloody gun before you get us all shot. That pistol is going to take some explaining away. And look at that. Jungpah has just found our passports. People who go to the Himalaya to climb mountains do not carry passports or pistols on their way to the summit.'

I walked over to the Dzongpon and the short officer and, drawing my Browning pistol out of my pocket, by the muzzle, I said, 'I think that you'd better have this. I found it up in the Jung Jung Khola. I think that it fell off the back of a truck.'

Fully expecting a burst of rapid fire 7.65 mm Kurz bullets, I closed my eyes, only to open them at the sound of laughter. The Dzongpon was holding my automatic pistol in his left hand while drawing his long barrelled Mauser with the other. He was comparing the minuscule size of my weapon with his. The Chinese all broke into smiles.

Jungpah said a few words to Gin Din Rhou. These were translated for Harrop and me. 'Jungpah says that he does not wish to embarrass you by a physical search of your bodies. If you will just show him the contents of your pockets he would be greatly obliged.'

Jungpah was a gentleman of the old school as far as the Chinese were concerned. I committed the error of thinking that all the Chinese we were going to meet would be like him. The Tibetans repacked and shouldered our loads and, on an order from Jungpah, set off for Khatang, escorted by two of the infantrymen. We struck camp and were packing our rucksacks when we saw our two missing porters, Koila and Ratti, arrive looking thoroughly dejected. Koila was in tears. As Sirdar of our porters he regarded himself as responsible for the safety of his two Sahibs, and now he believed that he was responsible for our forthcoming incarceration in Tibet.

'What will I tell Rajah Oom Jung?' he cried. 'I will be disgraced in my village.'

I told Damodar to tell Koila that if there was any blame to be levelled, then it should be aimed at me. The responsibility for our predicament was entirely mine. We picked up our ice axes, shouldered our rucksacks and set out for the Khatang pass and the village of one-eyed Phrupa.

We soon spaced out on the track. Harrop and I in front, Damodar somewhere behind, and our porters bringing up the rear. I noticed that Gin Din Rhou and the headman of Taklakot stayed close to Harrop and me all the time, perhaps because the Chinese made them responsible for our behaviour. After resting at the top of the pass, we descended the Khatang side and were intrigued by the numerous cave dwellings dotted all over a cliff face a few hundred yards from the village. The entrances to the caves were many feet above ground level. There was no sign of ladders and they appeared to have long since fallen into disuse.

The Tibetan side of the Khatang pass remains in shadow for the greater part of the day and in consequence was covered with hard, consolidated snow. The two senior Tibetans scampered down the snow slope like a couple of seasoned mountaineers, Gin Din Rhou being much the faster of the two. At the bottom we reached a small cantilever bridge over a river, where Gin Din Rhou and the Taklakot official had their ponies tethered. Gin Din Rhou and the headman mounted their steeds and signed for us to follow them. I stopped to drink some of the clear sparkling glacier water from that tiny river and, looking up, noticed that this small watercourse drained the whole of the Khatang valley, and then ran east to join the Jung Jung river through a narrow gorge. Gin Din Rhou explained that the tall Chinese, the Dzongpon of Taklakot, was from the western borders of China close to the Tibetan province of Kham and that was why he spoke Tibetan so fluently, and presumably why he had got the job.

I had a feeling that if Jungpah had been present when the PLA got their hands on Koila, Koila would not have been kicked and beaten. We later discovered that Jungpah's authority over the PLA was nil. He may have been the highest-ranking Chinese at Taklakot, but he was of the civil and not the military cadres.

We passed through a shallow gully where the ground was covered with great moraine boulders of enormous size, some as large as a two-storey house. Then the track, almost snow-free now, climbed out onto the tiny fields we had observed the previous day. We hopped over the three-foot-wide channels, some of them dry, some with just a trickle of water running through. Harrop commented that it must have been a fine feat of Tibetan engineering and a back-breaking job to cut and hew those channels all the way to the hanging glacier which overlooked Khatang from the south. Harrop should know, he was an agricultural scientist. We eventually arrived at a chorten, a Buddhist shrine, and a Mani wall, built of red sandstone. The phrase 'Om Mani Padme Hum', was engraved on each and every one of its several hundred separate stones. Harrop, Damodar and I and our porters took great care to pass the Mani wall on the left-hand side to avoid offending the religious feelings of the old lama, and he smiled graciously in acknowledgement.

Khatang village was now in sight and in a short time we reached the first of the houses. Khatang hardly ranks as a village, there being only four houses, three of which were in use. All three dwellings were occupied by the same family. The Tibetans came out to greet us, and we were to learn that twenty-two people lived in Phrupa's house, including Phrupa's parents. Phrupa was at least sixty. The house was square and flat-roofed, and all the windows looked onto a central courtyard. There was a small yard at the front of the house and this, surrounded by a low wall, was crowded with tiny Tibetan ponies and a few Chinese army mules, most of them saddled for an early departure. The sun was vanishing behind the mountains to the west.

Threading our way through the animals we crossed the yard, ducking our heads to enter a small passageway which connected with the main courtyard of the house. Doorways in Phrupa's house were seldom more than five feet high, and sometimes lower, and my perpetual collisions with low beams were a source of amusement to Phrupa's family.

Once in the central courtyard of the house Jungpah surprised us with, 'Please sit.' With that he gave us an expansive smile. 'Chai, yappa do?' (Chai is Hindustani for tea, yappa do Tibetan for yes.)

We nodded our assent and Jungpah departed through a distant doorway to arrange for a welcome brew of tea. We squatted on the mud floor of the courtyard, with our backs to a wall. I dropped my rucksack on to a wooden box covered with rags, only to be reviled by half a dozen Tibetans who were peering at us in the dusk through an open doorway. One of them entered the courtyard and screamed down a rectangular hole in the floor. Not until then did we notice this shaft leading down into the bowels of Phrupa's residence, and from it emerged three toothless old ladies. The oldest was blind in one eye and hardly able to walk. She crawled over the edge of the black, shadowy hole on hands and knees, her unkempt hair hanging in long greasy strands. Her face was deeply lined and heavily pock marked. I had never seen such a face before. She could have been a hundred years old.

In a land where the life expectancy is less than forty years, age is bought dearly, and the ravages of smallpox are apparent on the faces of many of the old people, some of whom walked with rigid gait, their knee joints locked by the effect of untreated syphilis. The old girl reached into the box, pushed my twenty-pound rucksack to one side and dug around amongst the rags. She lifted a naked baby out of the box and offered the child to me to hold, and I fell over Harrop's feet in my effort to get out of the way.

I backed around the yard, declining as gracefully as I could, and my salvation appeared in the form of old Phrupa himself, bearing a cast-iron kettle filled to the brim with yak butter tea. He was blind in one eye, and his good eye glared at us. I salaamed and he grunted an acknowledgement. Phrupa placed the kettle on the ground and produced small wooden cups from the folds of his voluminous sheepskin cloak.

The tea was Chinese, with yak butter, spices of undetermined type and ginger added. Being thirsty, we drank the first cup fairly eagerly, but not the second. The taste, certainly unique, was like split pea soup laced with rancid fat. The flavour of tea was virtually non-existent. Phrupa's entire family came out to watch the foreigners drinking tea. There must have been at least twenty people gathered around us. Some held small ghee lamps, from which a smoky flame provided minimal light. There was a great scramble for the foil coverings when we dined off three of our concentrated pemmican blocks. Dinner was interrupted by the Chinese, who appeared like shadows out of the darkness. It was time for us to depart, for what destination we knew not.

Phrupa, with Damodar translating, told us that he and his family wished us well and hoped that we would be able to return in a few days' time, not as prisoners of the Cheenee Burra Rajah Sahib, but as guests. As I thanked Phrupa for his hospitality, the Chinese PLA soldiers ushered us outside where Tibetans and Chinese were packing our loads onto ponies. Jungpah stated that he intended to carry only bare essentials for Harrop, Damodar and me for one night. Koila and the other three porters were detailed to follow the next day, on foot, with the remainder of our gear.

I had never ridden a horse before, and the pony I was offered had neither stirrups nor reins. Even more ominous was the absence of a saddle and, after much arguing, I was supplied with a Tibetan pack saddle. One look at the thing was enough for me to cry out for mercy. It was made of two wooden crosses joined together by bars of square sectioned timber running fore and aft, set with the sharp edges uppermost. On this I was to sit for a night ride of only heaven knows how many miles. But my protests were to no avail. The Tibetans led the animal to a low wall, and I climbed onto the pony.

The sharp edges of the wood cut into my flesh. But my complaints, uttered most vociferously, were cut short by Phrupa who handed me reins which he had just fitted onto the tiny pony. The reins amounted to no more than a single piece of string leading to the left-hand side of the creature's halter. A tentative pull on the string and my mount shot away from the wall, executed a couple of left-hand turns and galloped head-on into the Dzongpon's mule. That gentleman showed his displeasure by giving my steed a flick with his riding crop which sent it galloping off into the night. I dropped the string and grabbed the pony's mane with both hands as I began to slide off the pack saddle to the left.

Crisis overtook me when my pony charged head-on at a Mani wall. At the last moment he came to an abrupt halt, leaving me to continue my journey alone. Like a human cannon I hit the top of the wall and bounced down the other side, landing on my head and shoulders. Having made sure that no bones were broken, but feeling bruised in both flesh and spirit I got back onto my feet. I found the entire assembled company doubled up in merriment, Jungpah and the other officer having illuminated my 'John Jorrocks' ride with their battery-powered torches. Without more ado, the Tibetans lifted me back onto the Mani wall, from which I clambered back onto my pony. By now the creature had quietened down and accepted my presence as an inescapable and unfortunate burden.

From the heart of the mounted throng appeared the figure of Lama Gin Din Rhou. He rode past the head of the column and stopping by a chorten set in the middle of the Mani wall, muttered a prayer. His voice rose and fell. As he finished, he spurred his horse on, and each of the Tibetans on reaching the chorten followed Gin Din Rhou's pious example.

A whinnying from the yard behind us was answered by my pony, and a tiny all-white foal, no more than four feet in height, trotted into sight, nuzzling my mount which was obviously its mother. Thus began my first horse ride, bouncing up and down on that pain-inducing pack saddle, the tiny white foal running close alongside my diminutive steed.

6

I t was now so dark we had little idea of the outline of the countryside. The going was so steep that I had difficulty in stopping myself sliding backwards over my pony's tail. After about an hour we reached the top of a small pass, and in the last rays of the sun reflected from the snow slopes above our heads, we looked down onto the Tibetan plateau. Before us the valley of the Karnali river lay hidden in shadow. The horizon was fringed with the distant peaks of the Kailas range, the foreground being dominated by the huge majestic massif of Gurla Mandhata. The ethereal beauty of that pristine, unclimbed mountain took my breath away. It appeared to be suspended in mid-air, completely detached from the ocean swell of the plain lying in sombre garb below.

My contemplations were rudely interrupted by the Taklakot satrap who whipped my pony, causing it to gallop headlong down the snow-covered hillside. Rapidly I overtook every other member of the party. I saw a bend in the track bordering a drop of some thirty feet but, lacking the requisite horse control, I shot off at the corner, tucked my head between my knees and rolled down that slope like a ball. My journey ended abruptly in a snowdrift, out of which I staggered with some difficulty. The Tibetans helped me to remount, and had just succeeded when the pack saddle slipped under the pony's belly. Harrop was sitting in the snow. His horse, it appeared, kept falling down bodily, to the left.

'Just look at this,' Harrop said, as he clambered back onto his pony. 'We ought to report these beggars to the RSPCA, for cruelty to animals.' When properly mounted on his minuscule pony, Harrop's feet were only about a foot off the ground.

Two hours' riding made me painfully aware of the damage wooden pack saddles can do to the male anatomy. Damodar managed to relieve himself of most of the agony via the stratagem of lying flat on the animal, with both his arms around its neck. Surprisingly he managed the whole journey in this position without once falling off.

As my pony trotted across the darkened Tibetan plateau, I thought on the words of the Duke of Wellington, who said, 'No plan of battle survives contact with the enemy.' Unpaid, untrained, a rank amateur in the spy game, my operation had been rolled up by superior Chinese counter-intelligence operations before I had even set foot in the door. 'You must be a bloody idiot to have thought that it would be so easy, and that you could get away with it,' I said to myself. My mission was doomed to failure, or so I thought at the time. But fate has a knack of playing strange and unexpected tricks.

The night was cold and windless, and all that could be heard was the clatter of the horses' hooves on the still air. I looked apprehensively ahead. We were riding amongst the ruins of what must have been buildings of huge dimensions. Slowly the outline of a high-walled structure appeared. Flat-topped, and with slightly inward sloping sides, it looked far from inviting in the dim light. As we approached, heavy double doors opened. Beyond those doors and their creaking hinges there was nothing but blackness.

My pony trotted forward briskly in a manner which suggested that she had been here before and knew just where she was going. Sensing that we were back in the land of low beams, I took the precaution of lying flat along my pony's neck. Although I could hear the scuffling of feet, I could see neither faces nor figures. Hands gripped me around my middle and I was lifted bodily off my pony.

At last a flickering light moved towards us. As it came nearer I saw that we were standing in the middle of a courtyard, at the centre of which stood a flagpole, only visible in its lower reaches. The lamp was held by an old woman who pushed its smoking wick almost into my face to have a closer look at me. I was conscious of the strong smell of hot ghee-butter, the fuel for that tiny open-topped lamp. The bowl of the lamp was shaped from forged iron, hammered out from the red hot metal, with the wick floating in the melted butter.

In the shadows around us I could now make out a group of about twenty Tibetan monks, all hatless and with their heads shaven. In the yellow wavering light of the lamp our surroundings were eerie and mysterious. I felt that we were standing in a place impervious to time, where nothing had changed for centuries. Here was a way of life that was old when my ancestors, clad in skins, chased woolly mammoths around the mountains of Snowdonia.

The monks crowded around us, fingering my windproof Everest suit. Their investigations ended only when Gin Din Rhou ordered them to bed our ponies down for the night. By now our escort had shrunk to manageable proportions, and of the Chinese only the Dzongpon and the small officer remained. I realised that we were not in a Chinese fort but in a Tibetan lamasery. This was quickly confirmed by Gin Din Rhou. We were not in Taklakot, but in Jitkot Gompa. Gin Din Rhou was the head of the establishment and spiritual leader of the people of the surrounding area.

I was anxious to learn what was in store for us. The Dzongpon was in earnest conversation with the old lama and, when the discussion ended, Gin Din Rhou turned to Damodar for translation.

'The Dzongpon rides for another twenty-three miles tonight to see his commanding officer. He will show that officer your equipment and tell him your story, and probably you will be released within a few days. In the meantime, if you will give the Dzongpon your word not to try to escape, all Chinese soldiers will be withdrawn.'

The advantages of such an arrangement were obvious. Harrop and I felt that the immediate outlook was not as dismal as it had first appeared. We were to enjoy an unequalled opportunity to study Tibetan life at first hand. Harrop the agricultural scientist could question the Tibetans of Jitkot about their agronomy. The pact was made. We gave the Dzongpon our assurance that we would make no attempt to escape and, before his departure, the Dzongpon shook hands with all three of us. As he left, he turned and once again proffered his apologies for any inconvenience our temporary enforced stay at Jitkot might cause us. I formed the opinion that Jungpah would have made an ideal travel agent.

We were not only saddle sore, but very very tired. The three of us limped across the courtyard to a small doorway at the top of a short flight of steps. Three small prayer wheels were fixed to the wall at about chest height and as the Tibetans entered the buildings each gave all three wheels a spin. Once inside the door we lost contact with the lamp-carrying woman and found ourselves once again in complete darkness. We had to be led by the hand, but even this did not save us from the usual fate of having our skulls come into painful contact with low beams.

The stairways between the floors consisted of tree trunks set an an angle with notches for hands and feet. Fumbling our way along in the darkness, we were eventually shown into a room. We dropped our rucksacks onto the floor and for the first time that day we were left to our own devices. By flashlight we examined our new quarters. The room measured about sixteen feet by twelve. The floor and walls were of dried mud and the ceiling, supported by a carved centre cross-beam, consisted of a mixture of stones and mud which rested on roughly cut willow branches about two inches in diameter.

The three of us squatted on the bare floor, quite unable to foresee what the future held. Damodar was confident that when the Chinese saw his letter of authority issued by the Nepal Foreign Office, they would understand the situation and give us every assistance to return to our base camp in Nepal before the winter snows made crossing the Urai Lekh pass impossible. Damodar also added that as a Hindu, he would like to visit the sacred lake of Manasorawar and the holiest of mountains, Kailas. None of us expressed any doubts then that the Chinese authorities would be anything but friendly and co-operative. But at the back of my mind was the terrible thought that we might be wrong and the Chinese might suspect us of being 'imperialist spies'.

We inflated our air mattresses and, spreading our sleeping bags, turned in for the night. Something jarred in my memory. Jungpah had told Gin Din Rhou that he had to travel twenty-three miles that same night, to report in to his superiors. The known Chinese military and administrative centres were at Taklakot, only eight miles away to the north, and Gartok, about 120 miles to the north-west. Where could Jungpah's superiors be twenty-three miles from Jitkot? Not to the south, there lay Nepal. Not immediately to the east, for that would entail crossing the Nalkankar/Gurla Mandhata connecting ridge and there was no known pass over the divide. What about the west? Twenty-three miles to the west or north-west would place a Chinese encampment and HQ within sight of the Lipu Lekh pass on the Indo-Tibet border, where the Indians had a border post.

There was only one venue for Jungpah's PLA bosses, and it had to be north of Taklakot, near lake Manasorawar, with only the 16,000-foot Gurla pass to cross. Singh's guess that the Chinese had a large encampment hidden away in that area was undoubtedly right. 'Score one for our side,' I said to myself as I dozed off.

I was awakened the following morning at 8 a.m. by the most dreadful cacophony: beating drums and clashing cymbals, interspersed with the occasional deep booming note of a horn. Added to this was a spine-chilling high-pitched voice, which descended to a note so low it was barely discernible from the sound of the horn. The three of us sat bolt upright in our sleeping bags, dumbstruck by its penetration. A low humming sound replaced the solitary voice, and this grew in volume as a choir of monks murmured their way through Buddhist mantras. After about fifteen minutes, the sounds ceased as abruptly as they had begun.

The drums, cymbals and horn were eerie enough, but the singing was right out of this world. The spell was broken by Harrop, as always, for his sense of humour was equal to all occasions. 'If they start again, give them sixpence to go sing in the next gompa.'

We were exceedingly hungry, for we had not had a proper meal since breakfast the previous day, and Damodar valiantly offered to brave the mysterious monastic world in an effort to find food. 'A nice pot of tea would not go amiss, Damodar,' I called after him.

I had turned in thinking that our room had no windows. There was a trickle of light now. It came from a west-facing wall. Old sacks were nailed across the window, presumably to keep out the wind, for the window was innocent of glass. It consisted of a wooden lattice covered with thin white paper, but the paper was torn and allowed the wind to whistle through. In a far corner of the room stood a couple of ancient firelock muskets, muzzle loaders with twin-pronged forked rests attached to the barrels. From the butt to the muzzle these fearsome looking weapons were about six feet in length. My examination of them was interrupted by the appearance of the horn player. From the doorway he saw me handling the muskets, and placing his ten-foot-long brass and silver mounted horn on the floor, he took the guns out of harm's way. He then shouted at the top of his voice and in quick order the room was filled with monks. Gin Din Rhou pushed his way to the fore, but still halfway through a mantra he was chanting, he took no part in the proceedings. Damodar was brought back from the nearby kitchen and told to inform us that we were not to touch any lamasery property. There were some other items in the room and the monks closely examined them before carting them away, including three fine silver-decorated wooden saddles, some leather boots and a fur hat.

Alone once more in our bed-sitter, I decided to help Damodar with the breakfast preparations, and we set off for the lamasery kitchen to buy tsampa with which I hoped to make some passable porridge. An old woman appeared from the kitchen bearing a bowl of hot water which was set down on a small decorated table just outside the door of Gin Din Rhou's room. Squatting down, the old man proceeded to wash his face and hands, a proceeding which amazed me; for everything I had read about Tibetans had served to convince me that under no circumstances do they wash. I asked Damodar to enquire about this, and on hearing of my curiosity, Gin Din Rhou turned towards me, his face dripping with water. There was a look of injured dignity on his otherwise benign countenance. Damodar said that the old lama would under the circumstances forgive my obvious ignorance of Tibetan monastic life and customs. Washing in Tibet was evidently not unknown, but in all our stay in Tibet, I was to see only one other instance of morning ablutions. I offered Gin Din Rhou the small cake of soap I kept in a tin in my rucksack, but he declined the offer. Hot water was good enough for him.

Ablutions completed, a small mat was brought out and placed in the centre of the roof terrace, and on this Gin Din Rhou seated himself cross-legged. Next a small porcelain cup was placed at his right. A heavy silver-handworked cover was placed on top of the cup. Next some scrolls of paper were laid on his left-hand side, and a quill pen and a bottle of ink were set down. Still muttering his prayers, Gin Din Rhou started the day's business, which was tax collecting.

My attention was diverted by what seemed to be the sound of a small diesel engine running in the kitchen. There was a steady pulsating chug-chug-chug and, greatly intrigued, I went inside to investigate. I found myself in a black cavern of a room with one window the size of a pocket handkerchief. This provided inadequate light, and a tiny hole in the roof acted as a chimney flue. The whole place was wreathed in acrid smoke. I could hear Damodar coughing somewhere ahead. I placed a hand against a wall, and it came away covered with soot. Long sooty cobwebs festooned the roof and I kept wiping them off my face.

After a few moments my eyes became accustomed to the semi-darkness and I saw that the source of the engine sounds was a Tibetan tea-making cylinder operated by Gin Din Rhou's official tea-maker. The tea-man was standing at the side of the combined fireplace and oven. A tunnel penetrated the oven from one end to the other, and into it an old woman pushed handfuls of brushwood and dried yak dung. On top of the oven, which was constructed of unfired mud brick, large copper and brass pots stood covering circular holes through the edges of which licked an occasional tongue of flame. It was certainly an efficient cooker. Everything fed into it immediately roared into flame. Its major drawback was lack of a conventional chimney: the room filled with volumes of smoke.

Damodar introduced me to the tea-maker who claimed, rightly I believe, that he was the hardest working man in Jitkot Gompa. At least thirty, he had been making tea for the monks since the age of eight. He told Damodar that when he was a young boy, two Europeans like us had called at the Gompa and had taken Gin Din Rhou's photograph on the top roof of the lamasery. This must have been the Swiss, Heim and Gannser, who illegally entered Tibet in 1936.

Tea drinking is more than a habit with Tibetans. It is an obsession. Cinemas, theatres, radio and TV were non-existent. So what else was there to do but sit around the tea-urn exchanging gossip from Gyantse, Gartok or Lhasa? The tea-making machine was in action from morning to night and the tea-server was everlastingly carrying kettles of tea to Gin Din Rhou and his associates. The tea is first boiled in one of the kitchen pots which may hold up to two gallons. Afterwards it is poured into the wooden tea-mixing cylinder, yak butter, salt and spices generally being added. The mixing is done with the aid of a plunger, a wooden rod with a circular disc attached to the bottom with holes drilled in it.

A bout of long-winded haggling resulted in Damodar buying a small bowl of tsampa flour. The price was steep, ten times what we had been paying in Nepal. The high price reflected the time and effort and great difficulty the Tibetans experienced in collecting their barley or ready ground tsampa from India and Nepal.

Overriding the objections of the old woman stoking the fire, we borrowed a cooking pot and soon had a steaming bowl of tsampa porridge ready. Enamel plates were extracted from our rucksacks, and Harrop, Damodar and I squatted to eat in the middle of the lamasery roof terrace. Old Gin Din Rhou and his associates were greatly amused that we should take the trouble to cook the tsampa. Tibetans eat it uncooked, simply mixing water and tsampa, or more likely tea and tsampa in a small bowl until a hard ball or sausage of dough results. During our stay at Jitkot we never saw Tibetans eat meat, their diet consisting entirely of tsampa and tea. But I had seen a rather blackened-looking lump of dried meat hanging from the ceiling, and succeeded in buying it for three rupees.

I enquired how it came about that we were able to buy meat from people sworn by their religion never to take life, whether that of a human, an animal or even an insect. The tea-maker admitted that eating meat was permissible if the person eating it did not take life himself. 'There are people in the Taklakot area,' he said, 'who will kill a yak or a goat for a price. Usually they are satisfied with a portion of the meat. Sometimes meat is sold to the lamasery.'

Gin Din Rhou having completed his devotions, and hearing about my questions, assured us that we had nothing to fear from the piece of meat that we had bought. The goat from which it had been carved had not died of any serious disease, and the piece of flesh had only been hanging up in the lamasery for little more than a year. Reassured, I announced that we would boil the goat meat and eat it for dinner that night.

After breakfast, Harrop and I made a tour of the building. It was much larger than we had realised and was honeycombed with a maze of passages and small rooms. One room held a store of prayer flags; thousands of gaily coloured bits of bunting hanging from ropes stretched from one side of the room to the other. Quite by accident we walked into the holy of holies, strictly forbidden territory. I pushed aside a tattered curtain from a doorway. In front of me, on a dais, stood a four-foot-high Buddha, cast in brass. The floor was carpeted and bowls of incense lay smoking at the Buddha's feet. The room had two tiny windows through which streamed thin shafts of light to illuminate the face of the Buddha and two smaller images on either side. Small flowers like marigolds were strewn about the altar and there was an offering of tsampa dough on a plate before it.

The solemn atmosphere certainly discouraged levity on my part but not on Harrop's. As we slipped out of the room, he glanced over his shoulder, saying, 'No offence, Governor.' I am sure, had it been possible, the sunlit features of the Buddha would have broken into a smile. No one could be offended by John Harrop, not even the gods.

It was now midday and the sun shone from a cloudless blue sky. We walked out onto the roof terrace and sat down. Near us, a little girl was combing her long black hair with a bunch of twigs. Here at Jitkot lamasery, I had the finest view of my life. To the north towered the mighty Gurla Mandhata. From the foot of its south precipice stretched a series of ridges running right across the skyline, making a magnificent panorama of purple and brown rock peaks that culminated to the south-east in the Nalkankar massif on the Tibet-Nepal border. About eight miles to the north we could see the great lamasery of Taklakot perched on top of a cliff. Below it could be seen white painted houses and cave dwellings. Immediately below our lamasery, amongst the ruins of ancient Tibetan houses, we could see people going about their business, working in tiny fields, or grinding barley for tsampa, using two flat stones placed one on top of the other. It was obvious that some parts of the ancient ruined buildings had been repaired and were used for human habitation.

Irrigation channels provided water for the fields, the smallest of which was no more than ten feet square, the largest being about fifty yards by twenty. Jitkot Gompa was situated on the Tibetan plateau at about 14,500 feet. The edge of the plateau, on our eastern side, fell down to the banks of the Karnali river. The only greenery was by the banks of the river. Everywhere else, as far as the eye could see, was nothing but a brown, lifeless plateau enlivened by the occasional clump of willow trees.

Harrop wondered why Tibetans from this area had not migrated into west Nepal years ago, as had the inhabitants of what is now the Gurkha state in central Nepal. There was quite enough land in west Nepal, in the form of hills not yet terraced, which could have supplied sustenance for more than the Tibetan population of the Taklakot area.

As we discovered later, the truth was that with the advent of the Chinese and their draconian taxation, the population of the Taklakot area was decreasing rapidly. In ever increasing numbers the Tibetans were attempting to make a living begging in the northern provinces of India. This gives the lie to Chinese propaganda which claims that the lot of the Tibetans has been improved thanks to the advent of Marxism.

Koila and our porters appeared at 3 p.m. having been on the march from Khatang since late morning. Koila feared that Harrop and I would not see the outside world for at least ten years. Our assertion that we would all be on our way back into Nepal in a few days did little to reassure him. He and the other porters disappeared down a notched tree trunk ladder into the bowels of Jitkot lamasery. For some reason the Tibetans would not allow the porters to use the lamasery kitchen, and they were compelled to find a substitute. Wreaths of smoke emerged from the stairwell all afternoon long, suggesting that Koila and the boys were not going short of their ration of chapatis.

On the roof were window boxes made of dried mud. These were filled with soil, and a tiny crop of marigold-like flowers growing in them received constant attention from the monks, who shuffled in and out with copper bowls of water which they poured onto the parched soil. The window boxes quite obviously supplied the flowers for the offerings placed at the feet of the brass images of Buddha.

Jitkot lamasery having no supply of its own, all water was carried from a stream issuing from the hillside about 300 feet below. The woman who tended the fire in the kitchen had the unenviable task of keeping the cooking pots filled with water. She was properly thankful that, apart from Gin Din Rhou, few of the other occupants of Jitkot lamasery washed. In addition to twenty monks, there were about fifteen small boys in residence. In training for holy orders, they were dressed exactly like the men, even to the extent of having their heads shaved. They all wore long sleeved cloaks and highly coloured felt boots. These young boys were friendly and inquisitive and amused themselves by repeatedly ransacking our rucksacks. We put it all down to natural juvenile curiosity. It says much for their honesty that nothing was ever stolen.

Harrop went up onto the main roof to look for the lavatory. He called me up. 'Take a look at this.' The roof area was completely flat. There were four poles of willow, one at each corner of the roof, and strings of prayer flags hung from connecting rope lines. There were two small chortens on the roof, small pillar-box style structures, which were hollow and into which, through gaps in the side, votive offerings were made in the form of mud or plaster Buddha images, and lengthy scrolls of coarse hand-made paper, covered with Sanskrit writing. What interested Harrop was the John. There was a square hole in the roof. I looked down inside. A pyramid of freeze-dried human excrement reached almost up to the opening.

'They brick up a room,' Harrop commented. 'Then they cut a hole in the roof, and everyone craps or pees into that room. It must have taken donkey's years for the monks to fill that room. There is no smell, probably because of the ambient temperature. It's so damned cold up here.' Harrop sat on the edge of the roof, with legs dangling over the drop down to the Karnali river.

'What are you up to?' I enquired, as he scribbled on a notebook with a stub of a pencil.

'I'm working out the average weight of faeces excreted by a human being on a daily basis and, taking into account the number of people in this Gompa, they will be bricking up another room by this time next year, and sealing this one up. I reckon that in about a thousand years' time, this Gompa will be a huge block of excreta.'

But with the benefit of hindsight we now know that Harrop was wrong in his calculations. In 1955 the 'Young Red Guards' did not exist. They were some years later to destroy more than 99 per cent of all Tibetan lamaseries, and throw an equal percentage of lamas and monks into labour camps where most of them died. The great lamaseries at Taklakot and Kojarnath, and the smaller Jitkot Gompa were torn down brick by brick, the brass Buddhas melted for the base metal, the Sanskrit archives burned and the Mani wall stones with their 'Om Mane Padme Hom' inscriptions used as paving stones. Gin Din Rhou suffered the same fate as many other lamas and monks, and died in prison. But the Chinese wold never be able to capture his soul, which would fly off and up into the mystic state of Bardo, awaiting a summons to return to earth in human or some other form, or perhaps even to ascend to the ultimate state of grace, to Nirvana.

While Harrop sunbathed on the roof of the lamasery, I returned to the lower terrace to see if I could gain information from Gin Din Rhou. He was seated cross-legged on the floor, tax collecting, an assistant seated on his left. I was invited to sit at his right to watch as the local people came to pay their dues. They salaamed as they entered and, upon being informed that I was a guest, they favoured me with the same courtesy. The sums of money changing hands amounted to not many rupees and was presumably a tithe intended to pay for the upkeep of Jitkot lamasery. No opportunity was lost to make it clear to me, via Damodar's interpretation, how everybody resented the presence in Tibet of the Chinese and how the new Chinese taxes weighed grievously on the population.

While the tax gathering was in progress, yak butter tea was served in the now familiar wooden cups, which were devoid of handles. The tea-making cylinder could be heard at its endless task in the dark recesses of the kitchen. The tea-server scurried in and out bearing kettle after kettle of tea, and as fast as I emptied my cup it was filled again. I have heard that Tibetans can drink as many as sixty cups of tea a day. It was by no means as palatable as some Himalayan travellers make out, and I soon decided that I had consumed more than enough.

I kept asking questions about the daily routine and running of the lamasery, and I learned that Jitkot Gompa had its own fields and employed about forty men and women who worked continuously in them. As few of the fields were large enough to permit the use of a yak-drawn plough, the hoe was employed. The pay of the monastery employees was about ten rupees a month.

Meanwhile, my cup was refilled and, not wishing to offend my hosts, I drank the contents. Again my cup was refilled . . . for the tenth time. Damodar watched my tea-drinking marathon with a grin of amusement. For he knew a fact of which I was totally ignorant; that it is considered good manners in Tibet to walk away leaving a full cup untouched. He could have told me this, but preferred to sit and watch and enjoy my discomfiture as I drank each cup determined not to show what I assumed would have been a grave discourtesy. As I reached my thirteenth and my fourteenth cup, the monks looked at me with a puzzled air. My embarrassment mounted to such a degree that Damodar burst into uncontrollable laughter. At fifteen cups I had reached my maximum capacity. Nature called, and expressing my apologies, I made a hasty departure, my destination the roof-top urinal.

When I left, my cup was refilled, and Damodar told the monks of the misunderstanding. The joke was greatly appreciated, and I heard their guffaws as I stood relieving myself on top of the roof. When I returned to our room a monk followed me in, bearing a hot wrought iron shovel containing a heap of dried herbs which he ignited with a flint and tinder. They gave off a not unattractive odour. He piled the smoking mass in the centre of the room. Harrop had by now joined me, and our curiosity into this odd ritual was satisfied by Damodar. He questioned the incense wallah and then burst into laughter, so much so he held his sides in pain.

'What the hell's the joke, Damodar?' Harrop enquired.

'He said, John Sahib, that they will be doing this every day until they get used to the strange fragrance of the Sahibs.' With that, Damodar fell about still laughing.

Most of the monks and female members of the establishment came into our room in small groups. Harrop and I stood there wreathed in incense smoke, as the giggling monks and ladies took in the scene. Late in the afternoon we cooked our piece of meat over an open fire. It was as tough as leather, but it was protein.

The morning of 27 October was heralded for us by the din of the cymbal, the sound of the long silver horn with its low booming note, and the chanting of the monks at prayer. We had all slept the sleep of the just. Gin Din Rhou entered our room before we had left our sleeping bags just as soon as he had completed his devotions. He told us that the moment the Chinese Dzongpon had called to tell him that there were foreigners in the Jung Jung Khola, he had started a fast, and was continually praying for our safety and well-being. He had no doubt that the Chinese, whom he regarded as very suspicious people, would regard us as foreign agents. Gin Din Rhou stated that we would be told of all of the many injustices the Tibetan people suffered under the heel of their Chinese invaders, and he hoped that when released, we would carry to the outside world the story of his people's great misery, their hatred of the Chinese, and worst of all, the recent Chinese decree that tiny children would be taken from their parents for education in China, which meant political indoctrination.

Gin Din Rhou stated that he intended riding to Taklakot immediately to see the Chinese officers there, to plead for our release. He said that a higher ranking Chinese who could order our release was stationed beyond Taklakot but neither he nor his colleagues were allowed to visit that place. I gathered from this that he was referring to the secret encampment.

I asked Gin Din Rhou if he would consider making the six-day ride to the north-west to see the highest-ranking Tibetan in that part of Tibet, the Garpon of Gartok. Gin Din Rhou shook his head. The old Garpon had been replaced by a Tibetan satrap of the Chinese. 'We are not permitted,' he explained, 'to leave the Taklakot area for any other part of Tibet without the written permission of the Chinese, and that can only be granted to those who can prove that they have what the Chinese call "a purpose".'

So much for the so-called 'Liberation of Tibet' and the Tibetans' new-found 'freedom' under the aegis of Chinese communism. The old abbot left, not having broken his fast. He trotted his pony off through the huge double doors of the ground-floor courtyard, waving us adieu with his silver mounted riding crop as he went down the track towards Taklakot.

Harrop and I assumed that in his absence, we could undertake a little exploration of the Gompa's immediate surroundings. Harrop set off to look at the interiors of several of the chortens whose flag-bedecked roofs were only about fifty yards from the double doors of the Gompa. I decided to explore some old cave dwellings a few hundred yards away.

I went forth dressed in my filthy old navy blue sweater and windproof trousers, my feet encased in an enormous pair of insulated black leather high-altitude boots. When I passed a group of Tibetans they giggled at my clumsy footwear. In front of me a small child of about five was herding yaks along. He or she (the sex I could not determine) whacked the ungainly, slow-moving animals along with a stout stick and occasionally threw stones. The yaks showed no sign of resentment or fright and ignored both the stick-whacking and the stones which were thrown with considerable force. Some travellers have claimed that the yak averages about two miles an hour. This, I think, is an exaggeration.

To the north of the lamasery, concealed amongst old ruins, I chanced upon a single-storey house. Outside the front door were lined up a couple of dozen unfired earthenware pots which had obviously been thrown on a potter's wheel. Some were shaped like large teapots with finely worked spouts and handles. Others were simple water-carrying vessels similar to the amphorae of Asia Minor. I had seen few local examples of Tibetan craftsmanship; wishing to know more, I put my head through the open doorway and looked into the courtyard. Two men were there; one in his early twenties, the other anything from fifty to a hundred years old.

The old potter of Jitkot had suffered the ravages of untreated syphilis, which seemed to be so widespread in that part of Tibet. I recalled that Sherring and Dr Tom Longstaff, when writing of their visit to Taklakot in 1905, made mention of the high rate of syphilis in the area. The old man was blind in one eye and had little sight in the other and walked stiff-legged as if his knees lacked joints. The younger man beckoned me into the courtyard, and pointed to the roof where yak dung was drying. A woman was gathering dried yak dung into a wicker basket and passing it down into the arms of the old gentleman. The young man, his father behind him carrying the basket of dried dung, went out through the doorway and I followed them across some open ground to the top of a small hill.

There another score or more of clay vessels lay ready for firing. I looked around for the kiln, but nothing remotely resembling such a structure could be seen. As I watched, the Tibetans built a circle of mud bricks to a height of about a foot. The pots were placed inside, an inch or so separating them, then twigs were scattered in the spaces between the pots and yak dung piled on top. Twigs were also dropped inside the unfired pots followed by dried yak dung. With flint and tinder the fuel was lighted. At one side of the circle the old man worked a pair of leather bellows while his son, taking deep breaths, gave vent to formidable blasts of air that put the bellows to shame.

In little time the fire was under way, and I was surprised at the intensity of the heat. Never bursting into flame, as wood would have done, the yak dung gave a concentrated glow. It is said that glass can easily be melted by a yak-dung fire. As the fire grew, the fuel in the clay pots was ignited and the two Tibetans started to pile on more yak dung. I became so interested that I found myself helping with the fuelling of this outdoor kiln. My puny efforts at blowing into the red glow were not very rewarding and the younger Tibetan stopped his efforts to sit down and laugh at me. One of the most appealing facets of the Tibetan character is their tremendous sense of humour, and like all good-humoured people, they are not averse to making a joke about themselves. I have always felt that the most boring people are those who take themselves too seriously. The Tibetan people can never be accused of that.

I was aroused from my arts and crafts efforts by a voice bellowing from the roof of the monastery. It was the early morning horn-blowing monk. I knew that I had better head back before my loud-voiced friend roused the monks to come out and pull me back inside the Gompa by the ear.

Damodar was waiting for me at the front gates. He told me that the monks were far from pleased by our excursions and peregrinations. Harrop had already been apprehended and brought back. The tea-maker gave me a scolding and I mollified him by giving the three large prayer wheels at the foot of the stairs a couple of spins.

As I climbed into my sleeping bag that night I ruminated on our situation. In a few days' time, Nepalese porters from Chainpur and Dhuli would be arriving at our base camp to carry out our expedition loads. Henson, Dwyer and Roberts at base camp, not knowing of our plight, would have no choice but to depart south. The Seti Gorge would soon be closed for traffic until the following spring. Perhaps if the Cheenee Burra Raja Sahib was a sporting sort of chap and he allowed us to leave right away, we could be back at Saipal camp just in time to go out with the rest of the expedition?

7

The morning of 28 October saw all our hopes betrayed. Gin Din Rhou arrived back from Taklakot before we were out of our sleeping bags, bringing the depressing news that the Chinese had sent a courier post haste to the distant Chinese military encampment bearing his pleas for our release, only to return with the news that we were to be placed under close arrest immediately.

Disdaining to wait for the PLA armed escort, Harrop and I decided that we would pack our rucksacks and walk the eight miles from Jitkot to Taklakot in order to enjoy a final stroll in the sun, our last as free men for the foreseeable future. Damodar reminded us that the Dzongpon had now broken his word, and that our own word not to try to escape would now be invalid. Could the three of us and our four porters make a break for it now, without tents or high-altitude rations, and march back to Khatang on our way to the Urai Lekh before the Chinese arrived?

If the Chinese pursued us on horseback, which they undoubtedly would, our chances of escape were negligible. Reluctantly we decided that escape at this stage of the proceedings was not a viable option. In any case, why should we run away? The Chinese would interpret it as proof of our guilt. There was still the chance that we might be interrogated by someone like Jungpah, who would duly order our release.

As much as I wished to be free of the Chinese and the thought of possible imprisonment, there was still that task not yet completed. I had established to my satisfaction that the PLA had a military encampment to the north of Taklakot. But what about troop strengths, and that rumoured Strategic Military Highway to west Tibet? Remember the three maxims for counter-interrogation: 'Deny everything, admit nothing, but keep the other side talking to establish how much they know, and to try to glean intelligence from them.' In retrospect, I have to admit that the crack, the sense and the thrill of adventure, played some part in my decision not to make a break for the Urai Lekh and the safety of Nepal. An interrogation by the Chinese, at which I might learn something of value for Singh and Cricket Wallah, was something to look forward to. The sun was shining, it was a beautiful day, so what the hell?

Not feeling like eating, we eschewed breakfast and I broke the bad news to Koila, Ungya, Ratti and Giddy, and all four burst into tears. I felt sorry for them, until Damodar told me that they were crying not for their own misfortunes, but because they were sure that the two white Sahibs would never again see beyond the borders of communist China.

At that moment a new figure appeared in the shape of an Indian national. A young fellow in his middle twenties, he was dressed in the usual tight-fitting cotton trousers and an old tweed sports coat with holes in the elbows. Gin Din Rhou vouched for this young man, explaining that he was a trader from Almora, who also had a shop in the hill station of Pithoragarh. His business was selling cheap cotton cloth to the Tibetans, and he had arrived only the day before over the Lipu Lekh pass on the Indian border. He gave us the welcome news that the Lipu Lekh was still open for traffic. He complained to us of the treatment the Chinese meted out to Indian traders at Taklakot. Although the Chinese depended upon India for about 90 per cent of the grain and flour required for their garrison, they were making life difficult for the Indian traders. He also told us that the Chinese were building new fortifications with materials brought in from India, including sawn timber for roof supports.

I asked the young Indian trader to take a letter for me to Pithoragarh when he had completed his commercial transactions with the Chinese and the Tibetans. I addressed my letter to a Christian missionary we had met on our way in, Benson Greenwold, and who had kindly acted as our mail depot while we were in the hills. When the Indian trader told us that he would be taking a great risk, because the Chinese hand-search many of the traders, I told him that he should regard his own safety as paramount. He took some time to come to a decision, and after half a dozen bowls of yak-butter tea, he decided to act as our mailman. Harrop had sat through the tea-drinking session reminding the young Indian that we were all members of the British Commonwealth.

The trader said that he would be in Taklakot for about seventeen days, and hoped that he would not enjoy the fate of one trader who had recently been arrested by the Chinese for being in possession of a map, for it was against Chinese regulations to possess maps in Tibet. The map was not even remotely related to China or Tibet, and it consisted of the end-paper of a travel book on the South Pacific. Another Indian trader was found to be in possession of a cheap Box Brownie pre-war camera, and for that heinous crime spent nine months under the most appalling conditions in a cell at Taklakot on a starvation diet, emerging a mere skeleton. The trader also told us the story of the Indian professor on a pilgrimage to Manasorawar and Kailas who had been arrested because he possessed not only a camera but also a protractor and compass. The poor man was imprisoned at Taklakot, but unlike the camera-owning trader, his incarceration was short, because when Delhi heard about this flagrant abuse of human rights, and breach of the 1954 'right to travel' agreement in existence between India and Tibet, the Indian government objected in the strongest possible terms, and the professor was released after only a couple of weeks' incarceration.

As we had been found in possession of maps, survey instruments, magnetic compasses, binoculars and worst of all a loaded automatic pistol and a fifty-round box of ammunition, the outlook appeared to be none too rosy. The young Indian took my letter and a few rupees for postage. With luck our mailman would be back over the Lipu Lekh and handing my letter into an Indian post office in less than a month's time. In the event, my letter was never delivered, and I can only assume that my courier, on seeing Indian traders being searched as they approached the Lipu Lekh on their way back to India, destroyed it.

Gin Din Rhou summoned Harrop, Damodar and me to his roof terrace, where he gave us a moving little homily on the precious nature of the human soul, and how pain and adversity can never overcome or subjugate a truly free spirit. He advised us to spend many hours in meditation in the days and weeks ahead. He told us that he envisaged that we were about to face the greatest trial of our lives during which we would suffer great indignity, humiliation, and possibly death. After assuring us that he and the lamas and monks of Jitkot would pray for our safekeeping and welfare every day until our release, he told us that he would also visit the great lamaseries of Taklakot and Kojarnath to ask the abbots and monks to enter into daily prayer for us.

We sat in silence as all the monks assembled in the courtyard below. Our friend the horn blower drew a deep breath and produced a sombre sound from his long silver-mounted temple horn. The monks, seated on the ground in the courtyard below, sang in chorus, in that awe-inspiring resonant fashion peculiar to the lamaistic branch of the Buddhist faith. After half an hour, the chanting sombre chorus ceased, and the prayer ceremony was over.

We packed our rucksacks, and in mine I found a gaily coloured silk scarf Damodar had given to me when he joined our expedition. He had explained to me that to Nepalese and Tibetans, the giving of a scarf was deemed to be an act of great politeness when making a visit. I decided to present the scarf to Gin Din Rhou. Then I remembered that in Tibet a white scarf of pure silk was considered to be the most propitious of gifts. I had such a scarf in my sack. My wife Jean had bought it for me just before we left the UK and I had never worn it. As Gin Din Rhou escorted us to the gates of Jitkot Gompa, I made the presentation, in the approved formal fashion; Harrop took the two scarves and laid them across my outstretched forearms. I then made our offering to Gin Din Rhou, who accepted them most graciously.

At 11 a.m. we were off. At the last moment, Gin Din Rhou insisted on escorting us. He told Damodar that he was arranging for Tibetan ponies for Harrop, Damodar and me. We declined the offer, with Harrop saying, 'Tell him thank you, Damodar, but it's such a nice day, we think we'll walk.'

Gin Din Rhou had trotted his pony along the left-hand side of a Mani wall. We followed him, with Koila and the other three porters tagging along behind. The track dropped down to the bank of the Karnali river, and wound its way through irrigated fields. Occasionally we came across patches of grass. There was little evidence of crops, and Harrop the agricultural scientist claimed that most of the fields were neglected and were reverting to semi-desert. Nowhere between Jitkot and Taklakot did we see any sign of the 'mechanisation of Tibetan agriculture' the Chinese were boasting of in their propaganda.

In India, the left-wing radical press consistently publicised the alleged improvements in Tibetan agriculture bestowed on the fortunate Tibetan proletariat, who had been rescued from the near slavery of the neo-medieval system enforced by the Dalai Lama and the Tibetan hierarchy. This was all arrant nonsense which successfully deluded most of the Third World, and India in particular. We later learned that the neglect of the tiny fields in the Taklakot area was a deliberate act on the part of the Tibetans who, being underpaid for their barley by the Chinese, decided to cease production. Mao Tse-tung's army of occupation in Tibet was being exposed to the same kind of non-cooperation the Russian peasantry showed to Lenin's and Stalin's collectivisation of farming in the 1920s.

We came to the Tibetan village of Marsha Kalya, shown on the Indian maps as Lokpo, and sat down on the outskirts for a breather. Harrop was looking east towards the connecting ridges between Nalkankar in Nepal and Gurla Mandhata in Tibet.

'We could never have done it,' he commented. 'There's no way that we could have traversed that ground to reach Gurla Mandhata.'

I had to agree with him. Once again the Survey of India maps had been hopelessly inaccurate. The map showed a smooth ridge between the two mountains. The terrain was far more complex. There was a ridge of minor peaks between Nalkankar and Gurla Mandhata, but in the middle of that ridge system there was a huge cleft. The south side of the cleft rose up as a face more than 2,000 feet in height, and the top 500 feet or so overhung the chasm beneath. It was obvious now to both Harrop and me that the only way to get to Gurla Mandhata from the Urai Lekh, the Tinkar Lipu or the Lipu Lekh was by simply marching straight through Taklakot.

'The best laid plans of mice and men,' Harrop commented glumly.

Villagers soon gathered around us to look at the strangers. They answered our questions in a surprisingly open manner, stating that since the Chinese invasion, their standard of living had deteriorated sharply. One of their main complaints was in reference to fuel for their fires. It was explained to us that the amount of yak dung to be dried for fuel was, of course, limited by the size of the yak herds. Then there was the matter of dead dwarf juniper bushes, which formed a considerable part of the fuel system. Dwarf juniper dies at a constant rate. In the Taklakot area, production and consumption of yak dung and dwarf juniper were in balance. Then in comes the Cheenee Burra Rajah Sahib, who demands yak dung and dead dwarf juniper brushwood for his soldiers' fires and cooking arrangements. The balance was now thrown out of kilter by the Chinese, who brought with them nothing more than the clothes they stood up in, and the arms with which they subjugated the Tibetan people. To make matters worse, the Tibetans were forced to sell their yaks and sheep to the Chinese military commissary at a price fixed by the Chinese which was about half the normal commercial price for meat on the hoof. This reduced the numbers of yaks in the Taklakot area, and this again further reduced the supply of dried yak dung. The Chinese were also demanding more dead dwarf juniper wood, so Tibetan contractors were forced to travel further and further from Taklakot to find dead brushwood. Some of the Tibetans we spoke to were now burning live green dwarf juniper wood, which gave a poor flame and smoked terribly. This again diminished future supplies of firewood.

It was obvious that Tibetans in the Taklakot area were being treated like serfs by the invading Chinese. If the Chinese presence in west Tibet was not for the benefit of the Tibetan populace, then why were they there at all, so far from their own country? The obvious answer was chilling. There had to be substance to the fears of Singh and Cricket Wallah. The Chinese presence and that supposed Strategic Military Highway to west Tibet had to be for either a future invasion of the Indian sub-continent, or for use as a lever, a means of exerting pressure on India and the other Indian sub-continent states to accept a Chinese version of the Japanese World War Two 'Greater Co-Prosperity sphere'.

When we asked the Tibetans if they liked the Chinese, we always received the same reply, 'The Cheenee are our masters.'

'Nothing like theoretical Marxism and socialism for spreading a little comfort and joy,' Harrop so appositely suggested.

Gin Din Rhou, watering his pony by a stream, called out to Damodar. 'He says, Syd Sahib, when we meet the Chinese we must not speak to any Tibetan people who might be nearby. If we do, those Tibetans could be in serious trouble with the Chinese.'

'Tell Gin Din Rhou we have the score, Damodar,' I said.

Harrop responded, 'Hear all, see all, say sod all, in case Big Brother is watching.'

Our captors came into view. They had come expecting to escort us all the way from Jitkot to Taklakot and were obviously surprised to find that we were sauntering along the track of our volition. There were the now familiar figures clad in quilted cotton uniforms, hats with black fur earflaps and a red enamelled star on the front and the usual brown or blue basketball boots. Each man carried a PPSh assault rifle, with four spare magazines in pouches attached to his belt, and four stick grenades slung from the shoulder in a canvas holder.

'Looks like they've come prepared to fight a ruddy war,' Harrop commented.

With our armed escort came the Dzongpon, but he was no longer his former smiling affable self. We tried to strike up a conversation with him through Damodar and Gin Din Rhou, to remind him of his promise of our early release, but he retained a sullen silence. Our arguments were dismissed with a wave of the hand and we were told to keep close to the soldiers and not to speak to the local Tibetans. The black-clad Tibetan satrap from Taklakot was with them, and he gave us an ugly look. The PLA soldiers now formed up around us, and we started off again.

Arriving at a small Tibetan village, for reasons I could not fathom, all the ponies were handed into the care of some Tibetans who led them away. From here on the Dzongpon, the black-clad satrap and Gin Din Rhou would continue on foot. The track ran down to a small cantilever bridge which spanned a tiny river not shown on the map; a tributary of the Karnali. The great ridge and high escarpment overlooking Taklakot lay ahead and the huge lamasery with its rambling structure could be seen perched at the highest point. Taklakot lamasery was very much larger than Jitkot Gompa, but not as symmetrical in shape. It gave the impression that the original building had been much smaller and that odd rooms and outer walls had been added as need dictated throughout its long history. A picturesque place, its colours were totally different from those of the monasteries at Jitkot and Kojarnath. In addition to the usual monastic red, there were walls painted in white and yellow.

The colours of the lamasery contrasted with those of the scattered homesteads. The latter were covered with a kind of whitewash, the usual stacks of brushwood lining the upper edges of the roofs and walls. On occasion we passed a house which boasted a little clump of parched-looking willow trees. We crossed the bridge. There was a huge encampment of tents ahead. There must have been a hundred at least. But they did not, as I expected, contain Chinese infantry. The encampment was the bazaar populated by Bhotia traders from India. Tibetans from local villages came here to trade salt, borax and yak's tail fly-whisks, for articles ranging from cheap Indian shoes and watches to such strange headgear as bowler hats. A Tibetan clad in sheepskin and wearing a bowler hat adorned with a large pink silk bow is a sight for weary eyes. Soap was also sold at the Taklakot bazaar, but the main buyers were soldiers from the Chinese garrison. The Dzongpon was determined that we should have no chance of meeting Indians who might carry news of our arrest to the outside world. We turned sharp right and skirted the bottom of the ridge which overlooked the Karnali, and on which the trading bazaar was situated.

In spite of this, I thought that the Chinese idea of security measures was woefully inadequate. The Tibetans, who are notorious gossips, would be bound to talk about us to the Indians. It was obvious now that we were not to be quartered at Taklakot lamasery, for we had already passed the track leading up to it. The cliff face we were skirting was honeycombed with cave dwellings, some of them of quite elaborate design – the fronts being bricked up, entrance being gained via a well-fitting wooden door.

Others at the foot of the cliff face had small brick-walled courtyards in which ponies were tethered. The higher ones, however, were the most interesting, having terraced wooden verandahs built out of the rock face. These verandahs were made of slender willow branches and had hand rails running along the outer edge, and from them hung hundreds of brightly coloured prayer flags. In some instances, half a dozen caves were joined by a single verandah, the sole means of entrance and exit being a fifty-foot ladder made of poplar branches. Smoke issued from most of the cave entrances, and there was a great deal of activity, people constantly coming and going up and down the ladders. Most of the load-carrying appeared to be done by women.

'Just think,' Harrop commented, 'we're going to eat Chinese for a while and at no charge. Loads of chicken chop suey.'

I brightened up at the prospect. 'Do you think that they'll invite us to have dinner in the officers' mess?' I ventured.

'Bound to,' Harrop responded. He was blessed with an exuberant confidence. 'They can't be that uncivilised not to invite us into their mess.'

In this optimistic frame of mind we visualised the various tempting and exotic menus we would ask for.

Reaching a place where the river lapped up against the cliff face, we overcame that impasse by ascending a steep track to the top of the ridge. As the path levelled out, I turned to see that the Indian trading bazaar was well behind us now. I looked across the Karnali river. The river bank opposite rose into a vertical cliff which was at times overhanging in places. It was composed of a clay and boulder conglomerate structure which, judging by the heaps of rock debris at the foot of the face, was highly unstable. Beyond were two large buildings. One, painted red, was a former monks' residence. The other building, of more recent construction, was painted a dull flat grey. Both had only one storey, but each covered a much larger area than the average Tibetan house. The sides of the grey building were about fifty yards in length and the walls were about fifteen feet high. This we were to learn was a new Chinese army barracks; the timbers for roofs and doors had been packed over the Lipu Lekh from India. The red building had been commandeered from the monks and was now used as the officers' military HQ. Here resided the CO of Taklakot, a cold-blooded butcher of a man, who only a few months earlier had executed one of his soldiers, by a bullet in the back of the head, for the crime of agitating for leave.

Behind the two buildings was a hill several hundred feet high, and building work was in progress on the summit. The walls of a much larger building were in the final stages of completion, and scores of khaki-clad figures scurried in and out. They never walked, they always did everything at the double, on the trot.

A winding track led up to the top of the hill, and this was covered by a ceaseless procession of human figures and animals. Yaks carried huge bales of timber, and mules fitted with pack frames carried boxes of equipment or loads of rectangular four-gallon cans of water. Long lines of Tibetan women trudged slowly and wearily uphill, each bearing a basket on her back supported by a head-band. The baskets were filled with rocks, and each woman could not have been carrying much less than a hundred pounds.

A line of women carrying empty baskets ran nimbly down the hill, skilfully circumventing the clumsy slow-moving yaks which seemed to take up all the available space on the narrow track. Down by the bank, a platoon of Chinese soldiers was filling four-gallon cans with water and loading them onto mules, four cans to a mule. The production line never once became still in daylight hours during our coming weeks of imprisonment.

After skirting the top of the cliff face for a couple of hundred yards or so, the track descended again and we walked within a stone's throw of the river bank. The Tibetan dwellings to be seen were now few in number, and we came to the last one. I saw smoke rising from the yard of the single-storey structure, and to my surprise I saw smoke also issuing from the top of a huge boulder of conglomerate situated a few yards beyond the Tibetan house. I saw a woman stoop down and enter a small aperture at the foot of this thirty-foot-high rock. The Tibetans had hollowed out a home inside it. I was to learn that there were several other 'cave dwellings inside boulders' at the foot of the Taklakot escarpment.

Beyond the single-storey house was the Karnali, where a large wooden cantilever bridge of Tibetan construction was crawling with soldiers of the PLA. The single-storey house was to be our home and prison for the foreseeable future. At precisely 3 p.m. we stepped through the opened double doors into a courtyard, and dumped our rucksacks on the dried mud floor.

8

'It doesn't look like a luxury hotel, does it?' Harrop said. I had to agree with him. Our new quarters were depressing in the extreme. We were left standing in the middle of the yard, our armed escort having vanished through a doorway into the bowels of the building. Gin Din Rhou, the man in black and the Dzongpon, after a short conversation, followed the soldiers indoors. Left to our own devices, we decided to have a look around. The courtyard was in two parts, one higher than the other and connected by a small flight of steps. The higher part of the yard was surrounded by the living quarters comprising four rooms. The lower part had a wall running round it, equipped with a 'firing step' so that our guards could keep under observation anybody approaching the outside wall. On the right-hand side of the double entrance doors to the yard was a primitive kitchen which was nothing more than two walls with a tattered tarpaulin thrown over the top, the centre of the tarpaulin supported by a pole laid horizontally across the top of the two walls. The fireplace was the usual Tibetan affair made of dried mud. Three large urns were boiling way on top of it.

Opposite the kitchen area stood the primitive means of sanitation. This consisted of a walled enclosure with two holes in the floor which gave access to a pit under the foundations. At the rear of the yard stood the main part of the buildings, equipped with two windows. The smaller of the windows had iron strips fastened across it in a lattice formation. The large window, which allowed light into what was apparently our guards' quarters, was paned with glass, the first glass window we had seen in Tibet. The room with the barred window would be our cell.

On either side of the yard were two small cells, with tiny windows, mud-walled, mud-floored and deep in dust. The building, once a Tibetan house, was now used as the official Chinese prison. Two small dead trees were propped up at either end of the roof, and a string of tattered prayer flags hung dismally in between.

We sat on the bottom of the centre courtyard steps, and Damodar mentioned that he was hungry. Our appetites were further whetted by the smell of boiling mutton from the kitchen. I gained the impression that we were being observed through the glass window, and we could hear voices in the glass-paned guard room. I was surprised to see an Indian emerge from the guard's quarters. Friendly looking, his smile was made more noticeable by two gold-capped teeth. His hair was well greased and brushed back and he wore clothes that stamped him as of a higher order than the Indian traders and porters we had seen in the United Provinces of India. Most impressive were his boots, a fine pair of knee-high riding boots of excellent quality leather. They were unusual in that they laced up at the back.

He walked over to Damodar and sat down beside him. He spoke not only Urdu, but also the Nepalese classical language of Nuari. To our surprise he greeted all three of us with a handshake, instead of the usual salaam with both hands palms together. His coat was of expensive well-tailored cloth and light blue flannel trousers were tucked into his leather riding boots. His right hand was covered with gold rings, some set with stones.

He told us that he was a trader from Kalimpong in India, having a house and a shop there, and that he visited Taklakot once a year in pursuit of his trade as a cloth merchant. While in the tented bazaar at Taklakot he had heard of our predicament and feeling that one member of the Commonwealth should help another he had come along to render what small assistance he could.

When I asked if he was afraid of the Chinese, he replied that there was

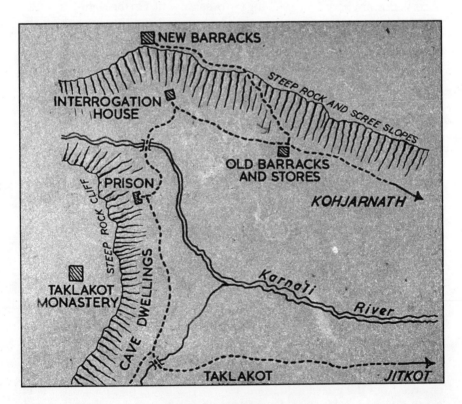

Plan of the Taklakot area

no cause to fear them. The Chinese were his best customers, buying a great deal of cloth from him. His manner was very reassuring, but I felt uneasy. He promised to have a chat with the Dzongpon and the CO of the PLA garrison and he was sure that matters would soon be put right. Our plight, he told us, was due to nothing more than a misunderstanding. The Chinese were naturally suspicious of our intentions, but an honest statement of our reasons for being in that part of the Himalaya would clear matters up.

He asked who we were, the name of our expedition, how long we had been in west Nepal, how many were in our entire party, and myriad other questions. But his questions as to who sent us created some difficulty. He seemed unable to believe that we were there because we wished to climb mountains. Coming a little closer, he said to me, 'If you tell me the real reason why you are here, I will be better placed to help you.'

That was enough. Both Harrop and I smelt a rat, and a Chinese stooge, an Indian 'brown nose', an agent of Peking who was working against the interests of his own country, India. I broke off the conversation. The demeanour of this Indian linguist, changed suddenly. Uttering Hindi curses he turned and spoke to the Dzongpon.

'The bastard is an agent of the Chinese,' Harrop commented.

At that the Indian spy called to the PLA soldiers, who appeared to be prepared to take orders from him. The three of us were lined up against a wall and told that we were to be searched. We were forced to stand with our hands clasped behind our heads while the Dzongpon ran his hands through our pockets, once again apologising for any inconvenience caused. To my great surprise the Indian spy rudely pushed Jungpah to one side, and went through our pockets and ran his hands over our bodies more thoroughly. He missed not a thing. We even had to remove our boots for him to see if they contained any concealed written material.

The search was in progress when Koila and the other porters arrived carrying our expedition gear. The Indian personally conducted the search of all our possessions item by item. Bars of chocolate and pemmican were unwrapped from their foil casing and the contents thrown back into our ration box, with expressions of disgust and disappointment.

The Dzongpon wished to end the search proceedings, but the Indian engaged him in a heated argument and finished up searching us for a second time. By now Harrop and I were beginning to lose our tempers. All of our equipment loads, including tents, stoves and survey gear, was taken away.

As our ration box was being removed with the rest of our property, Harrop bellowed, 'They're not getting away with that. God knows what the food is going to be like in here.' All three of us raised merry hell and, after a long argument, the food box was restored to us and we were told to place in it what they referred to as 'your room'. We were allowed to keep a few items of clothing, our inflatable air mattresses, rubber inflators, battery-powered torches and sleeping bags. My expedition log book, recording our journey from base camp at Saipal in Nepal up to and including our capture at gunpoint in the Jung Jung Khola was confiscated along with our only book, *The Century of Poetry from Pope to Keats*. Harrop's protestations about the loss of the book of poetry were to no avail, the Indian agent expressing the opinion that it might contain secret codes or cyphers.

We were motioned indoors and carried our air mattresses and sleeping bags into what was for the time being to be our communal cell. Damodar dropped his gear onto the floor in the middle of the room and a cloud of dust rose up to choke us. We soon learned that it was unwise to stamp about in our new home. The dust on the floor was like an inch-deep carpet, and in spite of our precautions, it succeeded in getting into everything we possessed. The dust was the room's only furnishing. We placed the food box in the middle of the floor to use a table, piling our sleeping bags on top of it out of the dust, until we had our air mattresses inflated and laid out on the floor. I bent down and looked through the iron strapped window to see the first of what would be a regular shift of guards coming on duty. Guard number one emerged from the guardroom with his PPSh assault rifle slung over his shoulder. Approaching our unglazed window, seeing my face, he unshouldered his weapon and pointing the muzzle in my face, shooed me away. We soon came to apply nicknames to our guards. The first guard on duty was the tallest of them all, so we called him Lofty. The others became Fatty, Monkey Face, Chubby, Marlo, Chungnya and Schickelgruber. Marlo's name was an abbreviation of an obscenity with which he prefaced or ended almost every sentence he uttered.

Guard duties never lasted longer than two hours, so we saw different faces at frequent intervals. Not for a moment were we without supervision, the guards standing outside our cell twenty-four hours a day. At 5 p.m., when we had settled into our new abode, dinner was brought in. The soldier who brought it was cook for that day, the cook being changed every three days, without any reference to skill. As luck would have it, only one knew how to cook properly, and it was he who brought us our first meal. We asked his name. He responded by pointing to his nose, a trait the Chinese have when referring to themselves, and said something that sounded like Chungnya. In fact we got it wrong. When I pointed to my chest and said 'Syd' and Harrop likewise referred to himself as 'John', Chungnya thought that we were talking about nationalities. He thought that I was a 'Sydman' and Harrop was a 'Johnman'. He could never pronounce our names properly and called me 'Chid' and Harrop 'Jung'. When he said 'Chungnya' he was really saying 'Chunghua', Chinese for 'The Middle Kingdom' which is the name the Chinese to this day use for their homeland.

The name stuck, and although we later learned that his real name was Sun Tian-sun, the title 'Chungnya' stayed with him. Whenever we wanted attention we just had to shout 'Chungnya' and he came running. He was twenty-two and a very likeable young man, as was his friend Chubby. The rest of them were far from friendly and at times were downright disagreeable.

That first dinner consisted of curried mutton and rice. We had barely started eating it when there was a commotion outside. We leapt up to see Koila put his face to the bars.

'They are sending us away,' he shouted to Damodar in Urdu. 'We shall never see you again.'

The cell door was open, and Harrop and Damodar ran outside to see our faithful Dhotial porters being shoved out of the prison yard gates. One of the guards ran over to push Koila out through the door, who was putting up quite a struggle. I seized the opportunity to scribble a note on a scrap of paper, addressed to Jack Henson at our base camp in Nepal. I stated briefly that we had been kidnapped at gunpoint by the Chinese and that he must get word out to the UK High Commission in Delhi without delay. I ran out into the yard to find Koila gone. He was walking down the track with the other three Dhoties, but when I called out to him he came back. I got one leg through the prison yard door, but was seized bodily by the guards. Koila, tears streaming down his face, threw his arms round my neck. As the Chinese tore us apart I managed to stuff the tiny piece of paper into his hand. With that he was gone. As they went off along the track towards Taklakot, I told Damodar to call after them and tell them that they had served us well, and they could keep all the gear they were using; the clothing, boots and sleeping bags.

I sighed with relief as the Chinese soldiers dragged me bodily back to my cell. Very soon, if Koila and company made it safely back into Nepal to Saipal, the outside world would know of our plight. But would they be able to make it back over the backbone of the Himalayas, when the Urai Lekh was officially closed until next spring? The Chinese had allowed them neither food nor money, and refused to let them have a tent, ice axes, or one of our two paraffin pressure-stoves. It was going to be a damn close-run thing for Koila and our porters.

That note, which Jack Henson still has, was essential in getting things moving without loss of time. The other members of our expedition would break camp the moment the hired porters arrived from Chainpur and Dhuli, and head off down the Seti Gorge with news that we had been kidnapped at gunpoint by the PLA. Thanks to dear old one-eyed Phrupa, Koila and the others were stocked up with ata and tsampa flour for that awful journey back. They made one camp, a bivouac, at Tharedunga, and then forced the Urai Lekh and down to our base camp in one day, arriving in the final stages of exhaustion. Koila proved himself to be a stout fellow and a thoroughly resourceful chap.

I was thankful that when the Chinese took our gear, they left me with the stub of a pencil, my Parker 51 fountain pen, a block of Chinese ink powder I had acquired in Jitkot, and a few scraps of writing paper. As we were to learn (for the Chinese communists everything has a purpose) the reason for leaving us with minimal writing requirements was that in due course we would write our confessions.

We ate our meal, prepared by Chungnya, and I did not enjoy it one little bit, hungry as I was. Trepidation about the future appeared not to spoil Harrop's and Damodar's appetites and they swallowed their curried mutton with rice like a couple of gannets.

Sleep on that first night in prison was fitful and troubled. I had to get out of my sleeping back once to make a trip to the lavatory, the guard at the door accompanying me to my destination and back, his assault rifle pointed at me at all times. After that I slept a little, my dozing interrupted by torch beams on my face through the window every five minutes or so.

For me, morning could not come too quickly, and it was heralded by the sunlight projecting the pattern of the barred window onto the wall by the foot of Harrop's bed. As it was bitterly cold in our unheated cell we simply sat upright in our sleeping bags waiting to see what the day would bring. At 8.30 a.m. a young soldier entered bearing a bowl of hot water. Sorting out my possessions I came across a small piece of soap. It was a very tiny cube, intended to rub on the lenses of our snow goggles to prevent them misting over. Harrop and I used it to have a wash, but Damodar preferred plain water.

Breakfast arrived at 9.30 a.m., a thin soup of small turnips which the guards called 'chigada', in which the bones of last night's supper had been boiled. There was rice as a filler, so we tucked in to that. After breakfast, the guards left the door of our cell open, and we were allowed out into the yard. There were small pools of ice on the ground where the Chinese had emptied tea from their mugs the night before.

Breakfast was being served to the guards. Six of them sat in a circle on the ground, cross-legged. A seventh soldier remained at his post on the firing-step by the outer wall. Each man had a small bowl containing rice, and before them in the middle of the circle was a huge brass pot filled with a turnip and meat stew. We observed that the guards' food rations were more than treble the amount fed to us. Each man dug into the communal stewpot with a pair of chopsticks and fished out a piece of meat. Anything not to his taste, he just spat out onto the floor. If the meat fell off the chopsticks, a grimy hand was thrust into the pot. This had a strange effect on the others. Once one man failed to use his chopsticks and used his hands, the others all immediately followed suit, as if some rule of the game had been broken. My curiosity as to how the guards picked up the boiled rice with their chopsticks was solved when they just placed the lip of the rice bowl in their mouths and shovelled the rice in. This was accompanied by a most awful noise, like water vanishing down a bath plug. We started to laugh and tried to imitate their gurglings, but our parody of their actions had no effect on them. They simply went on eating bowl after bowl of rice followed by enormous quantities of meat.

We were motioned to the kitchen to obtain our morning mug of tea. One of the soldiers interrupted his gargantuan meal to follow us inside the tarpaulin-covered enclosure. Lifting the lid off one of the pots he revealed the 'tea'. The raw product of this Chinese tea comes in brick form, the slab being about a foot square and two inches thick. The guards broke up the tea-brick with an axe, lumps flying all over the prison yard as they did so. Pieces of brick-tea weighing about half a pound were placed into a cotton bag and this was immersed in the brass or copper tea urn. It mattered not whether the water was hot or cold. The tea did not appear to infuse quickly as does Indian leaf tea, to which we were accustomed. It had to be boiled for some time before it began to colour the water.

Tea was on the boil day and night and the contents of the bag were only changed once a week. The longer it stewed the more darkly it stained the water, but the taste remained the same: mild and insipid. As the tea was consumed, the urn was topped up with ever more cold water and by the end of the week the brew had neither taste nor colour.

Our guards had a small supply of sugar which for all the world looked like rock salt, supplied by Indian traders. The troops had to purchase it at their own expense, along with soap, toothpaste, hair cream and cheap perfumes. We were surprised to see them coming out of their quarters rubbing the stuff over their faces.

We devised a rationing system over the next few days. If the main meal of the day was reasonably adequate, we could manage. If the food was poor, we supplemented it with a bar of pemmican apiece. We had a couple of pounds of sugar, and a few tubes of condensed milk, with which we laced our tea. Breakfast over, the remains of the guards' bowl of meat was tossed over the wall, where it was fought over by growling Tibetan mastiff dogs. Our expedition issue enamelled tin plates were taken from us by the guards, to be washed in the kitchen. I had not anticipated hotel style service and followed the kitchen-porter under the tarpaulin to witness Chinese hygiene at first hand. I could not believe what I saw. The soldier first placed a medical face mask of cotton wadding over his mouth, tied by a bow at the back of his neck. This was something we were never able to figure out, and which still puzzles me to this day. Every time cooking took place, the cook tied on his mask, just like a surgeon about to operate, and repeated the process when washing dishes.

I was sorry that I went in to witness the washing up procedure. Our plates and enamelled mugs were dropped into a cauldron of lukewarm greasy water. I could imagine salmonella bugs the size of fleas swimming around in that filthy pot. The dishes, still greasy, were fished out by the washer-up and hand dried on a piece of cotton cloth, once white. If the lousy diet further weakened us, the microbes would probably finish us off. The washer-up was guard Lofty, and several times during the proceedings he paused to clear his throat and then spat on the floor. Monkey Face sat on the ground by the stove cutting up lumps of raw mutton by hacking them on the mud floor with an axe, every so often thrusting a piece of raw meat into his mouth and eating it with obvious relish. He interspersed his gourmandising by spitting on the floor, right between my feet.

Harrop was quick to discover what we could and could not do. Approaching the prison yard door or even looking through it when it was open was sufficient to bring a stern reproof from the guards, who on occasion did their duty turn on the roof instead of on the firing-step by the yard wall. Our requests for permission to exercise outside the prison yard, in writing, to the unseen officers quartered on the other side of the Karnali river were ignored.

At 5 p.m. we were ushered into our cell at gunpoint and the long night began. Once the sun went down it was too cold to stay out of our sleeping bags, and it was too cold to emerge from them until 9 a.m. the following day. Thus we were compelled to spend no less than sixteen hours of every day in our sleeping bags. During the daytime, if the guards refused to open our cell door, we put on our down-filled jackets and walked about the cell. We did this in the evenings after being locked in for the night. It soon became dark and not wishing to waste what little life was left in our battery torches, into our sleeping bags we had to go. Then deep down inside my bag, by the glimmer of my torch, I wrote up my diary of the day's events.

For two days I kept a diary in this manner, but on the third day the guards came in and subjected the three of us to a body search. My journal, written on scraps of paper, was confiscated and I suspended my diary writing for the time being. The guard who confiscated my journal signified by mime and sign language that he was riding off that day to see officers who were on their way from Gartok. I was puzzled by this. There were PLA officers in the barracks on the other side of the Karnali, and there must be more senior officers at the place twenty-three miles from Jitkot, to which Jungpah had ridden to advise of our apprehension by the PLA. Why were we not being interrogated by the local officers?

In fact our presence at Taklakot was deemed to be a matter of considerable importance to the Chinese in west Tibet. We were to be interrogated by no less a personage than the commanding officer of all Chinese forces in Tibet, a full general of the PLA, who was on an inspection visit to Gartok.

We were allowed out into the prison yard and we watched the PLA dispatch rider, bearing my harmless pieces of paper, ride off on a horse of better quality than the usual Tibetan pony. He was a fine horseman, and he gave us a yell and a grin as he rode off to the west.

'The Lone Star ranger rides tonight, Hi Ho Silver,' Harrop and I called after him. It was then that I noticed that he was wearing black leather riding boots, laced up at the back, just like the Indian trader.

The following morning a new and by no means pleasant face appeared in the prison yard. We were sitting down on the top of the steps above the lower yard, eating a breakfast of boiled turnip soup when two of our regular guards, Chubby and Marlo, came in through the yard door bearing a load of bedding, including a straw-filled palliasse. Behind them came a man who was to become the bane of our existence. He had been appointed sergeant of our guards, probably for the purpose of stiffening up discipline before the officers from Gartok arrived.

An ugly character with a mean, bad tempered air, he looked more Japanese than Chinese, and we soon christened him Schickelgruber. His bedding was taken into the guards' room and he stood looking at us.

'Here's a character to be watched,' Harrop suggested.

Harrop had barely spoken when Schickelgruber screamed an order. The guard on duty ran up and handed over his own PPSh assault rifle. Advancing towards us, Schickelgruber waved the muzzle of the weapon from one of us to the other. We stopped eating, and watched his face. His eyes appeared to bulge out of his head, and he yelled at us in a screaming high-pitched voice. He held the gun in his right hand, and I watched his left hand clenching and unclenching. Then he stopped screaming and muttered under his breath. I formed the opinion that he was a psychopath, and the type of person who should not have power placed in his hands.

The rest of the guards came into the yard, their preparations for breakfast disturbed by their new NCO's coarse voice. He levelled his gun at my head with both hands, and screamed at the other guards, who started to usher us into our cell. We started to kick up a fuss at being sent indoors so early in the day, but without avail.

I wrote a strong note of complaint to the officers and shouted to Chungnya through the window. He took the note and went off across the river to the officers' quarters, but I never received a reply.

That night I resolved that I would somehow manage to keep a diary, which all three of us regarded as essential. But where was I to conceal my journal? How could I prevent the guards from finding it? An entry damaging to the Chinese, if discovered, could result in a worsening of our situation. I was in my sleeping bag when I found the answer to the problem. I felt the hard ground beneath me. My air mattress had developed a slight leak, so I turned over to blow air into the inflation tube. There was the solution. I would roll my daily diary up into a slim tube and slide it down the inflation tube of my pillow. If I kept the pillow constantly inflated, the Chinese might never discover my trick. I was running short of paper, but we still had some of our expedition rations left, and the chocolate, Kendal Mint Cake, and Ovosport wrappers all had a plain side. I would use the wrappers. Eventually I got hold of a broken chopstick and used that instrument to push my daily diary down into the pillow of my air bed.

Toilet paper was a luxury; we only had two rolls between the three of us. But the daily journal was of greater consequence and I used up some of my precious toilet paper for pages of my diary. Harrop decided that a calendar was also needed. The top foot of the cell wall was painted blue and white; a simple decoration with a continuous zig-zag swastika motif running through it. Harrop used the white-painted sections to write the date and day of the week, adding pertinent and insulting remarks about the intellect and habits of the Chinese communists. In large bold type I wrote the following on the wall: 'Harrop, Wignall and Suwal of the Welsh Himalayan Expedition. Kidnapped at gunpoint by the Chinese communists on 25 October 1955, and imprisoned in this cell on 28 October until . . .'

I left the rest blank. The final date could only be filled in by the Chinese.

The days dragged slowly by. Harrop, writing the November days one by one on the wall, remarked, 'There are not many shopping days left before Christmas.'

I had promised my wife Jean that I would be home for Christmas. I was beginning to wonder which Christmas? Would I be home for Christmas 1955, or 1975?

'Let's see what the Chinese officers are like when they come,' Harrop suggested. 'If they don't act in a civilised and reasonable manner, I vote that we all go over the wall one dark night.' With that we were all in agreement.

That night I was awakened by something crawling over my face. The duty guard happened to shine his torch through our cell window just at that moment, and I found myself looking into the face of a very under-nourished rat perching on the lip of my sleeping bag. He beat a hasty retreat and vanished behind Damodar's head. After that I heard the rat chewing something, but for all Damodar cared, it could have been his left ear, for nothing ever disturbed him once he fell asleep.

After that the rats became more cheeky and came into our cell during the daytime. There were also tiny chubby little pug-nosed mice. Once we heard a mouse chewing something in the corner of our cell. On examination it was found to be a very old dried portion of chapati. As neither the Chinese nor the Tibetans we came into contact with ever ate chapatis, we pondered over its origin. It became obvious that we were not the first people to be incarcerated in that room. There had been an earlier prisoner, and he was probably an Indian.

On 3 November Harrop decided that he wanted a few personal items out of our equipment loads which were being stored in the guardroom, and he tackled Chungnya about it. We were allowed to follow two of the guards into a small annexe off their living quarters and after a great deal of argument we managed to carry away our last packet of toilet paper, a pair of surgical scissors, our last two spare flashlight batteries and some sulpha pills; the latter as a precaution in case I had a recurrence of dysentery.

Schickelgruber was away at the time, and had he been there I am sure that he would have denied us access to our kit. Later in the day, Chungnya brought in two tiny Tibetan stools for us to use as tables or seats. We piled our few precious possessions on them and thanked that nice young man for his kindness.

The following day I went down with a dose of dysentery. The symptoms as before. Soon I was passing nothing more than blood-stained water, and my appetite completely vanished.

'Get a pemmican bar inside you, you are going to need it,' Harrop insisted, but the thought of food made me throw up. I sat on the top step in the prison yard, my head swimming. Harrop brought me a cup of warm water from the kitchen. 'Take three of these sulphaguanadine tablets,' he said. 'You should be back on your feet tomorrow, once these have gone through your system.'

I swallowed the three pills, and accepted the bottle of pills from Harrop. At that moment, Monkey Face entered the yard accompanied by Schickelgruber. Schickelgruber screamed at me and Monkey Face ran over and snatched the bottle of pills out of my hand, handing it triumphantly to his unpleasant colleague. I started to protest, and Harrop and Damodar, attempting to intervene, were pushed back into our communal cell at gunpoint.

The final indignity was to have to make trips to the lavatory hole every fifteen minutes or so during the whole of the afternoon. My legs felt weak, and whenever I was not on my way to and from the lavatory, I lay flat on my back in my sleeping bag, feeling like death warmed up. Each and every time I went to the thunder hole I squatted with a PPSh assault rifle muzzle held about three inches from my head by a grinning Monkey Face.

Harrop, in great indignation over the inhuman treatment of his expedition leader, wrote a brusque letter to the Chinese commandant. There was, of course, no response. Harrop eventually came up with the possible reason why our communications to the PLA HQ were being ignored. 'It's feasible that the Chinese don't have anybody who can speak English, other than that Indian trader, and if he is off over the Lipu Lekh into India, we have fat chance of engaging in any meaningful dialogue with these people.'

Harrop was, of course, right. The only Chinese national who was reasonably fluent in English was the assistant to the military governor of Tibet, and that gentleman was yet to make his appearance. On 4 November, feeling little better, I remarked that I could not face boiled turnips for breakfast-cum-lunch, so Harrop and Damodar went into the yard with a modicum of our minuscule supply of expedition Indian tea in leaf form. I looked forward to a decent brew, because the brick-tea by that morning had the colour of gnats' urine.

Within a minute, Damodar was back at the cell window. 'Marlo is on duty and he won't let us have any boiling water. John Sahib is going to light our own fire in the yard.' I staggered over to the lattice window to see what was going on. Harrop gathered some brushwood from the kitchen, and jamming a stout branch of juniper in a crack in the yard wall, suspended our only billy can from it, filled with cold water. He soon had a fire going and I was anticipating a cup of tea when a fearful hubbub broke out. Marlo was shouting his head off and the hullabaloo brought the rest of the guards out of their room. Schickelgruber started to push Damodar around, and when Harrop told Schickelgruber to lay off Damodar, the NCO kicked our can of water across the yard. He then picked up a stick about five feet in length and threw it at Damodar's head. The latter ducked nimbly out of the way. Harrop's physical intervention was restricted by two of the guards who seized him by both of his arms. Both the Chinese were small and light in weight and Harrop, who was strong and well built, managed to work his way across the yard, carrying the Chinese with him.

The guard whom we called Fatty now joined in the fray and started to push Damodar back towards our cell door with the barrel of his assault rifle. I shouted insults at the Chinese from my haven of comparative safety inside the cell, plus yells of encouragement to Harrop. This only brought more Chinese out of their quarters, and soon six of them were involved in the mêlée in the yard. Damodar headed for the safety of the door, followed by Harrop, who now had five Chinese soldiers hanging onto him. He literally carried them to our cell. There was a body jam at the door, and Harrop shouted, 'Sod this for a game of soldiers, I'm damned if I will go in to please these bastards.'

It was obvious now to both me and Damodar that Harrop was in fact thoroughly enjoying himself. It was fast becoming apparent that we were going to be interrogated by the senior officers from Gartok, and therefore we would not be shot or seriously harmed for the time being. Even so, one of the guards cocked his gun and kept it aimed at Harrop. Harrop grabbed the loathsome Marlo by the jaw with the thumb and forefingers of his right hand, and squeezed. Marlo screamed in agony, and for a moment I thought Harrop was going to break his jaw. Monkey Face swung from Harrop's right arm. Harrop lifted Marlo off the floor by his jaw, and such was Harrop's strength, Monkey Face went up in the air as well. Schickelgruber grabbed Harrop by the throat from behind, but Harrop deliberately lurched backwards, slamming Schickelgruber against the wall. Schickelgruber released his hold on Harrop's throat and sank groaning to the ground.

In my excitement the words of encouragement I uttered were a combination of a north-east English local cry, and my old schoolmaster Albert William Heap's favourite poem: 'Away the lads . . . play up . . . play up . . . and play the game.'

At last, Harrop slammed the moaning Marlo against the opposite wall in the passage between our cell and the smaller cell opposite, and Marlo slumped to the ground. That left two guards holding onto Harrop, plus Fatty with his assault rifle. Shaking the two remaining guards off like a terrier shakes off water, Harrop turned on his heel, and walking nonchalantly through the doorway of our cell, said, over his shoulder, 'That will be all for the time being, gentlemen. I'm going in now. Busy morning, eh,' he commented as he joined Damodar and me. With that our cell door was locked and we were denied further access to the yard for two days. We just spent all day in that freezing cold room. In the afternoon I went to sleep, and Harrop retired to his sleeping bag and busied himself searching for the Tibetan fleas which were making our lives a torment. The fleas must have been well camouflaged, for search as he might, he could find none in his sleeping bag. Nonetheless the fleas multiplied and our efforts to sleep were often nullified by a combination of flea bites and the bitter cold.

9

Feeling feverish, the perspiration pouring down my face, I stayed in my bed, other than when nature called, which was frequent. The Chinese refused to return my pills, and requests from Harrop for medical assistance for me were ignored. I began to fear that my condition might deteriorate to such a degree that I would be unfit for the march back to India when our day of release or our escape came.

My feeling of depression was lightened by Damodar as he kept watch through the window. 'Marlo is holding his head in both hands. Perhaps John Sahib has broken his jaw or his skull. Perhaps poor little bastard is going to die?'

Despite my condition, I had to laugh. The Chinese went indoors bemoaning their fate, and Chubby took over the kitchen duties for the rest of the day. Shortly afterwards, all the guards came out of their room, and sat cross-legged on the ground in the middle of the yard for what was obviously a discussion about their prisoners, for they occasionally turned and pointed to our cell window as they talked.

'They are sending Chungnya in,' Damodar said.

It was at that point that I realised that Chungnya had taken no part in the Battle of Taklakot. Perhaps he was out of the yard, or perhaps he saw no point in the episode of the tea can. Harrop and I decided that we needed at least one friend while held under such foul conditions, and so we greeted Chungnya as if nothing had happened.

By now Chungnya was able to pronounce our names reasonably well. Sitting at the edge of my bed, he said nothing for a few moments, and then he grinned and pointed to Harrop, saying, 'Jung, Ha . . . Ha . . . Ha . . . Yappa Do,' meaning that when John Harrop was in a good humour he was considered to be all right by the Chinese. Then Chungnya clenched his hands, and adopted an angry expression and said, 'Jung, Yappa Mindo,' the latter two words being Tibetan for 'bad' or 'no good', or just 'no'.

The sign language thereafter became very involved, as we tried to put over our side of the case. At last he realised that I was ill, and he acknowledged our repeated requests for the Dzongpon with the word 'lalasso', which appeared to mean 'yes'.

Chungnya had barely left our cell when Schickelgruber appeared in the yard accompanied by a tall soldier who was greeted by the other guards with a sort of sloppy salute. His clothing differed not at all from the garb of the common infantryman, for he wore a padded suit, fur-trimmed Davy Crockett hat and the usual basketball boots. Nevertheless he was obviously superior in rank to Schickelgruber, who was explaining to the newcomer the events of the morning.

Schickelgruber's exaggerated mime was most amusing as he described how he had kicked the deadly tea can out of Harrop's hands and how he and his comrades, unaided, had managed to force Harrop back into our cell. The newcomer, apparently impressed, gave Schickelgruber an encouraging pat on the shoulder. There was no holding the poisonous NCO after that, and he strutted around the yard like a rooster.

Marlo argued with Schickelgruber, holding his sore head and jaw in his hands, pointing after the receding figure, apparently asking for some form of decoration for his conduct in battle, and to compensate him for injuries sustained. He and Schickelgruber ended up cursing each other roundly, their profanity consisting of Tibetan words we now understood.

Harrop grinned at me from his vantage point alongside Damodar by the window. 'Looks,' he said, 'as though Marlo is going to start a counter-revolution.'

'Only because he has got a swollen head,' said Damodar, causing us all to laugh.

Schickelgruber suspended his altercation with Marlo to reprimand someone coming out of the guardroom. This was Chungnya, who ignored him and came into our cell, carrying an eiderdown quilt from his own bed. It was decorated with beautifully coloured patterns including a central green silk panel with a fearsome looking dragon rampant in the centre. I was now suffering from a fever and I was excessively hot in my sleeping bag, but Chungnya ignored my protests and tucked the eiderdown all round me.

About half an hour later he appeared again, this time with a small bowl of thin noodle soup on top of which floated a poached egg. I could hardly believe my eyes. We had seen one or two scraggy looking hens running around outside, but we never thought we would see an egg in that prison. Ill as I was, the sight of such a dish restored my jaded appetite, and I smiled my appreciation. Chungnya was the only PLA soldier we ever saw who appeared to be able to think and act independently.

'That boy should be the next Chinese Ambassador to the UK,' said Harrop, as Chungnya departed.

I was inclined to agree. Chungnya was a perfect example of everything that is good in China. No amount of political indoctrination or 'thought reform' could subdue his strong personality. He refused to be forced into the communist mould which was shaping the minds of young people in China. Chungnya was a thoroughly nice young man, and I felt privileged that he regarded me as a friend.

Darkness fell and Fatty came in bearing a small oil lamp which he set on one of the two Tibetan stools. He signified that the light must be left on all night so that the duty guard would be able to see into our cell. This was a new departure. We didn't object, for at least we could sit up and see something. Spending up to sixteen hours at a stretch in our beds, it broke up what was becoming an almost endless night.

When supper was brought in, happy with my egg noodles, I wanted nothing. The meal consisted of yak intestines with perhaps a tablespoonful of rice, with a handful of burning chillies added. Both Damodar and Harrop had to give up eating after a mouthful or two, the chillies scorching their mouths, the tears streaming down their faces. We were to learn by observing the cooking procedures that the 'red hot chilli' routine was especially for our benefit. The Chinese liked their chillies, but we always got a handful of crushed whole chilli peppers added on top of our meals. I think that this was Schickelgruber's doing, as retribution for Harrop's one-man Samson act. The proof of this became apparent whenever Chungnya cooked the meal. No extra chillies were added to our dishes.

We found yak meat almost uneatable. Some days we got a bowl of rice, some days a small portion of tough mutton, and on bad days yak belly or yak intestines. At 6 p.m. that night, Chungnya entered our cell followed by the Dzongpon, a Tibetan interpreter and a medical orderly who wore a stethoscope around his neck, and a gauze mask protecting his nose and mouth (just like our cook in the kitchen). Finally Schickelgruber and the rest of our guards swarmed in. The Dzongpon bowed to us and extended his usual polite greetings. His plausible bonhomie was back, but we now knew that his promises were worthless.

The medical orderly (his actions did not suggest that he was qualified as a doctor), appeared to be in his early twenties, and he asked me to undo my shirt. Harrop became annoyed at this futile attempt at diagnosis as the orderly placed his stethoscope on my chest.

'Tell the idiot that Syd has dysentery and not a ruddy cough,' he said to Damodar, who spoke to the Tibetan interpreter in Urdu.

The medical orderly took not the least notice, other than lowering his gauze mask so that he could clear his throat and spit on the floor by my sleeping bag. Harrop blew up into a rage about this and told Damodar to inform them that in England, people do not spit, and even pigs do not spit. This aroused the ire of the Chinese soldiers, and without more ado all of them, excluding Chungnya, cleared their throats and spat on the dusty floor of our cell.

'Philistines and bloody barbarians,' Harrop commented.

'I don't know how to interpret that, John Sahib,' Damodar said.

When this perfunctory chest examination was completed, the Dzongpon asked how long I had been ill.

Harrop explained that I had been plagued by recurring dysentery for three and a half months and that if my pills were not returned, the Chinese would have to accept responsibility for my deteriorating health.

This brought a response from the Dzongpon. He told us that there was a qualified medical practitioner at Taklakot, and that the doctor's medication would be superior to my own, and that I could not have my pills returned until they had been examined by the responsible authorities and that he, the Dzongpon, and the real doctor would return the following day.

The visitors departed, but not before the Dzongpon had promised that he would pay us a daily visit to attend to our needs. My dysentery was to get worse, the Dzongpon did not bring that doctor, and none of his promises were kept.

The next morning, the usual bowl of washing water was brought into our cell, followed by boiled turnip soup, of which I did not partake. Harrop suggested that I might feel better if I sat in the sun, and he and Damodar carried my air mattress and sleeping bag out into the prison yard. Chungnya came out of the kitchen enclosure shouting 'Chai' (Indian for tea) and bearing an enamelled mug decorated with a red star.

'Yappa do,' I said, taking the proffered cup. As I did so I looked across the river towards the grey barracks and something caught my attention. Two tall wooden masts had been erected at either end of the roof and between them I noticed the reflected gleam of an aerial wire. A radio, which had not been there a couple of days before, had been installed. This could mean that the PLA interrogators from Gartok were now drawing near and everything was being prepared for the transmission of signals direct to Lhasa or even China proper.

I drank the tea abstractedly. Koila should by now have reached our base camp and passed my message to the other members of our expedition. It was almost certain, subject to Koila's safe passage over the Uria Lekh, that the outside world would shortly be made aware of our predicament. In the meantime, I decided that we must keep a close watch on all movements at the other side of the Karnali. After that we kept a constant watch throughout daylight hours, with frequent trips to the lavatory, from which we could command a view of both the river and the cantilever bridge.

The usual activity was going on at the top of the hill overlooking the Chinese quarters on the opposite side of the river. We could see the endless line of men, animals and load-carrying Tibetan women winding their way up and down the track. In the early afternoon a party of soldiers emerged from the grey barracks and started carrying furniture to the red building. I was surprised to see seven modern tubular steel chairs, followed by a wooden table.

Our guards then carried all our kit, including tents, away to the grey building at the opposite side of the river. The reason for that move was obvious. Without tents, stoves and fuel, our chances of getting over the mountains, if we escaped, were virtually nil.

A group of Tibetans I had not seen before glanced up at me from the opposite side of the wall. They were sitting in the open dishing out yak-butter tea from an urn. Behind them smoke billowed from the top of the large boulder house. One of the Tibetans came over to the wall, looked up at me and held an empty bowl in his outstretched hand, begging for food. I sadly shook my head and turned away. The guard, coming out of the kitchen, waved me away from the wall. I sat on my bed in the prison yard. Damodar was leaning against the wall of the guardroom, with his head a few inches away from the glass. He appeared to be listening to something.

'Come away from there,' I said, 'or you'll get into trouble.'

He came over to where I was sitting. 'I think,' he said, 'the Chinese have a small cat.'

'Don't talk daft,' I responded. 'We haven't seen any cats since we entered Tibet. They wouldn't live long, with all those big mastiff dogs prowling around at night.'

Every family in Taklakot appeared to have one of these large dogs. Intended in the main to protect herds of sheep from marauding wolves, which roam the plateau in packs in winter, the mastiffs were let out at night, and heaven help the unwary traveller who should chance to be abroad during the hours of darkness. Strangely enough, these fierce looking dogs could be gentle and docile in the daytime. We saw Tibetan children and even Chinese soldiers playing with them. In areas where the wolf threat was greatest, the mastiffs wore a wooden collar, fitted with three-inch-long protruding iron spikes; this is to prevent a wolf taking the dog by the throat.

Damodar, to prove that his suspicions were well founded, walked over to the guardroom door and called, 'Puss, puss, puss.' The guard on the roof shouted for Damodar to get away from the door, cocking his gun, and raising it to his shoulder. Chungnya came out and said, 'Yappa mindo.'

The answer was evidently 'no'. We kept badgering the guards until finally Chungnya's friend Chubby came out carrying a pretty little black kitten, a piece of string tied to its neck and the other ended attached to a rock. The kitten was set down in the middle of the yard, its freedom being restricted to three feet of string. Damodar and I undid the string. The guards tied it on the kitten again, and we undid it once more until they gave up and the cat was allowed to roam around the yard.

Watching the charming little creature frolic about I thought that it might be that we and these Chinese at last had some common level of understanding in a love of animals. In this belief I was utterly wrong, for the kitten never enjoyed a moment's respite from persistent cruelty from the moment Damodar brought about its shortlived freedom.

Before the cat had played for half an hour, Marlo picked it up and blew cigarette smoke down the helpless creature's nose. Then he stubbed his lighted cigarette against the complaining kitten's face. That was only the beginning. Later in the day one of the guards took a running kick at the kitten and sent it flying across the yard. Our intervention was to no avail.

The cat was taken indoors, where its plaintive cries confirmed that it was being subjected to further cruelties.

Later in the day the kitten was brought out again, and Monkey Face, seeing how I tended to the injured little animal's burned face, took it from me, and swinging the kitten round and round by the tail, threw the wretched creature against the prison wall with all the force he could muster. Needless to say, the kitten died shortly afterwards.

I was beginning to feel a little better and enjoyed the Tibetan winter sunshine while it lasted. On the same day that I saw the radio masts, I heard sounds coming from behind our prison, in the area between the rear wall and the cliff face. Soldiers kept appearing, disappearing and then appearing again. Something was afoot. I looked to the top of the cliff just behind our prison. A crowd of Tibetan children who had gathered to see what was going on were not allowed to stay for long. Schickelgruber ran up the cliff top and drove them away with his assault rifle, clipping one or two on the ear with the muzzle.

My apprehension did not decrease when Chungnya came over and tried hard to convey something to me by sign language. He pointed over the lavatory wall towards Lhasa, and aiming his PPSh in that direction, said, 'TATATATATATATAT.' Then turning in the direction of Taklakot, and looking through the yard door towards the Indian frontier, he again said, 'TATATATATATATAT. Hindustan, Yappa mindo.' (Tibetan for India, no.)

I could not quite fathom what he was trying to tell me. Then he pointed to my climbing boots and motioned towards the cliff face behind our prison, and pressing the palms of his hands together and closing his eyes, signified that he was referring to night time. Finally he stamped his foot on the ground and said in a loud voice, 'Boom!'

'Oh no, not landmines!' I exclaimed.

With a pencil stub he traced the shape of a landmine in the dust, and then scraping away the dust, he placed a pebble in the hole and covered it over. I was still incredulous. Admittedly the cliff face was one way of circumventing the track at night, and thereby reducing the risk of running into guards, but the laying of mines seemed a big step to take merely to prevent the escape of two Englishmen and an eighteen-year-old Nepalese youth.

The idea that the Chinese apparently regarded us as Very Important Prisoners did nothing to assuage my anxiety. We began to gain the impression that whatever lay in store for us made escape imperative, even a matter of life and death, and the Chinese were taking every precaution to ensure that escape was impossible.

'I have the mine laying and the cruelty to animals worked out now,' Harrop called over to me.

'So have I,' I responded. 'They are trying to soften us up.'

Damodar cut in with, 'Great hopes, Syd Sahib, that Schickelgruber or

Marlo will go for a walk one dark night and get a totally unpleasant Chinese hot foot behind our hotel.' At that we all laughed.

'Nil desperandum illegitimo carberundum, Damodar,' Harrop said.

'Not understand. What that means?' Damodar said, looking puzzled.

I translated for him. 'It's dog Latin, Damodar, for never let the bastards wear you down.'

Thereafter, during daylight hours, there was always a guard with a loaded PPSh sitting on top of the cliff behind our prison, ready to drive away any Tibetans who chanced to come near to the rear of our jail.

On 6 November I went to the lavatory, to find a cluster of chubby little tail-less snub-nosed Tibetan rats eating human faeces for their lunch. There had been a hard frost the night before and these attractive little creatures presumably were not averse to eating their meal 'freeze-dried'. I looked over the wall, just as a cortege rode past. I shouted, 'Strangers in the mess.'

Harrop came over and joined me. 'This looks like it. This is what we've been waiting for,' I commented.

There were six Chinese on mules, riding down towards the cantilever bridge. Three wore the usual khaki, and the other three wore the dark blue uniforms of the political corps, the Communist Party cadres. These were indeed the 'Boys from Gartok'. Our waiting was at an end.

I scrutinised the faces of our guards. They were watching the arrival of the officers as intently as I was, and all conversation ceased. The six officers were escorted by a PLA detachment of about thirty soldiers, also on mules. Then there were about another dozen mules, carrying metal and wooden boxes, and bedding palliasses.

'I think that they are kitted up for a long winter holiday,' Harrop muttered to me under his breath.

There was a different atmosphere that night. Into it had crept an urgency which affected us all, even the guards. Their faces were expressionless as they stared at us through the window. Our efforts to crack jokes failed pathetically. Even Damodar, the born tumbler and court jester, failed to raise a laugh when he gave an imitation of Fatty. With remarkable aptness for mime, Damodar reproduced Fatty's belch, throat clearing, spitting, flea-hunting and, finally, reading, an occupation which Fatty carried out with sagging jaw.

My own thoughts were unhappily engaged with the possibility that perhaps Koila had not been able to cross the Urai Lekh. If so, our friends at base camp would have no knowledge of our fate. We would be presumed dead, and the Chinese would be able to hold us as long as they liked, maybe forever. The blow would fall most severely on my wife Jean, and our nine-year-old son. At least we knew what was happening to us. But for them there would only be a sudden ending to the regular air mail letters and then silence and torment.

I slept badly that night and kept dreaming of a Chinese 'People's Court'.

In my nightmare, the characters had the ugliest and most evil faces I had ever seen. One kept placing the muzzle of a PPSh assault rifle against my head, and I sweated, waiting for the explosion. I woke up in the night, in urgent need to go to the lavatory. Lofty was on guard duty, and he opened the cell door when I hammered on it, and then conducted me to the thunder hole. He shone his torch in my face and held the muzzle of his PPSh about an inch from my head. Hating the indignity, I performed my needs as quickly as possible. I stood up and looked over the wall. It was a sharp clear night, but with no wind, and the temperature well below zero. The heavens were full of stars. It was wonderful to behold. To the south, over the Himalaya, hung a solitary bright star. Was it Sirius, the brightest star in the heavens, or was it the planet Venus?

'What a wonderful place this would be for an observatory,' I mused to myself. No polluted atmosphere, no clouds, no haze caused by civilised society's artificial street lighting. I was roused from my reverie by Lofty. He gave me a far from comradely thump on the back of my head with the muzzle of his assault rifle. I returned to my bed.

10

B reakfast was eaten in absolute silence disturbed only by the sounds of a rat making his daily attempt to nibble sustenance from the ancient chapati in the corner of the cell. When we had completed our meal of turnip soup and tea, Damodar spoke first.

'What do you think will happen, Syd Sahib?'

'Possibly interrogation if we are lucky, and if we are unlucky, trial by a People's Court.'

Damodar, who had read little about international politics, enquired what a People's Court was. I explained that according to Chinese internal propaganda, People's Courts were essential to stamp out what were called deviationist and counter-revolutionary tendencies. China herself admitted that at that time no less than two million people had been condemned to death by People's Courts. The outcome of such trials is always a foregone conclusion. Nobody has ever been found Not Guilty in a Chinese Communist People's Court. The prime requirement, as in Stalin's Russia, is a signed confession unaccompanied by any physical, documentary or even circumstantial evidence.

The proceedings always followed the same stereotyped pattern. The accused acknowledges and laments his faults and shortcomings to the court, and judges nod their heads in agreement with the reformed views of the penitent. The proceedings at times include the accused being 'Struggled Against'. This takes the form (if the accused is a person of note) of the victim being made to appear in front of a crowd of ranting screaming accusers, sometimes thousands strong, in a football stadium or public square. Denunciation by a party worker is deemed sufficient evidence for a prosecution, just like in Caligula's Rome. The minimum sentence ever handed down by a People's Court was three years. Most sentences were for ten or twenty years or life, and the death penalty was usually carried out with a single bullet in the base of the skull.

I was interrupted by a click in the lock mechanism of our cell door. For the first time since our incarceration began, we were locked in. I knocked at the cell door and it was unlocked by Lofty, who followed me to the lavatory, and then to the kitchen where I signified that I wanted hot water for a shave. If I was to be interrogated then I intended to put up a reasonable front and appear in good order.

To my surprise my request was granted and Chungnya produced a cheap bakelite safety razor of Indian manufacture. There was only one blade and it was as blunt as a barrel hoop. I had but little soap, and making a lather minus shaving brush and with lukewarm water was virtually impossible. Nevertheless, I managed to remove a month's growth of beard, but not without considerable suffering, and my face resembled a raw beefsteak.

Every few minutes one of the soldiers went onto the firing-step on the outer wall and looked towards the grey and red buildings on the other side of the Karnali. I made repeated trips to the lavatory to take note of developments. It was like hanging around a dentist's waiting room, and I felt apprehensive. At 11 a.m. I saw a group of khaki- and blue-clad figures leave the grey barracks and walk the intervening distance across rubbly ground to the red building.

A few minutes later, a PLA soldier emerged from the red building and waved a hand in our direction. That was the signal. Schickelgruber tapped me on the shoulder and called Marlo and Lofty over. They pointed to the yard door, and I stepped outside our prison for the first time since our arrival at Taklakot eleven days earlier.

The bridge was larger than it had appeared from our prison, being wide enough for two yaks or mules side by side. A group of young Chinese soldiers in fatigue kit, some minus jackets and sporting bright green cotton sweatshirts, passed in the opposite direction, and stopped one by one to have a closer look as I went by. Lack of exercise and the effects of dysentery had left me in a run-down condition, and I arrived at the door of the interrogation building panting for breath.

I turned to look back across the Karnali, to see Harrop and Damodar still standing on the top step in the centre of the prison yard. They gave me a cheery wave. 'Thank God I'm not alone,' I thought to myself. Inside the courtyard stood an impassive-looking group of Tibetan officials who indicated a curtain-covered doorway to my left. I walked over to it. Someone inside the room pushed the curtain open and stepped out. It was the self-styled Indian trader who had tried to trap us on the day of our arrival at Taklakot. He gave me a weak smile and with that my fears started to disappear. This slimy creep was no unknown quantity. The emotion he aroused inside me was one of indignation and disgust. All I wanted to do was punch him in the face and knock his gold teeth out.

Ignoring his sickly grin and bending to avoid the usual bump on the head when negotiating Tibetan doorways, I stepped inside. The single step transported me from the world of sanity and reason and into a phantasmagoria of unbalanced values, lies and deceit. I was entering the domain of a Chinese general who envisaged himself as a sort of Tamerlaine of Tibet. I hesitated on the threshold while I tried to adjust my vision to the dim room. The only natural light came through a small window covered with thin white paper. The room was no more than ten feet square, and part of it was hidden by a folding wood and paper screen that stood to my right. To my left stood a small stove made out of a five-gallon oil drum, which in the absence of a chimney, sent smoke coiling up to the ceiling where it hung in wreaths.

Two armed PLA soldiers pushed me past the screen to my right, and it led into a larger room. I noticed a number of people seated around a small table. There were six of them. This was Big Brother's interrogation committee.

None of the six addressed me, and most of them ignored my presence. Occasionally one would look up from his notes and say a few words in subdued tones, as if they feared that I understood Mandarin and might overhear what they said.

They were decidedly unpleasant looking sextet. On the whole I preferred the look of our guards, even Schickelgruber. The ones in the blue political cadres' suits also wore peaked caps of the same colour. The khaki-clad individuals wore hats with ear flaps trimmed with beautiful Tibetan fox fur. The familiar red star badge was pinned to the front of the hat. The table before them was spread with dishes of nuts and Indian sweetmeats. A pot of tea was passed around, and with their tea they took milk and sugar, the milk of the condensed canned variety, with an Indian label on it. These characters obviously enjoyed a better standard of living than the ordinary soldiers at Taklakot. Their professed equality had no reflection in reality.

Above and behind the seated figures were two Red Army recruiting posters, striking because of their bright colours and bold style. One depicted Mao Tse-tung standing on a balcony waving to a crowd of young people. He was garlanded with flowers and beamed down on his young flock like a Dutch uncle. On the second poster he was joined by General Chu Teh, who had been Mao's companion on the Long March. Both were waving, this time to battalions of young goose-stepping soldiers who gazed up at their self-appointed leaders with faces glowing with youthful adulation.

My examination of the posters was interrupted by a voice saying, 'Hello!'

I looked down to see that the chubby faced fellow in blue seated on the right-hand side of the table had spoken to me.

'And hello to you too, my old China,' I responded.

'Do you speak Chinese or Tibetan?'

'Neither,' I replied.

Having passed this information on to the others, he said, 'Please sit.'

He, like his companions, was seated on a modern tubular steel chair. Looking behind me I was surprised to see a tubular steel chair, folded up and leaning against a wall. I reached for it and opened it out, recalling as I did so Singh and Cricket Wallah telling me that the Chinese even imported their barrack and messroom furniture over the Lipu Lekh from India.

The chubby character watched my every move, and just as I was about to take my seat, he spoke in Mandarin; the two guards placed the muzzles of their assault rifles against my temples, and the chubby character said, 'No, you must sit on the floor.'

I went hot with anger as I realised that, in accordance with Chinese tradition, I had deliberately been made to lose face. The Foreign Devil had to be shown that he was inferior to representatives of the People's Republic of China. 'No thanks,' I responded. 'If it's all the same to you, I'll stand.'

The English-speaking character muttered an order to the two soldiers. One snatched the chair away, and the other brought the muzzle of his PPSh against my head. 'You must sit,' Chubby-face said.

Not feeling inclined to argue further, I sat down on the dried mud floor. My captors were running true to type, and as I looked at their mask-like faces a shiver ran down my spine.

'Who are you?'

I was until then on the defensive. 'First I demand to know who holds me prisoner and by what authority. Unless I receive such information I will refuse to answer your questions,' I said.

The English-speaking Chinaman, whom we later identified by calling him 'Smoothy', was annoyed by my impertinence.

'You must not ask questions. You must only answer them. But I will tell you that you are prisoners of the People's Republic of China, and that we are the authority in the Tibetan province of China, and you are in the presence of the general commanding all Chinese forces in Tibet. You would do well to answer our questions fully, it will be in your own interest.'

'Which one is he?' I enquired.

Smoothy looked annoyed. 'You will ask no more questions.'

I looked over my interrogation committee to try to work out which was which. The man on the left, a wizened little figure in army kit, we were later to learn was the CO of the Gartok garrison. Because of his facial expression and his gait, we called him 'The Ape Man of Gartok' or 'Monkey Face'. From that moment we ceased calling one of our guards Monkey Face and re-christened him 'Short Arse' or 'Shorty'. Next to the Ape Man of Gartok sprawled an ugly brute who had the unenviable distinction of being the most unpleasant-looking character it had ever been my misfortune to meet. He had large protruding ears that were slightly pointed at the top. His long face appeared to have hardly any forehead, his nose was flattened, and his jaw sagged loosely. His long chin on his chest, he looked at me from under his bushy eyebrows, and all the time he sat there, he drooled, the saliva running down the front of his stained and grubby khaki tunic. This character was the CO of the Taklakot garrison, and had blown the brains out of one of his soldiers in front of the rest of his men a few weeks earlier. I did not like the look of him, and I had the feeling that he was all the time mentally measuring me for a coffin, if such a luxury is afforded the victims of Chinese law in Tibet. We were to nickname this character 'Ug-Lug', because that was the sound that issued from his lips whenever he spoke. It was unlike the Chinese dialect spoken by most of our guards and the other officers, and we never figured out Ug-Lug's origin or place of birth.

Next to Ug-Lug sat the blue-coated military governor of Tibet. Although I did not realise it at that initial interrogation, he was wearing a disguise. He had shed his officer's military uniform with general's shoulder boards for the less conspicuous garb of the party political hack. He looked most unimportant to me, being smallish and about fifty years of age. His gaze constantly wandered about the room, as though he expected interesting events to take place on the walls or the ceiling. On the odd occasion his eyes met mine, his gaze was instantly averted. He only lost his temper twice; on one occasion when I accused the Boys from Gartok of being fascists, and the other when I called him to his face by Marlo's favourite obscenity. He always spoke quietly, and when he did venture to speak all the other members of the Taklakot Star Chamber courteously fell silent. (I was to learn years later that the Chinese military governor heading our interrogation committee was none other than General Chang Kuo-hua; he had been with Mao Tse-tung on the famous 'Long March', and had risen through the ranks. When the major Chinese invasion of Tibet was launched via Chamdo in 1950, General Chang was in command. Unlike European armies where a senior officer might be rotated after two to four years, General Chang ruled Tibet like a warlord for more than eighteen years. At the time of our capture, he had arrived in Gartok to speed up work on the western end of the strategic military road, which China later titled 'The Great Defence Highway'. Chang was responsible for the deaths of several hundred thousand Tibetans during his term in office. His 1950 progress across Tibet at the head of the advancing PLA has been likened to 'drawing a red hot poker across a blanket'.)

Next to him sat a nondescript blue-clad youth who took very little part in the proceedings. He served as a scrivener, a sort of secretary, writing out all the questions and answers in a minute-book which lay in front of him on the table. The book was an Indian children's exercise book. Well, he didn't exactly write *everything* down, only the items which appeared to please his superiors, to wit any statement by me that met with their approval. We called this pencil pusher 'The Bookworm', and he looked to be no more than eighteen years old.

The fifth member of the committee was another army officer who carried a Russian copy of the Leica 35 mm camera slung around his neck. We refrained from giving him a nickname because he never made a second appearance. His task was to take identification photographs for the record.

The sixth member was the chubby little fellow with the bland unsmiling countenance whom we called Smoothy, the only Chinese in west Tibet who could speak English. After he had made his brief and very sketchy introductions, silence reigned for a few moments and a cosy little tea party developed. Small Chinese cups were passed round, Smoothy pouring the tea for the others. Occasionally the silence was broken as a member of the committee cleared his throat and spat on the floor.

I was both surprised and disgusted to find that the highest officers in the PLA in west Tibet indulged in the same awful expectoration as their common soldiers. Had there been any awards going for frequency of expectoration and accompanying acoustic effects, then Ug-Lug and Smoothy qualified for the Chinese Olympic gold medal for spitting. Indian sweetmeats were passed around and they looked particularly tempting. The Boys from Gartok ate these to the usual accompaniment of sucking and chewing sounds reminiscent of our prison guards. I opened my mouth to speak, only to be silenced by Smoothy with a quick, 'Hello, shut up.'

I had the feeling that all this waiting and tea drinking enabled them to size me up and to keep me in suspense which, they hoped, would make me feel nervous. But the longer I sat there, squatting on the dried mud floor, the less scared I felt. Their performance roused my indignation, helping me to win the psychological battle. It was impossible to feel you had lost face in the presence of such an ill-mannered group. The wizened little Ape Man wiped his nose on his sleeve. The Bookworm went one better by blowing his nose on the floor, without using a handkerchief. Everyone went on eating and drinking and nobody seemed to mind.

I reached into my pocket for my handkerchief, only to be given a blow on my right ear with the muzzle of an assault rifle. I persisted, as if nothing had happened, and when the handkerchief appeared it brought smiles to the faces of my two guards. It seemed that the idiots thought that I was about to produce a bomb or a gun.

Then I saw something that made my heart miss a beat. I noticed for the first time a small Tibetan stool-cum-table, on the far side of the room. On it lay my Browning pistol, and alongside it lay the 50-round box of ammunition. I was going to have some problems explaining that one away. Himalayan explorers do not carry firearms.

The military governor spoke a few words to Smoothy who, after examining some notes, set the ball rolling. 'Hello, we are going to ask you some questions and these questions you must answer honestly. You are forbidden to speak other than to answer a question.' Smoothy cleared his throat and spat a couple of inches from my feet. 'First, what is your name? Also your age, your nationality and your address.'

I supplied this information and then was asked my mother's name, my father's name, and also those of my wife and son, and my occupation, and so on. It was like applying for a job, only in this case the term of employment could be anything from five years to life. To the question of nationality, I replied, 'British, and damned proud of it.'

Smoothy interrupted me. 'You must not swear in the presence of the governor of the Tibetan Region of the People's Republic of China. You must conduct yourself well at all times when you are in our house.' Smoothy said a few words to the general, and then turned to me. 'You are not an American, then?'

Knowing how popular Americans were with the Chinese communists, I was thankful that I was not indeed a citizen of the USA. I answered, 'No, like I said, I'm British and proud of it.'

Smoothy thought for a moment, and then uttered the most stupid statement of the day: 'Are you sure?'

I smiled at this, and received another thump with a gun muzzle, this time on my other ear.

'You must not be facetious,' Smoothy said.

'Take a look in my passport,' I suggested. 'Look at the quality of the cover and the pages. The American passport is a bit of cheap rubbish compared to that.'

Smoothy turned to the Bookworm who produced my passport from inside his briefcase. Holding up the passport, Smoothy showed me the identification photograph. 'Is this you?'

I had to admit that my appearance had changed somewhat. I had lost weight and was hollow eyed, due to the combination of the dysentery I was unable to shake off and the lousy prison diet. I replied in the affirmative. I had a feeling that Smoothy was working up to something.

'We believe that this document is fictitious and that it is not your true passport. It is forged.'

I asked how they had come to such a conclusion.

'Because it says that you are an engineer, and you say that you are a manager. Either the document is false or you are lying.'

Patiently I tried to explain that I was manager of an engineering company. Smoothy would have none of this. 'What you say is a lie. You must answer more honestly.'

I was asked what my wife's occupation was, to which I replied. 'She is my wife. She is a housewife.'

Smoothy looked incredulous. 'But how does your wife live if she does not work?'

I pointed out that many English wives are supported by their husbands. I could only assume that in communist China every able-bodied woman must go out and work and that home life was considered terribly bourgeois and deviationist. Smoothy even wanted to know why I lived in North Wales when my mother lived fifty miles away in Cheshire. He evidently believed in the Confucian philosophy of filial piety and of maintaining the unity of the family.

The Boys from Gartok appeared to be wasting time, but of course they were not. These seemingly unimportant questions which went on for more than an hour, and which were occasionally repeated, were par for the course in counter-intelligence interrogation. If my cover story was false, there was always the possibility that I might slip up and forget a detail in my make-believe identity. And so some of the original questions were oft repeated.

As my background was not a work of fiction, they were unable to trip me up. Smoothy then asked the critical question. 'Who sent you here? Who gave you your instructions?'

I replied that nobody sent me anywhere, and that I was in the Himalaya because that is where I wanted to be.

Smoothy's attitude was one of disbelief. 'What you say is a lie,' he retorted. 'You must answer more honestly.'

We were the first mountaineers ever to be captured by the Chinese and now we faced the inevitable and unanswerable questions, such as, 'Why do you climb mountains?' and, 'Why do you visit the Himalayas?' When I am asked such questions by my fellow countrymen I always have difficulty in offering an explanation which makes sense to anyone not imbued with what I would call the spirit of the hills. So out it came, the inevitable unanswerable question. 'Why are you in the Himalayas?'

'Because I am a mountaineer. I do it for pleasure. It is my hobby.'

'That is not a satisfactory answer,' Smoothy said. 'What is the real reason you climb mountains?'

I repeated my original answer.

'What is the real reason why you climb mountains? What is the purpose? It will go badly for you if you do not answer more honestly,' Smoothy threatened. 'Now, you must tell us who sponsored your so-called expedition.'

'The Mountaineering Club of North Wales, a newspaper called the *Liverpool Daily Post*, and the American *Life* magazine.'

'How did you get to know this club?'

'That's easy, you could say that I founded it.'

'What is the club's purpose?'

'To bring together those in North Wales who are interested in mountaineering.'

'Ah yes,' responded Smoothy, 'but what is the club's other purpose, its real purpose?'

At this I laughed, but growls from Ug-Lug and Monkey Face caused Smoothy to suggest, 'You are not treating our investigating committee with proper respect. You cannot hide this club's purpose from us,' he said. 'We will if necessary find it out from your two companions. Now, what are the club's politics?'

'It's a mountaineering club and therefore strictly non-political,' I countered.

'That cannot be true,' Smoothy said. 'As Comrade Mao tells us, every organisation has its political beliefs and motives.'

'Not the Mountaineering Club of North Wales. It's a private members' club, not an instrument of the state.'

'You are being deliberately obstructionist,' Smoothy accused me. 'You are only making things difficult for yourself. You must answer more honestly.'

I blew up at this. 'Do you expect me to pervert the truth and make up fanciful lies, just to fit in with the answers you want to hear? If you don't like what you hear, you say that it's a lie. There appears to be no common ground for understanding between us. We come from different worlds, from different cultures.'

Smoothy choked on this and I noticed that he did not interpret my last remarks to the other members of the interrogation committee. They started to sort out the next set of questions and the Ape Man kept pointing to me and smashing his fist into the palm of his other hand. Ug-Lug smote the table with a huge ugly hand, making the pots leap in the air. The Bookworm, in his efforts to steady the crockery, was distracted from his notetaking. The general-cum-governor remained placid. He sat, his hands resting on his crossed knees, his gaze pursuing endless wanderings.

A Tibetan brought in a bowl of nuts and a further pot of tea. I was feeling thirsty and I was tempted to ask for a cup, but pride prevented me from making such a humiliating request, so I suffered in silence, and my captors, of course, did not offer me a drink. The interlude ended, the questions started again.

'Who sent you here to China?'

'Nobody sent us here. Your troops kidnapped us in the Jung Jung Khola at gunpoint.'

'What you say is a lie. You were arrested by the People's Liberation Army of the Republic of China. That is proof that you were illegally in Tibet. You came here to carry out an illegal invasion of China.'

'How the hell can two climbers and an eighteen-year-old youth comprise an invasion?' I asked.

'It is an illegal invasion,' Smoothy continued, 'and it was your intention to spy on the People's Liberation Army.'

'What the hell is there to spy on here in Tibet?' I answered.

'What was the name of the mountain you proposed to visit?' Smoothy enquired.

'Nalkankar,' I replied.

'Where is this mountain, Nalkankar?'

'The summit looks down on Kojarnath. It's half in Tibet and half in Nepal.'

'Why did you wish to climb it?'

'I can't answer that. I just like to climb mountains.'

'Admit the truth. You wished to illegally occupy this mountain for some purpose. What was the political motive?'

I had never heard anything like this before. According to the Chinese, mountains are not climbed, they are occupied. Smoothy was writing something in long-hand, and not in Chinese calligraphy. I waited for the result.

Smoothy pushed the document over to me. 'Please read this and sign it. Your guilt is already established.'

I took the note and read, 'I confess to participating in an illegal armed invasion of China.'

The armed part of it was obviously a reference to my pistol. I answered, 'I can't sign this because it is not true. I have never invaded China. When your men kidnapped us in the Jung Jung Khola we were in Nepal.'

'The Jung Jung Khola is inside China. All the people in the many villages in the Jung Jung Khola pay taxes to China.' I was no longer disposed to laugh, not even at this preposterous claim.

'That's impossible. No one lives in the Jung Jung Khola. It's uninhabited and always has been. It is a high mountain valley unsuitable for habitation, agriculture or grazing.'

'You are lying. There are many houses in the Jung Jung Khola and you must have spoken to the inhabitants when you illegally made your armed invasion of China.' Smoothy decided that he was getting nowhere with this tack and tried another avenue. 'You and Mr Harrop have sent us many letters asking for better conditions and better food. Sign this confession and all your requests will be granted. Also your punishment will be light.'

'I won't sign your stupid confession, and you can stick it up your anus. If you object to our presence, why not adopt the simple expedient of deporting us?'

Fortunately for me, Smoothy did not appear to know what an anus was. 'No. You have attempted to commit an act of armed espionage against the People's Republic of China and must be punished as a warning to other imperialist agents.'

Smoothy produced my expedition flags. These I had had made in London and they were small in size, of the type one attaches to the shaft of an ice axe, to be flown and photographed on the summit of a mountain. We had the Welsh flag, the flags of Nepal and the United Nations and the Union Jack. I had included in my stock of tiny national flags that of the People's Republic of China, so that we could, as a matter of courtesy, fly it with the others when we reached the summit of Gurla Mandhata. Smoothy ignored the Chinese flag, with its gold stars on a red background. He held up the flag of the United Nations. 'This is the United Nations flag. The UN has repeatedly declined to give communist China a seat at the UN. Why did the UN send you here? What is the connection between the UN flag and your illegal armed invasion of China?'

Before I could reply, Smoothy held up the Chinese flag. 'Look at this flag. This is the flag of the People's Republic of China. There can be only one reason for you possessing this flag. You intended disguising your illegal armed invasion of China so that Tibetans would not know that you are agents of a foreign power, Western Fascist Lackey Imperialist Running Dogs.'

'That's nonsense,' I countered. 'Nalkankar is half in Tibet, so if we reached the summit, we intended flying all these flags, and we thought that it would be courteous to fly the Chinese flag.'

'What you say is a lie, you Western Fascist Lackey Imperialist Running Dog,' Smoothy screamed at me.

He translated my answers to the other members of the Gartok Concert Party, and they all screamed their rage, their eyes almost popping out. I have never seen such fury. They chanted at me in unison like a Greek chorus: I was being 'Struggled Against'.

'Tell the truth about the United Nations,' Smoothy shouted at me. 'Tell this committee how the UN lackeys of American imperialism recruited you as mercenaries for an illegal armed invasion of China.'

I tried to explain that the UN flag had been flown from the summits of a great many mountains by expeditions that had reached the summit.

'Why did you not tell us that there were other illegal expeditions?' Smoothy bellowed. 'Who are they? Where do they come from?'

I sighed heavily. 'There are scores of expeditions. I can't tell you where they all come from, but I can tell you that they have no connection with our expedition. There have been not only British, but also Italian, French, German and Polish expeditions. A few hundred of the members of foreign expeditions are members of the Himalayan Club, like me.'

'Where is the headquarters of this Himalayan Club?' Smoothy asked. 'It's in India.'

Smoothy conveyed all this to the committee. 'Then this Himalayan Club is composed of Western Imperialist agents. We know that Nehru is a stooge of the American organisation called the CIA, whose head is John Foster Dulles. Nehru is a Western Fascist Lackey Imperialist Running Dog.'

'Bullshit,' I countered. 'Nehru's motto is Hindee Cheenee Bhai-Bhai, Indians and Chinese are brothers. Nehru is dedicated to friendship with China.'

'What you say is a lie,' Smoothy shouted at me. 'Nehru only pretends to be a friend of communist China. Nehru is an agent of the West. He is not a true representative of the aspirations of the freedom-loving peoples of Hindustan. He is a lackey of CIA chief John Foster Dulles.'

I just had to put Smoothy right. 'Look, old chum. John Foster Dulles is not the head of the Central Intelligence Agency. He is the American Secretary of State. His brother Allen Dulles is CIA chief. You can't mistake one for the other. Allen Dulles has a domed head, they call him Egg Head.'

Smoothy again acquainted the Boys from Gartok with my new high-quality intelligence data. They all spoke together, and then Smoothy turned to me. 'You have admitted that there are many espionage organisations operating in the Himalayas. We know for a fact that they are all part of the same anti-communist spy ring, and that all receive instructions from the same headquarters. Tell us everything and it will be much easier for you. The People's Republic of China is lenient with repentant criminals.'

'You are nuts,' I shouted back at Smoothy. 'They are what they claim to be, they are climbing groups, they are mountaineers. They are not spies.'

'What you say is a lie,' Smoothy screamed at me at the top of his voice. 'There are no such things as Himalayan expeditions. If there were, we would read about them in our Chinese newspapers, and once they were established as such, we would have a party line, a party directive on how we were to treat such people if we came across them.'

I thought to myself, oh my God. How can one deal with such ignorance? To their minds, everything in their idea of creation, of the cosmos, of the order of things, had to be in Mao's teachings of theoretical Marxism or it did not exist. Himalayan exploration was dismissed as a fiction at a stroke of a pen. I decided to take the heat off myself and pervert the truth, ever so slightly. 'The central HQ for the British illegal invasion organisations known as Himalayan expeditions is called the Everest Foundation. The leader is Sir John Hunt. He is a brigadier in the British Army.' I looked at Smoothy. He was beginning to look like the cat that swallowed the cream. At last he had broken down this Western Fascist Lackey Imperialist Running Dog, and the truth was about to emerge.

Smoothy talked to the others, and the Bookworm scribbled furiously. The faces opposite were keyed up with anticipation. British scheming against the People's Republic of China was about to be laid bare.

'You admit that this Brigadier Hunt is the chief of this Everest Foundation nest of spies, and that you take your orders from him?'

'Actually we only met once, at a climbing club dinner in the Lake District. But I don't take orders from him.'

Smoothy turned to the Bookworm, who produced our tiny Chinese red flag from his briefcase. 'This flag is evidence of your guilt. The penalty for espionage in China is death. At the very least you will go to prison for a great many years. Why do you not sign this confession? We will be very lenient with you if you do so.'

'I am not a spy, I only wished to climb the mountain Nalkankar.'

'What do you do when you get to the top of these mountains you have occupied?' Smoothy queried.

'We come down again,' I replied.

At this Smoothy gave the self-satisfied smirk of a man who knows that someone is trying to pull the yak wool over his eyes. The Boys from Gartok went into a 'Party Group Meeting' over the question of political motives for illegally occupying mountains, and started to shout not at me, but at each other. Smoothy returned to the matter of our sponsors. 'This *Life* magazine. Who owns it?'

I explained that *Life* magazine was a sister magazine to *Time* magazine, both of Time-Life International, New York, with bureaus in most of the world's capitals.

'This Time-Life International is an agency of the American imperialist CIA,' Smoothy threw at me. 'This Time-Life uses its offices all over the world to obtain intelligence data for the American CIA. It also dispenses capitalist lies about peace-loving China, and all the other peace-loving Marxist people's democracies. The fact that you were sent here by this Time-Life CIA organisation is proof of your guilt.'

I too was of the opinion that some of Time-Life's overseas operators were CIA stringers, but I kept my own counsel about that. Smoothy returned to the attack. 'Admit that it was this Time-Life organisation that recruited you into the American CIA spy organisation. Admit the truth.'

Ug-Lug bellowed at the two guards, and they pulled back the cocking levers of their PPSh assault rifles, and placed the muzzles against my temples.

'You must sign this confession. You are a member of this armed invasion of communist China. Sign the confession that you are a Western Fascist Lackey Imperialist Running Dog of the American CIA and we will be very good to you. Otherwise you will be severely punished,' Smoothy said.

I realised that I held the cards and not they. This bunch of thugs had to get a confession or their careers could be in jeopardy. If they blew my brains out, there would be no signed confession.

'I want to go back to my cell, which incidentally is filthy and rat-infested.'

'You are not in a cell. You have rooms, good accommodation provided due to the generosity of the People's Republic of China.'

Smoothy tried again, after a further 'Party Group Meeting' with his committee. 'If you sign this confession, we will let you have better rooms, and improved food.'

'What about my dysentery pills?'

'Your pills have to be examined by experts. In the meantime, if you will sign this simple confession, the finest medical skills in China will be made available.'

I shook my head. 'No deal. You and your committee can go and get stuffed.'

At that Smoothy lost his cool, and the others all took up the formal 'Struggle Against' stance and gestures. All six of them stood up and pointed their right forefinger at me, and at a command from His Excellency the Governor, the formerly impassive general, they screamed and chanted at me as I sat cross-legged on the ground. I could not understand a word of what they were shouting, but I guessed that it was something like, 'One, two, three, four, Western bastard on the floor. Five, six, seven, eight, you're the swine we love to hate.'

My two guards joined in the chants. This must have gone on for about ten minutes and my head was reeling with the racket they made. It was ever so nice and quiet when they stopped.

The general signalled to the photographer, and he closed up on me and sighted his camera for a head and shoulders shot. Not wishing to look anything but my best, regardless of my scratched and bleeding face – the effects of that blunt razor – I took a comb from my pocket and slowly and methodically combed my hair. 'It's the form that counts,' I thought to myself. Then I noticed that the Chinese military photographer was going to take my photograph with the lens cap on. 'Excuse me, old chap,' I said, 'you'll have a blank negative if you don't take that lens cap off.'

Smoothy glared at me, and barked an order to the photographer.

Smoothy rounded off the proceedings. 'You have not answered honestly today. Next time you come to our house you must tell the truth.'

The two guards prodded me with their rifles, and feeling stiff, with cramp in both legs, I got up off the floor. I had been squatting for more than two and a half hours. Bidding my hosts a very good day, I walked out into the courtyard, my eyes blinded by the strong sunlight. My first interrogation was over.

11

I paused for a few seconds to shield my eyes and to become accustomed to the light. The Dzongpon and the Indian agent provocateur stood by the courtyard door. Both greeted me, but I ignored them. Out in the open and away from that world of Orwell and Kafka I began to feel a little brighter. It was too nice a day to feel miserable. My guards stopped to light a cigarette and I sat on a rock to take advantage of the view.

All too visible across the river was our prison, and the thought of returning to its filthy, confining dreariness was depressing. I had only a few moments to take everything in, and sights and sounds I would not have noticed at any other time assumed unusual and poignant significance. Everything that was new I tried to register indelibly in my memory. 'This is Tibet,' I said. 'In spite of the Chinese, it is wonderful to be here.'

Resuming our journey, the guards and I passed over the bridge on up the hill to our prison. The yard was full of Chinese troops, most of them new to me. Harrop stood on top of the yard steps, and came down to greet me, but was stopped in his tracks by two guards who thrust gun muzzles in his stomach. Two other signified that I was to hold my hands above my head and stand with my back to the lavatory wall. Schickelgruber walked over to me, and pointing a finger at his mouth said, 'Mindo.' I was not to speak to Harrop.

'How did it go?' Harrop shouted to me.

'These Chinese are bloody impossible,' I replied. 'They are convinced that we are spies.'

Schickelgruber raged at me, waving his gun in my face.

'Then it's Lhasa or Peking next stop,' Harrop shouted.

'I'm afraid so,' I responded. This time, Schickelgruber reversed his assault rifle and signified that I was about to have my skull split open.

Everyone quietened down except Damodar, who muttered, 'These Chinese are bastards.'

Chubby stood on the firing step looking over the wall towards the red building. He answered a signal with a wave of his hand. It was Harrop's turn to appear before the Boys from Gartok.

With Harrop gone over the river, Damodar and I were forced to sit cross-legged on the ground, facing each other, with PPSh muzzles, about a dozen of them, pointed at us at all times.

Chungnya came out of the kitchen and stood behind the rest of the guards, looking curiously at me over their shoulders, doubt and confusion written on his face. Our inability to speak each other's language and the different mental outlook of East and West had not prevented a friendship from developing between us. Chungnya had good cause to look troubled. He had now met two of the so-called imperialists, and he had sufficient objectivity of outlook to see that they were nothing like he had been led to believe. I grinned at Chungnya, over the shoulders of our armed guards. Chungnya grinned back. 'Damodar isn't quite right,' I thought to myself. 'Not all Chinese are bastards.'

Schickelgruber turned and gave Chungnya an order, and he went into our communal cell to emerge carrying my sleeping bag and air mattress. Chungnya took these to the small cell at the right of the yard. At a signal, I followed Chungnya inside. Although my separation from Harrop and Damodar was an obvious move, it had not occurred to me. We were to be prevented from conversing with each other, or exchanging notes concerning our respective interrogations.

I was allowed to return to the larger cell for a few moments to sort out a few of my personal possessions. I shared out the last of our Nestlé's chocolate, Ovosport bars, Kendal Mint Cake, and our final tin of boiled sweets. There was enough condensed milk for half a tube each. Finally, we had about half a pound of sugar cubes apiece. Soon these remnants of expedition fare would be gone and there would be nothing to supplement the atrocious diet of yak belly or intestines, or improve the taste of the insipid brick-tea.

Along with my torch, one of the tiny Tibetan tables and the Chinese eiderdown bedcover Chungnya had given me, I went back to the cell that was to be my new home. The smallest room of all, it had once been used as a vegetable store. There was a raised ramp at the back of the room, about six inches off the dried mud floor, consisting of hard packed dried mud. This platform had once held bags of turnips and a few dried up specimens of these still littered the floor. My cell boasted two windows. One looked out onto the courtyard, and across it to the Himalaya, and the other provided a grandstand view of the interior of the lavatory enclosure.

The ceiling was too low for me to stand upright. If anything, my new cell was even filthier than the one I had just vacated. The lower parts of the walls were extensively riddled with rat holes. A piece of white paper glued to the wall by the yard window proved to be the remains of a Chinese calendar. As a little space remained, I scribbled in the date: 7 November 1955, adding '7 is my lucky number!'

There was a great deal of commotion in the prison yard that afternoon, and I did not hear Harrop return, or Damodar depart for his interrogation. My cell door was kept locked, and only opened for my excursions to the thunder hole. Dinner consisted of a small portion of cabbage, overloaded with throat-searing chillies. I ate what little I could, but had to give up when tears began to stream down my face. The chillies were hot enough to burn a hole in the plate. Looking through my window, I saw our guards dining off mutton-stew and a huge bowl of rice.

After dark, I was allowed out for tea, and took my pint mug to the kitchen. Harrop was there, as well as Damodar and Chungnya, and Chungnya's friend Chubby. The latter placed his fingers to his lips, indicating that there must be no talking. I decided that we would observe the rules for the time being, but we had to communicate. We had to know what questions had been asked and answers given.

I looked at Harrop, and it was obvious that there were things he was bursting to tell me about his interrogation. I grinned at him and he blurted out, 'Silly lot of beggars, aren't they?' I nodded my agreement.

Chungnya shook his head admonitorily at Harrop. 'Mindo.'

I reached under the kitchen table, which consisted of an old wooden door set on mud-brick supports, and pulled out a bag of dried chilli peppers, saying, 'Yappa mindo.' I repeated my complaint to Chungnya and Chubby: 'Chid, Jung, Damodar . . . Yappa mindo, mumbo mumbo.' (Tibetan for no good, a large quantity.)

Chungnya, who was devouring a bowl of cabbage, as a dessert after his

Chinese prison in Tibet, previously a Tibetan farmhouse.
  A. Chinese guard's quarters
  B. Author Wignall's cell
  C. John Harrop's cell
  D. Damodar's cell
  E. Kitchen
  F. Latrine

mutton-stew and rice dinner, understood. He nodded his head, and spoke a few words in Chubby's ear. There would be none of the flame-thrower chilli-peppers in our meals when Chungnya or Chubby was cook for the day.

At a signal from Chungnya, Chubby thrust his hands inside his tunic and produced two packets of Chinese cigarettes, one decorated with the emblem of a flying horse, the other with a clenched fist. I was given one packet, and Harrop the other. I gave mine to Damodar who, like Harrop, smoked like a chimney whenever he got the chance. Chungnya signified that I was to follow him out of the kitchen. He pointed to our original communal cell, and said, 'Jung.' So that was Harrop's cell. Chungnya pointed to the tiny room opposite Harrop's, and said, 'Damda.'

The thoughts that must have been plaguing Damodar also disturbed me. A few months earlier, Damodar had been studying at the University of Benares in India, his first term, in fact. This was Damodar's second expedition, his first being with the Kenya expedition to Himalchuli in central Nepal. He voiced anxiety only the day before our interrogations began, stating that he had already missed part of his autumn term at college. I did not dishearten him further by telling him that there was a serious possibility that he might miss many more terms at college and possibly live to draw his old age pension in China. For a boy of eighteen, Damodar had a dauntless spirit and a sense of humour equal to almost any situation. Nothing seemed to depress him.

It was dark now, and past our normal bedtime. I looked south at the great peaks of the Himalaya, Nepal and freedom. Chungnya signified that it was time for us to return to our cells. He shouldered his rifle, and I followed him as he first locked Harrop and then Damodar in their cells. I led the way and as I passed through my cell doorway, Chungnya stuck out his right hand. I shook it. No words passed between us.

It was now bitterly cold in my cell, and after a few minutes I heard the key turn in the lock, and Chubby entered carrying a tiny Indian made hurricane lamp, which allowed the guards to keep me under observation, possibly to ascertain if I was keeping an illicit diary. I donned my down-filled jacket and climbed into the comfort of my sleeping bag. I was in no mood for sleep. Some record had to be kept of the day's interrogation. I was interrupted in my thoughts when Chungnya entered my cell. He was carrying the plywood lid of our now empty expedition food box. He slapped the board down on my knees, and then produced from his tunic pocket a very dog-eared and dilapidated set of playing cards. The cards were Indian in origin and their backs were adorned with a daring pin-up of Miss Vina Rai, then one of India's most popular film stars.

Chungnya laid his rifle against the wall, in easy reach of my right hand, and sat down on the edge of my air mattress. We sat looking at each other for some moments. I had a feeling that this lad had something on his mind, and that he wished to convey a message to me. There was little I could do but show him, as indeed Harrop and Damodar also did, that we greatly appreciated his kindness. I offered him my last bar of chocolate, but he shook his head. He, like the others, called it 'coffee', and also like the others would not accept anything we offered to him. This was presumably orders from the Boys from Gartok. Chungnya tried to explain a Chinese game of cards to me, but as it seemed to consist simply of slapping cards down hard on our makeshift table, and he who slapped the cards down fastest and hardest always won, I had to give up the game after a couple of hands. I tried to show Chungnya how to play Patience but he could not get the hang of it.

At eight o'clock I heard voices from the guardroom, followed by the clank of metal. Chungnya looked quickly at my watch and, stubbing out the cigarette he had been smoking, he stood up, shouldered his PPSh, and adopted a business-like military pose. The door was pushed open by Lofty, who looked in, nodded a greeting to Chungnya, and went out into the yard. Chungnya grinned, and gave me a playful cuff over the ear and departed.

Fishing down in the bottom of my sleeping bag I found a few pieces of chocolate wrapper and toilet paper. Armed with the stub of a pencil I sought sanctuary in my bag, and with the top pulled over my head, in the failing light of my torch, wrote down the salient points of my interview with the Boys from Gartok. The diary completed, I relaxed. Sounds of tiny feet scuttering on the dirt floor told me that the rats were paying me a visit. Very soon they would be crawling not over, but also inside my sleeping bag.

The following morning I decided that I wanted a cup of tea, and a quick dash to the thunder hole, so slipping on my boots, I stood up, and immediately went flat on my back. Some of my washing water which had been spilled on the floor earlier on had turned to ice. The temperature in my tiny cell could not have been above freezing point for more than two hours a day at that time. Very shortly, my cell would be freezing night and day. Our guards lived better. They had some kind of a metal stove in their quarters.

I got back onto my feet and pocketed a few sugar cubes and my tube of condensed milk, to add to my morning mug of chai. Then something occurred to me. I had to know what Harrop had said to the Boys from Gartok, and vice versa. The slightest difference in our stories would be bound to complicate matters. As we were forbidden to talk, some other means of communication had to be devised. I returned to my bed and scribbled a few notes down on a scrap of paper. I would try to pass it to Harrop in the prison yard. The message completed, I knocked on my cell door; it was opened, and out I went for my mug of tea. Harrop and Damodar were seated on either side of the yard, Schickelgruber between them, looking from the one to the other, his PPSh held at the ready. There was no hope of passing a message to Harrop under such circumstances, and collecting my mug of weak tea, I returned to my cell thoroughly disappointed, my note undelivered. Another method had to be found, and one which could be carried out quite openly in front of the guards without them being any the wiser. One lump of sugar went into my cup, and then a squeeze of condensed milk from the tube. It was at that moment that the solution to the problem occurred to me.

The tube of condensed milk provided the answer. If I unrolled the bottom of the tube I could slip a note inside. But how was I to prevent my note from becoming plastered with condensed milk? The answer was provided in the form of the half dozen polythene bags that had once kept our pemmican rations waterproof, and which now resided in the pocket of my anorak. Cutting out a small square of polythene, I wrapped the note in it and, having scooped some of the condensed milk into my cup, pushed the note into the tube.

Dragging my sleeping bag and air mattress outside to sit on, I took up a position against the wall of my cell and waited for a few moments, hoping that Schickelgruber's vigilance would relax. But not for a moment did he cease to look from one of us to the other. Although I was not aware of it, harm had been done to our position already. For whilst I had said that our expedition had been sponsored by the Mountaineering Club of North Wales, the *Liverpool Daily Post* and *Life* magazine, Harrop had stated that our sponsors were the Royal Geographical Society. That discrepancy in our stories was all the Chinese needed to convince them that one, or more probably both of us, had lied.

Deciding that the message had to be passed without delay, in case there was to be another interrogation session that day, I squeezed a little milk into my cup, rather ostentatiously in order to draw attention to what I was doing. Then, screwing the cap back on, I threw the tube to Harrop. As he had his own tube of condensed milk in his anorak pocket, he must have thought my actions somewhat peculiar.

The tube landed about three feet short of where Harrop was seated, and before Harrop could move, Schickelgruber dived and snatched it off the ground. I felt as though the bottom had fallen out of my stomach. Schickelgruber, apparently suspecting something, was turning the tube over in his hand and inspecting it with curiosity. Walking away from Harrop, he seated himself on the top of the steps which led down into the yard. Turning round, he surveyed all three of us individually, and while I tried to appear unconcerned I felt sure that my mounting anxiety must reveal itself, thereby betraying me. Harrop caught my eye, and I winked. His expression assured me that he now knew something was afoot.

After a few moments, which to me stretched to as many years, Schickelgruber unscrewed the cap and squeezed some of the condensed milk onto his forefinger. He tasted it, and grinning said, 'Newfan.' This was the word our guards used for milk. The cap was screwed in place and Schickelgruber walked down the steps and over to Harrop. He accentuated

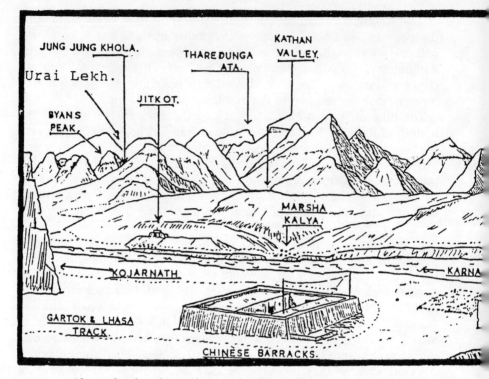

Above sketch redrawn from author Wignall's orginals on toilet paper,
Viewpoint at the foot of the great Taklakot escarpment.

my apprehension still further by opening the tube again, but this time, he
squeezed some of the contents into Harrop's cup. He turned and was
about to throw the tube back to me, when I pulled a second tube out of
my anorak pocket, and held it up for Schickelgruber to see. It was in fact
empty, but I had hung onto it with the idea of cutting it open to extract
the last drop of milk out of it that I could.

With that, Schickelgruber shrugged, and handed the tube to Harrop.
The moment Schickelgruber turned his back to walk back up the steps,
Harrop and I exchanged winks. My companion had more sense than to
go indoors right way. He pocketed the tube, and made no move until the
guards had been changed, at which point Schickelgruber departed for the
other side of the river.

When he returned he had a sheaf of papers with him. He handed one
to each of us, and then pointed over the Karnali. For some inexplicable
reason we were to write to the Boys from Gartok, but no indication was
given as to the nature our communications were to take. Did they expect
us to sit down and scribble out a confession?

I decided to take the opportunity to furnish Smoothy and company
with an impressive list of complaints, which occupied almost a full sheet

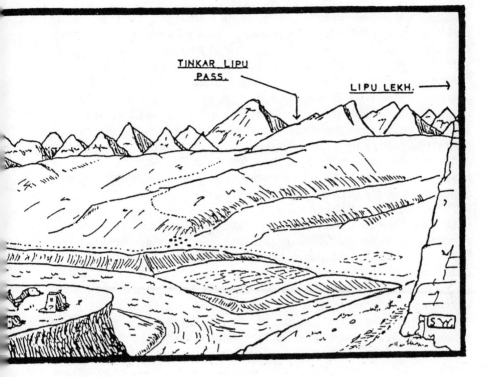

of foolscap paper. Later I discovered that both Harrop and Damodar had done the same thing. Nothing came of it, but it helped kill the time, the only commodity of which we had an excess supply.

Later that afternoon I went back in my cell and curled up in my bag. I had a feeling that another bout of dysentery was on the way, and I felt unsteady on my feet, my head swimming when I stood up. Harrop seized the opportunity to send a reply to my note. It was much easier for him to pass a message to me. I had no legitimate reason to go anywhere near his cell, but he had to pass my cell on his way to the lavatory, and once there he could, if the duty guard was not watching, slip a note into my cell window. I did not see the note come through my window, but I heard Harrop say, 'Damnation to the Chinese,' as he passed by. The note lay on the floor of my cell until the following day, when I found it by accident. That I found it at all was due to my unwelcome cell mates, the Tibetan rats. The previous night these creatures had awakened me several times. On the last occasion, I was disturbed by a rat nibbling through the neck of my sweater. The rats were not eating the wool, but purloining it to make nests. I determined to put an end to their depredations. There were about a dozen rat holes in the wall of my cell. Most of them led out into the thunder hole, where in the early morning I often surprised rats eating their breakfast of freeze-dried human excrement. I scoured the yard that morning, looking for small stones, some of which I prised out of the walls with my expedition cutlery set. One by one I had all the holes blocked up. I was just blocking up the last hole when I noticed a partially chewed ball of paper on the floor. It was Harrop's note to me. A rat had nibbled at it, and fortunately for me, had not taken it away for nest building.

In his note Harrop suggested that bringing Damodar into the clandestine correspondence game might be too unwieldy. So, Harrop suggested that as his cell door was only about three feet from Damodar's and directly facing it, he should whisper a few words across or, in an emergency, toss a note through the door during the daytime.

To help while away the time, I decided to make a sketch of the mountain ranges that stretched away across the skyline to the south. From my cell window I could see the whole of the west Nepal Himalaya from the Urai Lekh pass to the Tinkar Lipu, and almost to the Lipu Lekh on the border of India. I was, in fact, occupying a wonderful viewpoint and survey station, for no Indian or Nepalese surveyors had ever been granted permission to enter the Tibetan plateau and survey the Nepal Himalaya. I made the sketch on one of my last few pieces of toilet paper, in the form of a panorama. As the paper was not long enough for my purpose, I had to draw the sketch in several parts, one section drawn beneath the other. As I took several days to complete my sketching, I was unable to push the day's work down the inflation tube of my air mattress pillow. Instead, I hid it inside the plastic backing of a cheap mirror I had purchased in Cologne on my way by road to the Himalaya. Each day, over a four-day period, I would prise the back off the mirror, fish out my piece of toilet paper, and continue with my primitive sketch.

On the morning of Friday 11 November, Schickelgruber entered my cell at breakfast time and signified that I was to hurry up and finish my feast of boiled turnip soup. I was destined for my second interrogation. As I was being escorted out of my cell by two armed guards, Harrop and Damodar came out of their cells and Harrop gave me the thumbs up sign. I started off down the hill, but my way was barred by a soldier placing the muzzle of his PPSh in my chest. He signalled to me to march off towards Taklakot. This was a new departure.

12

My new interrogation chamber turned out to be a Tibetan house built partly into the cliff face and situated only fifty yards or so from our prison. Half a dozen army mules were tied to a rail outside the door, and two PLA soldiers stood in the doorway talking to the gold-toothed Indian spy.

I was ushered down a passageway so dark that I tripped over a saddle and bumped into another armed soldier. Within a few feet of the entrance I had picked up no less than six armed infantrymen as escort. The new interrogation room proved to be smaller than the previous one and there was barely sufficient room for everyone to crowd inside. Most of the guards had to remain jammed in the doorway. The room boasted one small window about nine inches square. Through this tiny aperture enough light percolated for me to see and recognise the faces of my inquisitors. All but one were familiar: the photo-bug had been replaced by a Chinese who wore the largest fur hat I had ever seen. A table was in evidence, and the Boys from Gartok occupied the same tubular steel folding chairs as before. I looked around the room for a sight of my trusty Browning automatic pistol, but was relieved to see that it was not on public display this bright November morning. Glancing behind me I was not surprised to see a tubular steel chair, folded up and standing against the wall.

The drill was as before. I reached for the chair, only to have a gun muzzle thrust in my face as Smoothy so predictably said, 'Hello, no. You must sit on the floor.'

I sat cross-legged on the ground. There were two or three minutes' silence. They all smoked English cigarettes; a tin of fifty stood on the table. Tea was poured out and, as before, I was not offered any.

The tea-drinking ceremony over, Smoothy cleared his throat, spat on the floor right in front of my feet and said, 'Hello. We have brought you here to answer some more questions. The last time you did not answer honestly. This time you must speak only truth.' He paused. 'What is your name?'

'Sydney Wignall.'

'What you say is a lie, you Western Fascist Lackey Imperialist Running Dog of the American CIA. We want to know your real name.'

I replied as before, unable to work out what he was getting at.

'What you say is a lie. You use other names. You have many aliases. You will tell to us all the false identities you have used in your dirty imperialist spy network.' I thought that Smoothy had started to go round the twist. 'We have proof that your passport is false.'

'That's a load of poppycock. I know that Sydney Wignall is an odd sort of name, but that was my parents' fault, and it would be grossly unfair to place the responsibility on the CIA.'

Smoothy opened his briefcase and, fishing inside it, he threw onto the table a handful of visiting cards. 'We found these amongst your personal belongings. These are your other aliases. Here is the proof that you are a spy and a British agent.' Smoothy handed the cards to me and I burst out laughing as I saw what they were. I had collected these cards on the 6,500-mile road journey to the Himalaya. They included the name of a German newspaper reporter in Aachen, local government officials in Wiesbaden, the British vice-consul in Innsbruck, a Reuter's correspondent, a customs officer on the Greek border, an American civil engineer from Istanbul, the personal secretary to His Majesty the Shah of Iran, an Afghan accountant from Kandahar, and finally the names of an English couple who were travelling from the UK to Australia by car. How on earth was I to talk my way out of this situation?

With difficulty I explained how the cards came into my possession. I went through the names one by one, trying to convince the Boys from Gartok that Sydney Wignall was the only identity to which I had ever laid claim. When I reached the calling card of a Turkish student named Ozcan Kocabiyikoglu, I decided that this false identity would be the one that would get me hanged. I tried to keep a straight face, but was unable to do so. I started to giggle.

'You must not insult this People's Committee by laughing in our presence,' Smoothy shouted at me. The rest of them were by now beginning to lose their cool, and Ug-Lug was Ug-Lugging away to beat the band.

'OK,' I said. 'Sorry if I upset you. I'll have a go at this one. It's the card of a young Turkish student. On our way to India, we stopped off in Istanbul and we were accommodated by the American, Robert College. This student's first name is Ozcan, like in Atlantic Ozcan. The other name Kocabiyikoglu, interprets as . . .' and at this point I was unable to contain myself and burst out laughing.

Smoothy bellowed at the guards, and my enjoyment of the situation was contained by a thump on both sides of my head by PPSh muzzles. I tried to simmer down, but could not help chuntering and smirking to myself.

'You must continue. What does that name mean?' Smoothy demanded.

'It means, in English,' I said, 'Son of the big moustache.' At that I fell about on the floor roaring my head off. For this I received a forceful reminder that Chinese and English humour had little in common.

When Smoothy translated my words to the other members of the committee, they quite literally screamed with rage. 'Here we go again,' I said to myself, as they all got to their feet, and shouted at me in unison, with Ug–Lug this time being the cheer leader. I presumed that this was the well rehearsed procedure of being 'Struggled Against.'

It took some time for them to go through their liturgy, but I eventually arrived at the conclusion that it was in fact very good for them. It relieved tension and emotions, and I'm sure they all felt much better for it.

Smoothy glared at me as they all sat down. 'Now speak more honestly and do not try to make fools of this committee.' He produced another card. 'Now tell us who you are, this is evidence of false identity.'

I let Smoothy have both barrels. 'It's perfectly simple, old chap. You see here, my name is Fields, I'm Mr Fields, and you will observe that I am also his wife Mary. Perhaps I should wear a skirt and a pair of knickers.'

I expected the usual uproar, and dress rehearsal for the Taklakot PLA concert-party. But it did not come. This time Smoothy looked puzzled. I notice that he did not translate my last sentence to the others.

'All of these false identities prove that you are an agent of a foreign power. A great deal of trouble will be saved if you sign this confession.'

The by now familiar document was produced, and again I refused to have anything to do with it.

The governor, the general, interposed to say a few words in a soft voice. Smoothy asked the question the governor had fed to him. 'Who is the big leader of your illegal expedition to occupy mountains?'

'I am,' I replied.

This quite obviously came as a surprise to all of them. They had not expected me to tell the truth, and it was at that point that I realised that the subject of who was our expedition leader had not been raised at the earlier interrogation.

Smoothy, after consulting the other members of the committee, then asked me a question which I found to be almost unanswerable.

'If you are the big leader of this illegal armed invasion of the Tibetan province of the People's Republic of China, why did you come here? Why did you not send somebody else?'

I repeated that I was in the Himalaya for climbing and exploration and nothing more. I also accused the Chinese of kidnapping us at gunpoint on what I believed was Nepalese territory, and I added, 'This is not the first time your PLA has illegally invaded Nepal. Two years ago, Chinese troops illegally entered Nepal north-east of Kathmandu and were arrested by Gurkha soldiers. One of the Chinese soldiers was still a prisoner in Kathmandu less than a year ago, and my liaison officer, young Damodar Narayan Suwal, saw him being exercised in the streets. He was escorted by unarmed Nepalese soldiers and given far greater freedom than you allow us.'

Smoothy translated that piece of information to the others and they reacted by screaming at me again. Only the governor remained calm. This Chinese general was, I thought, a shrewd person, and I thought that he was far more intelligent than the others. But the old boy never smiled, so I gave him his new nickname. Henceforth he would be the Pheasant Plucker.

The Pheasant Plucker raised a hand and the others quietened, giving him undisputed possession of the floor. In subdued tones he made a brief statement to Smoothy, who translated for him. 'The People's Republic of China has never committed an act of armed aggression against any nation. China's peaceful record is proof of that.'

I asked for details of China's peaceful record, to be told by Smoothy that I was there to answer questions and not ask them. A new piece of foolscap paper was produced and Smoothy, after writing on it, handed it to me. 'Sign this.'

I read, 'I confess to having organised an armed illegal invasion of China.'

'Sign this,' Smoothy said, 'and your conditions will be improved.'

'What improvements do you have in mind?' I enquired. 'Will our guards carry only two hand grenades instead of four?'

'You will receive cigarettes and soap and any other small items you might desire,' was Smoothy's response.

As I did not propose to trade my future for a tablet of soap and a tin of cigarettes I declined the offer. Smoothy then tried what must be the oldest trick in the book. 'During their first interrogation, both your companions signed confessions that they are Western Fascist Lackey Imperialist Running Dogs of the American CIA and foreign spies. You are the only one not to confess. If you do not sign, your punishment will be harder than theirs.'

Being fully aware that I was the only spy in Taklakot at that time, and that Harrop and Damodar were innocent of any of the charges, I treated that statement with the contempt it deserved. 'That's a load of codswallop, and you know it. I'm not signing anything.'

'Here is proof that you entered Tibet illegally long before you were arrested by our PLA,' Smoothy said, producing a piece of Tibetan Sanskrit writing Harrop had taken from a chorten at Jitkot.

'This document was found in Harrop's possession when we searched your belongings on the day of your arrest, on 28 October. That was in the Jung Jung Khola. That is proof that you had already been in Tibet.'

'That is a lie,' I responded. 'John Harrop took that piece of Tibetan writing, some form of Buddhist mantra, from a chorten close to Jitkot Gompa.'

'That is not true,' Smoothy continued. 'You have never been to Jitkot Gompa. Our border guards brought you straight to Taklakot from your place of capture in the Jung Jung Khola.'

Astounded at this blatant lie, I realised that the Boys from Gartok were now trying to frame us. I responded by asking Smoothy to bring the Abbot of Jitkot, Gin Din Rhou, and the Chinese Dzongpon, both of whom would testify to the truth of the matter.

Smoothy's response was that I was clouding the subject and trying to hold up the proceedings. 'You have never met the Abbot of Jitkot,' Smoothy said. 'We are in no hurry and are prepared to wait many years if necessary until you take a more reasonable attitude and confess your crimes.'

With that it was my turn to lose my cool. 'What the hell are you doing in Tibet? Tibet is not China. Why did you invade Tibet? The Tibetans are a pacific people. They offer no threat to the security of communist China.'

Smoothy was enjoying a small bowl of tea, and he paused with the bowl halfway to his mouth. 'China has not invaded Tibet. Tibet has always been an integral part of China. *We are liberating Tibet from the threat of foreign invasion.* Our task is the complete emancipation of the people of Tibet from the medieval rule of the lamas who oppress them.'

I was puzzled by this. 'But you are in complete control of Tibet. How can you suggest that you are still liberating the Tibetans?'

'You must be aware,' Smoothy said, 'that there are parts of Tibet that are not yet liberated?'

I was not aware of any such thing, but I was quite willing to have a Chinese geography lesson as a change from the usual demands for me to sign a confession. 'To which unliberated part of Tibet do you refer? My memory is a little hazy,' I said.

'We will not allow our subjects to live under foreign domination,' Smoothy continued.

This claim opened up possibilities. Could it be that the Chinese communists included as their subjects all people of Tibetan origin who lived in various parts of Nepal? Surely not, for to claim suzerainty over the Bhotias, Sherpas and Gurkhas was nothing less that a threat to annex parts of the independent kingdom of Nepal. But if Comrade Mao claimed that Bhotias, Sherpas and Gurkhas were of Tibetan origin and therefore Chinese subjects, that would be good enough for the People's Liberation Army.

I decided to explore this possibility. 'Are you referring to the peoples of Nepal who are originally of Tibetan ethnic stock?'

Smoothy deliberated for a few seconds, and then deferred to the military governor, General Pheasant Plucker, who gave him the answer he required. 'They do not live in Nepal. Where Tibetans live, there is Tibet, and part of China, and not Nepal.'

'That's ridiculous,' I countered. 'The people you refer to have long since renounced Tibetan nationality and live in border areas of Nepal.'

Smoothy rounded on me. 'Again what you say is a lie and not a true statement. A Chinese subject can never renounce his true nationality. Where these people live is Tibet and therefore China. The people you mention have witnessed the peaceful liberation of Tibet by the People's Liberation Army of the Republic of China, and are all looking forward to the day when they too will be liberated from their lives of serfdom under the bourgeoisie. Name these areas you have mentioned,' he said.

I asked for a map, and my own eighth-of-an-inch scale map of Nepal was produced.

'Haven't you got any maps of this area yourselves?' I queried.

'We have never seen maps of this area of Tibet,' Smoothy answered. 'This map of yours,' he continued, 'shows substantial areas of Tibet and some parts of Nepal.'

'No,' I countered. 'This is a map entirely of Nepal. Show me the parts you believe are Tibet.'

Smoothy chatted to the governor, and the latter placed a short podgy finger on the area of Nepal known as Mustang. It lies in central Nepal, just north of the Annapurna range. It occurred to me that Mustang lay very close to the route any Chinese Strategic Military Highway was bound to take. By now I was on my feet to look at the map. The Pheasant Plucker signalled to one of my guards. I expected a gun muzzle in my ear but instead I heard Smoothy say, 'Hello, please sit.'

The guard behind me had opened up a folding steel chair, and I was invited to sit on it.

'No thanks,' I said. 'I've been through all that before.'

'Hello, please sit,' Smoothy said. 'No harm will come to you.'

And so I sat on a comfortable seat for the first time in weeks.

'You can have a cigarette,' Smoothy offered. Being a non-smoker I declined.

'Perhaps you are right,' I said, trying to lead Smoothy and the Pheasant Plucker on. 'Perhaps I am mistaken. Try and refresh my memory. What about these areas, this is where the Bhotias live, this is the area where the Sherpas live, close to Mount Everest. This is the Gurkhali state, where the Gurkhas live.'

All this was translated to the governor by Smoothy. 'The governor, our general, says that all of those areas are Tibet and therefore Chinese territory. The governor says that he believes that your main purpose here is not only to spy on the PLA, but also to create a rebellion by trying to influence these Tibetan peoples, those we have liberated and those we have not yet liberated, to fight against China.'

'I would like to see a larger map,' I suggested. 'I might be able to assist you.'

The chance of help from a CIA spy was just what the doctor ordered as far as the Boys from Gartok were concerned. One of the others opened a small wooden box and drew from it a battered old copy of the Oxford atlas of pre-war origin. The Pheasant Plucker located the appropriate pages.

'The governor wishes you to indicate to him what your imperialist masters have told you is not part of China.'

'Anything to oblige,' I commented, and proceeded to pore over the pages showing Central Asia. As I pointed to the countries which border Tibet, the governor would nod or shake his head.

'You have been filled with Western Imperialist Colonialist propaganda,' Smoothy said. 'Look, we will show you. Here is Tibet, and here, and here.'

I could not believe my eyes. The Chinese governor's interpretation of the maps suggested that parts of the border between Pakistan and Tibet, hitherto regarded as Pakistan territory, were really parts of China. My mind boggled when I saw the governor's interpretation of the map. He placed his finger on a huge slice of Pakistani Kashmir and his claims to Indian territory were even larger – the entire Aksai Chin plateau. This area of India's province of Jammu and Kashmir north of Ladakh bordering on Chinese-occupied Sinkiang was 150 miles in depth.

I led them on, and on and on. There was no hesitation on the part of the Pheasant Plucker. He knew which parts of the border area communist China was claiming. I was horrified when he included the whole of the then independent kingdom of Sikkim (since taken under Indian suzerainty), and the kingdom of Bhutan. Not content with that he included a fair slice of the northern area of Burma, plus the area of northern India which lies between Bhutan and Burma, which under the Raj was know as NEFA (North East Frontier Agency) and which independent India calls Arunachal Pradesh.

The governor pointed to Sinkiang, or Chinese Turkestan. Well, we all knew that China had invaded and occupied Sinkiang immediately after the revolution and the overthrow of the Kuomintang government. But that was not all. 'We want back the whole of Mongolia,' Smoothy told me. 'The Soviet Union holds half of Mongolia. Some day we will liberate that part of China from Soviet domination.'

'Good on you, chum,' I responded. 'I can't wait for the day. I wish you all the luck in the world,' to which I added under my breath, 'You're going to need it, buster.'

'All of this ground we have looked at; surely the rest of the world recognises this as part of communist China?' Smoothy suggested.

'Actually, old man,' I responded, 'I'm afraid they don't. I must admit to having been terribly misinformed by my superiors before I left the UK.'

One thing was certain, Singh's three principles of counter-interrogation were working. I was denying everything, admitting very little, and I was keeping the other side talking and most certainly learning more from them than they were learning from me. It was obvious now that Harrop and Damodar, under questioning, had told Smoothy that I was leader of the expedition. It was to become painfully obvious in the very near future that I was going to be the main target, I was the one they had to break.

Smoothy spoke. 'There is a resurgence of nationalist feeling abroad in

Asia today. All Asiatics see in communist China the embodiment of their desire for political emancipation.'

At this I smiled, and at an order from Smoothy I received another blow on my right ear with a PPSh muzzle. This stung me to retaliate. 'Does this emancipation extend only to nations not under Chinese domination? You can't by any stretch of the imagination describe China's occupation of Tibet as the emancipation of the Tibetan people, can you?'

Smoothy vented his anger at my complete ignorance of the history of China. 'Tibet is and always has been recognised throughout the world as an integral part of China. Only last year, China and India signed a mutual-friendship treaty, in which Nehru recognised China's claim to Tibet.'

I responded. 'But history does not bear out your claims. By all the principles of international law Tibet is or was an independent free country.'

Smoothy, horror writ all over his visage, transmitted my statement of Tibetan national independence to the rest of the Boys from Gartok. Once again they exploded into the well worn ritual of 'Struggling Against', all on foot, chanting in unison.

Eventually they all quietened down and resumed their seats, and once again I felt that the interlude of raucous bellowing had done them all a great deal of good. I tried to recall the last time I had heard such a din. It was probably the occasion when I attended a Welsh rugby match, and the crowd were in the process of lynching the referee.

Smoothy had a few words with the others, and I noticed smirks on their faces. They were working up to something. The Bookworm fished into his briefcase and handed something to Smoothy. I was hoping that it wasn't my pistol. I was agreeably surprised to see it was only the small cotton bag in which Harrop had stored his collection of ammonite fossils. I was due for a surprise.

'What was the real reason for you wanting to illegally occupy the mountain Nalkankar?' Smoothy demanded.

'We simply wished to be the first to climb it,' I answered.

'What you say is a lie,' Smoothy said. 'What did you hope to find on the summit of that mountain?'

'Only snow,' I said.

'Once again you lie. What are these?' With a bigger smirk than before, Smoothy emptied Harrop's bag, disclosing a dozen or so ammonite fossils. 'What are these?' he repeated.

'Well, actually, and you're not going to believe this, these are fossils of sea shells which lived on the ocean floor millions of years ago.'

Smoothy then perpetrated a first-class schoolboy howler. 'You did not find these in the sea, you stole them illegally in Tibet, a province of China.'

I sighed with despair. 'Millions of years ago,' I explained, 'Tibet was under the sea. We found these fossils near the Nepal–Tibet border, at a height of about 16,500 feet.'

Smoothy's expression betrayed that he believed not a word that I had spoken. 'You think that we are ignorant. We are not. We know that the sea is a thousand miles from Tibet. What you say is a lie.' Smoothy then delivered what he believed to be a bombshell. 'I will tell you why you and your colleagues were sent here by the British government to illegally occupy the summits of mountains. You are here to search for radioactive minerals such as these samples you have collected in Tibet.'

'Oh my God,' I thought to myself. 'Harrop really has dropped us in it, with his penchant for picking up odd useless bits of rock.'

'We hoped to present those items to the British Museum of London,' I said.

'Is this British Museum an arm of the British Imperialist Government?' Smoothy enquired.

'Well, I suppose that it is,' I responded.

Smoothy turned to the Bookworm with a 'get all this down, it's very important' look on his face.

Smoothy's amanuensis scribbled furiously away in his Indian school exercise book.

'Are there other illegal climbing expeditions searching for these radio-active materials?' Smoothy enquired.

'Loads of them,' I responded. 'There are German, Austrian, Japanese, American and British expeditions, all doing the same thing, on the mountains of Nepal.'

'How do you keep in touch with them? How do you get your orders?' Smoothy demanded.

'We get sealed orders before we leave,' I replied.

'Where is the nearest expedition seeking these radioactive materials?' Smoothy pressed.

'There is a Swiss expedition, led by a former mountaineering guide by the name of Raymond Lambert,' I threw in, 'in central Nepal.'

'Is this Switzerland a People's Democracy?' Smoothy enquired.

'Not of the type that you would recognise,' I answered. 'Lambert went very high on Everest,' I added.

'Where is this Everest?' Smoothy further enquired.

Geography was obviously not his subject. 'Mount Everest, which is called Chomolungma by the Tibetans and Nepalese, is the highest mountain in the world. It straddles the border between Nepal and Tibet. It lies in the Sola Khumbu area of Nepal. Look, I'll show you where it is.' My map was laid on the table, and I indicated where Sola Khumbu was.

'That area is Tibet,' Smoothy countered. 'That expedition of the Swiss was an illegal possession of territory of the People's Republic of China.'

'Actually, you can't lay all the blame on the Swiss,' I said. 'You see it was a British expedition that first climbed Everest, and that was only two years ago, in 1953. The leader was Colonel John Hunt of the British Army. He received a knighthood from Her Majesty the Queen, as did one of the two climbers who reached the summit, New Zealander Edmund Hillary. The other summiteer was a Nepalese Sherpa guide by the name of Tenzing Norgay. He received a British decoration as well. They used oxygen to reach the top. The summit would have been reached earlier by an acquaintance of mine, Charles Evans, but Evans' oxygen apparatus failed just below the summit.'

'This Colonel Hunt. Is he the same as the Brigadier Hunt who operates the Everest Foundation illegal espionage organisation?'

'Self same,' I replied. 'The one and only. He was promoted from full colonel to brigadier only recently.'

'For his espionage work?' Smoothy enquired.

'Can't think of a better reason,' I replied.

'You mentioned just now that foreign agent Charles Evans failed to complete the illegal occupation of the summit of this Tibetan mountain Chomolungma due to the failure of his oxygen apparatus.'

I nodded my assent, and then Smoothy sprung on me the classic bloomer of the year. 'This Evans, *what was he carrying inside his oxygen apparatus?*'

I succeeded in keeping a straight face. 'This bloke should be in the movies, with Laurel and Hardy,' I thought to myself. I was stuck for words.

Smoothy fed me my next lines. 'When these Hillary and Tenzing illegally occupied the summit of this Chomolungma, did they also carry oxygen equipment?'

'Oh yes they did. The oxygen was contained in metal cylinders.'

'What did they do with these oxygen cylinders, when they illegally occupied that summit? We must know.' Smoothy insisted.

Knowing that Hillary and Tenzing were still using oxygen on their descent of Everest, I realised that such an answer would confound Smoothy. It would not fit in with his belief that 'everything has a political motive'. 'They deposited them on the summit on the orders of John Hunt,' I said.

'But that is not good enough,' Smoothy continued. 'You have not told what these imperialist agents were carrying inside their oxygen cylinders.'

I was about to say, 'Oxygen, you bloody fool,' when I realised that such a simple sensible answer would not suffice for people who saw Western imperialist plots behind everything. I sighed. 'I don't know, and your military people at this table will understand when I tell you why. I am a very small cog in a big wheel. I am not privy to all the major decisions of British Intelligence.'

'You lie. It will go hard for you if you do not tell the truth. Now tell us what was inside those oxygen cylinders.'

I had to feed him something so I said, 'Uranium 235.'

That did it. Smoothy beamed all over his face, as he conveyed my confession to the rest of the Boys from Gartok. Judging by the expressions of complete satisfaction on their faces, followed by a serious, heated discussion, it was obvious that I had made their day.

Smoothy turned to me, saying, 'You have been more truthful and honest today. Now you must sketch a map of this Chomolungma, including the route taken by these Hillary and Tenzing, including the exact place where they deposited these cylinders of uranium.'

I had difficulty in suppressing a giggle when, as I was completing my sketch, Smoothy interjected. 'Hello, please, you will mark where the oxygen cylinders were deposited with an x.' On orders from Smoothy, Bookworm scribbled notes, which Smoothy translated into English, on a page of the Indian exercise book.

'We require you to sign this simple confession.'

I was about to tell Smoothy to get stuffed, when I read what he had written. I signed with a flourish, and with an easy mind. The note read: 'On an unknown date in the year 1953 a Mr Hillary and a Mr Tenzing illegally occupied a mountain in Tibet and left on the summit two oxygen cylinders filled with uranium, for an unknown purpose.'

The document, with appropriate Chinese translation, was passed round the table and the Boys from Gartok appeared to be completely satisfied with the day's work.

Deeming this to be the appropriate opportunity to obtain a concession from my captors, I asked to have returned to me colour photographs of my wife Jean, and my nine-year-old son Michael. Smoothy passed my request on to the governor, the Pheasant Plucker, who agreed to it. The photographs were produced from Smoothy's briefcase and handed to me.

'Next time you come before us, you must answer more honestly, as you have done today,' Smoothy said. 'Now we will give you three minutes in which to reconsider your position, and sign your confession that you are an agent of the CIA.'

My three minutes having expired, I was led out of the room by my two armed guards. My second interrogation was at an end.

13

In our prison dinner was being served early that day. Harrop and Damodar were eating a meal of rice and cabbage. The guards ate the same, but with added lumps of mutton. Today there was a welcome addition to the menu which the Chinese called 'pin-sa'. This was a flat cake of dough about twelve inches across and an inch thick, baked on a tin lid placed on the fire. It was, by European standards, very stodgy, but we liked it. It was as near to bread as we could get and appeared on the menu only occasionally.

With my back to my cell wall, I sat with legs outstretched to relieve the cramp that tormented me from the thighs down. I took a bite of pin-sa, and it hit the bottom of my stomach like a lump of lead. As I walked past Harrop to get my tea mug filled, he muttered, 'Sign any dud cheques lately?' meaning had I signed a confession. In answer I shook my head. I returned to the wall of my cell and sat down to finish my meal and drink my tea.

Schickelgruber came over to me and, producing a piece of paper and a pencil, thrust them into my hands. He pointed to the path that I had just taken from that interrogation room. Was he on about that bloody confession? I decided to ignore Schickelgruber, but he was not to be ignored. He presented his rifle for me to see, close up. Then he pressed the release catch and pulled the box magazine from out of the underside of the breech. He held the magazine towards me, about six inches in front of my face, so that I could see the topmost of the 35 rounds it contained. It was a full metal jacketed copper-nosed bullet. Schickelgruber then motioned towards the piece of paper and the pencil in my hands. I shook my head defiantly, and whispered, 'Piss off,' which he appeared to get the gist of.

He then rammed the magazine into the loading gate, and cocked the gun. He then placed it against the side of my head. Lofty came over and pointed to the piece of paper, and then turned and pointed down the track. Again I shook my head. Schickelgruber pulled the trigger. There was a resounding 'clack' and the bolt slammed forward onto an empty breech. The 'clack' almost made me jump out of my skin. I realised what Schickelgruber had done. When the weapon was against my temple, and out of my sight, he had pulled the magazine release catch, and lowered the magazine about a quarter of an inch, so that when he pulled the trigger, the bolt just missed scooping the first round off the top of the magazine, thus 'clacking' home, and releasing its firing pin into an empty chamber. A few days earlier, Schickelgruber had played that trick on me, but with the safety catch in the 'on' position. As there was no clack, because the bolt was not released, this had failed to unnerve me. Neither Harrop nor Damodar was privileged to enjoy this kind of treatment. It was reserved for me. I was the leader of the expedition, the spy-master. I had been caught in possession of a loaded automatic pistol, an offence which by itself was sufficient for a People's Court to hand down a death sentence.

This Chinese roulette happened about thirty to forty times. I never got used to it. It never failed to unnerve me, and I always tried not to show it, keeping up that pretence of the British stiff upper lip, which only we British know is simply suppressed hysteria. The PPSh had a muzzle velocity of 1,600 feet per second, and what with blood, brains, and a handful or so of splintered skull bone flying across the room, some poor beggar's cleaning up job would have been thoroughly distasteful. I was fully aware that the Chinese would never intentionally shoot me while my confession lay unsigned on the table. My main fear was not only the possible poor judgement of the man with his finger on the magazine catch, but also the mechanical reliability of a Russian-designed mass produced Chinese weapon.

As I refused to sign that confession, my plate was snatched out of my hands, and I was ushered into my cell at 3 p.m. Apart from frequent trips to the lavatory, I had seen my last bit of sunshine for the next five days. The weather now became much colder, and the temperature in our cells remained below freezing point night and day. I looked out of my cell window, and yelled my defiance. 'You can all go to hell, you miserable cowardly bastards.'

Hearing me, Harrop and Damodar gave an encouraging cheer, and this resulted in Lofty standing with his back to my tiny window while he was on duty, so that I could not see out into the yard. I still had one tiny window left, the one that looked out onto the lavatory. Frozen stiff, wrapped up in every piece of clothing I possessed, I spent the rest of the hours of daylight making a social survey of the sanitary and hygienic habits of the PLA.

Even wearing three pairs of wool socks, two pairs of trousers, underpants and string vest, a shirt, two sweaters, a thin one innermost, and a thick one outer, plus my windproof Everest anorak jacket and a down-filled duvet-style coat, with a woollen balaclava hat, I still froze in my cell. I had a woollen scarf which I wound round the lower part of my face. It was too cold to stand around, so I retired to my quadruple-layered sleeping bag.

At 5.30 p.m. Marlo came in and lit my small hurricane lamp. I grew bored with spending up to eighteen hours a day in my sleeping bag during that period of solitary confinement, with no spells in the watery sunshine outdoors. I tried to play patience with the pack of Indian cards Chungnya had lent to me a few days before. My luck was out, and I did not win a single hand, but those failed games of patience allowed me to stumble on the means of conveying to Harrop the substance of the questions and answers given during my recent interrogation. The lid of our now empty food box, which Chungnya and I had used as a makeshift table, was made of plywood, and the layers were now in a process of delaminating.

I wrote down everything of substance, and then folded the paper double, and slid it between two layers of plywood. With the note well concealed, I called Chungnya by name, over and over again until he came. I then handed him the pack of cards, and the plywood lid, saying, 'Jung, yappa do.' Chungnya grinned and took the cards and wooden box top to Harrop's cell. I could only hope that Harrop understood my motive in sending him the cards. Later that night, I heard Harrop banging on his cell door to be allowed out to the lavatory. As he stood urinating in front of my tiny window in the dark, I heard him mutter almost under his breath, 'OK, I've got the drift.' As he left, he flicked a small ball of paper through my window, and it hit me on the nose. Harrop was now in a position to be able to marry his answers to mine, when next confronted by the Boys from Gartok.

On the morning of 12 November I was awakened by the noise of dishes being rattled in the kitchen. I banged on the door and Fatty opened it, but when I tried to step outside, he hit me in the chest with the muzzle of his rifle. Fatty called Schickelgruber, who came to my cell door, and again offered me a piece of paper and a pencil stub. I told him to go to hell, and the door was slammed in my face.

As I had slept fully dressed in my sleeping bag, and fully kitted out for a morning over the hills, I decided that I could do just as well walking around my cell. A simple calculation told me that if I walked round the room 176 times I would cover close on a mile. Soon, because of the smallness of the room, I became dizzy, and I countered this by doing twenty-five trips clockwise followed by a similar number anti-clockwise. This involved ducking my head to avoid a low roof beam 352 times for each mile covered. Between meal times I managed about three miles a day. After the first day I no longer needed to count, for I could judge the distance by recording the time on my watch.

My guards never ceased to marvel at this performance and vied with each other to push their fur-hatted heads into the tiny window space to witness my peregrinations. Boredom was my most dangerous enemy, and I was determined that come what may, I would emerge from my incarceration as sane as when I went in. Rats invaded my solitude again, and I discovered that they ignored the holes I had blocked up with stones and now burrowed new holes through the crumbly dried mud walls. I now regarded the rats as company, liking them better than the Chinese.

I would let one rat in, and then bung up its entrance hole. The rat would scurry around the floor taking not the slightest bit of notice of me. I tossed one male rat a tiny bit of boiled turnip, a left-over from breakfast, but he turned his nose up at it. When the little beggar started to chew the corner of my sleeping bag, I took a stone out of a hole in my cell wall, and ushered the rat out. I let him in once a day, and we became good friends. When I got a bit of mutton with my main evening meal, my rat received a morsel. When it was yak intestines, he got the lot. It was at about this time that the female rat I called Megan came into my cell. She was pregnant and her tummy stuck out like a galleon in full sail. I began to take notice of my Tibetan rats, and their habits. Megan was a breed of rat, which to me were peculiar to the Taklakot area of Tibet. They were all snub nosed, and minus tails. They looked more like voles. Perhaps they were. Perhaps they lived down by the Karnali, and only came up to our prison for food.

On the third day of my isolation my dysentery returned. I kept passing watery blood, my legs felt like jelly, and my head swam whenever I stood up. All I wanted to do was lie down. I sent a note to the Boys from Gartok, requesting medical attention, but it was ignored. My letter probably played into their hands, signalling to them my weakened state, and the probability that I would break down and sign a confession at my next interrogation session.

All this time my guards never ever once went for a walk or indulged in any form of exercise. I now understood why they thought that there must be a purpose or political motive for climbing mountains. If there was no purpose why undertake it? In late afternoon Chungnya visited my cell, and realised that I was sick. He handed me a piece of paper and a pencil, and indicated with a big grin that I was to write something on it. 'Oh, not you too,' I moaned. So just to please Chungnya I wrote a damning note to the Pheasant Plucker and his acolytes, accusing them of being fascist and no better than the Nazis or the Japanese in World War Two.

Chungnya handed the note to Schickelgruber who, thoroughly delighted with the thought that the Foreign Devil had at last signed a confession, rushed across the river with it. The note was just a ploy on Chungnya's part. Once our hated sergeant of the guards had gone Chungnya repaired to the kitchen and returned later with a bowl full of noodle soup, with dried shrimps, and a real, genuine, poached egg floating on top. Chungnya could only have obtained those dried shrimps and the egg from Indian traders, and at a considerable financial sacrifice to himself. As I sat slurping away at this delicious meal, Chungnya, joined now by Chubby and Shorty, sat on the edge of my inflatable air mattress, smiling at me, and saying 'Chid, yappa do.'

Chubby and Shorty pulled their knitting gear out of their tunic pockets, and going over to the window, where there was more light, they continued with their tasks of knitting socks, or gloves. All of the guards knitted. Later they were joined by Marlo, who to my surprise was spinning his own wool, drawn through the fingers of his left hand and wrapped around a wooden bobbin that spun below his right hand, dangling on the end of the thread. It must have been handicraft week in the PLA. Shorty suspended his knitting and produced two paperback books from inside his padded tunic. I asked to see the books and they were passed to me. One was a simple text book through which Shorty was learning to read. The pages were filled with tiny sketches, each one adjacent to the appropriate Chinese symbol. I was struck by the fact that most of the illustrations were of a military nature, although it was not a military manual as it contained pictures of houses, clocks, children and animals. Three pictures out of four represented weapons of war, including rifles, machine-guns, helmets, tanks, mines and many other items. It was, I thought, a miserable vehicle for education.

The second book took the form of an illustrated Chinese comic paper. It told one long story in picture form, the Chinese equivalent of *Superman*, only the Chinese protagonist was a monkey king, who lived in a palace on a mountain top surrounded by thousands of chimpanzee-like subjects.

At 7 p.m. Lofty handed over his guard duty to Shorty. The rest of the guards retired for the night and I was left alone in my cell once more. For a long time I sat looking at the photographs of my wife and son. I did not hear Schickelgruber return. I hoped that he was reprimanded by the Boys from Gartok for not obtaining my confession. The next morning I was awakened by Schickelgruber who came into my cell screaming his head off. His eyes seemed to be bulging out of his head. He clenched one fist and thrust it in my face, inferring that I was due for some rough treatment. Weak though I was, I decided that this man was both a bully and a coward. Standing upright, I grabbed hold of the lapel of his khaki padded jacket with my left hand. He jerked away from me, and losing his footing over the edge of the raised platform on which my bed lay, he fell on his back. He got to his feet, still screaming at me, but seeing that on this occasion Schickelgruber was unarmed, and in no position to resume his game of Chinese Roulette, I followed him to the door. He, retreating backwards with my right fist just under his nose, fell a second time, on this occasion over the raised step of the entrance to my cell.

He got to his feet and continued to retreat, backing away from me, and I followed him through the guardroom door. Without his trusty rifle Schickelgruber was an abject coward. Out of the corner of my eye I saw his PPSh standing against the wall about three feet from my right hand. I was in a mind to seize it and beat his head in, when Lofty grabbed me from behind, and with arms around my chest, called for assistance. I decided that resistance was useless and returned to my cell. Losing my cool with Schickelgruber was, on reflection, an error of judgement on my part. He had lost face in front of his men, and I could count on him being even nastier from now on.

Harrop and Damodar were taken separately for further interrogation that same morning, but to the other side of the river, and not to the small Tibetan house where I had been questioned. That night, Harrop, on his way to the thunder hole in the dark, flipped a note through the window of my cell. He informed me that the Chinese wanted to know how we communicated between our campsite at Saipal in Nepal and our headquarters. Harrop informed them that we had blundered badly by leaving our carrier pigeons in Bombay. The Boys from Gartok accepted Harrop's explanation without question.

At about 6 p.m. Chungnya unlocked the door of my cell and came in bearing half the book of poetry that we had brought from our base camp in Nepal and which the Chinese had confiscated on the day we were moved to Taklakot. It appeared that Harrop had sent notes requesting the return of *The Century of Poetry from Pope to Keats*, and the Chinese, no doubt feeling that Harrop had been co-operative in supplying details of our 'live drop' carrier pigeons, had duly rewarded him. Thanks to Chungnya, I now had half the book, Harrop having ripped it in two down the spine, right through the middle of Samuel Taylor Coleridge's 'Rime of the Ancient Mariner'.

What a joy that half-book of poetry was, and how it boosted my morale. I read and re-read every line, learning Byron's 'Don Juan' by heart, scribbling some passages with my pencil stub on a small patch of white-painted wall over my bed. I found one of Alexander Pope's poems remarkably apt.

> In the worst inn's worst room with mat half hung,
> The floors of plaster and the walls of dung.

It was while I was scribbling away on the wall that I noticed someone had been writing there before me. There was something in Sanskrit, and what I took to be the same message in English. I read from the short English section, 'I am a poor Indian trader. The Chini have put me . . .' The rest was indecipherable. I was quite obviously not the first prisoner to occupy that tiny cell.

It was 15 November, my fifth day of enforced solitary confinement. Each day I looked through the window to see Harrop and Damodar sitting in the yard enjoying the sunshine. But I had to stay in my freezing cold rat-infested cell until I broke, and signed a confession. A squeamish person might have been driven out of their minds by the ever-present rats, who swarmed over my sleeping bag during the night. The Chinese were not to know it, but the rats were now my companions and also my allies. I found that I could have a reasonably intelligent conversation, albeit one way, with little fat pregnant Megan, who nightly enlarged the hole in the chest of my woollen sweater as she raided it for the lining of her nest. The rats proved harmless. They never bit, and on the red-letter days when Chungnya brought me a piece of the Chinese steam-baked bread, I saved a morsel to share with my little tail-less, snub-nosed cell mates. Megan would sit on my shoulder when I was huddled in my sleeping bag, my head covered, writing up my diary on paper scraps. To get rid of her, I only had to place my hands around her fat tummy, and picking her up, shoo her down her personal rat hole.

My dizzy spells were more frequent now and I felt light-headed most of the time. When I stood up nausea assailed me and the room started to spin round. I could no longer look at the boiled turnip soup at breakfast. I spent most of the time asleep. I longed for fresh air and sunlight.

I was awakened at midday by Schickelgruber prodding his gun muzzle in my face. He was accompanied by the bodyguard of His Excellency the Governor, General Pheasant Plucker carrying an ex-US Army MI.30 calibre carbine. This could only mean another command-performance in front of the Boys from Gartok, and I felt too ill to accept their invitation. I shook my head and turned over, only to be grabbed bodily by the feet, and tipped out of my sleeping bag onto the floor. I was then dragged to my feet, and Shorty and Lofty joined the other two as my escort, and for the short pull up the hill from the bridge I had to accept the assistance of both Lofty and Shorty, who showed a degree of humanity completely alien to Schickelgruber.

This questioning session took place in the same red building as my interrogation on 7 November. I waited for the usual 'Hello, please sit,' followed by a thump from a gun muzzle when I reached for the chair. Nobody spoke for several minutes. There were six of them, and they all started chanting, ranting, and the 'Struggle Against' ran its cacophonic course.

I leaned against the wall behind me.

'Stand up straight,' Smoothy screamed at me.

'You go to hell,' I responded, feeling that I didn't care a damn what they did to me.

Smoothy's chubby little face was working with passion. He waved the note I had sent across with Schickelgruber. 'You sent this insulting letter to us. You likened us to the German and Japanese war criminals. You call the People's Republic of China a Colonialist-Imperialist state because of our liberation of Tibet and the political emancipation of the downtrodden Tibetan proletariat. We are not fascists. We are very democratic. You are being treated very well. You complain about your accommodation. It is not a cell. You have a good room in a guest house reserved for visitors to the People's Republic of China. We do not usually treat criminals as well as we have treated you.'

'Does this posh hotel accommodation extend also to the Indians, the citizens of Hindustan? Like the poor bugger who occupied my cell before I came here? Was he the one you arrested for the crime of possessing a map?' I enquired.

Smoothy went almost purple with rage. 'There has never been anyone else accommodated in your hotel room,' he thundered.

'I'm not alone in there,' I responded. 'I have my own private cavalry.

They are increasing in numbers day by day. Pretty soon they will come out and surround you.' I was, of course, referring to my friends the rats.

Smoothy looked taken aback and somewhat puzzled by this, and had to converse with the others. It began to look as though the officers were questioning our prison discipline. They shouted for Schickelgruber, and he came in snivelling and hand wringing, as Ug-Lug bawled at him. 'The prisoner is no longer allowed to have visitors in his cell,' they in all probability shouted at him.

Quite literally touching his forelock, Schickelgruber bowed his way out of the room. There was a moment's silence, and then Smoothy said, 'Hello, please sit.' He motioned me towards the steel chair. I ignored the officer. Smoothy signalled to one of the two guards who had been standing on either side of me, their rifles pointed at me. The guard duly opened up the steel folding chair and placed it behind me, indicating that on this occasion I could have a comfortable seat. My backside had hardly touched the chair when the other guard hit me on the shoulder with the butt of his rifle.

'No, you must sit on the floor,' Smoothy said.

I looked along the row of faces on the opposite side of the table. They were all smiling. The foreign devil was about to lose face. The chair was withdrawn and once again I squatted on the dried mud floor. For about twenty minutes we went through the same routine as on the other two occasions, questions about my identity and my family, all in an attempt to catch me out with my alleged fake identity.

Then Smoothy took a new tack. 'You have to be able to make contact with those who sent you here. How do you do that?'

'Carrier pigeons,' I said, taking my cue from John Harrop. 'But we had to leave them in Bombay, due to Indian regulations on the import of livestock.'

This seemed to satisfy Smoothy for a moment. Then I had to make a request. 'I have a recurrence of dysentery, I have to go to the lavatory, right away now.'

'You will stay where you are,' Smoothy said.

'All right,' I responded. 'Any second now I will defecate blood and liquid in my pants and all over your floor. I am almost incontinent.'

Smoothy spoke to the guards, and I was escorted out of the red building, and had to squat in a corner of the yard, surrounded by a curious crowd of Chinese soldiers and Tibetans. I was too ill to experience any feeling of embarrassment. The Tibetans shook their heads and tut-tutted. Eventually I was assisted onto my feet by two guards, and escorted back into the star chamber. The guards gave Smoothy a lengthy description of what had taken place, for they had seen the pool of blood I had left on the ground. Smoothy could no longer claim that I was malingering.

I seized the opportunity to request medical attention, and Smoothy advised me that the matter was still under consideration, and that my signature on that vital piece of paper would in all probability ensure that

I received treatment for my dysentery. 'You are being kept in your cell [Smoothy slipped up here and actually said cell and not room] because you have made an illegal armed invasion of the People's Republic of China. You are a criminal and as such you will be punished in accordance with Chinese law.'

Unable to stomach his self-righteousness I retorted, 'According to the principles of democracy, a man is not punished for a crime until he has been tried and found guilty by a properly constituted court. You cannot punish us without a conviction.'

Smoothy's reply was indicative of the degree of justice one can expect in a Marxist state. 'You will be tried by a People's Court. You will be convicted and you will be punished heavily.'

'Who will represent us as defence counsel at the trial?' I enquired.

'You do not need a defence,' Smoothy retorted. 'We know that you are guilty. In the fight against the bourgeoisie, Comrade Mao has decreed that "Defence is Revolt".'

Smoothy translated this appalling piece of Marxist theory to the rest of the Boys from Gartok, and they all nodded their heads in agreement, the Pheasant Plucker emphasising his feelings with polite clapping.

Pointing to the governor, I said, 'Tell that parchment faced bastard that he is a fascist.'

Smoothy passed on the compliment and the Pheasant Plucker lost his usual imperturbable demeanour, and shouted to the guards. They grabbed me by the shoulders and shook me. I fell over from my sitting position.

'You must apologise,' Smoothy said.

'You can all go to hell,' I responded.

'You have little time to change your mind,' Smoothy said. 'Sign this, and your punishment will be lighter. Your trial will be held shortly. We have taken every precaution to prevent your escape. The rest of your illegal expedition cannot help you. They are all in hiding in Hindustan.'

I began to daydream and the voiced kept fading away. The guards kept prodding me into wakefulness with their gun muzzles. I told Smoothy in one of my few clear-headed moments that I just had to lie down. Smoothy responded by giving my guards an order and they hauled me to my feet. I thought that this was the signal that the Taklakot Concert Party had finished with me for the day, and staggered towards the door. My way was blocked by the governor's bodyguard, who rammed the muzzle of his American MI carbine under my chin.

The guards dragged me back before the committee, and I tried to lean against the wall, my legs now beginning to collapse under me. I was roughly pushed away from the wall by one of the guards, and I fell down. One of the guards caught me, and pulled me upright. I could faintly hear Chinese voices, but they sounded as though they were reaching me down a long tunnel. Things became a little clearer, and I heard a voice say, 'Sign this and all will be well.'

At that moment I felt that I would be willing to sign anything to escape from that nightmare chamber. I had one last defence. 'I'm too ill to read what it says. I need a doctor. I need medical attention.'

'Medical attention is now on hand,' Smoothy replied. 'We have a doctor waiting outside the door. Sign this simple confession, and we will call him in, and you will receive the very best of medical attention.'

'And if I don't sign?'

'Then you will get no medical attention.'

My vision was coming back and I looked along that line of Chinese communist faces, one by one. The worst thing they could do was kill me, and in the state I was in, I didn't give a damn if I lived or died, so I said, 'I'll see you in hell first.'

An order was almost whispered to my guards. It came from the governor, the Pheasant Plucker. The guard on my right grabbed me from behind and put his left arm round my throat. With his right hand he grabbed my hair, holding me so that I could only look straight ahead. The other guard stood in front of me and released the magazine from his PPSh assault rifle. I knew what was coming. I was shown the gleaming copper nose of the topmost cartridge in the magazine. The magazine was slammed into the loading gate.

Smoothy spoke once more. 'It will be easier for you if you sign this simple confession that you are a Western Fascist Lackey Imperialist Running Dog of the American CIA and leader of an armed invasion of the People's Republic of China.'

I just spoke one word. 'No.'

The guard in front of me raised his PPSh up to eye level, and pulled back the cocking lever. The guard holding me took his arm from around my neck, and stood to one side, still holding onto my hair, keeping me facing the gun muzzle. He was making sure that if the gun-toting guard made a cock-up of the imminent session of Chinese Roulette, he would be out of the line of fire.

The gun muzzle was placed about an inch from my right eye. It was too close for my eyes to focus on. But I clearly saw his right hand, and his finger on the trigger. I was certain in my mind that the gun's magazine had been lowered about a quarter of an inch, so that when the bolt slammed forward, it would not scoop the topmost round out of the magazine, and send it down the barrel and through my skull. Then horror upon horrors, at an order from someone seated at the table, I could not see who, the gunman took his right hand away from the trigger, and slammed the magazine up tight into the locked position. That magazine was firm home. If the PLA soldier pulled the trigger now, my brains would be all over the wall behind me.

'One last chance,' Smoothy said. 'Say yes, that you will sign this confession, and you will come to no harm.'

A voice inside me said, 'Go on, sign the damn thing. You have done enough. You're not a professional spy. Why have your brains blown out? Go on and sign it.' Another voice was saying, 'Twenty, maybe thirty years in prison in Peking, and with no medical attention. You'd be better off dead, old chum.'

'No.'

I heard an order given. I remember the clack and that is all. When I came round, I realised that I had had one of my famous turns. When subjected to severe pain or fed too much garlic, my body revolts, and I faint. I had passed out. I lay with my right cheek on the dried mud floor. 'Remember the rules, Wignall. Don't try to get up too soon. If you do, the blood will drain from your head, and you can suffer brain damage.'

Brain damage . . . well, my brains hadn't been blown out, had they? Or was this all a bad dream and I was really dead? I could hear the murmur of Chinese voices. I started to collect my thoughts. Just what the hell had happened? The answer was obvious. While one guard was holding my head by my hair, forcing me to look ahead, the guard with the gun had either made a quick switch with another guard's gun, one with an empty magazine, or he had changed his loaded magazine for an empty one.

Eventually I was able to sit upright, but the room swam round and round.

'Sign this confession.'

'No.'

Same performance as before. But this time I did not faint when the bolt mechanism slammed home. But it made me jump. This must have happened about ten or more times. I lost count. Of all the games of chance I have played, I found none so unenjoyable as Chinese Roulette. I have never been one to hate easily. Now for the first time in my life I hated passionately and so fiercely that, had I possessed a gun, I would cheerfully have killed every one of them. Given the opportunity I would have snuffed out their lives with no more compunction than I would a candle. Smoothy, after a chat with the Pheasant Plucker, handed me a sheet of blue notepaper.

'Take this back to your cell and write a criticism of your insulting and unco-operative behaviour. Tomorrow is Self-Criticism Day for all the soldiers in our command. You too must criticise yourself.'

I stuffed the paper in my pocket, and stumbled through the door. The two guards who had been making sport with Chinese Roulette stayed behind. I was greeted outside the Taklakot Concert Hall by two different guards. Dear old Chungnya and his pal Chubby. I only remember them placing my arms around their shoulders, in an effort to help me walk back down the hill, and over the bridge back to my cell. I must have had another of my famous turns. I didn't remember any more until I came round when Chungnya and Chubby were struggling to get me inside my sleeping bag. I feel asleep and lost consciousness, having been deprived of food all day and having had nothing to drink since my breakfast mug of tea. Due to my dysentery, my body was fast dehydrating.

The following morning I was turned out of my bed at 9 a.m. To my astonishment my sleeping bag and air mattress were taken out into the prison yard, and placed in the sunniest corner. My enforced stay indoors was at an end. It had failed to produced the oft-demanded confession, and perhaps my accusation of fascist treatment had struck a sensitive spot.

That day was like a holiday. I basked in the sunshine and read Byron. At midday Harrop and I exchanged respective halves of the Penguin book of poetry. Harrop started to learn Gray's 'Elegy Written in a Country Churchyard' off by heart. Damodar red Shorty's book about the Chinese ape king. He roared with laughter to such a degree that Shorty, frowning, snatched the book off Damodar and took it indoors. It was obvious that Chinese monkeys are no subject for undue levity.

Later in the day, all of our guards sat in a circle, and carried out what must have been their Self-Criticism session, after which they wrote down the Self-Criticism essays in an exercise book.

The toilet paper situation was now becoming desperate. We had none left and in my condition my need was urgent. I went into the kitchen and appropriated an old padded army tunic our guards sometimes wore when cooking. When Marlo argued and tried to take this stained and greasy garment from me, I raised merry hell, going through the mime act of suggesting that I needed it for a pillow. Chungnya came to my rescue, and I returned to my cell in triumph.

Taking the jacket indoors I tore open the lining. It was padded with layers of soft cotton wool. This would do admirably. In point of fact I can recommend old Chinese PLA padded jackets for the abstersion of one's fundament. Much gentler, softer and more caressing than common toilet paper. Harrop was in the process of tearing up his spare shirt.

That night the guards brought in a sheep for the kitchen table, and what followed was one of the most callous, brutal and disgusting scenes of cruelty I have ever witnessed. Watching through my cell window, just as it was turning dusk, I saw Marlo and Shorty tie the creature's four legs together and start to kick the poor helpless animal. Tiring of kicking it in the ribs, they went to work on its face. Marlo wore rubber basketball boots and, judging by the expression on his face, was enjoying a great deal of sadistic pleasure. When the animal lay still, they started pointing to its eyes. I recalled that whenever a dead sheep was delivered to our prison (this was the first live one) there was a great deal of competition about who should have the dead animal's eyeballs, which our Chinese guards regarded as a great delicacy, eating them raw.

An argument started between Marlo and Shorty as to who should have the eyeballs. The argument developed into a scrimmage with both men punching each other. They ended up rolling around the floor. While they were fighting they were pre-empted by Schickelgruber who, emerging from the guardroom and seeing what was afoot, ran past the two bodies writhing on the floor and over to the hog-tied sheep. The poor thing had regained consciousness, and I saw it struggling against its bonds and, as I watched, to my unspeakable horror, Schickelgruber bent down, and using his two thumbs, gouged out the eyes of the still-living animal. The sheep bleated in pain, and Schickelgruber, pushing the two eyes into his mouth, chewed and swallowed them. It was only then that he drew a pocket knife, opened it, and slit the sheep's throat.

I screamed at Schickelgruber through my tiny window, 'You lousy rotten Chinese communist bastard.'

Schickelgruber ignored my cries, for after all he could not understand a word I said. He sauntered back into the guardroom, looking very pleased with himself. The other two guards gave up their fight, only to find that the Taklakot chef's suggestion for the day had already been purloined.

I went back to my bed thoroughly dispirited. 'So this is Marxism put into practice. God help the people of Tibet and God help China,' I thought to myself. Almost subconsciously, I went over to the wall of my cell and pulled out one of the stones blocking up a rat hole. As luck would have it, little fat pregnant Megan appeared immediately. She sat on her haunches looking up at me, her long whiskers waggling as she sniffed the air. I reached down and picked her up, and sliding into my sleeping bag, sat cuddling her to my chest. 'You are the nicest little rat around here,' I said to her. 'Don't have anything to do with these Chinese, they are bloody awful people.'

14

The days passed with irksome tedium, enlivened by my totally inexcusable enjoyment of Harrop's discomfort brought about by the shortage of toilet paper. I relented from my Scrooge-like possessiveness, and when I heard Harrop going into the lavatory area in the night, I whispered through my tunnel-like window, 'Here's a present for you.' I thrust a complete armful of cotton wool wadding from my purloined Chinese jacket into the tunnel. Harrop grabbed it, and I presume he stuck it up the front of his sweater. I favoured Damodar in a similar fashion that same night.

There was to be competition for my lovely soft toilet requisite. Megan the rat took a fancy to it. In order to conceal it from the unspeakable Schickelgruber, I had rammed it down into the bottom of my sleeping bag, and wrapped it around my cold feet in an effort to keep warm. Megan, being constantly lifted out of my sleeping bag when she made further holes in my sweater, burrowed further into my bag and would wriggle out past my face in the night, with a bundle of cotton wool in her mouth. I was in darkness, with only a stub of a candle, our guards having evidently run out of paraffin for our tiny Indian hurricane lamps.

Music became a mental safeguard while in my solitary cell. I sat with my eyes shut and meditated on orchestral concerts I had attended in the past. Gradually I was able to remember and hum to myself whole passages of classical music. Tchaikovsky's Fifth Symphony was the first major piece I was able to hum right through from beginning to end. My greatest achievement was Beethoven's Eroica Symphony in its entirety. I was also fond of film music, and remembered passages from the composer I regarded as one of the finest film composers, Erich Wolfgang Korngold. I hummed parts of the incidental music to *The Sea Hawk* and *Robin Hood*, and finally what to me is still the most perfect film score, that from *King's Row*.

To keep warm in daylight hours, I stood fully dressed, humming a piece of orchestral music, while conducting my imaginary hundred-piece orchestra with the aid of my broken PLA-issue wooden chopstick. At night, when it was too cold to stir outside my sleeping bag, I sat upright, and using my chopstick as a bow, played the 'Adagietta' string section of Mahler's Fifth Symphony on my imaginary violin. The rats would watch this performance, and sad to say, the music from my imaginary orchestra and equally imaginary violin fell on their 'deaf' ears.

In his teachings, Buddha said, '*I can teach you only two things: suffering and relief from suffering.*' I found my relief from suffering in music. In my enforced solitude in my freezing cold prison cell I escaped from earthly bonds, and transported by the music of the great composers of the past I found an inner peace and serenity of spirit I had never before experienced.

Came the dawn and I had ideas about a different kind of music. As we were forbidden to speak to one another in the prison yard, what about singing a song? None of our guards spoke English. I decided to give the matter a try, thinking that getting our guards into a good humour with a little levity would not go amiss. I possessed a pair of woollen mittens, gloves minus half the fingers, that my wife Jean had knitted for me before we set off for the Himalayas. I proposed to use these as theatrical props.

Most of our guards were in the yard, preparing the evening meal, skinning and dressing the sheep, the eyes of which Schickelgruber had gouged out. Harrop and Damodar sat by each of their cell walls. I stood on the top step, and went into my song and dance routine. I gave the Chinese my rendition of a very jolly Edwardian music hall song, made famous by the late Miss Vesta Tilley. (I'm not that old. It was taught to me by my late father, who was a mediocre singer but an expert tap dancer.) The song was 'Burlington Bertie From Bow', and it went like this.

> I'm Burlington Bertie, I rise at ten thirty
> and saunter along like a toff.
> I walk down the Strand with my gloves on my hands,
> and I walk down again with them off.
> The Prince of Wales' brother, and
> some chappie or other, said
> Come to the Palace have supper with Mother.
> I'm Bert, Bert, and royalty's hurt.
> When they ask me to dine I say No.
> I've just had a banana with Lady Diana,
> I'm Burlington Bertie from Bow.

The Chinese roared at this, especially when I very theatrically took off my fingerless gloves and waved them in the air. At this Chungnya joined me on the top step, and parodied my actions when I did a repeat performance. I then announced that Harrop and Damodar and I would sing the Welsh national anthem. The Chinese did not understand what I was saying, but they hugely enjoyed our parody of the hymn 'Onward Christian Soldiers', to which we sang the repetitive line, 'Lloyd George knew my father, Father knew Lloyd George.' It just went on and on, the same line repeated over and over again. My parody of the Irish national anthem was also well received, and I boast not when I claim that there was hardly a dry eye in that prison yard when I sang that emotive line, 'Don't sit on the billiard table, cos you're wearing off the green.'

This led to calls for a repeat of 'Burlington Bertie'. My encore, perhaps due to my inclusion of a tap dance, in waltz time, may not have looked very elegant, me in my enormous high-altitude boots, but it laid the People's Liberation Army of the Republic of China in the aisles.

I was working up to something, and I could tell by the twinkle in Harrop's eyes that he had rumbled what I was about. I sang several old First World War songs like 'Silver Lining' and 'Good Byee', but using my own words. Song by song, I took Harrop and Damodar through my interrogation and 'thought reform' sessions.

Then Harrop stood up and sang 'Ilkley Moor'. It is one of those interminable songs that seem to go on forever and ever. By the time he had completed his solo virtuoso performance, I was fully in the picture. I was the target as far as the Boys from Gartok and the Pheasant Plucker were concerned. I had to be broken. It was essential that the leader of the expedition confess that we were foreign spies, and forerunners of a future armed invasion of Tibet and China by Western imperialist forces.

Harrop was also under the impression that there was a degree of urgency in the matter, and that the delays between interrogations were due to communications difficulties the Chinese were experiencing. Harrop had it worked out that our material was first evaluated in the PLA HQ at Taklakot, and then transmitted by radio to Chinese military HQ in Lhasa, from where, after further evaluation, it was sent on to possibly Chungking, China's main army base for the occupation of Tibet. As the Chinese communists appear to work only on instructions, the Chungking PLA would then send all the material to Peking. It was a case of buck passing all the way down the line, because nobody was prepared to take any responsibility without the OK from higher up.

The Pheasant Plucker needed a speedy confession, and Harrop was now of the opinion that Koila and our porters had got through to Saipal, and that the other members of our expedition would by now be back in India, presuming that they regarded speed as of the essence and that the British government and the Indian authorities would be asking China what on earth they were doing arresting Himalayan explorers at gunpoint. The Chinese in fact lied to both governments, and also to the Nepalese government who later asked for clarification of the situation, by stating that they had no prisoners at Taklakot, and that they had never heard of Wignall, Harrop and Suwal.

The Chinese lies were exposed when Jack Henson, in New Delhi, produced my scribbled note, carried over the Himalaya by Koila, which specifically stated that we had been captured. In the House of Commons, Welsh MPs demanded that the British government do all in its power to obtain the release of the three members of the first Welsh

Himalayan Expedition. My MP Peter Thomas was very active on our behalf.

By now Peking must have realised that if they did not obtain a confession from us, they would very soon have to yield to international pressure and release us. It was therefore essential that the Boys from Gartok obtain a confession as soon as possible. Once that confession was in the bag, the contents would be released to the world and Harrop, Damodar and I could be convicted of espionage and given harsh prison sentences.

Our major ally in the struggle for freedom, although I was not aware of the fact until some weeks after our release, was the Indian government. India at that time was canvassing for China to be given a seat at the United Nations, and India advised that arresting and imprisoning innocent Himalayan explorers could do China's case for a seat in the UN considerable harm. In the Indian army those who knew the facts were quite wisely keeping their heads below the parapet. Nobody told Krishan Menon or Nehru that I was an unpaid agent of Indian Military Intelligence.

I was now in full possession, as were Harrop and Damodar, of the answers each of us had given to the Boys from Gartok, and thus felt better equipped for the next question and answer session. Later in the day Schickelgruber indicated that I had been invited to spend the afternoon with the Taklakot Concert Party, and off over the Karnali river I went.

It was the same procedure as before. Offered a chair, and told, 'Hello, you must sit on the floor.'

After an interminable load of questions which went over old ground, trying to catch me out, and after declining to sign a confession, I was again subjected to the game of Chinese Roulette with the ubiquitous PPSh assault rifle. It still shook me, but I kept silent and tried not to show any emotion.

The Pheasant Plucker spoke to Smoothy, and Smoothy turned to me. 'This is your last chance. You will tell us the truth now, or very unpleasant things will happen to you. You will never see your wife and son again. Now speak the truth.'

I stared Smoothy in the face and said,

> The isles of Greece the isles of Greece,
> Where burning Sappho loved and sung,
> Where grew the arts of war and peace,
> Where Delos rose and Phoebus sprung,
> Eternal summers gild them yet and all
> Except their sun is set.

I followed this with, 'In Xanadu did Kubla Khan a stately pleasure-dome decree, where Alf my nextdoor neighbour ran through caverns measureless to man, down to a sunless sea.'

'What is that you are saying? I do not understand you,' Smoothy bellowed at me.

I continued: 'A king sat on a rocky brow o'erlooking sea borne Salamis.' I was of course quoting Byron and Coleridge from our paperback copy of *The Century of Poetry from Pope to Keats*.

I could manage the whole of 'Don Juan', and also parts of Gray's 'Elegy Written in a Country Churchyard'. 'The Rime of the Ancient Mariner' was not a complete success simply because Harrop had the second half of the book, and me the first. Smoothy could not for the life of him figure out what a 'painted ship upon a painted ocean' had to do with espionage and Tibet.

'Is it a code?' He shouted at me.

'Brilliant, old chap,' I responded. That was something that had not occurred to me. 'Yes. You want the truth. Well, I've had enough. I will tell you the facts. But I want some concessions. I want sugar, and a few cigarettes for John Harrop. I also want some nice home-made bread. I would also like to see some meat on my plate. And I'm fed up being by myself. Put the three of us back in the same cell, and I will reveal all to you.'

Smoothy conferred with the rest of the committee. 'If your information is genuine, you will have your concessions.'

'What I have been reciting to you,' I said, 'are a string of coded or encyphered signals, to be distributed amongst the illegal spying operations called Himalayan expeditions.'

'Who were you to pass them on to?' Smoothy enquired.

'You fouled all that up,' I responded. 'When you took us at gunpoint in the Jung Jung Khola, we were only two days away from meeting a high-ranking CIA officer. He was to be found in the caves near Phrupa's village of Khatang.'

'Describe this Western Fascist Lackey Imperalist Running Dog,' Smoothy insisted.

'Sorry. I have no idea what he looks like, but his name is – ' I had to make something up in a hurry – 'Brown, Charles Brown.'

'Then there has to be a code sign. A secret sign. What is it?' Smoothy continued.

I had to think of something fast and also plausible. I came up with the Welsh rubgy player's equivalent to the 'Sailor's Farewell'. 'Keep passing to the left, Boyo,' I said.

Smoothy wrote this down. Then he looked up. 'You will now repeat to us all the coded messages you learned. You will pass them to us, but first, how do we decypher these messages?'

'That's something I can't answer. You see I'm only a very small cog in a very big wheel. I just carry messages. I have no idea what the contents are. I was supposed to collect similar messages from this CIA spy and carry them back over the Urai Lekh, through Nepal, to India.'

And so, at Smoothy's behest, I had a very quiet afternoon, and for several hours I repeated my poetry very slowly, so that Smoothy could translate it to the Bookworm, who laboriously scribbled it all down in his little book. It was a pleasant change from Chinese Roulette.

When I ran out of remembered poetry, I threw in what few lines from Shakespeare I remembered from my school days. I shrank back from uttering, 'God for Harry, England and St George,' in case it sounded too chauvinistically British.

'We shall see what concessions you can have,' Smoothy commented as he signalled my two guards to escort me back to my cell.

I arrived back just as an old Tibetan, accompanied by a young boy, delivered a load of dead juniper firewood. They argued with Schickelgruber about the price, and the latter cuffed the boy over the ear, and pushed the old gentleman forcefully through the door and out of the yard. Later a concentration of troops came marching along the track which passed to the east of the Taklakot ridge. They had come from the Lhasa track, and I presumed that they were from that secret encampment. Marlo was standing on the roof, and when he saw me staring at the troops, he shouted for Lofty to send me, Harrop and Damodar indoors. But not before I had estimated that there were four or five hundred PLA men. Most were on foot, some on mules. I saw heavy and light machine guns and also mortars packed on some of the mules.

That night we were served with the most awful meal of rubbery yak intestines, and a small amount of rice, all smothered in throat-searing chillies. Quite obviously my plea for concessions, with an emphasis on better food, was to be ignored. Our guards dined off the sheep that had been so cruelly treated and killed the night before.

Then something very strange happened. Schickelgruber came into my cell. I had made notes about the passing of that troop concentration, and fortunately had thrust it down the inflation tube of my air-mattress pillow just before our sergeant of the guards walked in. Schickelgruber ordered me out of my cell and to my surprise he seized hold of my inflated air-mattress and sleeping bag, and went off with them. I followed him. I was amazed when he walked into Harrop's cell, our original communal cell, and threw my gear down on the floor. My ruse had worked to a degree. Damodar's personal belongings joined mine. We were no longer to be held in solitary confinement.

'Who the blazes do we have to thank for this?' a surprised Harrop enquired.

'I am not quite sure,' I replied. 'Could be thanks are due to Lord Byron, or Coleridge, Dean Swift, or even the Bard of Avon. What about swapping halves of that book of poetry? It's the hottest piece of espionage intelligence in west Tibet right now.' I then recounted to my colleagues what had transpired. We all had a good laugh at the expense of the Cheenee Burra Rajah Sahib.

We went out into the yard to have a mug of tea to celebrate our renewed and very welcome close association. Our guards caught the mood, and insisted that I give another performance of 'Burlington Bertie', and I was happy to oblige.

That night we had much to discuss. We debated all the permutations of what could happen to us, and how long the Chinese might hold us in detention. The most optimistic estimate was three to five years. We had to get out. Burrowing out through the mud brick wall would not have given us any great difficulty. We had our camp knife-fork-spoon sets, and we practised on the adobe style wall. It was like digging into chalk. 'A piece of cake,' Harrop commented. But it was out of the question. Our guards were changed every two hours, and while we were conversing, Fatty entered our cell with a can of oil for the tiny hurricane lamp. There was no way that we could dig through that wall and not be seen doing it.

There was only one answer. We had to disarm a guard, in the middle of the night. Once that was done, Damodar, being the smallest, and of about the same height and size as most of our guards, could wear the guard's uniform, basketball boots and cap, and carry the guard's assault rifle. We could make it look as though Harrop and I were being conducted past Taklakot by a Chinese soldier. We would have to wait until one guard went off duty, and the next guard arrived for his spell of sentry detail. We would give the departed soldier half an hour to bed down and get to sleep, and then create a situation that would draw a guard into our cell, where we would have to render him unconscious and then make our break.

Once out of the prison, under cover of darkness, we would have to proceed at the double, past Taklakot, and south-west to the Indian frontier avoiding any border guards stationed in the vicinity of the pass. It could not be more than ten miles to the Lipu Lekh pass, and we would have one and a half hour's start on the Chinese, before the next guard came on duty, and looked for his missing predecessor.

But which of our seven guards would we slug over the head? The problem was complicated by the fact that only two guards did not train weapons on us when entering our cells, and they were Chungnya and his equally pleasant young comrade-in-arms, Chubby. The most vulnerable of all had to be Chungnya. Whenever he had entered my cell in the past, he had always laid his gun to one side, or stood it against the wall, and sat on the side of my bed. So that was it then. It had to be Chungnya. But who was to strike the blow?

The answer to that problem was painfully obvious. Chungnya was most relaxed in my company. I would have to crack the skull of the nicest Chinese soldier in the whole of Tibet. What about a weapon? Harrop already had that sorted out. 'I picked this up in the kitchen area,' he said. 'It's the round stone the Chinese use for grinding their rock salt.' The proposed weapon weighed about five pounds, and it was an almost perfectly rounded river washed pebble. 'The buggers have missed it. They keep arguing about who last used it,' Harrop commented. 'I hid it on top of that beam that holds up the middle of the roof.'

We kept putting off that awful decision for the next two weeks until, unable to stand the constant suspense, we agreed that the first night that Chungnya came on duty, if it was about two or three a.m. when he came into our cell, which he always did, I would pretend to wake up, and Chungnya would probably sit on the edge of my air mattress. I would have the rock contained in a woollen climbing sock, and when Chungnya was looking the other way, I would swing the rock through the air, and bring it down on his skull. I had no idea what amount of force would be required to render a man unconscious, but not kill him.

The fateful night arrived. We were in our beds at 6 p.m. Chungnya replaced Marlo as duty-guard at about two in the morning. Our Chinese friend entered our cell. He could see by the light of the small hurricane lamp that I was awake. I sat up in my sleeping bag. Harrop and Damodar snored so effectively, I was afraid that Chungnya would rumble to the fact that they were only playing possum. Chungnya sat on my bed, and taking a ballpoint pen out of his pocket, he wrote something on the rubberised cloth of my air mattress, and then he pointed to his nose.

I looked down at what he had written. It was not in Chinese calligraphy, and I read 'Sun Tian sun'. Chungnya was confiding to me his real name, something he and all the other guards were forbidden by their superiors to do. I was deeply touched by this. When I read the words aloud he grinned broadly and said, 'Chid, yappa do.'

A Tibetan mastiff dog howled outside our prison gate. Chungnya turned to look in that direction. The moment had come. I clutched the sock and felt the weight of that lethal rock. I pulled the primitive weapon out of my sleeping bag with my right hand. I swung it up in the air. Chungnya's back was to me. and then I slowly lowered my 'skull-cracker' and hid it back in my sleeping bag. I just could not do it. Not even for freedom. Not even to save the three of us from perhaps twenty years in prison. Chungnya turned, and made doggy-howling noises, and we both laughed. Then Chungnya picked up his rifle and departed.

In a moment he was back, and bending down, his Indian ballpoint pen in hand, he laboriously and very carefully blacked out the words Sun Tian-sun he had earlier written on my air mattress. Placing a forefinger to his lips, he pointed to the wall that divided our communal cell from the guardroom. I knew what he meant. He did not want Sergeant Schickelgruber to know that he had revealed his true identity to a Foreign Devil. Then he was gone.

Harrop and Damodar turned over in their sleeping bags.

'Sorry. I just could not do it,' I said, as I fought back tears. 'He's much too decent a chap.'

'I know, I know,' Harrop responded. 'I agree. How the hell could we have lived with ourselves if we had killed Chungnya?'

'I know his real name,' I muttered through my tears. 'I'll tell you tomorrow.'

'Would not have worked, would it, Syd Sahib?' Damodar suggested none too convincingly.

'No,' Harrop agreed. 'Forgotten factor we did not take into consideration. Those bloody Tibetan mastiff dogs they let loose at night. They raise one hell of a racket every time anyone passes by. Give you a nasty nip on the ankles. The noise they would make would wake the dead.'

'And possibly might bite our balls off,' said Damodar, in an effort to cheer me up.

'What about a good old sing-song?' Harrop suggested.

I realised that they were trying to jolly me along. Harrop was not to be put off, and so first he, then Damodar, and then I went into that most moving of poems, William Blake's 'Jerusalem'.

'And did those feet in ancient times, walk upon England's pastures green?'

Chungnya stuck his face against the slatted metal bars of our cell window and grinned at us. We sang louder and louder. Eventually there were cries of complaint from the guardroom next door. We were spoiling the sleep of the PLA. Nothing daunted, we continued, now in full voice. Words I had half forgotten since my school days, but which were contained in our paperback book of poetry.

Our voices echoed off the cliff face behind the prison, almost loud enough to wake the dead, or even detonate those landmines planted just to the rear of our cell. Tibetan mastiff dogs joined in the chorus, howling and baying, as we sang the final words: 'Till we have built Jerusalem in England's green and pleasant land.'

The fine sunny days became less frequent. The winter sky was now often overcast and the great range of mountains that stood between us and Nepal was screened with snow-bearing clouds.

We were looking at it one morning when Harrop said, 'Thank God we won't be going back over the Urai Lekh, and through the Seti Gorge. I don't much fancy that place in winter. When they decide to release us let's return over the Lipu Lekh into India.'

The 18,482-foot-high Urai Lekh pass had never been traversed at this time of the year. Happily, we thought, it was not for us. We were to discover that the military governor of Tibet, General Pheasant Plucker, had ideas of his own on that matter.

Schickelgruber and Fatty never adopted the more liberal attitude of some of our guards. Fatty always made a point of closing the yard door whenever he saw us looking through it. We were never allowed to go anywhere near the yard door when it was unlocked. We discovered that if we paid no attention to what was happening outside, Schickelgruber and Fatty did not mind the door remaining open, so just to annoy them, we made a point of staring fixedly and intently through the doorway as if something of great importance claimed our interest. We always did this whenever Fatty or Schickelgruber was on the roof, on guard duty. They would leave their rooftop perch, climb down and peer outside, and after favouring us with a hostile look, they would close and lock the yard door.

We made a point of pulling this trick whenever one of the other unpleasant guards such as Marlo went down to the Karnali river to fetch water for the prison kitchen. The water was carried in two four-gallon mustard-oil cans, suspended on either end of a pole carried across the shoulders. The load must have been close on ninety pounds in weight, and it was quite a haul up the steep slope from the river bank. When the water wallah arrived back, he found the yard gate shut and locked on the inside, and he would shout and curse at the guard on the roof, who had to come down and unlock the door. Day in, day out, we repeated this joke. It gave us something to do.

The weekly slaughtering of sheep and yaks took place over a two-day period, Saturday and Sunday. Standing urinating in the lavatory area, I could see this victualling process going on. Chinese troop strength in the Taklakot area: did not Singh and Cricket Wallah ask me to try to ascertain the strength of the PLA? As there was at that time no wheeled transport in the vicinity of Taklakot, all sheep and goats slaughtered could only be for the consumption of local troops. Our guards were provided with one sheep per week. There were seven guards and we three prisoners, and that made a total of ten. We enjoyed little of the mutton, but our guards ate more than a reasonable fill. Ergo, one dead sheep fed ten PLA soldiers for a week. I presumed that the sheep and animals killed at Taklakot must have been for the consumption of not only the local garrison, but also for the larger encampment of troops at that secret base twenty-three miles from Jitkot. I had totted up more than a hundred dead sheep, and twenty-five yaks, when Marlo, up on the roof, ordered me out of the lavatory area. I sat by Harrop in the yard.

'I would like to know how many sheep there are, tethered waiting for slaughter, just to the left of the Chinese who are cutting up carcasses and cleaning out viscera,' I said. 'Marlo shooed me away. You have a go.'

Harrop went into the toilet area. He was back within a few minutes. 'Didn't count the dead ones. But there must be about three hundred sheep awaiting slaughter.'

'Well done,' I said, congratulating him. 'How did you manage to do it so fast?'

'Just simple mathematics,' Harrop responded. 'You count the legs and divide by four.'

Hearts, liver, kidneys and intestines were cooked on the spot by the river bank in huge cauldrons, and the usual crowd of Tibetans, both children and adults, stood around, hoping for a scrap of meat to be thrown their way.

I called to Shickelgruber, and drew a picture of a sheep in the dust with my forefinger, and rubbing my tummy I said, 'Yummy, yummy,' which of course he did not understand. I tried another tack, using Tibetan words with which he was well acquainted. I said, 'Mumbo mumbo, yappa do,' meaning, 'Lots of it, very good,' and again pointed to my crude drawing of a sheep. Schickelgruber pointed to the sheep's eyes on my drawing and rubbed his stomach.

'Oh yes, I know you like sheep's eyes, you disgusting sod,' I said to his face. 'And much tastier if they are from a living and not a dead sheep.'

Schickelgruber grinned at me. I pointed to the sheep, and raised one finger, and then to its eyes, and raised two fingers. Schickelgruber nodded. I pointed across the river and raised my hands in the air, as if something mystified me. Schickelgruber caught on at once, for was not the Foreign Devil referring to that favourite snack, the eyeball? He walked over to the firing-step, and then to my complete surprise called me over to join him. I did so. He looked across the river, and pointed to the sheep, and then bending down scratched the Arabic numerals 380 in the dust. He then pointed to the yaks, and wrote 60 in the dust.

He grinned at me, again patting his stomach. I grinned back at him, and thanked him, saying, 'That's just what I wanted to know, you stupid Chinese communist bastard.'

I rejoined Harrop. He spoke before I could get the words out of my mouth. 'Come on, what did he tell you?'

'Nearly four hundred sheep and sixty yaks. That's once a week, on a Saturday and Sunday.'

Harrop's mind, that of the agricultural scientist, was not tuned to the same wavelength as mine. He said, 'At that rate, they are consuming Tibetan livestock at an irreplaceable rate. The local Tibetans will soon starve to death. The Chinese are destroying the entire economy of the greater Taklakot area. They take all the yaks and sheep and they take all the juniper firewood. I've seen up to eighty yaks carrying firewood, herded along by PLA soldiers. They are stripping away all the Tibetans' winter fuel to supply their lousy army of occupation. The price they pay the Tibetans for their home-grown barley is so low and uneconomic, the people have ceased farming. I predict famine, and starvation for the Tibetan people. The Chinese are blood suckers.'

I had other matters on my mind. The original Indian estimate of 200 Chinese at Taklakot, and Perimal's estimate of 2,000, were both gross underestimates. The weekly slaughter of sheep and yaks suggested a Chinese troop strength in the area of around 5,000 to 6,000 PLA soldiers.

Whenever I found the answer to a question, the answer in itself raised further questions. It was perfectly obvious that 6,000 Chinese could not be concealed at Taklakot. But why kill the sheep and yaks here? Why not drive them to the secret encampment which must be about seventeen miles away? I watched the Chinese throwing yak and sheep skins and hooves in the Karnali. The answer must be that the other PLA army base was not close to a river such as the Karnali, which was ideal for waste disposal. But the Chinese must have water. From this I surmised that the secret base was close by a suitable water supply such as the sacred lake of Manasarowar, or a stream flowing into it. This would place that base en route to the Lhasa-Ladakh track, and it provided confirmation of why the Chinese were now turning back Indian pilgrims who had to take that route to the holy mountain Kailas.

I now had in my possession three important items of intelligence my Indian contacts required. There was a fourth, and I deemed that just about impossible to ascertain, and that was, when the Strategic Military Highway to west Tibet would be completed.

15

Schickelgruber tapped me on the shoulder, and pointed across the river. 'Here we go again,' I said to myself as I set off, two guards marching behind me, their assault rifles pointed at the small of my back. I entered the courtyard of the red building and pulled aside the curtain. It was just like going home. I was getting used to the place. But this time, I had prepared my own question and answer session, and was well prepared for my forthcoming interrogation.

It was the same as before. I was offered a chair. When I reached for it, it was snatched away and Smoothy would shout 'Hello. You must sit on the floor.'

I waited for the usual few minutes' silence, and then at a signal from Smoothy, both guards showed me their fully loaded PPSh magazines, and slid them into the loading gates of their weapons, awaiting the expected order.

'You must answer more honestly when you are in our house. We have some very serious questions for you. You must confess all to this investigating committee of the People's Republic of China.'

I said nothing.

'Now we wish to know what the code-breaking key is for the book codes you told us at your recent interrogation.'

'I don't know the key. I told you. I was just carrying the messages for the CIA spymaster whom I should have met in the caves at Khatang.'

'What you say is a lie. You must answer more honestly.'

'The code-key. Could it be that phrase you said you were to use as a watch-word, or call-sign, when you met that American Charles Brown in the Khatang caves?'

'You mean, Keep passing to the left, Boyo?' I enquired.

At this the governor, old Pheasant Plucker himself, had a try at English, and cut in with, 'Gepp pizzin to the leff, Boy-oh.'

'But not into my right boot, please,' I muttered to myself as I started to smile. I expected a thump over the ear from a PPSh muzzle for my facetious facial expression, but the Boys from Gartok took my half-smile as a mark of my approbation for the Pheasant Plucker's attempt at a colloquial Welsh rugby farewell.

Then Smoothy threw what he thought was a fast ball. 'Who is the big leader of the British Communist Party?' I thought hard for a second and said, 'Harry Pollit.'

To my amazement, the entire committee chanted, 'Arreepollit, Arrippollit,' and their faces again broke into smiles. I breathed a sigh of relief. I wasn't all that sure of my facts.

'Who is the big leader of the CIA?' Smoothy asked.

'Same man I mentioned before,' I said. 'Allen Dulles.'

'What you say is a lie,' Smoothy snarled at me. 'You are trying to disguise the truth. John Foster Dulles is the big leader of the American Fascist Lackey Imperialist Running Dog CIA. Does your CIA sypmaster Charles Brown also control the Western Fascist Lackey Imperialist Running Dog espionage service of Hindustan?' Smoothy further enquired.

'Hardly,' I responded. 'India is an independent country. The Americans have no say in Indian foreign policy, nor do they in any way control India's secret service.'

'Again you lie,' Smoothy shouted. 'Hindustan Prime Minister Nehru is a running dog of the Americans.'

I could hardly believe my ears. 'But China and India signed a treaty last year. It was negotiated between your Foreign Minister Chou En-lai and India's Krishna Menon.' Smoothy conveyed my answer to the Boys from Gartok. 'Part of what you say is true. Krishna Menon is a true friend of communist China. He is anti-colonialist and anti-imperialist, just like communist China. But Nehru has fallen under the influence of the Western Imperialists.'

Smoothy ordered one of my guards to enjoy a little Chinese Roulette, and again I tried not to show any emotion when the bolt of the PPSh clacked home into that empty chamber.

'Now we want to question you about those cylinders of Uranium 235. We have been in contact with our superiors in China, and they say that cylinders filled with Uranium 235 could not serve any useful purpose. Could it be that the cylinders contained something else as well as the Uranium 235, and that you are concealing this information from us?'

I had to think fast. 'You will be aware,' I said, 'that Uranium 235 is an energy source. Yes?'

Smoothy nodded his head, and spoke to the Bookworm, who scribbled away in his exercise book. The scribbling gave me time to think of my next move. 'Come on, Wignall,' I said to myself. 'Pull your ruddy finger out.' Then I hit pure form, and told the biggest and most convincing pack of lies imaginable. 'You have a huge army in Tibet. You have aircraft flying into and out of Tibet. You have what you believe to be secret bases. Nothing is secret now. I had a few drinks with one of the scientists who worked on that device that now lies on the summit of Mount Everest. In his cups he told me a little of what is going on. Electric batteries have a short life. They run down. The Americans have invented a system whereby the low-powered electric current required for high-powered long-range surveillance apparatus can be supplied from a small generator which is powered by Uranium 235. So you see, the Uranium 235 is not the most important part of that package of electronics Ed Hillary and Tenzing left on the summit of Everest. It's just the power source.'

It took Smoothy and the Bookworm some time to translate all this from English into jargon understandable to the others. The Boys from Gartok all had serious looks on their faces. At last, this cold-hearted diabolical Anglo-American espionage operation was to be laid bare.

'What is the range of this machine?' Smoothy enquired. 'How does it work?'

'I'll deal with the latter part first,' I said. 'I am not a scientist, I am an engineer. I don't know the technology, I just know what it can do.'

'Continue,' Smoothy demanded. 'What can it do?'

'Well, for starters, it can record the angle, and also the bearing and altitude and precise position of every Chinese aircraft flying within its range.'

'What is its range?' Smoothy demanded.

'This is going to make you unhappy,' I continued. 'Right across Tibet, all the way to Lop Nor and beyond. To the east as far as the Chinese mountain Minya Konka, and to the west as far as Kashmir and Ladakh, and the mountain Muztagh Ata.'

'Can this thing identify troops and trucks?' Smoothy further enquired.

'No problem,' I said, confirming his worst fears.

'How long will this machine last? When will its batteries need replacing?' Smoothy wanted to know.

'Never need replacing,' I said. 'The Uranium 235 energy source will ensure that the surveillance apparatus will work for a lifetime. No problems are envisaged unless the apparatus breaks down.'

'What will they do if it does break down?' Smoothy wanted to know.

'Lugging that thing up Everest was one hell of a task,' I said. 'I suppose that they may eventually take another one up Everest as a stand-by.'

'Do they intend placing any more of these surveillance machines on any other mountains?' Smoothy enquired.

'I don't know. I don't make policy,' I said.

This was not good enough. The Boys from Gartok had the bit between their teeth. They got on their feet, and I was once again Struggled Against. Six forefingers were pointed at me, as they screamed their combined heads off. I became weary of all this and, unable to think of a suitable epithet, I chose one that our guard Marlo used repeatedly; in fact he could hardly utter a sentence without including That Word. I pointed to the Pheasant Plucker and at the top of my voice I bellowed, 'Marlacapee.'

The chanting stopped. They all stared at me in disbelief. Then the sky quite literally opened up and the proverbial roof fell in. The Boys from Gartok yelled louder than ever, and their eyes appeared to bulge like organ stops. I received a couple of impolite thumps on the sides of my head with PPSh muzzles. My head was ringing. What the hell was it that I had said that upset the Boys from Gartok and the Pheasant Plucker so much? I had no idea.

It took them a long time to simmer down. Then Smoothy spoke: 'You have gravely insulted the most senior officer in the People's Liberation Army in Tibet. If you continue to insult us, and refuse to tell the truth, you will not leave Tibet alive. Now you must tell us where these other surveillance machines were to be placed.'

A moment earlier I had felt like a rat in a trap. But no longer. Now I saw my way out. 'Nalkankar,' I said. 'I was to meet Charlie Brown in the Khatang caves. He is not only CIA, he is also a top American scientist from Los Alamos. But he is not a mountaineer. I am not only a mountaineer, but as I told you when you first invited me to talk to you, I am also an engineer. Charlie Brown would deliver the apparatus to me, and I would take it to the top of Nalkankar, or better still, if we had been able to get past your border guards, the summit of Gurla Mandhata would have provided a better situation.'

'Where is this Gurla Mandhata?' Smoothy wanted to know.

'You are sitting right under it,' I said. 'This barracks of yours lies at the south-western foot of Gurla Mandhata. It's the highest mountain lying entirely in Tibet, it's over 25,000 feet high. You see, the height gives the apparatus extra range, so that it can see over the curvature of the earth.'

I was greatly relieved not to have Smoothy accuse me of lying, with a claim that the earth is flat.

'Look,' I said. 'I'm sorry if I upset the old boy. Didn't mean it really. Just got my rag out.'

Smoothy waited until Bookworm had scrivened away with all my data on the CIA-Los Alamos infernal long-range surveillance machine, and then he had a quiet word with the governor. The Pheasant Plucker nodded his agreement to whatever it was Smoothy had said, 'Can this machine really see that far? As far as Lop Nor?'

'Lop Nor was specifically mentioned in the design parameters of the apparatus,' I confirmed.

That appeared to do the trick. Smoothy signalled to my guards, and one of them opened up a steel chair, and offered it to me.

'No thanks,' I said. 'Thank you kindly, but I've played that game before.'

'Hello. Please sit on the chair,' Smoothy suggested. 'No harm will come to you. The general has accepted your apology, and we are pleased with the information you have given us. You have answered more honestly today.'

I proffered my thanks, and struggled to straighten my cramped legs. I then sat on the chair.

'You may have a cigarette,' Smoothy said, offering me one from a tin of fifty.

'No thank you. I don't smoke.'

'You may take some of these.' Smoothy offered me access to an open bowl of Indian sweets, each wrapped in paper. I took half a dozen, and unwrapped one. It wasn't half bad at that. Sticky and too sweet, perhaps, but a pleasant change from yak intestines.

'There must also be other stations where the American CIA plan to install these machines?' Smoothy suggested.

I decided to play along. But where oh where would the diabolically clever CIA place the damn things? Well, I thought to myself, if the CIA could place one on top of Gurla Mandhata, why not place others on peaks inside communist China? 'Minya Konka and Muztagh Ata,' I responded.

The Bookworm produced their battered copy of the Oxford atlas. I pointed out the situation of the two mountains. 'You see,' I said, 'from the summit of Muztagh Ata, one of these machines could look right across the Taklamakan Desert in Chinese Turkestan, to Lop Nor. The Americans would use a long-range bomber for such a trip, too far into Chinese territory for a manpowered expedition. They have facilities, the CIA, to fly out of Peshawar in Pakistan. For Minya Konka, in the east, the Americans would fly out of the airfield of Myitkyina, in Burma. They would fly low over the summit and drop the apparatus. The plan had to be abandoned due to the CIA's inability to guarantee pin-point accuracy and a soft landing for the highly expensive surveillance packages. The CIA practised drops on Mount Rainier in Washington State, and also on Mount Logan in Alaska. The failure rate was such that the idea was dropped.'

The CIA at that time was developing the U2 spy plane, which first flew out of Taiwan over China in 1961, five years after my release from imprisonment. At the time of my incarceration, hard intelligence data out of Tibet was hard to come by. Later US flights over Tibet photographed the Chinese atomic energy facility and nuclear weapons test site at Lop Nor, and collected samples of high-altitude irradiated dust immediately after the Chinese detonated their first nuclear weapon at Lop Nor in 1964.

My mention of Lop Nor must have caused fluttering in the dovecots in Peking. I had mentioned Lop Nor right off the top of my head. I continued, 'Now that the operation is blown, thanks to the alertness of the PLA here in west Tibet, the Nalkankar and Gurla Mandhata surveillance-apparatus locations will in all probability be abandoned. My best guess is that the CIA will have to stay with that one very important site on the summit of Mount Everest.'

Smoothy nodded. 'We have looked at your maps, and our atlas. We have found this Everest. This Western Imperialist piece of spy apparatus must be removed by the People's Liberation Army of the Republic of China,' Smoothy said.

'Well, it isn't as easy as all that,' I countered. 'Everest is more than 29,000 feet in height. You don't just walk up to the top. To aspire to climb the highest mountain in the Himalaya one must have a great many years' experience in rock and ice and snow mountaineering. It's a job for expert climbers, not infantrymen, regardless of how good soldiers they may be.'

Smoothy pondered on this and then deferred to the Pheasant Plucker. Their 'Party Group Meeting' must have gone on for about fifteen minutes. Then Smoothy spoke on behalf of all the Boys from Gartok. 'Comrade Mao has told us that we do not need formalistic Western ideas or expertise to attain just goals. This mountain Everest can be ascended by strict tactical application of the philosophy of Party Chairman Mao Tse-tung.'

'I only wish that I had been able to obtain a copy of the *Philosophy of Chairman Mao* when I started climbing more than ten years ago,' I told Smoothy. 'It would have saved me a great deal of trouble. It might have made life easier for me.'

'At that time, Comrade Mao was formulating his philosophy,' Smoothy said. 'You could not have benefited from Chairman Mao's wisdom at that time.'

I looked at the Pheasant Plucker. I could almost read his mind. He looked self-satisfied. I could hear him saying to himself, 'There might be promotions coming out of this.'

'Now,' said Smoothy. 'There is this letter in your belongings. It is from someone called Keki Bunshah, and he lives in Bombay. Tell us about him.'

I explained that Bunshah, a fellow member of the Himalayan Club, had been detailed to assist me in getting my expedition equipment through the Indian customs in Bombay and that I had invited him to come up to west Nepal and join my expedition.

'This Bunshah in his letter says that he plans to join you via the Tinkar Lipu pass into Tibet, and then travel via this place, Taklakot, to your illegal espionage headquarters in west Nepal, and that he is leaving his cameras behind to be sent on to him by runner. This Bunshah is obviously a Nehru Fascist Lackey Imperialist Running Dog Spy. According to the date on this letter, he should have passed through Taklakot weeks ago. We did not see him. What happened to him?'

I was delighted to learn that Keki Bunshah was not 'in the bag'. I learned later when I got back to India that his law practice had become overloaded with cases and he had been unable to join us. If Bunshah had arrived in Taklakot on the dates mentioned in his letter to me, he would undoubtedly have been in prison awaiting our arrival. After a great deal of arguing, Smoothy dropped the Keki Bunshah story. He accepted my explanation that as Bunshah had not turned up at Taklakot, he must have stayed home in Bombay.

'You have been much more honest this time,' Smoothy said, 'and when this valuable information about the CIA apparatus on top of this Chomolungma, this Everest, has been communicated to our authorities in China, we are going to recommend leniency for you, now that you have seen the error of your ways and are co-operating more fully with us. Now return to your room.' So off I went, secure in my mind that the most effective counter to the all pervading *Philosophy of Chairman Mao* was a combination of poetry and bullshit.

Back in our prison, Harrop was trying to copy out the flash on the breast of all the Chinese soldiers' tunics. There were several symbols and, unable to sketch them on paper in the presence of our guards, Harrop copied them one at a time on his left thumbnail with a pencil stub. Inside our cell, he redrew them on paper, one by one, and hid the paper in a crack in the cell wall. When it was completed, we slid it down the inflation tube of the pillow of my air mattress. Our hopes of having recorded a regimental insignia were to be dashed when we returned to India. The Chinese calligraphy simply read, 'People's Liberation Army of the Republic of China'.

There was evidently some kind of Chinese national holiday on 27 November, although what it was dedicated to we never discovered. Its importance was however brought home to us when some of our guards put on a clean shirt. Marlo even changed his long underwear.

Great effort was put into the preparation of dinner that afternoon. One by one we were conducted to the kitchen, and for our edification, Schickelgruber counted the number of courses on his fingers. There were noodles, eggs, pork scraps, mutton, dried shrimps, pin-sa bread cakes, mien-bo, a form of steamed dough, the old stand-by, turnips, peanuts, and other dishes we were unable to identify. Schickelgruber beamed all over his face. He was really putting on the dog, showing the Foreign Devils that communist China can outshine the Ritz when required to. PLA soldiers from other encampments kept dropping in to see what good things graced our menu. Chungnya was, fortunately, cook for the day, for he was the best cook out of our complement of seven guards. To display proper respect for food hygiene, he wore a cotton-gauze face-mask when busy in our kitchen.

I was doing my mental homework, stacking up my chronological dominoes. For my most recent interrogation to be transmitted and evaluated, and a response made to the Boys from Gartok, last night, 26 November would be just about right. This may have been a Chinese national day of some sort, but we prisoners had never before been allowed to share in any of the good things.

'They've bought my story,' I said to myself. 'Hook, line and bloody sinker.'

In the middle of the feast two strange guards came in bearing an old-fashioned wind-up gramophone. Lofty was Master of Ceremonies, and he set that diabolical scratchy-sounding contraption into operation. Half the records were devoted to Chinese military marches. The young soldiers were thrilled with this canned music and allowed their food to go cold, as open-mouthed, they watched the 78 rpm records spin round at an ungoverned 100 rpm or more.

The music was not to our taste, but the food was good, in fact it was excellent, and we stuffed ourselves with as much as we could hold. No limits were placed on our consumption by the guards. This was the sort of diet we needed to get our strength back for the trip over the Himalaya we hoped soon to make.

I added to the hilarity by trying to drum up a sign-language conversation with Marlo. I got nowhere. Eventually, all of our guards, plus about half a dozen visiting PLA soldiers were involved in my feeble efforts at communication. I wanted to know why the Pheasant Plucker had been so upset when I said 'Marlacapee' to him. I kept saying Marlacapee, and every time I said it the Chinese soldiers roared with laughter. Eventually young Chubby cottoned on. He turned his back to me, lowered his trousers, and bending over, pointed to his own posterior.

'You are not going to believe this,' I said to Harrop and Damodar, 'but I called the military governor of Tibet an arsehole.'

We had a good laugh over that one. It was at about this time that something struck a distant chord in my memory. That name, Charles Brown. Quite subconsciously I had given the Boys from Gartok the name of a character from an American comic strip, 'Peanuts', with Snoopy and Good Old Charlie Brown. I had a good snigger at this.

The following morning we breakfasted on scraps left over from the previous night's dinner. I took a lump of steam-baked dough and asked Chungnya to allow me into my old solitary confinement cell. He unlocked the door, willing to oblige, but unable to comprehend my purpose.

I pulled a stone out of the wall, and then another, until finally a snub-nosed tail-less rat appeared. I sat on the raised ramp on which my inflatable air mattress used to lie, and the rat climbed onto my knee. There was no doubting who this creature was. Only Megan had become that tame. I gave her a piece of bread, and she sat upright on my knee, munching away. Then the invasion began. As I noticed that Megan was no longer fat round the middle, her new family of tiny offspring emerged one by one out of the holes. They were little brown fellows, slightly lighter in colour than their mother. They would not venture too close, and I threw scraps of bread to them which, instead of eating on the premises, they treated as take-away food.

While all this was going on, Chungnya stood looking at me and my rats, shaking his head from side to side. He just could not comprehend what it is to be an animal lover. Eventually, my supply of bread almost exhausted, I picked Megan up and put her by the hole from which she had emerged. I then pushed a small piece of steam-bread into each of the other holes I had uncovered, and turned my back on my little Taklakot zoo.

Schickelgruber appeared carrying a book, and he sat against the wall, engrossed in it. After half an hour, he gave up reading, and Harrop politely indicated that he would like to have a read. Our sergeant handed Harrop the book. It was a Chinese-English dictionary and phrase book. Schickelgruber was trying to learn English, presumably to enable him to listen to our conversations. As Schickelgruber vanished inside the guardroom, something small fell out from between the pages of the book. Harrop placed his foot on it, and gave me a knowing wink. I recognised the green cotton-covered book as Smoothy's English dictionary.

Harrop eventually handed the book to Marlo. When nobody was looking, I picked up the tiny item. It was a postage stamp sized black and white picture of none other than our old friend Smoothy. I hid the minuscule photograph in my pocket until I returned to my cell, whereupon I again prised the back off my little mirror, and secreted the photograph of Smoothy inside it. That memento of Smoothy was eventually to cross the Himalaya with us, on our winter journey back to freedom. I have it still.

16

Harrop, who was no mean artist when it came to sketching landscapes or drawing portraits, decided as light relief to sketch his idealised version of a Chinese communist. He sketched a large fat pig, with a star on its forehead, surrounded by tiny starving Tibetans. Fatty snatched the drawing off Harrop, and took it in to Schickelgruber, who emerged from the guardroom, screaming his head off. Without more ado, he stormed off over the river to show the Boys from Gartok that Comrade John Harrop had not succumbed completely to the benefits of Thought Reform. Harrop was to hear more of the matter at his next interrogation.

One the morning of 10 December Harrop was duly marched over the river for further interrogation. I was sitting in the prison yard, enjoying a little sunshine when I heard a loud rumbling noise on the far river bank. I stood up and looked towards what I can only describe as a geological disturbance. Something nasty was happening up on the hillside above the red building. It was a landslide of sandstone boulders and rubble. Soon the hillside was enveloped in a cloud of dust. It swept over the red building and the grey barracks, and took several minutes to settle.

Eventually, his question and answer session over, Harrop returned to our prison. He was covered from head to foot in dust, and shook a cloud of it out of his shock of dark hair.

'Syd Sahib,' Damodar exclaimed. 'John Sahib has European cigarettes.'

This was one for the book. A few days earlier, I had come across Harrop and Damodar trying to roll their own cigarettes made up of Indian wrapping paper, scrounged off Chungnya, and used Chinese brick-tea, which consisted of leaves the size of fingernails. My two cigarette- addicted cell mates choked and coughed over their hand-made smokes, and had to give up.

'I hope you didn't sign anything to get those lousy cigs?' I ventured.

Harrop grinned, and pulled a tin of fifty cigarettes out of his pocket, shaking a dozen or so into Damodar's eager outstretched hands. I waited impatiently while they puffed away at their foul cigarettes, and finally I could no longer contain my impatience and curiosity.

'What the hell are you grinning for, like a Cheshire Cat? Come on, out with it.'

And so John Harrop told a tale, and halfway through he had both Damodar and me rolling about laughing. By the end of his story my merriment had subsided, and I gazed upon my prison companion with feelings of both pride and admiration.

The meeting had taken place out of doors, in the sunshine. Harrop was on this occasion allowed to sit on a steel chair. Two guards were assigned to stand either side of him, their assault rifles pointed at his head. The Gartok chorus-line seated at the other side of the table was the same one as before. The questions were also the same as before. And then suddenly, Smoothy sprang his surprise, producing Harrop's sketch of a fat pig with a star on its head, surrounded by starving miniature Tibetans.

'It is forbidden for you to draw pictures of your guards,' Smoothy bellowed at Harrop.

At this Harrop exploded with laughter, because there was nothing contained in his sketch that could in any way be associated with the PLA. He received a nudge on his right ear from a PPSh muzzle as a reward for his facetious behaviour.

The confession was pushed in front of Harrop several times, but he declined to sign it.

'Your big leader Wignall is a Western Fascist Lackey Imperialist Running Dog agent of the American CIA,' Smoothy informed Harrop. 'He has provided information which confirms what we have all along suspected. These Himalayan expeditions are really spy organisations, illegally occupying mountains to convert to CIA bases. We have discovered the political motive for these Western Imperialist missions, and the Chinese people, guided at all times by the philosophy of Chairman Mao, and assisted by the leading role of the Party, will use strategy and tactics to destroy these bases. Wignall is using you and Suwal as dupes, to cloak his imperialist operation in camouflage. You would do well to sign this simple confession.'

It was at that moment that Harrop heard a rumbling up on the cliff face. As a geologist, he had a feeling that something out of the ordinary was about to happen. 'I concentrate better over a cigarette,' he said to Smoothy.

'Then take this tin of English cigarettes,' Smoothy said, 'for it will confirm to you the generosity of the Chinese people.'

Harrop took the proffered tin of fifty cigarettes, and troubled one of his two guards for a light. The guard struck a match, and Harrop, displaying a hitherto unobserved element of greediness, lit three at once. He sat there, cross-legged, three cigarettes in mouth, puffing away quite happily, then in his own words, 'The bloody sky fell in.'

The avalanche of unstable sandstone conglomerate tumbled and roared down the cliff face behind the red building. The Boys from Gartok looked up, as did Harrop. He saw boulders the size of armchairs bouncing down the cliff face, accompanied by assorted rubble, from grapefruit-sized rocks down to pebbles and dust. A couple of bowler-hat-sized stones came over the yard wall and bounced on the ground, to burst and disintegrate. Then suddenly the cloud of dust enveloped the red building, its yard, the Boys from Gartok, Harrop and the entire proceedings. It took several minutes to settle, but when it did, Harrop found himself covered from head to foot in dust. He was still seated on his steel chair, puffing away at his three cigarettes. Of the Boys from Gartok there was no sign.

For this special occasion, the folding wooden table had been covered with a white tablecloth, and dishes of Indian sweetmeats, and bowls of tea had stood upon it. The whole was now covered in dust. Slowly, one by one, the Boys from Gartok showed their heads over the top of the table, emerging from their fraternal hiding place. They glared at Harrop, dusted off their seats, and were about to sit down when Ug-Lug saw where Harrop's two guards were hiding, and he screamed with rage. The rest of the Taklakot Entertainment Committee entered into a ranting 'Struggle Against' posture, pointing their right forefingers at Harrop's two guards, who were no longer armed, having dropped their PPSh assault rifles when the mountainside had descended upon them. Harrop looked down, and saw two khaki-clad Chinese backsides, one on either side of him, their owners' heads hidden under Harrop's chair.

Harrop, looking nonchalant, blew smoke rings up into the air, and then noticing that his trio of cigarettes had a layer of dust on them, blew the offending matter away.

When the committee had settled down, they glared at Harrop, because in his own words, 'The buggers lost face, and in front of a Foreign Devil at that.'

Harrop said that he thought that the Chinese would try to exact some form of revenge on us for their loss of face. He was to be proved right. But now he continued his story. He had handed Smoothy a letter addressed to his parents in the UK with a request that the Chinese send it to England over the Lipu Lekh via one of the Indian traders.

'There are no longer any Indian traders at Taklakot,' Smoothy rejoined. 'The trading season has ended and they have all returned to Hindustan. Besides, the Lipu Lekh pass into Hindustan is now closed for the winter.'

'If the Lipu Lekh is closed, then does that mean that both the Tinkar Lipu and the Urai Lekh into Nepal are also closed?' Harrop enquired.

'Yes,' Smoothy said, confirming Harrop's worst fears, 'All the passes between Tibet, Hindustan and Nepal are now closed due to heavy winter snow, until the spring of next year. When you leave here, it will be via China.'

Harrop then handed me a sheet of paper. 'They told me to hand you this, and you are to be given three minutes to sign it, it's your confession. You really should have confided in me, I didn't know that you were in the CIA. Any part-time jobs going?'

'I know what I would like to do with this,' I responded.

'Then why don't you do it?' Harrop replied with a laugh.

'All right, I will.' I took the sheet of paper and asked Schickelgruber for a pen. He produced a pencil. I signed the piece of paper, and ignoring Schickelgruber's outstretched hand I went into the lavatory enclosure, dropped my trousers, defecated, and then used the signed piece of paper, writing side uppermost, for the abstersion of my fundament. I threw the piece of paper down into the thunder hole, and hoisting up my pants, joined the others.

Schickelgruber bellowed an order, and Marlo and Fatty shoved me through the yard door back in the direction of the bridge over the Karnali. We were overtaken halfway across the bridge, by Shickelgruber, bearing my confession in his right hand.

The Boys from Gartok had taken the trouble to have Tibetan servants clean up the yard, and shake the dust off the no longer white tablecloth. There were no preliminaries now. No question and answer sessions on my name, age, address, my mother's address.

Smoothy launched into a tirade, waving my confession in my face. 'You have insulted the People's Liberation Army of the Republic of China,' he yelled at me. 'You have insulted this Committee of the Chinese Communist Party.' Then he quietened down. 'But at least you have signed your confession. You now admit that you are not Sydney Wignall, and you are in fact the CIA agent you told us you were to meet in the caves at Khatang. You have signed this confession with your real name, Charlie Brown.'

I shook my head. 'Good grief,' I said. 'I am not Charlie Brown. I am just a subordinate, and I sign his name on documents in his absence.'

Smoothy looked for his pen to write all this down in Chinese, but his pen was nowhere in sight.

'If you are looking for your pen,' I suggested, 'It's down there on the ground, under the table, where you dropped it when you were down there entertaining John Harrop.'

Smoothy glared at me, and bending down, retrieved his missing pen. I noted that he did not translate my last remarks to the other members of the committee, he had lost too much face already.

Then Smoothy delivered the bombshell. 'Now that you have signed your confession, that you, Charlie Brown, are the leader of an armed invasion of the territory of the People's Republic of China, and that you are the head of an illegal Western Fascist Lackey Imperialist Running Dog CIA group, wishing to illegally occupy the summits of mountains for the establishment of illegal surveillance apparatus, you will be released. But we also want another confession, the same as this one, but this time in the name of the alias that you have been using, that of Sydney Wignall.'

So I countered with, 'Give me a piece of paper and I will write out and sign my own confession.'

Smoothy beamed with undisguised pleasure and, handing me a piece of paper, chatted away to the rest of the Boys from Gartok. By now even Ug-Lug and the Pheasant Plucker were smiling.

I wrote as follows: 'If at any future date it is agreed between the governments of Nepal and Tibet that the place where Wignall, Harrop and Suwal were arrested is inside the frontiers of Tibet, then a formal apology for an accidental incursion over the Tibetan frontier will be made to the Chinese government representative in London. Signed, Sydney Wignall, 10 December 1955.'

Smoothy read it out to the others, shaking his head. To my surprise the Pheasant Plucker overruled Smoothy's objection that my confession under the name Wignall was unacceptable because it was conditional, and nodded his head. I had won. The only confession they had in their possession was in the name of an American comic-strip character. I was at that moment relieved that Smoothy had been educated in Shanghai (as he had informed me at an earlier interrogation) and not the USA.

Smoothy then produced a further confessional note, or rather it was more in the fashion of a Fodor's Guide testimonial. I read through it and smiled. It read:

I have so much enjoyed my stay with the representatives of the People's Republic of China, in the Tibetan province of China, I wish to place on record this my appreciation of their just and humane treatment of me and Harrop and Suwal, and I thank the People's Republic of China for the fine accommodation, and generous food rations given to us. It grieves me to leave my fraternal comrades of the People's Liberation Army of the Republic of China, and I salute the Great Helmsman Mao Tse-tung, and applaud the leading role the Communist Party has played in the reconstruction of the Chinese province of Tibet.

My mind boggled at the thought that grown-up people could not only write, but also believe in, such claptrap propaganda.

I shook my head. 'Sorry, no holiday-travel testimonials are to be had from me. I wouldn't recommend the accommodation to anyone. It's almost as bad as lodgings I once had in Scunthorpe.'

Smoothy could not comprehend my last remark, and he and the others accepted that they had got all they were going to get.

The Pheasant Plucker now stood up and made a lengthy speech, the substance of which was not translated for me, but everyone enjoyed the military governor's well-chosen few thousand words, so much so, they all on occasion applauded. I joined in the acclamation for the Pheasant Plucker's speechifying, and the entire Taklakot Entertainment Committee beamed at me whenever I applauded. As I smiled at the Pheasant Plucker he smiled back at me. When the speech was over, the Pheasant Plucker got a standing ovation, and I stood up and joined in the applause. True to form, the military governor also clapped, thereby applauding himself. I was not whacked with a gun muzzle for standing up, for this was a joyous occasion. The smiles, however, were soon to be wiped off my face.

When they had all settled down I raised a few points. 'Harrop says that you advised him that all three passes into Nepal and India are closed for the winter, and that we will have to travel back home via China. What are our travel arrangements?'

'You will not now go back through China,' Smoothy said. 'That is no longer necessary. You will go back over the Himalaya.' I realised why they had told Harrop that we would be going back via China. The China trip was for more professional interrogators to get their hands on us, to extract that much needed confession. Now that they had a confession, signed by Good Old Charlie Brown, they had completed their task. I realised at that moment that Koila and our other three porters must have got through to our expedition camp at Saipal, and that international pressure had been put on Peking to effect our release. Now that the Boys from Gartok had their confession, Peking could claim that we were in fact spies and that we had confessed.

But what of our fate now? Were they really planning to shove us over the Himalaya in December? I did not believe their story, told to Harrop, that the Lipu Lekh was closed. There are periods in the winter months when it must be possible to cross the 17,000-foot-high Lipu Lekh into India. 'You told Harrop earlier today that all the passes to the south, over the Himalaya, are closed for the winter,' I said.

'We just had information to the effect that one of the passes is now open.'

'That will be the Lipu Lekh, into India,' I responded. 'OK, we'll go back over the Lipu Lekh.'

Smoothy shook his head. 'No, the Lipu Lekh is closed.'

'The Tinkar Lipu, then,' I suggested. 'Once over it we could be on the Indian border and into the town of Garbyang within four days.'

Smoothy again shook his head. 'You will go back over the Urai Lekh. We have just learned that the Urai Lekh is once again open.' I knew that he was lying, and wondered what the motive was. It gradually dawned on me. There were two paramount reasons. One was that they had been made to lose face on several occasions, and for that we had to be punished. Another and more important reason was that I now knew too much about China's claims to large areas of territory bordering Tibet. When the Pheasant Plucker had pored over that atlas with me and uttered China's claims to chunks of Kashmir and Ladakh and the NEFA regions of India, he was under the impression that I would eventually be transported to China proper to serve a lengthy prison sentence, unable to communicate with the outside world until well after the Chinese embarked on their planned 'liberation' of parts of India.

I knew too much. If the authorities in Peking had realised at that time just how much I knew, I have little doubt that heads would have rolled in west Tibet, and the Pheasant Plucker would have been the most senior bird to have its neck wrung. So we had to be killed off, and the most convenient way to do that would be to send us back over the 18,482-foot-high Urai Lekh, and through the Seti Gorge, which the local Nepalese had on more than one occasion informed us had never been forced in winter.

'You will be released tomorrow,' Smoothy said, 'and we will give you sixty pounds of flour.'

'We can't survive on just plain flour,' I countered. 'We will need more than that to cross the Himalaya in winter.'

'We think that what we offer you is a very generous ration scale,' Smoothy replied.

'How the hell can we carry our gear, and a sack of flour?' I asked.

'We will let you have mules, and a military escort, and they will take you to the village of Khatang. There we will hire four porters for you, either from Khatang, or one of the many villages in the Jung Jung Khola.'

'The Urai Lekh is impassable at this time of the year,' I said. 'We will probably die of exposure up there.'

'Once you are released your lives are no longer our responsibility,' Smoothy reponded cold-bloodedly. The die was cast.

17

I entered the prison yard looking so troubled that Harrop thought our hopes of release had been disappointed. He was surprised when I said, 'We are going home tomorrow.' I gave Harrop and Damodar the bombshell a few moments later. 'They insist that we return over the Urai Lekh.'

Harrop and Damodar were incredulous. 'The Urai Lekh has never been crossed in December,' Harrop protested. 'They are going to deposit agricultural fertiliser on us, in an enormous quantity, and from a stupendous altitude.'

Damodar looked puzzled. I translated for him. 'What John is saying that the Chinese are going to shit on us, and from a great height.'

'The Seti Gorge, Syd Sahib,' Damodar said. 'When Koila and those porters returned to base camp from Dhuli with flour, they said that the Seti Gorge was swept by avalanches and was in a very dangerous condition. That was October, Syd Sahib. The Seti Gorge will be impassable now.'

'If we are to see the last of the lousy Chinese,' Harrop commented, 'then even the Urai Lekh and the Seti Gorge have their attractions, I suppose.'

Damodar crossed over to the lavatory wall to see what was claiming the attention of all seven of our guards, who were gazing towards the bridge. 'The officers are coming. They are coming here.'

This was a completely new departure, for not once during our incarceration had they visited our prison. They filed into the yard and nodded a greeting to Schickelgruber, who had run like a scalded hen to adopt his guard-duty position, assault rifle on his shoulder, at the door to our prison yard.

Food was on the go in the kitchen and it was soon produced. The officers sat cross-legged on the ground in a circle, and ate their food in the same way as the soldiers, picking food out of common bowls with their fingers, and either eating it direct or dunking it in chilli sauce. When they had finished eating we tackled Smoothy about food. We could not possibly cross the central Himalaya in winter on a diet of plain flour. After a great deal of argument he agreed that we could have a bag containing ten pounds of sugar. I remarked that we needed paraffin for our pressure stove, but Smoothy retorted that as we were being given a 'generous ration' of tsampa flour and tsampa does not require cooking, our need for paraffin was non-existent. As a sop he said that we could have one small piece of meat. Smoothy then offered the concession of a lump of Chinese tea in the form of a brick. It took too long to infuse at high altitude and I far from politely told him that he could stick it up his arse. I still had about two ounces of Indian tea left over from our expedition rations, which I had kept concealed in my sleeping bag. That would have to suffice for any tea parties we proposed to give on our journey back over the Himalaya.

I broached the question of porters. If we were to have four porters, the Chinese would have to recruit them from Taklakot. I explained that as Khatang was a small hamlet, Phrupa's family would not be able to furnish us with four able-bodied men.

Smoothy snorted in disgust. 'Khatang is a large town in the Chinese Autonomous Region of Tibet, and there will be ample labour available.' It was like talking to a brick wall. I gave up in disgust.

While all this was in progress, a detachment of soldiers strange to us brought in our previously confiscated kit. We were asked to examine it and sign a receipt. I regarded this as a farcical formality.

'Now you can have your cameras returned,' Smoothy said, 'but we must have the exposed films.'

Our cameras were stacked on the floor of the yard. I took up our 16 mm cine camera, wound up the motor and proceeded to run the film through the gate. 'Bang goes my lovely footage of Gurla Mandhata,' I said to myself. When I proceeded to open the back of the camera to extract the 100-foot spool of film, the Chinese officers backed away, and one of them shouted to our guards, who trained their rifles at us. I was flabbergasted.

'The silly buggers think that our cameras are booby trapped,' Harrop commented, winking at me, with a mischievous grin on his face. I watched with incredulity as Harrop opened the back of his 35 mm still camera without first winding on the film. Was he going to expose the film so that it would be of no value to the Chinese? I was wrong. He drew a pair of surgical scissors from his pocket, and cutting the film, withdrew the cassette which contained unexposed film, throwing it to the Chinese officers, who jumped aside and let it bounce off the prison yard floor. I cottoned on to Harrop's strategy. He would have lost some shots due to exposure to the light, but some might survive. It all happened so quickly. I bent down and fished inside our biscuit-tin camera-box, ostensibly for another 35 mm camera. I speedily grabbed an unexposed 35 mm cassette and making a semi-concealed attempt at opening one of my 35 mm cameras, threw an unexposed cassette to the Chinese.

It worked. No one was more surprised than I was. Now I realised why the Chinese had not opened our cameras and confiscated the film prior to bringing our cameras into the prison yard. They really did suspect that there could be explosive booby traps inside the mechanisms of our cameras.

Now came the crunch. Smoothy announced that we were to be subjected to a thorough body search. I peeled off my layers of clothes and stood shivering in my underwear. My garments were closely examined. I realised that the Chinese were looking for a written record. Having intended that we die of a combination of starvation and exposure on our journey back to Nepal, they wanted to assure themselves that if our bodies were discovered by Nepalese traders in the summer of the following year, no record of our interrogations and the Military Governor's gaffes would be found on our bodies. After me they searched Harrop and Damodar. Next came our gear. Our sleeping bags were turned inside out. Then came our inflatable rubber mattresses. My heart missed a beat. A Chinese officer picked mine up. It was still inflated. He pulled out the plug on the main body of the mattress and watched as the air whistled out. It must have sounded like music to him, because he cracked what was obviously a crude Chinese joke, pointing to his posterior. 'Smart arse,' I said to myself. The joke helped that inquisitive officer forget about any further investigation of my air mattress. With the pillow inflated, and all my pages of prison diary floating around inside it, he threw the mattress to the ground. I gave an audible sigh of relief.

'You lucky sod.' This from Harrop, in a stage whisper.

The officers departed. We were never to lay eyes on the Chinese military governor of Tibet, General Chang Kuo-hua, again. As they passed through the door of the prison yard, the governor spoke a few words to Smoothy. He smiled as he spoke. It was an icy smile. Smoothy turned to speak to me. He had a look on his face like the cat that ate all the cream. 'I am instructed to inform you that the People's Republic of China has only friendly feelings towards you, and we wish you a pleasant and happy journey back to your Hindustan CIA headquarters.'

The officer went back over the Tibetan cantilever bridge laughing at what they thought to be a huge joke. I watched them go with a determination that, come what may, we would win through, and when we did, the Cheenee Burra Rajah Sahib wold be laughing on the other side of his face. That night was to be the last we were to spend in that Chinese prison, and we celebrated in fine style. Chungnya brought in a really first-class meal which he had specially prepared for the occasion. Even Schickelgruber joined in and insisted on shaking hands with Harrop, Damodar and me. My two companions were plied with Chinese cigarettes and Chungnya handed me a bag of Indian sweetmeats he had purchased from one of the few remaining Indian traders at Taklakot.

Chungnya took away our paraffin can and returned with a smile. He had purchased half a gallon of paraffin from the Taklakot bazaar. I shuddered to think about the hole he had made in his minuscule Chinese army pay, just to help his two English and one Nepalese friends. The night was capped by a bottle of chang, Tibetan beer brewed from fermented barley, also purchased at the Taklakot bazaar. The chang was contained in a well finished Tibetan bottle of turned wood, bound with brass. It was thick milky stuff, slightly green in colour and all sorts of unidentified objects floated on the surface. After two drinks, neither Harrop nor I was any the worse for wear, but Damodar became decidedly merry. As Harrop had once remarked, Damodar would keel over at the smell of a cork.

Damodar stood up in his sleeping bag and attempted to execute what I can only describe as a Nepalese kangaroo dance, hopping around the cell, until he fell flat on his face. Harrop and I carried him to his corner of the room and laid him down to sleep. Schickelgruber said his farewells and left Harrop, Chungnya and me alone together. Chungnya kept grinning at us and saying 'Chid' and 'Jung'. I leaned forward and said 'Sun Tian-sun'. He frowned. So Harrop said 'Chungnya'. At that our friendly Chinese soldier grinned from ear to ear.

I drew a map of Europe, Asia Minor and part of Asia on the dust floor of our cell, using the tip of my fingers, and read off the countries Harrop and I had motored through on our way to India, Nepal and Tibet. I went through the motions of starting up an automobile, releasing the hand brake, putting it into gear, and steering my way through traffic.

Chungnya put his hand on my arm, and pointing to his nose said, 'Chungnya,' and then went through the motions of starting up a motorcycle and driving it. Harrop and I nodded. Then Chungnya repeated the performance, only this time demonstrating that he could drive a car. Neither Harrop nor I was prepared for what was about to follow. Chungnya pointed to his nose, then holding up his left hand, started to count off his fingers. When he had finished, he again pointed to his nose. Chungnya quite apparently was twenty-two years of age. Then he went through the motions of driving a car, and said, 'Chamdo, Lhasa, Taklakot,' followed by counting off on his fingers the numbers twenty-three and twenty-four. Grinning he pointed to the ground, and saying, 'Taklakot' he pulled on an imaginary handbrake and switched off an imaginary engine.

So there it was. Laid before me free, gratis, and for no effort at all: the date for the completion of the Strategic Military Highway to west Tibet. That road which bore such deadly portent for Nehru would be completed inside two years, and when the last load of stone ballast was packed into place, communist China would be able to place a huge well-trained and -equipped army within 250 miles of India's capital, New Delhi.

After Chungnya had slapped us both on the back and left us alone, Harrop and I discussed this vital piece of information into the early hours of the morning. We had little sleep that night, although Damodar slept like a dead man and snored like a ruptured hippopotamus. At daybreak, Harrop and I were up packing our gear. I was pleased to observe that not only had our cameras been returned, but also our cassettes of unexposed film. After a breakfast of tsampa and tea a Chinese officer arrived. He was new to us and was dressed in a voluminous padded PLA jacket and trousers which made him look like the Michelin man. We found him rather pleasant. As Harrop and I packed our rucksacks in the prison yard, Chungnya wound up the phonograph he and the other guards had borrowed from the officers' quarters and put on a Chinese marching tune. I used that musical interlude to deflate my air mattress and fold it up. I could feel the pages of my prison diary through the rubber outer skin. I tied the air mattress to the top of my rucksack and hoped for the best. It was now time to set off back in the direction of Jitkot Gompa, one-eyed Phrupa's village of Khatang, the Jung Jung Khola, the 18,482-foot-high Urai Lekh and, if we were able to cross that Himalayan watershed, the awful prospect of the Seti Gorge.

Our escort was to include the officer and a rather evil-looking little PLA soldier we immediately christened 'Runty' because of his small size. Runty had a furtive look about him, and displayed that obnoxious trait which is seen to surface in colourless mediocrities when power is placed in their hands. Runty would kick items of our equipment to one side as he passed by. He screamed at Harrop and me and made threatening gestures with his rifle.

Eventually, Harrop having had all he could take, pushed Runty's gun barrel to one side with his left hand, grabbed Runty's right ear and twisted hard. Runty let out a scream. The fat officer ordered our guards to release Runty from Harrop's vice-like grip. 'OK, I'll let go,' Harrop said. 'At least that nasty little sod will think twice about badgering us.'

I turned to Chungnya. He looked serious and shook his head. I realised that we had an enemy in Runty, who had been made to lose face. We were instructed via hand signals to get on our way. We were each allocated a mule, and two extra mules carried our porter loads which included our two Meade tents.

Our caravan consisted of Harrop, Damodar and me, the small fat officer and his batman Runty, plus Chungnya and Schickelgruber. The officer carried a pair of binoculars, and he and Schickelgruber had .32 calibre Chinese-manufactured semi-automatic pistols similar to the Walther PPK. Chungnya, Schickelgruber and Runty also carried the ubiquitous PPSh 7.65 mm assault rifle. I noticed a horse being brought up. It was a tiny off-white Tibetan pony, and this was mounted by the short fat officer. The poor creature could hardly carry his weight.

The trip back towards the Nepal border on that Chinese army mule was considerably more comfortable than the outward journey. We had Chinese military saddles, although the leather was worn, dried up, and would crack or break if any stress was put on it. My mule responded only to my jumping up and down yelling at the top of my voice. I galloped it round one of the huge hollowed out boulders of conglomerate which served as a home for a nearby Tibetan family, and Chungnya joined me in our impromptu Wild West display of far from competent riding. After several weeks cooped up in that tiny prison at Taklakot I was looking forward to the fifteen-mile ride to the village of Khatang, up in the foothills of the sacred snows of

Himachal. I looked to the south, and my heart chilled. The Himalayan divide was covered in cloud. That meant winter snow, and heavy snow could make the forcing of the Urai Lekh pass impossible. I tried not to think about that part of our journey, as we rode our mounts down to the Karnali river, and forded it to the other side. We rode along the east bank over river-washed stones, for the Karnali was no longer in flood because the monsoon season had ended and the waters had receded, leaving stretches of exposed river bed. I looked back towards the Taklakot ridge. I could see the huge lamasery plainly. The cave dwellings on the south-facing cliff were bedecked with Tibetan prayer flags. There was no sign of the tented Indian trader market.

I craned my neck to look backwards for a sign of our lost goal, Gurla Mandhata. For a fleeting moment the clouds cleared, and I could see part of the south-west ridge. Then it was gone, lost in grey swirling snow clouds. I concentrated on the route ahead. We recrossed the Karnali, the water here only a foot or so deep, and our mounts plodded up the bank onto the Jitkot-Taklakot track. After a few miles we passed through the tiny Tibetan hamlet of Marsha Kalya. Prayer flags fluttered from houses, from stupas, chortens and Mani walls. The unfeeling Chinese quite deliberately rode along the 'wrong side' of the Mani wall, presumably to offend the watching Tibetans. Harrop, Damodar and I also quite deliberately steered our mounts to the left hand, the correct side of the Mani walls. I bowed to the watching Tibetans, and they, solemn-faced, returned my greeting, which was repeated by Harrop and Damodar. Runty charged his mule at a group of watching Tibetan children and let out shouts of glee as he forced them to flee and hide behind rocks.

'They are no better than the rotten Nazis,' Harrop observed. I resolved to keep a close eye on Runty. He spelt trouble. Young and old Tibetans came out onto the track and they all bowed and salaamed their farewells, ignoring the Chinese. Runty, out of spite, forced the pack mules into a gallop and within seconds the loads were tumbling off the pack frames, rotten Chinese leather tack breaking in the process. More time was lost as the loads were retied. We suffered this performance twice. The crunch came when Runty galloped his mule past Harrop, and in passing whipped Harrop's pony's flanks, causing the animal to rear. John Harrop is a tall, heavily built and powerful man and, regardless of his weakened state due to two months' malnutrition, he was able to jump off his pony, and run after Runty, in an attempt to pull him off his mule and give him a good sock on the jaw. Runty screamed with fear and, dismounting, ran around his mule, eventually being cornered by Harrop up against a boulder. Regardless of the PPSh barrel sticking in his chest, Harrop grabbed him by the collar and shook him like a terrier shakes a rat. The little bully dropped his gun and yelled for help. Eventually he was saved from a well-deserved thrashing by the intervention of Chungnya and the fat officer. Harrop let go of Runty and, mounting his pony, wagged a finger in Runty's general direction. 'And next time, you creepy little Chinese sod, I'll break a couple of arms and legs.' And Harrop would have done it, too.

Damodar spoke next. 'We must be careful of that man, Syd Sahib. He is very dangerous. Please ask John Sahib not to thump him too hard.'

I was intrigued by the way that Chungnya and Schickelgruber gave disapproving looks in Runty's direction, and then broke into knowing grins when Runty bleated to the short fat officer about Harrop's beastly behaviour, and the fat officer patted his batman affectionately on the shoulder. I wondered if they were homosexual.

I dismounted, as did Damodar. We walked over and joined Harrop who by now was sitting on a rock, grinning all over his face. 'If we refuse to go on, we don't have to cross the lousy Urai Lekh,' he said.

'You want to spend the winter with the Chinese?' I enquired. It was obvious that by now, Chungnya and Schickelgruber had had enough of Runty's theatrical shenanigans, and they told the short fat officer so in no uncertain terms. The Chinese then sat on rocks and held what in Peking is called a 'Party Group Meeting'. Runty sat discomfited as he was 'Struggled Against'. Then we all remounted, and I presumed quite wrongly that we were not going to have any more trouble. We passed under the cliff-face at the top of which stood the towering walls of Jitkot lamasery. I reined in my mule and waited for Harrop to catch up with me.

'Let's have a try at going to see dear old Gin Din Rhou. We can thank the old boy for his advice and hospitality, and say our farewells.'

'I'll have a go with sign language,' Harrop suggested, only to be restrained by Damodar.

'I don't think that that would be a good idea, John Sahib. It could compromise Abbot Gin Din Rhou in the eyes of the Chinese. Before we left Jitkot, Gin Din Rhou told me that the Chinese were trying to discredit the Buddhist religion and planned to turn the people away from Buddhism. Gin Din Rhou said that he feared that all monks and lamas would eventually be imprisoned by the Chinese.'

I reflected for a moment. 'I think that we should defer to Damodar's wisdom, John. It's a great pity. I would have liked to have seen Gin Din Rhou just long enough to tell him that his attempts to instil spiritual strength into us had a sufficient degree of success for us to be able to withstand the threats of the Cheenee Burra Rajah Sahib.'

We steered our mounts past Jitkot lamasery, and the track wound its way up onto the plateau above. Ahead lay the foothills leading to Khatang valley. We gained height, and passed by a small Tibetan village not shown on the Indian Survey map. We toiled up the steep track. The going was awful, consisting of loose rocks which slid back under the mules' and horses' hooves. About a mile above the small village Chungnya held another 'Party Group Meeting' with the fat officer, Runty and Schickelgruber. Whatever the reason, they had problems coming to a decision. It appeared that Runty and the fat officer took a point of view opposed to that of our young friend Chungnya. Eventually, the fat officer shrugged his shoulders and signalled his acquiescence to Chungnya, who set off downhill, back in the direction of the village. We continued up the ridge.

I looked back now. The clouds to the north had cleared, and there was Gurla Mandhata in all its glory. I could clearly see the south-west ridge, which was split just to the west of the summit by a huge gash, one that had checked Dr Tom Longstaff's attempt by that route in 1905. The easily ascendable north-west ridge stood out clearly. I could see the notch in the ridge where we would have established camp. But I now had all the intelligence the Indian military required.

Turning to look east, I saw the summit of Nalkankar, that most mysterious of mountains. I was awakened from my reverie by a shout from Harrop. 'Look at what the silly sod has done now.' Runty had tried whipping a mule, and the animal had bucked and sent its load spilling onto the ground. Our billy can, in which we brewed tea or boiled soup, had gone tumbling down the khud. I reined my mule in and, to show willing, tried to assist Runty in retying the load. He growled at me and pointed down the gully to our billy can lying about fifty feet below, signalling me to go down and get it. I shook my head, and said, 'Up yours, chum.'

Runty started to become hysterical, screaming at me and prodding me in the chest with his rifle. I grabbed hold of the barrel of his gun; he took a step back, stumbled over a rock, and falling on his backside left me holding onto a loaded Chinese PPSh assault rifle. Back on his feet, he hung onto the butt end of the gun, with me gripping tight on the muzzle. I took a swing at him with my right fist, which did not connect because he hung back. I had a feeling that if he came forward far enough to get his finger on the trigger, I was a dead man. But he was too scared of my right fist, which was swinging past his face. Schickelgruber got between us, and poked his PPSh in my chest. The fat officer arrived on the scene, screaming in Chinese, but not daring to get involved in the fray. I let go of Runty's PPSh, and he made a further pratfall onto his back. Schickelgruber and the officer argued, as Schickelgruber hung onto the muzzle of Runty's gun, pointing it away from me.

To the astonishment of Harrop, Damodar and me, Schickelgruber was allowed to take possession of Runty's PPSh. Further loss of face for Runty. We were amazed at the almost instantaneous change in Runty's demeanour. Stripped of his symbol of authority, he became a whimpering coward, and made a point of keeping a respectable distance from us.

Damodar hit the nail on the head. 'I think that Runty was shouting that he was going to kill you, Syd Sahib. That's why the fat officer told Schickelgruber to take possession of Runty's gun.'

I had to concur. Chungnya caught up with us while the argument was still in progress. He was accompanied by a young Tibetan boy who was carrying a hand-woven sack. Smiling as always, he said, 'Tsampa.' The bag contained about fifteen pounds of tsampa, and a small piece of meat. The meat was perhaps sufficient for two meals for Harrop, Damodar and me for our week-long proposed journey over the backbone of the Himalaya. I smiled my thankful acknowledgement to Chungnya.

Harrop called out, 'Get a load of that.' The light was fading now, and Harrop was looking in the direction of Nalkankar. Great long white plumes of snow were being blown off the summit and the western ridge. 'It must be blowing seventy to a hundred miles an hour up there,' Harrop commented. 'I hope to Christ the Urai Lekh isn't going to be like that.'

I called to Chungnya. He turned round. I pointed to our billy can, lying about fifty feet down the gully to our left. Fat officer, Schickelgruber and Chungnya now turned on Runty and after an illustration of Chinese trial by hectoring, Runty, muttering under his breath, dismounted from his mule, and went down into the gully to collect the fallen item. It was obvious that he had been told that as he was the cause of all the problems, he could carry the can. We remounted and were on our way to Khatang; the young Tibetan boy tagging along behind on foot, carrying our rations for the march back to Nepal.

The going became steeper and my mule lagged behind the others. It also had a propensity for wandering off the track in search of clumps of thistles. Whacking the animal's flanks had little effect. My mule was both tired and half starved, its ribs showing through its skin. I dismounted and, leading my now lightened mount, caught up with the others. One by one they all dismounted, Harrop and Damodar first, Runty last. He had been whipping his mule unmercifully, until the fat officer called on him to desist.

We crested the pass. In the dim fading light I could see the cave dwellings, no longer occupied, in which Phrupa's ancestors had lived long before the village of Khatang was built. There were lights down below. Through the open doorway of two houses I could see the glimmer from yak-butter lamps. The Chinese remounted, but Harrop, Damodar and I elected to walk the remaining distance to Khatang. Schickelgruber's mule elbowed me off the track and I slithered for about fifty feet down the hillside. It was an accident, and everybody laughed except Runty, who glared as he whipped his mule past me.

18

It was pitch dark when we reached the village, and male members of Phrupa's family came out of their houses to help us unload our baggage animals. We entered the same dark passage and banged our heads on the same low beam as before. I now understood why the Chinese had sent the fat officer and Runty along. They were both fluent in Tibetan. Harrop, Damodar and I were shown into a room. It was so dark we could not see the walls, and Damodar fell over a Tibetan stool. Then Phrupa came in. He was holding a tiny yak-butter lamp, the light illuminated his lugubrious visage. Phrupa had the face of a Hollywood Fu Manchu screen villain, and his appearance was far from improved by his empty eye socket. But he wasn't a bad old geezer really. Harrop commented, 'With a face like that, old Phrupa could make a fortune haunting houses.'

We were then shown to our room for the night. In England it would have passed for a disused coal cellar. The walls were no more than five feet high, and we were unable to stand upright. The doorway was a 'hatch' and we had to almost crawl through it. The walls were covered with a thick layer of soot. We inflated our air mattresses and laid out our sleeping bags. Some young Tibetan boys carried in our kit and dumped it unceremoniously in the far corner of the room. This raised a cloud of soot and dust which sent the three of us scrambling for the door. The boys left us a small yak-butter lamp, which furnished us with a tiny smoky flame.

Old one-eyed Phrupa joined us. He held two small Indian paraffin lamps in his hands. He wanted some of our precious supply of paraffin. Damodar wisely suggested that in our present state, we needed at least one ally at Khatang. I filled up Phrupa's lamps and he expressed his gratitude. Next came Chungnya. He too had two small Indian oil lamps. Phrupa informed us that they belonged to the fat officer and he too wanted oil for his lamps. I watched our tiny supply of precious paraffin decrease further. I doubted if there were more than three days' supply for cooking the barest minimum of meals, and that for a seven- or eight-day march to the Nepalese village of Dhuli. Phrupa showed his gratitude by bringing in a large iron kettle filled with tea. A most welcome brew despite the addition of ginger and spices. I protested at this, to Harrop's comment of, 'You ungrateful beggar.' But old Phrupa was up to the challenge and within half an hour he returned with a kettle full of plain tea.

Our supper consisted of some of the tsampa Chungnya had bought for us. We ate in Tibetan style, mixing the tsampa flour with tea until a ball of dough was formed. I was of the opinion that a daily diet of Weetabix would not provide us with our nutritional requirements for that forthcoming hack back over the Himalaya. I reflected on Tilman's advice for our now failed attempt to clandestinely climb Gurla Mandhata. 'Work out your minimum ration requirements, and then reduce that by half. You will be hungry, but you will travel light and cover ground.' We were going to have to do just that, in spades.

Harrop opened up our small medicine box. 'How's your dysentery?'

'I haven't had a dose of the Tibetan Trots for a day or two,' I responded.

'Well,' Harrop continued. 'When the Chinese took your bottle of sulpha drugs, they failed to spot these. I have six sulpha pills in an unmarked bottle. If you take three a day for two days, you should be in better shape for that trip over the Urai Lekh and into the Seti Gorge. I suggest that I hang onto these for a day or two, just in case you start eating them like peanuts.'

I was delving into a box and to my surprise my hand closed on the butt of my trusty 7.65 mm Browning self-loading pistol. I drew it out and by the flickering yak-butter lamp, pointed it at Damodar. 'Look, got my pistol back, but no ammunition.'

Harrop was nonplussed. 'These people defy description. Didn't they interrogate you about that lousy pistol while we were in that filthy clink?'

'Never mentioned it once,' I replied. 'It puzzled me too. I fully expected that at every one of my "Thought Reform" sessions, that slimy sod Smoothy would ask me what harmless Himalayan explorers were doing carrying lethal weapons with them.'

'They appear to go by the book,' Harrop commented. 'The instructions for our release had to come from Peking. It would include confiscation of our exposed film, our diaries and our maps. And also our passports, but then again, surely they should have asked why two Englishmen and a Nepalese should find it necessary to carry passports when climbing a mountain. If Peking made no mention of your pistol, then it would not be on their local embargo list, and they would return it to you. And by the way, if it's not too inconvenient a question, why the hell did you carry a loaded automatic pistol for a clandestine mountain climb in Tibet?'

'I just felt comfortable with it in my front pocket,' I countered. 'You never know when we might have come across a marauding bear, a snow leopard, or even a voracious Yeti. Still, we will probably have problems if and when we cross the Nepalese frontier into India. The Taklakot Entertainment Committee took our passports. We have no real means of identification.'

'Chinese not take our passports, Syd Sahib,' Damodar interjected. 'Look here are all your documents and mine, and also your copy of the permit from Kathmandu to climb and explore in the Api-Nampa-Saipal ranges of Nepal.'

'Wonders will never cease,' Harrop said. With that we turned in.

At about 2 a.m. I woke up with a severe stomach cramp, and wandered out of the room by the light of my fading electric torch. Security was now lax, and the Chinese had all bedded down for the night, apparently of the opinion that as we were being released, there would be no point in us trying to escape. I located the ladder up to the roof and found the urinal. As at Jitkot Gompa, a room had been bricked up, and a hole cut in the roof.

I could see the faint outline of snow-clad peaks surrounding Khatang on three sides, their sharp summits silhouetted against a cloudless star-filled sky. On the roof, an old woman was snoring loudly under a pile of sheepskins, testifying to the hardiness of her race. Three little children shared her bed. They snuggled together for warmth, their pillow a log of wood.

Smoke rose out of a hole in the roof, and I bent down and looked inside. About a dozen members of Phrupa's family were seated around a tea cauldron. They invited me down. Squatting cross-legged in the circle of Tibetans I accepted a small wooden bowl of tea. The chattering stopped, yielding to a heavy and oppressive silence. This was totally unlike the Tibetans I had come to know, like and respect. They were usually full of gossip, and perpetually roaring with laughter at each other's jokes. Phrupa rose from his place in the circle and, retiring from the room, returned with Damodar, whom he had roused from his sleeping bag.

'Phrupa wants to talk to you now, Syd Sahib, while the Chinese are asleep.'

'Ask him why that old lady and three tiny tots are sleeping out in the open on the roof.'

Damodar translated for Phrupa. 'The Chinese evicted Phrupa and members of his family from their rooms to provide one room for each two Chinese and one for us three.'

'The miserable bastards,' I commented.

Damodar continued with the translation. 'Phrupa is worried because the Chinese may not obtain reliable men for your load carrying over the Urai Lekh. Phrupa thinks that the Chinese want you to die on the way back, otherwise they would have let you return to India over the Lipu Lekh. Phrupa also says that the Lipu Lekh is only a day's march from Taklakot, and he and other Tibetans know, from their conversations with Indian traders at Taklakot, that there is an Indian Army post just over the pass on the Indian side of the Lipu Lekh.'

'I guessed as much, Damodar. What about Koila and our porters?'

Damodar continued, 'Phrupa says that when Koila and our other three porters were released they were instructed by the Cheenee Burra Rajah Sahib what to say when they got back to Rajah Oom Jung at Chainpur.

They were told to say that the Tibetans were very happy living under Chinese rule, and that the Chinese paid for everything in silver coin and did not take anything from the Tibetans without paying for it, and that Koila was to say that he had seen tractors and other mechanical farm machinery that the Chinese have provided at no charge, to help the Tibetans improve their standard of living, and that the Tibetans love the Chinese communists and have rejected the lamaistic branch of the Buddhist faith, and have embraced Marxism voluntarily.'

'Fat chance of Koila saying that,' I countered. 'Koila will tell the truth exactly as he saw it.'

'That is what the Chinese suspected,' Damodar went on, 'and Koila talked about this to Phrupa. He told Phrupa that the Chinese threatened that if he and the other three porters did not do as the Chinese commanded, the Chinese would place an embargo on all trade coming over the Urai Lekh from Nepal.'

'What did Koila say he would do?' I enquired.

'Koila told Phrupa that he would have to do as the Chinese bid, for his livelihood depended on trade with Tibet, as did most of the people in Chainpur and Dhuli.'

'Tell Phrupa that I will square the matter with Rajah Oom Jung. I will tell him and the people of both Nepal and India, and the entire world what these bastards are doing to the people of Tibet, their religion and their culture.'

Damodar did as I asked, and all the Tibetans present grinned, and some came over to slap me on the back. But I had not finished.

'When we were at Saipal trading camp in Nepal, Damodar, and you asked on my behalf of the Tibetans there how they liked the Chinese, they all said that they liked the Chinese. I want the truth.'

Phrupa poured me a generous libation of chang rice wine, which I downed in one. It must have been real high-altitude vintage stuff because I felt its effect almost immediately.

Damodar talked to the Tibetans at length. 'They are told to say that they like the Chinese and hate the lamas. The Tibetans at Saipal are only allowed out of Tibet and into Nepal if they are supervised by a Tibetan in Chinese pay, an informer. That man in the red cloak at Saipal was an informer for the Chinese. He came back here to Khatang to tell Phrupa that there were Europeans at Saipal, and when Phrupa refused to help him, he carried on to Taklakot on one of Phrupa's ponies, to warn the Chinese of your presence in the area.'

'Has Phrupa had any more visits from the Chinese, since our arrest?' I asked.

The answer was in the affirmative. 'Phrupa says that the Chinese send regular patrols to Khatang now, but they never venture over the Khatang pass into the Jung Jung Khola. Phrupa also says that quite recently a Chinese patrol searched the nearby Khatang caves and asked Phrupa if there had been any Foreign Devils in the area other than ourselves.'

I presumed from this that Smoothy and the Boys from Gartok had believed my story that the CIA master spy, good old Charlie Brown, had been in hiding in the Khatang caves, awaiting his rendezvous with me.

Phrupa's eldest son, very dignified looking, wore modern European-style shoes imported from India. He offered me tea, which I drank, to be followed by further refills. I remembered the drill we learned at Jitkot Gompa when enjoying the hospitality of Abbot Gin Din Rhou. When you have had enough tea, always leave a full cup. I had finally to refuse the offer 'She-She' which means, 'Please have some more'. I replied 'Me-Me,' conveying that I had drunk an ample sufficiency. I then retired to my sleeping bag.

We were plagued by a crowd of urchins the next morning, who arrived from the other houses in Phrupa's tiny village. They found our kit more interesting than us, and we were perpetually hoisting little boys and girls out of our rucksacks, in which they tried to hide themselves.

Phrupa drew my attention to a tiny baby. Through Damodar's interpreting, Phrupa was pleased to tell me that the child was still alive, no thanks to me. I was nonplussed by all this until Damodar explained that when we entered Phrupa's house after our arrest and I had dropped my rucksack on a pile of old rags, this was the child underneath. The child had evidently absorbed the impact with no ill effect. The baby was still kept in the same wooden box, covered with old rags and skins. At midday, the toothless and half-blind old lady we had seen on that earlier occasion began to wash the baby. This was the only time during my time in Tibet I ever saw a Tibetan child given a bath. The old girl simply filled her mouth with cold water from a cup and then squirted the liquid from her mouth over the child. After some six such mouthfuls the baby, now wriggling and screaming fit to burst its tiny lungs, was considered to be clean enough to be wiped over with one of the rags which comprised its bedcover. It was then buried completely under rags and finally a sheepskin.

One of the married daughters of the family sat with a young girl of about six years of age on her knee, picking lice out of the child's hair. The woman did not kill the lice, but placed them carefully on the ground. True to her Buddhist religion she would not take life. I also learned that each of Phrupa's daughters was married by custom to all of her husband's brothers. According to Tibetan tradition all the children she bore were legally the offspring of her husband, and not his brothers. This applied to all the women at Khatang, and according to Phrupa it was the custom throughout the Gnari Korsum region of west Tibet, of which Taklakot was the local administrative centre. The strange thing about this Tibetan matrimonial arrangement is that it leads to the birth of far more girls than boys. The reason why has never been satisfactorily explained to me.

The short fat officer entered the room and in a fit of totalitarian pique instructed Phrupa that the Tibetans and the 'Foreign Devils' must not speak to each other. We observed this most unreasonable rule until midday when the officer retired to his room for a snooze, whereupon Damodar again assisted with interpretation as Phrupa wished to learn more about Europeans and I tried to glean as much as I could of the Tibetan way of life. Phrupa wanted to know, 'How wide is the tube, and how long is it?' Neither Damodar nor I could figure this one out until Phrupa told us that the Tibetans who came back over the Urai Lekh before winter set in had told him that the Europeans had a machine which 'talked' (our short-wave radio) and that it spoke in a strange tongue (English) and also in Urdu, and in Urdu it delivered messages from Delhi in India to Saipal in Nepal, even telling the Sahibs what the weather was going to be like, which to Phrupa made no sense at all because even a half-witted Tibetan always knew what the weather was going to do on the Nepal-Tibet border. Phrupa said that the Tibetan traders had lifted up the Sahib's radio (I saw them do this but at that time never learned what they were up to) to look for the tube which ran all the way from Delhi to Saipal, carrying the machine's voice.

I tried to explain that the messages were carried on a kind of 'wave' which travelled around the world. Phrupa frowned at this and gave me a look of disbelief. 'How can the Sahib's "waves", whatever they are, travel round the world? The world isn't round, it's flat.' There was no answer to that. I asked Phrupa about the disposal of the dead. We saw nothing remotely resembling a graveyard either at Khatang or Taklakot. Phrupa did not understand the word 'burial'. Damodar's translation suggested that Phrupa was talking about 'disposal' of the dead.

'Phrupa says that they dispose of the dead just like you do.'

I was puzzled by this. 'How does he know how Europeans dispose of the dead?'

'He says that surely you just throw the bodies away like he does?'

When I countered that we buried the dead in the ground, Phrupa was most upset, and implied that what we did was indecent and improper. 'Poor people just throw the body into a ravine for the vultures, lammergeyers and jackals to eat, leaving no flesh on the bones. Those who can afford an undertaker hire one, and he takes the body to a special place on the mountainside where he strips the flesh from the bones and breaks the bones with an axe. Everything is thrown into a river. In some areas, where there is a large community and people die more often, the lammergeyers and vultures settle in the area, and then get fat dining off the flesh which the disposers of the bodies throw to them. We do not regard the disposal of a body as a sacred rite. Once life departs, the soul flies off into the mystic state of Bardo, awaiting the summons to reappear on earth in a human or some other form. A very holy and pious person may after many reincarnations leading blameless existences be transported to Nirvana, a state of nothingness just like a drop of rain, merging into a lake or a river into which it falls. To aspire to Nirvana is in itself a selfish act and deemed by Buddha sufficient reason to deny entry to Nirvana to the aspirant. Then there is the Bodhisattva. He is one who after many reincarnations, dying, ascending to the mystic state of Bardo, in a state of grace, about to be absorbed into Nirvana, renounces Nirvana, and returns to earth to take upon himself the sins of mankind. The holiest of all people are the Bodhisattvas.'

I was deeply impressed by the dignity of old one-eyed Phrupa's delivery of that abbreviated lesson on the Buddhist faith. 'To take upon himself the sins of mankind, Damodar. Tell Phrupa that in our religion there was only one Bodhisattva, and his name was Jesus Christ.'

Phrupa took us onto the roof of his house, and pointed in the direction of the Khatang pass, over which we had come two months earlier, with our escort of Chinese soldiers and Gin Din Rhou. 'To the left, when you come close to the bottom of the pass, you will see a rock bluff, on the side of a cliff. That is where we dispose of our dead.'

The Chinese now appeared and ordered us back into Phrupa's house. The PLA wanted food, and Phrupa was insistent that he and his family were short of tsampa due to the late-running monsoon and early onset of winter weather reducing the trading season. They had no meat. Runty then opened our ration bags and took out the meagre portion of meat which was to last us for more than a week's march back to Dhuli. He cut off half of our total meat supply with a pocket knife, squatted on the floor and proceeded to eat the meat raw. Phrupa then told us that the Chinese had arrived with no food supplies, and that they always lived off the country wherever they travelled in Tibet. The fat officer demanded that Phrupa make a kettle of tea for him and his men, and proceeded to empty half of our sugar ration into it. Then he helped himself to our tsampa, snarling at me when I objected.

Damodar enquired of Phrupa if the Chinese paid for their rooms or the food they consumed. 'The Chinese take what they want,' Phrupa replied. 'Rooms, food and fuel, and they never pay for anything. When your porter Koila first arrived, the Chinese beat him savagely to make him confess that he was leading foreign spies into Tibet. When I told them not to beat Koila, they beat me also. We dare not ask for payment. We are afraid of the Cheenee Burra Rajah Sahib.' In the afternoon the fat officer handed over our rations for the march back over the Himalaya. I noted that nearly half of our precious tsampa had been eaten, mostly by the Chinese, and as a make-weight they handed me three small cotton bags of ata, plain flour which required cooking. I still had the spring balance scales we had brought with us, and the total weight of tsampa and ata was less than 30 pounds. It was not enough. I told the fat officer this. He grinned, and in Tibetan to Phrupa said, 'We don't care if they die on the way back to Hindustan.' I found what was left of our meat ration. It was no bigger

than our paperback poetry book. Damodar cooked it and made some
unleavened bread with ata flour. This was to be the nearest thing to a
meal we were going to get for the next seven days.

Then an argument took place between the fat officer and Phrupa. Phrupa
was accused of hiding food. 'Hoarding food in the Tibetan region of China
is a serious crime,' the fat officer shouted. With that he grabbed our
precious bags of flour. When Harrop tried to snatch back the bag he
had a muzzle of a rifle thrust in his face by Runty. We then had to watch
Runty make unleavened bread and tea-tsampa for all the Chinese with
our rations. A good ten pounds of ata and tsampa was used up. That
which was not eaten, instead of being offered to the Tibetans, was flung
outside onto the ground. The little Khatang urchins scrabbled on the bare
earth for pieces of steam-baked bread and tea-moistened tsampa. I had a
recurrence of dysentery and after passing blood I collapsed in my sleeping
bag. 'Take three of these sulpha tablets now,' Harrop said. 'We are going
to have a rough ride ahead. You have to get in better shape if you can.
I don't look forward to carrying you over the Urai Lekh.'

I downed the three tablets with a drink of water and lay on my back
feeling like death. Eventually I dozed off and I slept like a log until the next
morning. Our four specially hired Tibetan porters arrived and they were a
comical-looking quartet. The leading light was wearing a red Shuba and a
Gurkha felt hat with floppy brim. On top of the hat he had tied about half
a yard of lace and a pink silk bow. He was small in size. Two of the others
were of average build, but the fourth was a giant of a man. He boasted
that he had once been a brigand, preying on travellers to Kailas.

The four porters sat with their backs to the yard wall and insisted that
no loads would be carried or any forward movement on the track to
the Khatang pass would be made until they had been supplied with a
liberal quantity of chang. The fat officer whispered his instructions into
the ear of the big Tibetan who appeared to be the Sirdar of the group,
and then went indoors. Phrupa appeared with a bottle of chang. There
was an argument and the big Tibetan made threatening moves towards
old one-eyed Phrupa. In the event two more wooden bottles of chang
appeared.

It helped loosen the tongue of the big fellow. He called Damodar over
for a chat. 'Do you know how far we are to carry your loads for you?'

Damodar replied, 'The Chinese said that you would carry for us over
the Urai Lekh, through the Seti Gorge to Dhuli.'

The big man laughed and took another swig at his chang bottle. The
short one shook his head. The middle-sized one delivered the punch
line. 'We are instructed to carry for you over the Urai Lekh. We are to
drop your loads at Garanphu at the entrance to the Seti Gorge. We are
forbidden to carry to Dhuli. If the weather worsens and the clouds close
in on this side of the Lekh, we are to dump your loads and let you carry
for yourselves.'

Damodar came over to me. I was sitting on a small Tibetan stool, enjoying a few rays of sunshine in Phrupa's back yard. He told me what the Tibetans had said. 'Ask how much the Chinese are paying them, Damodar,' I suggested.

Damodar did so. 'Four rupees, Syd Sahib.'

'That's about the rate for load carrying,' I said. 'Four rupees a day.'

'No, Syd Sahib. They are getting four rupees each for the entire journey.'

'What skinflints these Chinese are,' Harrop commented as he joined us. 'You can see now why it matters little to these four ruffians where they drop our loads. They get no more than four rupees anyway.'

'Go back and talk to them, Damodar,' I suggested. 'Tell them that we have a little cash, and if they will carry for us we will pay them four rupees a day for the journey to Dhuli.'

Damodor did as he was bid, but the reply was not only negative, it was ominous. The big man spoke. 'Nobody can get through the Seti Gorge in winter. We would not try for fifty rupees a day. You and your two Sahibs are dead men.'

We exploded at this and went indoors to have it out with the fat officer. The four Chinese including Chungnya sat round a stove made from an old mustard-oil tin, feeding it with dwarf juniper brushwood and dried yak dung. Phrupa acted as interpreter for Damodar and we brought matters to a head by accusing the officer of deliberately trying to bring about our deaths. He denied any such instruction and stated that he had ordered the four Tibetans to carry our loads to Dhuli. I looked at the faces of the other three Chinese as the fat officer was speaking. Runty and Schickelgruber made no attempt to conceal their pleasure, while Chungnya looked troubled and avoided my gaze.

Harrop, Damodar and I were leaving the room when the fat officer made a statement. He said that no matter what happened to us, he was only obeying superior orders, and that orders had to be obeyed. He also informed us that his instructions were to remain at Khatang for a week to ensure that we did not return into Tibet. He threw in for good measure, 'If you do not like our porters, you can always hire new porters from one of the many villages in the Jung Jung Khola.' With that he laughed.

After Damodar and Phrupa had translated that statement I looked the short fat officer right in the eye. He held my gaze. I could tell by the half-amused gleam in his piggy little eyes that he was as fully aware as we were that there were no Tibetan villages in the Jung Jung Khola.

Damodar lightened the atmosphere for Harrop and me. 'Syd Sahib, if I die on the way back I will miss another term at college and my family will be very angry with me.'

'Time to go, Syd Sahib,' Damodar added, as the Chinese ordered the four Tibetans to pick up our loads. Harrop, Damodar and I hoisted our rucksacks onto our backs. We were away by 11 a.m. I was deeply concerned about the lack of sobriety on the part of the four Tibetans. The small one wearing a Gurkha hat was none too steady on his feet. They had consumed a considerable amount of highly potent chang. There was a Buddist chorten a few feet from Phrupa's front door, and all four porters dropped their loads, and going on their knees prayed to Prince Gautama Buddha. The fat officer swore at them until they picked up their loads.

Harrop, Damodar and I bade old one-eyed Phrupa and his delightful family farewell, assuring him that we held the Tibetan people in high esteem and we longed for the day when they would be free of the yoke of Chinese communism. The old man, greatly touched, cried, 'Khali-phe, Khali-phe,' which is 'Go gracefully and go well.'

19

The fat officer informed us that we would suffer the direst penalties if we indulged in photography. No still pictures, or cine footage. He remained at Khatang and we left the village accompanied by Chungnya, Runty and Schickelgruber. Harrop, Damodar and I travelled on foot, carrying rucksacks and ice axes. The Chinese brought mules, but after Runty's mount slipped on a patch of ice depositing him flat on his back, the PLA spent most of the time leading their mules. We soon passed the four Tibetan porters, who looked none too steady on their feet. We crossed over the tiny cantilever wooden bridge.

Conditions had changed since that fateful day when we had crossed the pass in the opposite direction. The lower part of the pass was now covered with a great avalanche cone of snow that had hardened into ice. Once this had been soft, but constant thawing and freezing gave it the texture and surface of a sloping ice rink. Harrop and I cut steps for the Chinese with our ice axes. Of the Tibetan porters there was no sign. The upper slope of the pass was free of snow, and Harrop, who was leading, commented that he was out of condition. I felt like death. My knees felt like jelly and my boots seemed to weigh about twenty pounds each. The sulpha tablets had temporarily stopped my bouts of dysentery but would I get over the Urai Lekh pass and through the Seti Gorge with only three pills?

We sat on a broad flat rock taking a well-earned rest while waiting for the others to catch us up. The Khatang side of the pass lay in shadow and it was bitterly cold. We sat and waited for nearly two hours with no sign of the porters, until eventually the big man came staggering into sight, followed by the others. They reached the small cantilever bridge, and I took my binoculars out of my rucksack to look at them. Runty screamed at me and pointed his rifle at my head. Not only were we forbidden to take photographs, we were evidently to be precluded from looking through our binoculars. But I had seen enough.

I said to Harrop, 'The Chinese said that they would hire four porters, and what they gave us is a bunch of boozers.'

The big Tibetan fell flat on his face. The smallest of the four leaned his back and load against a rock and slid down to a sitting position. The other two, staggering along arm in arm, dropped their packs and flopped down alongside the big man who was still lying face down. This was a discouraging start for our journey home and Harrop and I cursed the Chinese. There was nothing for it but to go back down the pass and try to revive our porters, who had consumed more than enough of Phrupa's chang.

When we reached the four Tibetans only one was conscious, and he quite sensibly suggested that we camp for the night at that spot, and set off early the next day. We pitched our two Meade tents, and set out our inflatable beds and sleeping bags. The four Tibetans were so drunk they ignored the tent offered to them and proceeded to spend the night out in the open wrapped in their fleece-lined shubas with extra sheep skins thrown over them which they carried with our loads.

The afternoon sun was going down, and we sat out enjoying its last warm rays. This was to be our first night camping out after nearly two months in those filthy cells at Taklakot. We looked forward to what was comparatively speaking a degree of freedom. To our disgust Schickelgruber, at gunpoint, insisted on taking some more of our precious ata flour. Damodar, aware what Schickelgruber was up to, hid our remaining tsampa behind a rock. I doubted if we had ten pounds left now, for a week-long march. Then the fat officer turned up and announced that he intended discharging the four drunken porters and would send a runner from Phrupa's house to find another four load carriers.

'That could take days,' Harrop said. 'And I doubt if these incompetent beggars will provide us with any more ata or tsampa.'

I agreed. 'Better the devil we know, even if he is a Tibetan boozer. Let's tell the fat officer that it's no deal, and if he wants to argue, we will all go back to Taklakot, and we will inform the Cheenee Burra Rajah Sahib that his fat twit of an officer allowed our Tibetan porters to get drunk. Tell that to him via the Tibetans, Damodar.'

Damodar did just that. The fat officer thought for a moment and then conceded to our demands. To our surprise he and all the other Chinese left us at dusk. For the first time in weeks there wasn't a Chinese in sight. We turned in. At 5 a.m. I was awakened by Chungnya shining a torch in my face. Runty was with him. We made breakfast off a can of tea and roused our porters, who were now fully recovered from their drunken orgy of the night before. They appreciated the speedy way we got a yak dung fire going for them, with our small rubber bellows-style air-mattress inflators. Once they had brewed up and partaken of a meal of tsampa, we were off for the summit of the Khatang pass and made it in good time.

To our complete surprise, Chungnya indicated to us that he and Runty would accompany us no further. Runty sat fiddling with his rifle, muttering in Tibetan to our porters. I thought it strange that the Chinese would not be accompanying us to the other side of the pass and could only presume from this that the Chinese were no longer sure that the Jung Jung Khola lay inside Tibet, as they had stated during our interrogations.

Chungyna first shook hands with the three of us, and then he insisted on embracing each of us with a bear hug. He was grinning all over his face, and appeared to be delighted that his Western friends would be on their way home. Runty gave us a sickly smile, and in an effort to bury the hatchet I offered him my right hand. He held it limply.

Harrop, Damodar and I and the four porters set off over the summit of the pass and down the other side. A few hundred feet of descent brought us to that fateful spot called Kalapani, place of Black Water, where we had been eating breakfast when surprised by the Chinese in October. I asked Harrop to pause by the small tree, alongside which our tents had been pitched. I loaded my 35 mm Edixa camera and took a picture. At that we heard a yell and the blowing of a whistle. I looked up. Runty was peering down at us through a pair of binoculars.

'Oh, no,' Harrop exclaimed. 'We are in Nepal, dammit. Surely it is not a crime to take a photograph here?'

The Tibetans put their loads down and told Damodar in Urdu that Runty had shouted for them to stop. My heart sank, and I had visions of us being marched back to Taklakot at gunpoint, for another wearying round of questions and answers about the legality or otherwise of taking photographs in a valley which consisted of limestone cliffs and rock debris.

Intent of saving my film, I went behind a rock which hid me from the gaze of Runty and Chungnya who were now running down the track. I quickly wound back the film and replaced it with an unexposed film. I dropped the exposed film down the waistband of my trousers, which were tucked into puttees.

Chungnya was first to reach us, and he looked upset, as if I had betrayed his trust. I opened up my camera and gave Chungnya the black and white film. I was trying to explain to Chungnya, via Damodar and the Tibetans that my picture was a harmless study of John Harrop against a backdrop of limestone cliff, when I was cut short by a vicious blow in the small of my back. Before I could recover and turn round, a second blow, from the butt of Runty's rifle, landed just below my right ear, sending me sprawling on my face on the track. Painfully turning over, feeling very dizzy, I saw Runty standing over me. His PPSh was held with its butt towards me. He reversed his weapon, pulled the cocking lever back and, bending down, placed the muzzle right between my eyes. I heard the click as he moved the safety catch to the off position, and I saw his right hand close around the stock, his forefinger on the trigger. Runty was screaming at the top of his voice, and I was certain that my last moment had come.

There was a flash of khaki and Chungnya, pulling the muzzle of Runty's PPSh away from my forehead, pointed it up towards the sky. Then I saw the pistol. Chungnya had a short-barrelled automatic pistol of Chinese manufacture in his right hand. To this day, I can still see the embossed emblem of a star on the left-hand side of the pistol's envelope. The star was enamelled red, in contrast to the gun-blue of the pistol. Chungnya held the pistol against the side of Runty's head, and as Runty screamed at me, Chungnya shouted back at him, but in a more commanding, lower, far from hysterical tone.

The crucial moment passed. Voices were lowered. Runty pointed his rifle away from me, and Chungnya holstered his pistol. Chungnya insisted on emptying Harrop's camera, and confiscating all our cameras. I now had one roll of film in my possession, and it was the most valuable film cassette our expedition had exposed. It included our descent of the Urai Lekh with our four Nepalese porters under those appalling snow conditions in October, our journey down the Jung Jung Khola, my photograph of Khatang valley and Phrupa's houses, at a time when Chinese PLA mules were actually tethered outside. I was determined not to lose it now.

Runty shouted a change of orders to our porters in their own language, which Chungnya did not fully understand. We gained the impression that Chungnya was the senior of the two men, but Runty was the fat officer's blue-eyed boy, and Runty was threatening Chungnya with all kinds of disciplinary problems when they got back to the fat officer, who was still comfortably ensconced at Phrupa's house.

'Runty is telling the Tibetans that they must turn back and take us to Khatang, and that we should go to Taklakot for punishment for taking illegal photographs,' Damodar commented.

It was obvious that Chungnya's mind was troubled by a dichotomy. On the one hand I had broken regulations, and should be brought before the Boys from Gartok to be Struggled Against, and on the other hand, his orders were that we be taken to the Khatang pass, and pushed over the border, forbidden under pain either of death or life imprisonment ever to enter Tibet again.

Chungnya knew enough Tibetan to get his message across to our four porters. We were to get on our way, and we must not stop before nightfall. If the Chinese wanted us returned to Tibet, he and Runty, and presumably Schickelgruber and the fat officer, would come after us. If we were not to be rearrested, a Tibetan runner would be sent after us with a message, telling us to move out next morning, on over the Urai Lekh. I somehow had the feeling that Chungnya was placing both his career as a soldier and his personal safety on the line, just to help us.

Runty simmered down, and both he and Chungnya waved us on our way, the Tibetan porters being instructed that they must wait at our next campsite, wherever that was, below the Urai Lekh, for the Chinese to come and arrest us if such orders came from the fat officer. The small of my back and my head ached. I felt shaky, but was determined to put as much distance as possible between us and the PLA before nightfall. We tried to persuade the four Tibetans to make haste, but they refused to exceed their own set pace, which equated to the Swiss mountain-guide maxim of 'hurry slowly'.

Losing height we approached the Jung Jung river and crossed the small wooden cantilever bridge. I turned to look back, and saw that Chungnya and Runty were sitting on a rock, watching us through binoculars. That was an encouraging sign, for they were not rushing back to Khatang. I deemed this due to Chungnya's influence. All three of us now voiced our fears.

'The fat officer will probably send them after us, when he gets the gist of what happened,' I suggested.

'We can only hope that he plays it the way the Chinese appear to play everything,' Harrop said. 'By the ruddy book.'

'You mean that the fat officer will not take it on himself to have us rearrested?' I asked.

'That's right,' Harrop continued. 'My guess is that he will send a runner on a mule back to Taklakot, for guidance from the senior officers. That gives us twenty-four hours' clear start ahead of them. If we don't dawdle, we could be climbing up the final slope of the Urai Lekh tomorrow. That is if we can persuade these porters to go on, and not stop for either the PLA or a Tibetan runner to catch up with us.'

To our dismay, when we had covered a bare three miles, our four Tibetans stopped at a stream and announced that they were going to make a brew of tea. We argued, but this only made them more obstinate. They set about collecting brushwood and yak dung in a leisurely fashion and placed their brass pot on to boil. The thing held almost a gallon and half an hour was lost before the water was hot enough to infuse tea. When the container was empty, we picked up our rucksacks ready to be on our way, only to be told that one urn of tea was not enough, and they proposed to make another brew.

We felt completely helpless, knowing that by now, Chungnya and Runty would be in Khatang, and Runty would be screaming for the fat officer to enter the Jung Jung Khola, overtake and arrest us. We lost an hour and a half due to the Tibetans' extended tea break.

Eventually we got on the march again, and approached the twin lakes of Tharedunga. No need to skirt around the lakes now. They were frozen over, and we walked across ice that must have been at least a foot thick. At 3.30 p.m. we reached the site where we had camped on our way into Tibet in October. I pleaded with the Tibetans to carry on, but they decided that they had carried far enough for one day. Nothing would persuade them to continue even though there was daylight left. They even refused to make camp out of sight amongst huge glacial boulders, and dumped their loads at a spot in full view of anyone coming along the track from the direction of Khatang.

Feeling thoroughly depressed, Harrop, Damodar and I pitched one of our two Meade tents. The primus stove was lit and we made a brew of tea. The Tibetans made tea, and mixed tsampa in it, in their tiny shallow wooden drinking bowls. We three had no appetite, and for that matter, we had little flour for tsampa-Weetabix or for chapatis, and besides, we needed to conserve our paraffin supplies from now on.

At dusk the Tibetans built up their fire, and it bathed the surrounding rocks in a yellow light. When we protested, they heaped more brushwood on the fire and produced a blaze that betrayed our exact location over a region of several miles.

Damodar expressed the thoughts of both Harrop and me, when he said, 'I think that the fat one will get troops from Taklakot, and take us back.'

We crawled into our sleeping bags, but none of us could sleep. At about 10 p.m. we were startled by a shout from the track. Looking through the tunnel entrance to our tent I saw a torch light bobbing about. Harrop and Damodar were both sitting upright in their sleeping bags, sharing my conviction that the PLA had come to rearrest us. The man with the torch ran past our tent, and we could hear him talking to the Tibetans, who were bivouacked under a huge overhanging boulder. Damodar was listening to the voices.

'It's a Tibetan, and he's come alone.'

We leapt from the tent and joined the Tibetans who were now grouped around their huge fire. Another container of tea was on the go, and the thirsty runner, who had travelled from Khatang, swallowed one cupful after another. His thirst slaked, he handed over our two cameras. That was a good sign. My camera was in good order, but Harrop's camera had evidently had a large rock dropped on it, presumably by Runty, perhaps mistakenly thinking that the camera was mine.

Our runner then produced three unexposed cassettes of film, and handed them back to us. Then quite unbelievably, he fished inside his shuba, and out came the 50-round box of ammunition for my Browning pistol.

'Is there any fathoming the Chinese mind?' Harrop enquired.

'Looks like a good sign,' I suggested. 'It's obvious that the Boys from Gartok don't want to detain us any longer.'

'Not so, Syd Sahib,' Damodar interjected. 'This Tibetan says that the fat officer wants to have us rearrested and taken back to Taklakot, but he can't do that without orders from above. So he has sent Runty back to Taklakot with a report about your picture-taking, Syd Sahib, and in the meantime, he must act entirely to his original orders, which were to free us at the top of the Khatang pass, and send a runner on after us with the box of ammunition for your pistol, but only after you were so far away there was no risk of you shooting one of the Cheenee soldiers.'

'What the hell kind of logic do these people work by?' Harrop enquired.

'Everything must be by the book,' I said. 'It is to our advantage to get these Tibetans on the road before sun-up.'

Damodar had a further chat with the Tibetan runner, and he proved to be a sterling fellow. 'The Chinese are our masters,' he said, 'but we hate them. I will tell the fat Cheenee Burra Rajah Sahib that when I caught up with you, you were close to the foot of the Urai Lekh, and they would have little chance of overtaking you.'

When I suggested that the Chinese would have a good idea how far we could have gone up the Jung Jung Khola on this first day's march, he dissented.

'The Chinese never come up the Jung Jung Khola. They have no idea how far it is to the Urai Lekh.'

I counted out my remaining rupee notes, and handed a third of them to our fleet-of-foot Tibetan ally. He told Damodar that he would start back right away, in the dark, and would travel through the night, but would hide from the Chinese when he got back to Khatang, in Phrupa's grain store. The Chinese had told him that he must return right away, regardless of the conditions, and by hiding until daybreak, he hoped to convince the Chinese that he had covered too great a distance to get back during the night, and we were therefore too far ahead for the Chinese to catch up with us. With that he was gone, his torch light bobbing about along the track back to the Khatang pass.

Thanks to the reassuring manner of our visitor, we felt relaxed, and sat chatting to the Tibetans, roasted by their enormous fire. Eventually we turned in, sleeping fitfully, and woke up at 6 a.m. It took some considerable persuasion to get the Tibetans up and under way, and they complained about the weather, pointing up the Jung Jung Khola. My heart sank. It was snowing hard over the Urai Lekh. Less than an hour's walking brought us to an old glacial terminal moraine. The snow advanced down the Jung Jung Khola, and then swept over us. We sat amongst the boulders waiting for the Tibetans. Suddenly the snow stopped, and the sun came out. We were about to cheer when an icy wind sprang up, and it cut right through us. This deterioration in the weather did not augur well for that crucial passage over the Lekh and forcing of the Seti Gorge. We sheltered behind a twenty-foot-high boulder, and Harrop mentioned that my nose was turning blue. This was the onset of frostbite. I rubbed my nose vigorously to restore circulation.

The Tibetans eventually reached us, and announced that they were not going any further that day. I was shaken by this, for we had been on the march only for an hour. There was nowhere flat enough to pitch both tents, so Harrop, Damodar and I spent half an hour levelling a thirty-degree snow slope, so that both Meade tents could be pitched. The Tibetans would have none of it and told Damodar that they were going back to the previous night's campsite because there was brushwood and yak dung there to light a fire. They would have nothing to do with our paraffin pressure stove. They also said that if the weather did not improve by next morning, they would go back to Khatang and leave us to our fate.

We were now in the business of survival. I opened the box of ammunition for my Browning, and in plain view of the Tibetans, I loaded the magazine, slammed it into the butt of my pistol, worked the first found into the breech and said, 'OK, Damodar. Tell them that they can go back, with just what they stand up in. Everything they own stays with us. They can go to hell for all I care. But if they want their food, their tea urns, and all their belongings, they can come back here and get them in the morning. With that the four Tibetans set off back towards the campsite only one and a half miles behind us. It was apparent to the three of us that if the Chinese at Taklakot decided to come and grab us, they would have little difficulty.

We pitched our tent and crawled inside. The stove was lit and we boiled up a can of snow for tea. Damodar mixed a few handfuls of ata flour with warm water. It was tasteless, and far from nourishing. A wind blew up, and the temperature dropped. I could not sleep, and sitting up in my sleeping bag, I commented, 'Going to be a jolly night.'

From Harrop's bag, his head hidden, I heard the grunted rejoinder, 'Yes. Like carnival night on the *Marie-Celeste*.'

The wind dropped, and so did the temperature. I presumed that our four Tibetans would have a blazing fire going all night. The thermometer hanging from the top flap of Harrop's rucksack read forty below. At that moment I knew fear.

At 9 a.m. the next morning, after far too many hours of precious daylight had gone by, our four Tibetan porters appeared. We were agreeably surprised. They told Damodar that they knew the weather, and the outlook was far from favourable. They forecast snow. There was no time to hang about, no more perverse delays. We must now try to get over the Lekh in one march.

Once the Tibetans had gone on ahead, carrying our loads, I loaded my camera and took a number of photographs of the surrounding mountains. Only the lower reaches were blanketed with snow. Above 20,000 feet, summits which were white when we marched down into the Jung Jung Khola were now devoid of their pristine mantle, and revealed bare rock.

Having completed my photography session, I carried on, slowly plodding my way up the Jung Jung Khola, until eventually I caught up with Harrop and Damodar.

'We're going to have a little ceremony,' Harrop said, 'and you have the ceremonial appurtenance in your rucksack.'

'I would like to have a crap, Syd Sahib,' Damodar said, 'and I have no toilet paper.'

'You've been too profligate with that armful of cotton wool out of the PLA jacket I gave you,' I muttered, fearful that my companions might gang up on me, and make off with the remainder of my share.

'It's not cotton wool, it's kapok,' Harrop said, 'and it's full of nasty little hard seeds.'

My mean streak was coming to the fore. 'Call it what you like. It's all I've got, and with my dose of the Tibetan Trots, my need is greater than yours, and Damodar will have to use a handful of snow.'

They were both grinning. 'Don't want your cotton wool, Syd Sahib,' Damodar said. 'I would like to wipe my whatsit on that small red Chinese communist flag you brought from England with you.'

At that I brightened up. 'What a jolly good idea,' I said, as I unpacked my rucksack. 'Look here, Damodar, you can't have the British flag, but you can have the expedition flag of Nepal to take home as a souvenir. Here's your Chinese flag. Help yourself.'

It was a fitting end to that embarrassing item, and an appropriate expression of our shared feelings of contempt towards the Chinese occupiers of Tibet.

Then we got down to more serious matters, as Harrop said, 'Look at these pills. There are two kinds. The first is for frostbite. They will, hopefully, keep our blood circulating more efficiently. I suggest that we take three each now, and three more tomorrow morning, before we go into the Seti Gorge.'

Damodar and I nodded our assent.

Harrop continued, 'This next lot are some sort of pep pills. They give you a much needed boost when your eyeballs are down near your ankles, and help you keep going. But, and in our predicament it's a very big but, once the boost effect wears off, lethargy and depression can set in. So if you are going to take them, you have to be sure that whatever trial or crisis you have to get through, you are out of it and safe before the adverse reaction sets in. So what do we do?' Harrop was staring at me. I was the weak link and we all knew it.

'I seem to remember something about a Himalayan expedition. I think that it was to make a traverse of Nanda Devi. The two summit men took these pills, and they were so euphoric that when they left their highest camp, one of the two forgot to wear his high-altitude climbing boots, and went off wearing crampons on top of soft lambswool camp-boots. Neither of them was ever heard of again.'

'I don't want to take those pep pills, John Sahib,' Damodar said.

'As Mr Sam Goldwyn once said, you can include me out. I'll go as I am. I haven't had a bout of dysentery since you gave me those sulpha pills at Khatang,' I told Harrop.

'OK,' Harrop said. 'Then you take the last three anti-dysentery pills. We've no water. You'll have to melt snow in your mouth. And here's the anti-frostbite pills. We all take them now. I'll hang on to the pep pills, in case we need them on the way up the Urai Lekh, or on our way through the Seti Gorge.'

We now resumed our journey. In the back of my mind I worried about our young Chinese friend Chungnya. I had a gut feeling that his friendship with Foreign Devils could possibly create difficulties for him. At last we reached the final ice slope at the foot of the pass. Harrop led the way, cutting steps with his ice axe. Damodar followed, the four Tibetans came after Damodar, and I tagged on behind. Staying in the rear allowed me to ensure that the Tibetans did not cut and run. It also gave me ample opportunity to take a rest, which amounted to five or six deep breaths for one step upwards. I was suffering from what Tilman referred to as 'Mountaineer's Foot', a reluctance to place one in front of the other.

My nose froze, and then the fingers of my right hand, clamped around the head of my ice axe. I adhered to the advice of F. S. Smythe of Everest fame in the years before World War Two: 'Always keep your toes waggling.' I had been waggling my toes all the way up the slope, and now at about 19,000 feet, I could waggle them no more. I had lost all sensation in my feet. Frostbite could not be far away. Then it started to snow, heavily, but thankfully there was no wind.

I caught up with the rearmost Tibetan. It was the big fellow, and he was straggling behind the others. He was in better shape than me, but he was being bloody-minded and perverse. I placed my ice axe against the back of his load, and gave him a gentle push. He turned and glared at me and shouted, 'Khatang, Taklakot!' pointing back down the Jung Jung Khola.

The others had gone ahead. Visibility was reduced to about ten feet. It was now or never. I pulled off my right-hand windproof mitt, unzipped the kangaroo pocket on the front of my anorak with difficulty, as I was losing sensation in my fingers. The big Tibetan vanished in a flurry of snow. I was alone on the pass. I had no horizon. It was a white-out.

Then the wind blew the snow away, and the big Tibetan half-turned in the ice steps Harrop had cut for us and looked downhill, straight into the muzzle of my pathetic little 7.65 mm Browning automatic pistol. I had no intention of shooting him, but he did not know that. Then he grinned at me and laughed. I grinned back, and placed the pistol back in my kangaroo pocket. The big Tibetan climbed on up after the others. I didn't try to zip up my kangaroo pocket. I looked for my windproof right-hand mitt. It had gone, slipped out of my hand, and by now would be several hundred feet down the ice slope. All I had was my woollen fingerless glove. I gritted my teeth and continued, my by now white and lifeless right hand gripping the head of my ice axe.

Then we halted again. The big Tibetan had caught up with the others, and they were stationary on the steep slope, bawling at Damodar.

'Syd Sahib. They want to know what time of day it is. They think that it is too late to get over the Lekh and down the other side to a place where we can shelter for the night!'

I looked at my Rolex. It was 1.15 p.m. I shouted back up to Damodar, 'Tell them that it's still morning and only 11.45 a.m. by the Sahib's watch. We still have plenty of time to get over the Lekh well before dark.'

Damodar conveyed this vital information to the four Tibetans, and they, believing that a Sahib's watch could not possibly give the wrong time, continued on their way. I was so weak, I found difficulty in placing my climbing boots securely in the steps Harrop had cut for us. I longed for my crampons, but they were strapped to the back of my rucksack, and there was no way that I was going to unzip my rucksack and untie those crampons, and then try to strap them onto my boots, with frozen fingers, standing on one foot on that bloody awful steep incline.

Then suddenly the snow stopped falling, and the sun came out, and I could see the huge sentinel-like rock pillar on the eastern side of the summit of the pass. I tried to cut intermediate steps to compensate for Harrop's long stride, but I did not have the stamina; I felt completely exhausted.

Suddenly something snaked down past me. 'Grab hold of this. We'll give you a pull. I've still got that small hip flask full of cherry brandy I bought in Cortina D'Ampezzo on our way through the Dolomites.' The thing that snaked past me was a climbing rope. I looked up. I was alone on the face of the pass. Harrop, Damodar and the four Tibetans were on the summit of the Urai Lekh. I grabbed hold of the rope, and Harrop and Damodar hauled, hand over hand, until I was with them, 'On the Roof of the World'.

'Now let's drink that cherry brandy,' Harrop suggested.

I collapsed in the snow. 'Come on, look. No snow on the very top of the Lekh,' Harrop shouted to me. He was right. The high winds of winter had stripped off the snow cover. I staggered over onto bare rock. To my left stood a Tibetan Mani wall of crumbling mountain rocks. A solitary willow pole stood proud of it, with a dozen tattered Tibetan prayer flags sagging limply. Harrop sat at the foot of the cairn of Mani stones. I joined him and, asking Damodar to do the honours with my camera, took a swig of his delightful Italian cherry brandy. I spent the next few minutes blowing on my lifeless right hand, trying to unfreeze my fingers. There was no sensation in my toes. As the circulation returned to my right hand, I was in agony, and could not stem my tears.

Suddenly a blast of ice-cold air stormed up the Urai Lekh and over the summit of the pass, where in those close confines between huge rock pillars, it funnelled and concentrated its fury. We huddled down behind the Mani cairn, all seven of us, and waited for the squall to subside.

'God, we are lucky,' Harrop commented. 'Do you realise that if we had met those damn winds we could see from our prison, blowing snow off the tops at about a hundred miles an hour, we would never have survived.'

This day, 16 December 1955, had been such a relatively fine day. We needed two more, preferably with less snow and no wind, both of which could be fatal to us either on the descent of the Lekh, or in the Seti Gorge.

'Let's go,' Harrop said, and he set off down the slope into the upper reaches of the Seti valley, back towards the old campsite at Saipal. Damodar followed, the Tibetans last. The smallest one, who was something of a comedian, slipped on his backside, and the other Tibetans roared their heads off.

I was feeling warmer now, thanks to that cherry brandy, although I was aware that in a situation such as ours, alcohol is not recommended. 'But the hell with it,' I thought. 'We have something to celebrate. We have hopefully seen the last of the Cheenee Burra Rajah Sahib, and I'm bringing out of communist-occupied Tibet every last piece of information Singh and Cricket Wallah wanted.'

I plodded slowly back to the north side of the pass and looked down the Jung Jung Khola, into Tibet, that fabled land I had learned to love. I was more contented at that moment than I have ever been in the whole of my existence. At that sublime moment, when we stood together on the summit of the Urai Lekh, we were the highest men in the world. Winter Himalayan climbing was way into the future. Anybody else at that altitude, on that day, would be warm and cosy in the pressurised cabin of an air liner.

Then I saw something down on the valley floor in the Jung Jung Khola. It was a flash of light. Then I saw it again. It was light reflected from something, possibly the lens of a pair of binoculars. The PLA were coming after us. But they were at least two miles behind us, did not possess ice axes or climbing ropes, and were completely unskilled in the craft of ice and snow mountaineering. They were too late. I decide to say nothing to Harrop and Damodar. No point in sharing a trouble unnecessarily. I could not imagine the Chinese ascending the Urai Lekh in near darkness, and without high-altitude tents and sleeping bags. We were safe from the oppressors of Tibet. We had only the elements to worry about now. I turned my back on Tibet knowing that that wonderful land would be denied me for the rest of my days.

20

Going down is usually easier than going up. But on this occasion, descending the upper reaches of the Urai Lekh did have its problems. We came face to face with a type of ice terrain I had seen in photographs and books about climbing in the Andes. I had no idea that such conditions could prevail in the Himalaya. As far as the eye could see, for at least a couple of miles, the descending slope consisted of small ice pinnacles called 'neve penitente.' This ice structure originates as a smooth ice slope, but with constant thawing and refreezing, the once flat ground becomes a carpet of serac-like spikes, looking for all the world like the penitent monks they are named after, the tops of the spiky ice pinnacles having the semblance of a monk's cloak.

The Urai Lekh neve penitente ice spikes were about two or three feet in height, and up to a foot wide and two inches thick at the base. They did not point straight up into the air, they lay at an angle, like the stakes used to disable cavalry in the middle ages. Each spike pointed at the angle the sun followed across the horizon. One could not place a foot on flat ground. One had to step on the spiky top of each neve pentitente as one walked. Trip over and you got badly cut and bruised. Take a wrong step, and fall with a leg in the gap between two neve penitente, and a wrenched, fractured or broken ankle would be expected.

Progress on this bed of ice nails was painfully slow. We were all carrying loads, and our Tibetan porters' loads were heaviest of all. Great care had to be taken to avoid a fall. In the event nobody made a false step. Occasionally an ice blade collapsed, but apart from one or two bruised shins, no serious injury was sustained. A broken ankle in that situation could have only one result. I remembered Tilman's remark to me: 'My view is that all a doctor can do for you in the Himalaya is diagnose what you died of.'

Several hours of very slow progress over the descending plain of ice spikes took us no more than halfway down to our old base camp at Saipal, and we found ourselves stumbling along in the dark. At last we reached the gravel bed where the other members of our expedition had left us on 19 October. Here he hoped to find water. A shout of 'Pani' from Damodar confirmed our hopes. Damodar could hear water running under the ice. It was a small stream, flowing too fast to freeze over. Miraculously there was a small patch of clear snow-free gravel, and we pitched our two Meade tents. Initial attempts to light our two paraffin stoves were to no avail. The paraffin was of poor quality, and the altitude did not help. I rummaged in one of the porter loads and came up with a half bottle of cheap rot-gut Greek brandy I had bought in the town of Kavalla on our way to the Himalaya.

'Here goes nothing,' I said as I poured a generous libation into the filler cap. A match was struck, the stove was pumped up, and the resulting explosion nearly blew the three of us out of the tent. Then the thing settled down to a roar, and what a roar, like a disembowelled steam train. But it worked. On the other stove, also charged with Greek 'rocket booster', I tried to boil the Tibetans' enormous brass tea urn. The stove was not up to it, and they had to make do with lukewarm tea to mix with their tsampa.

We dined off a mix of tsampa and ata flour, to which tea was added, in true Tibetan fashion. It was all we had, and we were very hungry. I mentioned my fears about our coming trials in the Seti Gorge. 'Look, I'm not sure that I have it in me to get through that bloody place. I'm not in good nick. Let's get it clear and understood now. I'm the weak link. We don't rope up for the passage through the far end of the gorge. If we rope up, and belay for the difficult bits, we will lose so much time, moving one at a time, we will not get through in daylight, and if it's as bad or worse than described to us by Koila, when he went out to Dhuli and back for extra ata and spuds during the monsoon, and anyone falls, the rope will become an instrument of mutual destruction. I say we jettison the two climbing ropes, with all the other useless crap we are carrying in those porter loads, when we get to Garanphu.'

Harrop disagreed. 'You've always been a stickler for correct climbing procedures, on the grounds of safety. Passing through that place in winter, unroped, means that any poor sod who goes down the khud is finished. It's a thousand-foot drop or more in places.'

'Sorry,' I responded. 'I'm pulling rank on you. We throw the rope away, and that's my decision as leader of this expedition.'

Nothing more was said on the matter. I had come to realise that Harrop would have been prepared to rope up, and in places where a belay was unobtainable, try to hold me if I fell. His chances of saving himself, let alone me, were just about nil. He knew it, but he was that kind of man. There are some people you would not like to be back-to-back with in a fox hole in a theatre of war. There are others you would trust with your life. I would at that moment rather have had one John Frederick Harrop than fifty of anyone else.

I was aware that in the back of Harrop's mind was the ever present problem that I might just simply collapse, due to another onset of dysentery; and if that happened what would he be able to do for me in that situation? I had relieved him of that unenviable decision.

As we snuggled down in our sleeping bags, Damodar had the last word. 'It could have been worse, Syd Sahib. Just think what might have happened if we really had been spies. My golly, we could have been in very serious trouble.' I made no effort to disillusion him.

That night was the coldest we experienced in the Himalaya. A down-draught of icy wind from the summit of the pass gradually penetrated our sleeping bags. None of us slept. We shivered all night and I heard our porters chuntering and complaining almost non-stop in their nearby tent.

It was during that bitterly cold night, when the ambient temperature and wind-chill factor combined to give us a private record of about 70 degrees Fahrenheit below freezing, that we had a brief visit from some unidentified person or creature. After the wind dropped, in the early morning, I heard a snuffling sound close to my face, on the other side of the tent. I thought that I was perhaps dreaming.

I had to go out for a natural purpose, and shone my tired torch onto the ground. There were tracks outside our tent. Then the temperature rose suddenly, and it started to snow. Snow was what we did not need for our passage through the Seti Gorge. I was not in the mood to investigate the tracks and repaired to my sleeping bag as quickly as I could.

At dawn, we looked out of our tent to see the first light touching the summit of Kapkot, a 21,000-foot mountain that overlooked our Saipal base camp. Its west face fell straight down into the Seti Gorge, 7,000 feet below its summit. We wriggled back into our sleeping bags and made no attempt to move until sunlight reached our tent at about 8 a.m. With no thought for a tsampa breakfast, or even a brew of tea, we packed our gear as speedily as we could to get down below those continuing fields of ice blades. We had indeed been fortunate to find that one flat piece of ground on which to pitch our tents the night before. There were at least another two or three miles of neve penitente to cover before we reached Saipal.

We reached the level plateau at Saipal at midday. The morning was sunny and we sat with our backs to the walls of one of those beehive-shaped stone shelters. There was still some tsampa left, so we had a watery bowl of Tibetan Weetabix apiece, followed by a mug of hot but very weak tea. At 1.30 p.m. we set off for Garanphu, the furthest place south the Tibetan traders ever reached, situated as it was on the last substantial flat piece of ground in the Seti Gorge, before the difficult parts are encountered. A great deal of the Tibetan trade was carried on yaks, and yaks could not, like the Nepali sheep, negotiate the steep sections of track built out on saplings jammed into the cliff face.

The ground between Saipal and Garanphu is normally easy, but conditions had changed since September. Where a safe track had meandered across steep grass slopes, huge avalanche cones now lay. Some had fallen athwart the Seti river, and had temporarily blocked it, but the river had eventually worn a passage under and through the ice field, and water flowed through huge cavernous tunnels. In some places, these ice tunnels had collapsed and the snow and ice had been worn away by the river, leaving almost vertical ice faces, which one had to traverse to continue along the east face of the gorge.

Crossing the first avalanche snout proved to be the most difficult. Harrop, who was ahead of me, had to cut steps in the hard slope and then surmount a steep slippery corner. When rounding the corner, Harrop slipped and for a tense moment I feared that he was gone. He managed to steady himself by snatching at a sharp blade of ice, cutting his fingers badly in so doing.

The Tibetans now used ice axes, yes, the ice axes we had issued to Koila and our other three Nepalese porters, which the Chinese had refused to return to them for their October journey back over the Urai Lekh. I was pleasantly surprised how well these Tibetans managed over this difficult ground, showing all the ingrained skills possessed by hill people, swinging and cutting away in a manner that would not have displeased a Swiss mountain guide.

The big fellow ran into trouble, and trying to get round Harrop's slippery corner, he started to fall. Intent on survival, he slipped the head-band on which he was carrying his load by a swift tip of his head, and that precious pack of comparatively useless but expensive expedition gear went down the khud, into the Seti river, never to be seen again. Down went our 16 mm camera and lenses, several lenses for 35 mm cameras and, the greatest tragedy of all, our last full bags of tsampa and ata flour. All we had to eat now was a small amount of flour in one of the other loads.

The big fellow turned to assist the smallest of the four, and as he swung up, hanging onto his colleague's hand, two kit bags of gear fell from his load into the river. This was not going to be our day. When we reached the other side of the avalanche cone, Harrop and I went down to the river's edge to look for our lost loads, but they had been swept down the gorge by the fast-flowing Seti.

'Apart from the flour, there was nothing in there of survival value,' Harrop commented. I had to agree.

Garanphu was reached without further incident, and we sorted out a comfortable stone shelter for ourselves. We were indeed lucky, for we found one that had escaped our attention when we passed through in September on our way north. This shelter was different, having a complete roof and constructed on the lines of an Eskimo igloo. Each circle of stones overlapped the one below, until a solitary flat stone capped the top. We raised this capstone and jammed smaller stones under it to allow for ventilation. This also allowed a little light to enter. We found out to our joy that the previous tenants had left a pile of dead juniper wood. Using our bellows inflators we soon had a roaring fire going.

We decided to 'blow out our kites' on one last meal. We would mix most of the small amount of tsampa and ata we had left into a dough, and make one chapati each. This was the only time we ate anything cooked on that march from Khatang to Dhuli. We made a small oil lamp out of

Harrop's now empty cigarette tin, and using a piece of Harrop's shirt as a wick, and melting some Tibetan yak butter over the fire mixed with a small amount of paraffin, we soon had illumination in our primitive Stone-Age hut. A fire, artificial lighting, a chapati, and a mug of tea; this was luxury indeed.

I shook my bottle of Greek fire-water brandy. There was a little left. 'Do we save this for the primus stoves?' I asked. 'Or do we drink it now?'

'I don't want you to think that I am an alcoholic,' Harrop replied, 'but I can't see us, without porters, carrying primus stoves on our backs through the gorge. Can you?'

I had to agree. 'OK. There is enough wood left for a fire for boiling tea in the morning. We've used the paraffin stoves for the last time. Let's drink the brandy.'

I held up my flask and made a toast: 'Iechyd da pob cymro a phob sais twll deen pob Chinese.'

Damodar looked at me in wonderment. Harrop translated for me. 'It's Welsh, Damodar, for good health to the Welsh and the English and arseholes to the Chinese.'

I took a swig, and choked. It was the most awful firewater I have ever tasted. Harrop took a dram, and spat it out. Damodar, taking the hint, decided that modern Greek culture was not for him. What little was left I poured onto our brushwood fire, and got my eyebrows partially singed off in the ensuing explosion. We turned in. During the night I had to go outside, and was deeply concerned to find snow flakes falling, large ones.

'Any Yetis out there?' Harrop enquired.

'No, but we had one, or something like it, snuffling around our tent up near the Lekh last night,' I responded.

'I heard that,' Harrop cut in, 'but I thought that it was either you or Damodar snoring.'

'I took some pictures when I left the tent,' I commented. 'Some on soft snow, and one small group of pug marks on a patch of hard-packed snow. No giant, that.'

'No,' Harrop agreed. 'The size of a dog. On all fours. Occasionally on two hind legs for a look-see. I've examined droppings and they are those of a herbivore, not a carnivore. I look forward to seeing the slides when you get them processed when we get home.'

I did not express my thoughts, my apprehension. When we get home. But would we ever see home again? 'It's snowing hard out there. Bloody big wet flakes,' I offered.

There was no reply. What was there to say? The one thing we did not require on the difficult stretches scheduled for the morrow was fresh snow.

Came the morning, Damodar got our fire going and made a brew of tea. The Tibetans appeared to announce that they were heading off back to Khatang right away. They were worried about the change in the weather, and feared that a full day's heavy snowfall might make their return journey over the Urai Lekh impossible.

I asked them to disobey Chinese orders and carry for us as far as Dhuli, offering them a substantial cash reward. They replied that they feared to disobey the Cheenee Burra Rajah Sahib, for not only they, but also their families would be punished. They also added that they would not attempt to force the Seti Gorge at that time of the year for a thousand rupees a day, and repeated to Damodar what they had said to him at Khatang, several days earlier: 'We think that you and your Sahibs are dead men.'

With that, the smallest of the four showed us the true worth of the sorely tried Tibetan people. He opened up his shuba and produced his far from commodious bag of tsampa, and tipped some of the contents onto the lid of our billy-can. His three companions shamefacedly followed suit. They had several days' march back across the watershed of the Himalaya, in mid-winter, and refusing our offer of a gift of a tent, they now shared with us the only thing of real value up there in the Seti Gorge. Food.

I felt like bursting into tears, but managed to hold myself in check. Reaching into my anorak, I produced our rupee notes. 'I want them to have ten rupees between them, Damodar. I would like to make it more, but we have to buy food when we get to Dhuli.'

To my complete amazement they entered into an argument, and took my rupees only after Damodar persuaded them vigorously.

'Christ, these people are the salt of the earth,' Harrop said. 'They don't deserve the lousy Chinese communists.'

'We now have enough tsampa for one big sausage each,' Damodar said, 'and some for tomorrow, and we still have a little sugar left.'

With that our Tibetan friends departed, picking up their pack frames and wicker baskets. They trotted at the double along the track which led to Saipal and the Urai Lekh. A few minutes later they vanished round a corner. We were alone now, just us and the Seti Gorge.

I asked Harrop and Damodar to carry out a ruthless pruning of our porter loads, to ensure that we carried only what was required for bare survival. While they busied themselves, I sat down to write two important letters, each on a Chinese cigarette packet cover. One was addressed to Indian Intelligence in Delhi, the other to Harrop. When I had written what under the circumstances might well have been my farewell notes, I folded both letters up together, and placed them inside the rear flap pocket of Harrop's rucksack. If I did not make it through the Seti Gorge, he would find my notes the next morning, for that was where he kept his toothbrush. I then waited until Harrop and Damodar were fully engrossed in their task and, unpacking Harrop's rucksack and mine, I swapped Lilo inflatable air mattresses. Harrop would now be carrying my air bed, and my prison diary. If I fell by the wayside he might still get through, and one of those two notes, addressed to Harrop personally, requested that he hand the second note, containing my intelligence on Chinese activities in west Tibet to 'Cricket Wallah' in Delhi. As I did not know Cricket Wallah's name, I addressed my data to 'Timmy', one of whose boys Cricket Wallah said I was. I tucked the notes into Harrop's rucksack with a feeling of deep satisfaction. (See page 13 of the picture section and also page 211 for a transcription of the hand-written notes.)

There was spare clothing in those unwanted pack loads, and we piled it up inside the igloo hut. Both primus stoves had to stay behind, along with the paraffin can, which now contained about a cupful of fuel. I watched Harrop throw one lightweight nylon climbing rope onto the pile, and then turn towards me with the other rope in his hands.

'No, John. Like I said. If we rope up in that place, and one falls, we all go. Leave it, old son.'

Harrop shrugged his broad shoulders and complied with my wishes. 'Crampons; do we take crampons?' he enquired.

'I think not,' I replied. 'If there is ice that's that bad in any of these gullies, we'll never get through the gorge by nightfall, and as there is no place large and flat enough on that face to pitch a tent, we either get through the gorge today, or we die of exposure on the face during the night.'

Harrop nodded his agreement, and threw his, mine and Damodar's crampons onto the growing pile. I saw only one of our two Meade tents.

'Where's the other tent? We are not taking a tent. It weighs over 16 pounds. Too much dead weight, and too bulky to carry. We will have to get down into the tree line, and we'll be all right.'

Harrop shook his head. 'Look, I don't want to argue with you. But just for this once let's accept that although you are the leader of this expedition, right now you have a minor revolt on your hands and no matter what you say, we are taking that tent, and I'm going to carry it.'

There was no answer to that. I was too weak to carry a tent, and Damodar just did not have the physical strength for such an extra load. Such was the self-effacing modesty and self-sacrificing courage of my companion. It was what I had come to expect of John Harrop. This was no time for argument or even lengthy discussion, for every minute of daylight was a precious commodity. For the first time in six months I felt incapable of making light of a situation, or cracking a joke.

'So really, we're taking nothing out of those surviving loads?' I said.

'Afraid not,' Harrop responded. 'Just our sleeping bags, air-beds, one still camera apiece, and if you've still got it, that bloody silly piece of Browning artillery you've been carrying.'

'That stays here,' I said, dropping the pistol and its box of ammunition wrapped in a piece of tent cloth onto the pile. 'Rajah Oom Jung might like it. He can have it, when his men come up here to reinstate the track in the spring.'

'One of the ropes is lightweight,' Harrop said, looking hard at me.

'It's not the bloody weight. It's the temptation to put it on for the difficult passages and then lose time traversing one at a time in the gorge.'

Harrop shrugged his shoulders. The die was now well and truly cast.

There was no snow now, and the sun was shining. At Garanphu, 7,000 feet below the summit of Kapkot, we were in shadow, and would be until the afternoon, when the sun would bathe our side of the gorge with totally unwanted light. Strong sunlight would warm up the snow and ice on the west face of Kapkot, loosening rocks which would hurtle down the face like some form of mountain artillery. This was a hazard we had to face, an obstacle to be overcome, but right now, the sight of a sunny blue sky was good for morale.

Harrop set off first, his heavy bulky pack surmounted by the Meade tent, which hid his head. Damodar followed. I came up in the rear.

As I plodded along the track, the easy part, which for two miles amounted to no more than a goat track on a steep grass slope, I looked ahead to the most difficult part of the day's journey. There were dark purple flying-buttresses of rock ahead, and it was amongst those buttresses and the intervening gullies, where the track was built out onto the face, that we were going to have our ordeal, not by fire, but by ice.

As I followed my two companions I reflected on Sir Jacob Astley's prayer before the battle of Edgehill, in the Civil War: 'Oh Lord, thou knowest how busy I must be this day; if I forget thee, do not thou forget me.'

18/12/55

John, I feel all in. I doubt if I can get through this place. It scares me stiff. If I fail, you will appreciate why I decided that we would not rope up. The rope would be an instrument of mutual destruction. I intend swapping our Lilo's when we pack our gear. You will have mine, and you will find my prison diary in the pillow. The attached note is for a contact in Indian Intelligence in Delhi. If I don't make it, they will probably contact you. If not, then use your own judgement. I am dumping my .32 Browning automatic pistol with our surplus gear.

When you reach Chainpur tell Rajah Oom-Jung he can have all our (jettisoned) expedition gear and the pistol, to be collected when the Nepalese come up here to reinstate the track through the Seti Gorge next spring.

I'm grateful to you and Damodar for your support. Also proud of the way you both stood up to the Chinese Communists. I hope that my wife Jean and my son Mike get looked after.

Syd.

Signal
to Shri Timmy. Indian Intelligence.
From S. Wignall, Welsh Himalayan Expedition.
Subject Chinese PLA at Taklakot
Date December 18th 1955
Origin Seti Gorge. W. Nepal.

1 Chinese PLA strength Taklakot approx. 500.
2 PLA have larger base. Site not known. 23 miles from Jitkot, 17 miles from Taklakot.
3 Troop strength (of above) approx. 4,000 to 6,000 men.
4 Strategic Highway from Lhasa will reach Taklakot 1957 at latest. Confirmed by PLA soldier who will drive trucks.
5 Chinese Military Governor (of Gartok, capital of West Tibet) laid claim, in my presence to India/Aksai-Chin and whole of NEFA. Nepal/Mustang-Manangbhot salient; Gurka state and Sola Khumbu (south side of Everest situated in Nepal). Also parts of Pakistan/Kashmir. Whole of Sikkim. Whole of Bhutan. Parts of northern Burma.
Will use force if necessary.
Signed,
Sydney Wignall,
Expedition Leader

Transcription of the notes for Harrop

21

We soon became spaced out as I fell further and further behind. The ground became steeper and the track narrower, as we climbed away from the river bed. There were two miles of easy going, made uncomfortable because the soft wet snow from the night before began balling-up on the Vibram soles of our climbing boots. Every few steps, we had to stop and knock huge clumps of snow off the soles.

Eventually, the easy part of the track was behind us. We had made good progress, covering those two miles to the rock-bound steeper section of the gorge in little more than an hour. Harrop and Damodar vanished around a corner. I looked down to my right. The Seti river lay more than a thousand feet below me. I rounded a corner, and was faced with the sight of Harrop chipping steps in an ice-filled gully. The track had vanished down the khud. The cliff face in this section consisted of hard rock, but it was occasionally split almost vertically by gullies of softer conglomerate material. Rocks and pebbles occasionally protruded through the ice. Whenever possible, Harrop used these as hand- and foot-holds. When they petered out, he was forced to resume chipping steps in the ice with his axe. The angle was steep, and a slip would mean certain disaster. Harrop made it across the face of the gully, and then called to Damodar who, relieved of the need to cut steps, crossed that gully showing a remarkable degree of agility. I looked across at Harrop. His load appeared enormous, mainly because our rucksacks were lightweight, not heavy-duty metal-framed load-carrying models. He wobbled over to one side as he hung onto a handhold, just showing his head round the corner, looking back in the direction from which he had come, directing Damodar's hands and feet by shouted instructions.

Now it was my turn. I just hoped that in my weak state I would not get a dose of the knee-shakes if I had to stand on one small hold for any length of time. Bit by bit, I edged across that ice gully, and ended up rounding the corner to join Harrop and Damodar. Another similar gully lay ahead. 'Where's the bloody track?' I shouted to Harrop.

'Don't you remember?' he called back. 'That was one of the easy places in September. The track has been swept down the khud.'

There was a huge rock overhang just beyond the gully facing us, and icicles ten to fifteen feet in length hung from it, poised over an ice bulge. Ice walls are one thing, but ice bulges are another. One of the main principles of rock and ice climbing is to maintain correct posture, and thus ensure safe balance. With an ice face two to three feet from one's chin, one can stand upright in footholds, and hold oneself in a vertical position by placing hand or ice axe against the face. But ice bulges demand chipped-out footsteps, and no face to balance against. The trick is not to lean in towards the face, for if you do, your feet are prone to shoot out into space.

Harrop ducked under the icicles, leaving a perfect set of cut steps behind him for Damodar and me. Then he was onto the ice bulge, and Damodar and I watched, unable to offer any assistance, as Harrop gradually chipped his way round the corner out of sight. Then we heard his voice. 'Back on the track again.'

Damodar and I let out a cheer, for the delay caused in cutting steps across those two gullies had taken more than half an hour of our precious daylight. I heard Harrop, out of sight now, chipping away with his axe, and below the ice bulge I saw the ice flakes he was cutting out, sparkling and tinkling down the gully wall, until they vanished from view.

Harrop was waiting round that corner ready to give advice. If any one of us slipped, there was nothing the other two could do to arrest his fall. We were back on the track for a hundred yards or so, just flat rocks placed on top of saplings jammed into crevices and cracks on the cliff face. Ahead lay another section of vanished track. We were back cutting steps in the ice. Midway across this section, the angle eased in a shallow snow-filled gully. There was danger here.

'Watch out, John,' I shouted. 'That lot looks like windslab. It could slide off down the khud.'

Harrop nodded in my direction, and then launched himself into the snow-filled gully. Gingerly kicking steps in the snow, standing straight upright, ice axe held almost horizontal against the snow face, he worked his way quickly across, to be followed by Damodar, with me in the rear. I took a lower line than Harrop and Damodar, with the intention of not making too deep a single line of steps across that snow slab. I made it with a sigh of relief, but no sooner had I reached a rock stance on the far wall of the gully, than I heard a rushing-swishing sound, and looking behind me, I watched a thousand tons or so of snow avalanche down that gully, until it vanished over an overhang. If any one of us had been in the middle of that snow slide, he would have gone down into the river Seti, more than a thousand feet below.

Then we were back on the track again, part man-made, part natural fault line across the face of the gorge. We came to another corner, and once again had to move one at a time. Standing still for several minutes I found that I was no longer able to wiggle my toes; they were frozen and lifeless. The fingers of my right hand, holding onto my ice axe, also became lifeless. I followed Damodar, and across another gully I could see Harrop chipping steps round another of those interminable bloody corners.

Damodar crossed the gully using Harrop's steps. I waited for a few moments, blowing onto my frozen fingers, trying to get circulation back into them. I took one step into the gully, and then another, and then saw only sky, ice, sky, and then felt a jolt. I had come off on a climb only once before in my life, and that was on a cliff in Snowdonia. Tales of one's life history flashing through one's mind as one falls are sheer bunkum. There is no sensation attached to falling off a mountain. No fear, no screams, no cries, just sheer bewilderment. On this occasion, after my slide had turned into a cartwheel, I felt that thump, and ended right side up, in a sitting position, my progress down the cliff face temporarily terminated by whatever had hit me on the base of my spine. I was in agony, with pain shooting up my back. I felt sick (I am a cissy when it comes to enduring pain). I just hoped that I would not have one of my famous 'turns' and pass out, in what was quite obviously going to be a very interesting situation. I heard a ripping sound from behind, and I slid down that slope, still in a sitting position, for a few inches. I looked down. 'Christ, never do that, you twit,' I said to myself. My boots dangled over the ice edge of my shallow gully which at that point issued out over an overhang. I could see the far wall of the Seti Gorge just a few hundred feet away. I could not see the bottom of the gorge, but I could hear the sound of the rushing water. 'Try to turn over, get on your face, that way you can bang the pick of your ice axe into the ice, you prick, but where is the bloody ice axe?'

Luckily for me, I was of the school of mountaineers who believed in a sling, by which one can let go of the axe, and it will dangle from one's wrist. So there was my trusty Swiss ice axe, dangling from my right wrist. When I tried to turn on my face, I heard that ripping sound again, and I slid another couple of inches down the slope. I realised what had saved my life; it was the back of my Everest anorak, which had hooked onto a small sharp rock projecting through the ice. My weight was slowly pulling that rock flake through the material. On my face I had to go, and pretty damn quick.

It was at that moment that something intangible happened, something I had heard others talk about, but which I had disbelieved, and in my philistine arrogance had even sneered at. I felt that I was no longer alone. There was someone there with me, on that bloody awful face of the Seti Gorge. I looked around. No visible sign of another person, and yet I felt that I only had to close my eyes and reach out, and there would be a reassuring hand there, ready to guide and assist me.

Another grunt from the tail of my anorak jacket, and I knew that it was now or never. I swung over to my right, hearing the rock rip clean through and out of the rear of my anorak and, as I started to slide, I slammed the pick of my axe into the face and hung on with both hands. I was secure for the moment. Then I let my right hand slip out of the wrist-strap, and while holding onto my axe with my left hand, my right hand groped across the face, until I located and grabbed hold of that life-saving sliver of rock. Then I worked my right knee up onto it; took a quick two handed swing with the pick of my axe a couple of feet higher up the ice face, and hauled up until I could get my right foot onto that tiny piece of rock. I felt better now, but I knew that too long a spell in that position, with all my weight on one foot, and I would get the knee-trembles. Then it happened, it was quite indescribable, I felt like the man who, trying to avoid getting wet in pouring rain, dodges in and out of doorways until eventually he is soaked through to the skin, and realising that he cannot get any wetter, just walks in the rain and enjoys it.

All my fears and apprehensions vanished like a puff of smoke. The worst the lousy gorge could do was kill me. I started chipping steps for the fifty feet that separated me from the ones Harrop had cut in the ice above. He was still there, that other presence, whoever he was. I was reminded of Frank Smythe, that great populariser of mountaineering through his many books and hundreds of superb mountain photographs. When alone, exhausted and dispirited, at 28,000 feet on the north face of Everest, he had been conscious of a second person being close by, giving him moral support. I had heard similar stories from both Arctic and Antarctic explorers. In some cases, two climbers had spoken of the feeling of a 'third man on the rope'.

I knew how Frank Smythe felt, and how all those other tired, weary, exhausted climbers and travellers must have felt, when that invisible presence cast a kind of warm glow over me. Little did I know, that at that time, at least one congregation of Welsh parishioners was praying for us, in a chapel in the Conway valley. Gin Din Rhou had told us that he would pray for us. I was later to learn that the hill villagers at Dhuli were praying for our safekeeping. Three separate religions, Christian, Hindu and Buddhist, all praying to what they believe to be separate deities. Is it possible that there is such a thing as the 'power of prayer'? Could it be that mass, sustained prayer creates a force of psychic energy, that can manifest itself in a physical dynamic way? The gods were certainly working hard for the three of us that day.

Slowly but methodically I cut steps up that ice slope, until I reached the place where I had slipped. No knee-shakes now. I felt completely exhausted, but all my fears had dissipated. I steadied myself on two good footholds, and cut my way across to where Harrop and Damodar had disappeared round a corner. I breasted the corner, to see my two companions on a lower level. They had lost the line of the vanished track, and were seeking a way across steep overlapping boiler-plate slabs of rock which curved down into the void. The slabs were ice-covered, and now they held the added danger of last night's snow lying on the ice and disguising its presence.

Harrop used the head of his axe to first sweep away the snow cover and then snick away at the ice to expose bare rock for a safe foothold. I moved gingerly across the intervening face, turning to look behind me, about to say, 'Come on, it's all right now,' when I realised that I was alone up in that corner. My unidentified invisible comrade who had helped me recover from my fall and carve my way up that gully had departed. He must have decided that I was no longer in need of help. I was alone. He had gone perhaps to render assistance to others in need on that December morning amongst the sacred snows of Himachal. Perhaps he had gone off to the Urai Lekh to give a helping hand to our Tibetan porters plodding their way over that desolate pass.

I caught up with Damodar as he moved across Harrop's expertly carved footholds. It was nice to place one's feet on rock and not ice or snow for a change. Then we came to the big overhang, and Harrop shouted the obvious to me and Damodar, 'We're back on the track now.'

This part of the track through the gorge is a most impressive place. The track runs into a narrow gully, and then turns right across the far face, under a great overhang in the cliff wall. I watched Damodar as he approached a huge projecting boulder. He would have to edge under it because the track at that point had collapsed down the khud. I struggled with my camera, with frozen fingers. The track was in a good state beyond where Damodar was, and it consisted of dry-stone walling. Then it passed under the overhang proper, and Harrop stood in its shadow. Ahead lay a huge boulder, just beyond the overhang and right on the next corner to be turned. I remembered that great boulder as being a very dodgy place when we entered the gorge in September. One must climb onto a six-inch-wide outwardly sloping ledge, with no further handholds, shuffle along the ledge, and then step down onto the track again. I clicked the shutter and I decided there and then that come what may, I would make a photographic record of our ordeal by ice whenever the terrain allowed two hands free for camera and exposure meter.

I followed Damodar and, sitting on my backside, wriggled under and past the big overhanging boulder, my legs dangling over the void. 'What the hell,' I thought. 'A thousand feet down. You can get killed falling ten feet. The length of fall is of little consequence, it's the sudden stop at the bottom that can give one cause for concern.'

Damodar was just ahead of me when I heard Harrop call back, from his highly dangerous traverse, edging across that six-inch-wide ledge, 'Not very good tidings. A piece of track just beyond this boulder has gone. The next bit is going to be very naughty.' Damodar was edging along the narrow ledge. Harrop was trying to balance, denied handholds, the forty-pound load swaying on his back. Then he was gone. I heard a thud. 'OK, I made it.'

Now it was Damodar's turn. He shuffled sideways, face in, until he reached the end of that narrow snow-covered ledge. He looked round the corner, and then turned back, and facing into the big boulder, he closed his eyes and started talking to himself. This was not Urdu. This was his own classical Nepali language of the Kathmandu valley. Damodar was praying

in Nuari, to which god I knew not. 'Pity you're a devout practising atheist,'
I said to myself. 'Good job that bloke who helped you in that gully didn't
know it. He might have left you to slide down into perdition.'

Damodar steeled himself, edged back to the far corner of the tiny shelf,
muttered a religious imprecation out loud, and made the leap. I heard a
thud, followed by Harrop's voice. 'Come on, it's your turn now.'

I followed my companions, edging inch by inch, until, leaning away
from the boulder face to maintain correct posture and balance, I was able
to look round the corner. It was as Harrop had said: 'A bit naughty.' The
built-up section of track had broken away for about three feet. One had to
jump across. Jumping three feet should not under normal circumstances
have given me anything to worry about. But facing in to a rock wall,
with no handholds, depending entirely on balance, and then having to
change feet with left foot in front, my body turned partially outwards,
to get into the right position for a leap was not only difficult, I found it
almost impossible.

'Go on. You can do it.' This from Harrop. I made it a point not to look
down into the gorge. Then I jumped.

My right foot hit the edge of the far gap in the track, and my left missed.
My right foot slipped, and I fell forward and down. As my hands grasped
for the passing edge of the broken track, I was grabbed by someone. I
looked up. It was, of course, dear old ever-present when needed, tower of
strength, Welsh Himalayan Expedition Rock of Gibraltar, John Frederick
Harrop.

Half pulled up by Harrop, I scrambled up onto the track. Harrop was
grinning at me. I noticed that he had shed his rucksack load, fearing that
I might have problems with that leap. Damodar sat on Harrop's sack, a
few feet further along the track.

'You won't do that again, will you?' Harrop said, still with a smile on
his face. But his eyes were not smiling, and I could see through his mask
of Janus, and realised how deep his concern was for my safety.

'No. I promise. Honest injun. Won't do it again.' I confirmed.

'Better not tell him about that fall down the gully,' I said to myself.
'He'll begin to get the idea that you are something of a liability. And don't
mention your trip back up to the track, accompanied by the Fairy Godfather
of the Seti Gorge. He'll think that you really are round the bend.'

We plodded on. It was after midday now, and a danger we had already
anticipated revealed itself. We were on good piece of undamaged man-
made track when a bomb, or something very like it, exploded on a ledge
about twenty feet ahead of us. There was an acrid smell of sulphur in the air,
and fragments of rock flew off into space. The sun, somewhere high above,
out of sight to us poor mortals deep in that narrow gorge, was loosening ice-
bound rocks from the western face of Kapkot. Now it was to be ordeal by
mountain artillery. Those were the days when mountaineers did not wear
crash-helmets. We would have regarded them as fit only for pansies.

We made as much of a dash for it as our cumbersome loads would allow, pausing only when we had a near vertical face above us, for that protected us, the stones falling away from the rock wall, hurtling past us with a nerve shaking 'zooooze' sound. When the terrain offered no protection, we just hoped for the best, as mountain bomb after mountain bomb burst on the steep track.

Then we were lost. It was well into the afternoon now, and so many parts of the track had vanished down into the gorge, we could not find the correct line of traverse. Eventually we came to a huge wide gully. It led down to the bottom of the gorge about a thousand feet below. It looked easy going, and moraine rocks jumbled together at the bottom, with the Seti flowing up against them. The route down was denied us by a short rock wall, which we would have to descend. There was nothing else for it. We would have to go down that wall, into the gully, and climb down it until we reached the bottom of the gorge, and hope to hell that there was a way through. But if there was a way through, at low level, the Nepalese would have made use of it, and not constructed their ingenious track.

Harrop went first, as always, followed by Damodar. I was in the rear. I watched Harrop work his way across the gully wall beneath me. Then he was almost there.

'My hands. Lost all feeling. Christ, my axe.'

I watched Harrop's ice axe fall from his frozen fingers, and down into the gully. Unlike me, Harrop did not like webbing slings, he said that they flapped about (true) when cutting steps. The loss of an ice axe was not to be contemplated in our situation, and both Damodar and I let out a yell of delight when we saw Harrop's ice axe, flying down like a dart, bury itself in a patch of snow, which fortunately covered a grass ledge. It took Harrop half an hour to make his way down that rock pitch, and across to his ice axe. Damodar and I followed as quickly as we could.

I took a couple of tumbles getting down that thousand-foot gully, but we were never in any danger. At dusk we stood on top of huge boulders, with the Seti river flowing rapidly by close to our feet.

'Too late to make our way across any more of that cliff face,' I said.

'The river. No other choice. We'll have to go into the river,' Harrop responded.

'How deep will it be, Syd Sahib? I can't swim,' Damodar complained.

'Neither can I, Damodar,' I responded. 'We could always blow up one of our air beds, and sail down the damn river!'

'Look ahead,' Harrop called in the fading light. 'The gorge becomes a narrow canyon. Water is going through like the clappers, but the monsoon has gone. Can't be all that deep. Problem is we don't know how far we would have to continue in the river bed.'

'We'd have to stay close to the left-hand wall,' I said, 'and try to stay upright, and hope to God it isn't so deep we'd have to swim, because if we have, Damodar and I are goners.'

'Rolling stones,' Harrop rejoined. 'Remember when we crossed all those rivers marching into base camp? The force of the water rolls big stones along, and you can fall over them. Important not to stumble.'

'You sound like you are talking yourself into something,' I commented. 'Do we go in or don't we?'

Harrop shrugged. 'No choice!'

At that moment I felt my knees buckle. I had been surviving on what reserves of physical and nervous energy I had left, and now I felt what little remained was draining away. We stood on a huge boulder. It would have been underwater during the monsoon. I peered closely in what light was left at the thermometer tied to the rear of Harrop's rucksack.

It's about thirty below freezing, Fahrenheit,' I said. 'Do you realise that the water temperature will be higher than the air temperature? That glacial water will be just above freezing point?'

'In that case, we are in for the first warm bath we've had in months,' Harrop jested.

That was the first humorous remark any of us had made since we left Garanphu.

'I'm all in, John.' At last I had the courage to face up to things and tell my two companions that physically I had just about reached the end of the road.

'It's the dysentery. It took too much out of you. Had any recurrences since you took those last three pills?'

'No,' I replied. 'No Tibetan Trots, just feel washed out. Legs like rubber now. I just want to lie down and go to sleep.'

'Not here,' Harrop responded. 'Can't pitch a tent on these boulders, and what if the temperature rose in the night, and the snow started to melt? We would either wake up underwater, or have to climb back up that damn gully. Sorry, this is it. It's the Seti or nothing.' And then he added, 'There are those pep pills, those boosters, they might see you through the next bit.'

'And if the next bit become a long distance marathon, and the after effects hit me, I'll just keel over. No thanks. I'll stick with jellied legs,' I rejoined.

'Then let's go,' Harrop said, moving off towards the left-hand wall of the dark canyon that lay ahead. After stumbling down the boulder-strewn slope, we reached the canyon wall. It was dark in there. I could hardly see a thing. I looked up, to see that I could still recognise the darkening sky overhead.

Harrop went first. This time I followed him, for I felt reassured by the close proximity of his strength. When he was shin-deep in water, he turned to me, and above the roar of the Seti river shouted, 'Up the creek, and without a ruddy paddle.'

We were soon stumbling over loose rounded river-washed stones, as the water tore at our legs. We were knee-deep now. I saw the dark shape of the canyon wall, and at that moment I lost sight of Harrop. I shouted to him, to see if he was all right, but my cry was lost in the roar of the Seti. I felt Damodar bump up against me. 'Christ, one collision in this place, and if you can't get on your feet and drop your load, you could drown.'

So much for the water being warmer than the air. It felt icy cold around my legs, through two pairs of trousers, but I felt the circulation returning to my feet, and it hurt. I was in agony. I steadied myself against the cliff face with the shaft of my ice axe. That helped. I was in complete darkness. Now the water was over my knees, and washing up to my thighs. 'Much deeper than this and we'll cash in our chips,' I said to myself as I felt a football-size boulder being forced against the back of my legs by the fast flowing current. I raised my right foot, to let the boulder go past, and on placing my foot down, it landed on top of another rounded river stone. I stumbled, and quickly brought my ice axe down off the canyon wall, and just in time rammed the pick into the stony river bed in front of me, thereby avoiding what would have been a fatal fall.

Now the water was thigh-deep, and the odd wave washed up against my backside. I felt the force of the water trying to hurry me along, and knock me off my feet. God knows how many times I stumbled, but retained my balance. At one point, I recovered from a stumble, and on reaching out again for the left-hand wall of the gorge with the point of my ice axe, I felt nothing.

'Oh, Jesus, this is it,' I said to myself. Lost in the middle of a Himalayan river, in December, in the dark. It was a situation I would not have wished on my worst enemy. Then something occurred to me. If I had lost the left-hand wall of the gorge, it must be because it had curved away from me. Perhaps we were close to a place where we could leave the river? I edged further to the left. Still no rock wall. The water was knee-deep. It had shallowed out. Further left again I went, and tripping over a round stone in that Stygian blackness, I fell on my face. I was soaked through with icy cold water, but there was no raging torrent. I was not being swept away. Then I saw a light. It was a match. It had to be Harrop. Fortunately there was no wind down there in the bottom of the Seti Gorge, and he held onto his match until I heard him grunt as it burnt his fingers.

'Over here,' he said as he struck a second match.

'I see it, John Sahib,' Damodar cried as he caught up with me.

'Where the hell have you been?' Harrop enquired somewhat facetiously.

'I've been having that bloody bath you were talking about,' I growled.

'Not too loud,' Harrop said, lighting a third match off the last one, 'or every Yeti in the upper Seti will want one.'

'Where are we, Syd Sahib?' Damodar enquired.

'Buggered if I know,' I responded.

'We are in a ruddy great terminal moraine of boulders the size of houses,' Harrop offered. 'This lot must have been deposited here by a glacier, thousands of years ago.'

Damodar sat on a stone and taking off his rucksack had a look at what life was left in his torch. Just a glimmer.

'Now for tent country,' Harrop suggested. 'We have got to find a place large enough to pitch this tent, or we will freeze to death.'

Damodar passed me in the dark, shining his torch on the huge boulders. They were all clustered together, and any route out of that gorge bottom would have to be to the left, scrambling up one side of a twenty-foot-high boulder, only to slide down the far side, not knowing what the hell you would land on.

After an hour of this kind of terrain I realised that I was spent and physically completely finished. I lay on my face on an upward sloping slab. My legs would not move, it was like they were set in concrete, or belonged to somebody else. A voice called, 'Are you all right, Syd Sahib?'

I felt too shattered to shout a reply. I must have passed out. I was woken up by Harrop shaking me. 'Come on, we can't have far to go now,' he said.

I didn't even have the strength to shake my head. I just lay there on that slab, my right cheek placed against the cold rock. 'Leave me here,' I muttered. 'Can't go on. Nothing left. You two try to get out and get to Dhuli, and send some porters back to collect me.'

'Bullshit,' Harrop replied. 'You will die of exposure. You can't stay here.'

'Not die of exposure.' I was having problems articulating. 'I don't feel cold any more. I feel warm now.'

This must have aroused Harrop's concern, because my soaking wet trousers and anorak were now starting to freeze hard.

'Let me have some kip. Gotta sleep. Feel better in the spring,' I muttered, and to myself ruminated on: 'Well, winter's here, can spring be far behind?' Then they were gone. 'Sensible fellows,' I thought to myself, 'I'll be all right. That fellow Harrop nags like a wife.' I must have dozed off, and I was awakened by someone pulling my boots off. Harrop and Damodar were back. I had no idea of time. They were rubbing my now lifeless feet. Then they went to work on my hands. Then they rammed my feet back into my boots.

'Come on, Damodar, give me a hand,' I heard Harrop grunt.

Then I felt myself being lifted up into the air. I was across Harrop's broad shoulders; he had me in a fireman's lift. Damodar steadied Harrop, and he started to stumble up a great slab of rock, with Damodar pushing behind. I was coming to now, and I realised that Harrop was not carrying his rucksack.

'Where the hell are we, where is your sack?' I asked him.

'Dumped it with Damodar's,' he replied. 'Found a place where we will be above any rising water level in the night, and there is enough space to half-pitch the tent, and Damodar found a small tree, and we are going to break some branches off it, and we are going to have a fire.'

That was as far as Harrop got; then he crested the slab and all three of us cascaded down the other side in the dark. By now we were all bruised, but we did not feel it. Damodar led the way through and over that purgatorial labyrinth. If Harrop had committed any sins in a former existence, then he purged them away that December night. He was a prime candidate for old Gin Din Rhou's Nirvana.

In some places, Harrop and Damodar hauled me. In others they carried me. I heard Damodar sink down with a sigh. 'Couple of minutes' rest, John Sahib, then I'll have a bash with my ice axe at that little tree.'

We had arrived. Harrop thrust some sectional tent poles into my hands. 'Here, you stick these together.'

As I fumbled in the dark, I realised what Harrop was up to. He wanted to get me into a frame of mind where I could find an interest in life.

Eventually, Harrop and I rigged up the tent with poles in one end, the other end unsupported. Damodar by now had returned with some broken tree branches.

'Green wood, Syd Sahib. It will smoke.'

'Bugger the smoke, Damodar,' I replied. 'Let's have a jolly good bonfire.'

It took some effort on Damodar's part, but eventually he got a twig of wood to glow. He worked on it with our bellows inflator, and eventually we had a fire. It did smoke, and we didn't care, even when we choked on it. We were able to boil enough water for one mug of tea each, but not enough to mix a tsampa-Weetabix sausage. We had half-pitched our tent on snow, in a small space between a boulder and what in the flickering firelight was obviously the face of a cliff.

'Hear that water rushing. Does it ring any bells?' Harrop asked me.

'No. I must be thick. Go on, tell me. There's only one river, and that's the Seti. We've just come down it. So what.'

Harrop flashed a smile. 'It's louder than the ruddy river. Don't you remember when you and I came up here ahead of the others in September? That waterfall tumbling out of the south end of the Seti Gorge. That roaring sound. It has to be it.'

'Then we've made it, if we are close to that waterfall, John Sahib,' Damodar said.

'We must be pretty damn close to it, Damodar,' I offered.

We tried to thaw out our frozen socks, boots and the bottoms of our trousers in front of that completely inadequate fire.

'If we get into our bags and leave our clothes and socks out for the night wet, they will freeze again like a brick,' I said.

'Yes. We'll have to wear them wet inside our sleeping bags,' Harrop commented. 'That way may give us a miserable wet night, but we'll be wearing warm wet clothes in the morning.'

And so we turned in. I looked at my watch in the firelight. 'God. It's only 7 p.m. It seems like we've been going for about twenty-four hours. That was the longest day of my life.'

There was no room to lie down. So we sat up in our sleeping bags. Harrop and Damodar packed me into the far end of our half-pitched tent, with my back against a rock wall, which for some strange reason was packed with broken tree branches. 'Here we go again,' I said to myself. At Kalapani I had spent two nights at the lower end of the tent, with Damodar rolling onto Harrop, and Harrop rolling onto me. In my uncomfortable position, inside my now warming bag, it took some time for me to realise what my unselfish companions had done. The tree branches were designed to insulate my back from the cold rock face; and by placing me at the back of the half-pitched tent, Harrop and Damodar were further insulating me with their bodies. We were very hungry, having eaten nothing other than a chapati each the night before, and a tsampa sausage for breakfast. I dozed off, and I doubt if 18-inch naval guns detonating outside that tent would have woken us up that night. We slept straight through for fourteen hours, coming to just before 9.30 a.m.

Damodar looked out through the end of the tent. It was the unsupported end, and he had to wriggle through the collapsed part to reach the tunnel entrance.

'Syd Sahib, John Sahib. Come and look at this. You will not believe what I am seeing this moment.'

We crawled out of our sleeping bags, bleary eyed, and joined Damodar. It was like a fairy tale come true. It was a wonderland. The sun was shining. The sky was blue. We had pitched our tent on the only piece of uncomfortable real estate in sight. There were trees and a carpet of pine needles, and over to our right, only a couple of hundred yards away, that magic waterfall roared its way out of the Seti Gorge, from which we had unknowingly emerged the night before.

Damodar leapt about like some half-crazed leprechaun. He seized his ice axe, and started to hack away at tree branches for a fire, and in the process broke off the head of the axe.

We had done it. We had made it. The first men ever to not only force the Urai Lekh, but also the Seti Gorge in winter. To my knowledge, no one has done it since. I stumbled out of the tent, and lay on my face, burying it in pine needles. Then I staggered over to a tree and clutched at a pine branch. I snatched up a tiny alpine flower and held it to my lips.

Harrop was cheering, as was Damodar. I walked away from the tent. I had to be alone for a few moments. I found a flat rock and sat on it. Birds flew over my head, and I was awash with birdsong. 'Oh, how wonderful it is to be alive,' I thought to myself. Then I buried my head in my hands and I burst into tears. I cried like I have never cried before in my life, not even when I was a child. It took some time to recover my composure. I returned to the pine needle carpet and sat cross-legged on it. Damodar had a fire going, and our billy can was on the boil.

'Let's have a Christmas feast,' Harrop suggested. 'Why don't we blow out our kites, and eat all the flour at one go.'

'That's right,' I said. 'We'll all make pigs of ourselves. It can't be more than two or three days' march to Dhuli, and we'll manage without grub until then, if we have to.'

So that is what we did. We had a brew of tea, and made tsampa-Weetabix sausages with the flour the four Tibetans had given us, with the last of our sugar mixed into them, and we thought when we had completed our breakfast that we had dined like kings.

I looked hard at John Harrop and Damodar Narayan Suwal as I supped from my tea mug. 'How did you manage to find such men?' I asked myself. I could not have achieved anything on my own. I could not have made that awful journey over the Urai Lekh and through the Seti Gorge solo, but I'm quite convinced that John Harrop could have won through by himself. He was that kind of chap. He epitomised to me the indestructibility of the free human spirit. That is something our Chinese captors could never comprehend in 1955. That same indestructible free human spirit was displayed thirty-four years later in Tiananmen Square in Peking and all the power of the Chinese communist state, supported by the PLA, failed to crush it.

We further celebrated with another can of tea, for Damodar had found a small stream and there was no further need to melt snow. We were no longer under pressure. No need to hurry slowly. We could plod our tired and weary way to Dhuli at our own pace. Harrop busied himself packing up the tent. I fished my farewell notes from the rear pocket of his rucksack. My air bed could stay inside Harrop's rucksack, for we had slept sitting upright just in our sleeping bags, with no room to place inflated air beds in our half-pitched tent. I would make the swap when we camped later that night.

'Torn the back of your anorak, Syd Sahib,' Damodar offered.

I pulled my anorak off for the first time in days. There was a rip up the back, where that rock spike had saved my life. My nose was no longer blue, the frost nip from the ascent of the Urai Lekh having vanished. All of the toes on my right foot were tipped with blue, as were three of my left toes. The middle finger on my right hand was also blue. Harrop appeared not to have any frostbite symptoms, although for some strange reason both his ankles were swollen. Damodar appeared to have suffered no ill effects whatsoever.

Damodar eyed up his broken Austrian ice axe ruefully.

'Never mind, Damodar,' I said. 'When we get to Delhi, you can have my

Swiss Mischabel axe. It was a present from my wife, who hates mountains and mountaineering, though I can't think why.'

With that, Damodar was content. We packed up our loads and, saying goodbye to the Seti Gorge, we trudged off along the track to Dhuli.

22

I had to some extent recovered from the exhaustion brought on by my exertions and our tribulations in the Seti Gorge, but my legs felt wobbly, and I found difficulty in walking in a straight line. Harrop and Damodar soon outdistanced me, and I enjoyed the solitude offered by that forest track. After a few miles we came across a shrine set into the face of a cliff, under a huge overhang. It was a Hindu shrine, and passers by made their offerings to the gods in the form of small brass bells, or tiny silver shields, the latter fashioned from either Nepalese or Indian silver rupee coins. Prayers said at that shrine would hopefully protect those heading for the Seti Gorge. Those returning from the gorge would offer prayers of thanksgiving for a safe return.

I decided that an offering would be appropriate, and hid a few anna coins and some paper rupees under a stone in the centre of the shrine. Hoping that I would not offend the gods, I took from the shrine one small brass bell and four hammered silver rupee shields. Perhaps they would protect us for the remaining part of our journey home. Harrop and Damodar, having waited for me to catch up with them, set off once more. I took a breather, and then remembered that there might be one or two Nepalese silver rupees in the pocket of my rucksack. I fished them out to place on the shrine, and found in my hand another, much larger silver coin. I had seen that coin before. It had on its obverse side a relief picture of 'The Old General', whoever he was, and that coin was Chinese.

It was Chungnya's good luck charm, which he had once shown me. Chungnya must have slipped it into the rear pocket of my rucksack as we said goodbye on the summit of the Khatang pass six days earlier. Perhaps it helped. Who knows. My wife has it now, and occasionally wears it on a silver chain.

I followed on after my two companions and found them making camp for the night. Harrop had the tent rigged up and Damodar was lighting a fire. My socks were still wet and I hung them on a branch to dry, close to the fire. Damodar heaped on a log of great size, which sent up a tremendous blaze. By now we were almost counting out our tea leaves as we dropped them into our billy can. Our tea was of the palest amber hue, and almost pure water. There was nothing to eat, and on this occasion nobody made jokes about food.

We slept for twelve hours, and awoke to the sound of birdsong. On emerging from our tent, Harrop smelt burning. It was our climbing stockings. Damodar's big log had burnt most of the feet out of our socks. This upset me more than it did Harrop. On our journey into Nepal, he had on some days taken off his boots and socks and marched in his bare feet, to toughen them up.

Bare feet in boots, even weaker tea, and no breakfast and we were off on the march again. We passed through a spot I had called 'the Fairy Meadow' on our way north in September. It consisted of a grassy area surrounding by rhododendrons and azaleas, and in winter, appeared just as beautiful to me. Giant conifers formed the boundary to the Fairy Meadow, and there was a backdrop of mountains. The Seti river sparkled and roared nearby.

When one thinks about coming out of the Himalayas, one has in mind a continual downhill walk. Would that it were so. The track did descend for a few hundred yards, but then it climbed again, and although I felt relief on the downhill sections, I grew to dread those interminable uphill parts of the track to Dhuli. I found that I had to pause between each footstep. Simply placing one foot in front of the other was an effort, and I knew that I had reached a state of exhaustion whereby I could no longer have a rest every couple of miles or so. If I sat down, I knew that I would not be able to get on my feet again. I eventually caught up with Harrop and Damodar, seated on a rock, and without pausing I plodded wearily on past them. They soon overtook me and vanished ahead out of sight. They must have taken five or six rest spells like that, but I took none.

Just after midday we heard sounds of voices on the track ahead. I came upon Harrop and Damodar chatting to two Dhotials, a man of middle age and a boy of about ten years. Regardless of our scruffy appearance, they immediately recognised us and salaamed. The man said that the people of Dhuli had prayed for us daily since hearing of our capture by the Chinese. He was pleased that we were alive but thought that we had found some new magical way over the Himalaya because he insisted that the Urai Lekh and Seti Gorge were impassable at this time of the year. Nothing would persuade him or his friends to attempt a journey to Saipal trading camp until the spring of the following year.

The man gave little hope for Rajah Oom Jung being able to benefit from the equipment we had left behind at Garanphu. He said that the Urai Lekh would be negotiable long before the track through the Seti Gorge could be repaired and reinstated by the Nepalese, and as the Tibetans would be first on the scene, they would undoubtedly help themselves to our gear, including the Browning pistol. I just hoped that some unfortunate Tibetan would not accidentally shoot himself with my discarded hand gun.

The Dhuli villager showed us little snares he was setting, aided by his grandson, to catch tiny deer, no bigger than a dog, which frequent these forests. The snares were set up on deer 'runs' which, though apparent to the trained eye, were invisible to ours. The man told us that the village of Dhuli was only half a mile away. It must have been an Irish half mile, for it was in fact more than three miles. Perhaps he was trying to cheer us up, for in the Irish story, two weary travellers ask Paddy how far it is to Ballybunion, to which he replies, 'Well, it's about eight miles, but as you look very tired, I'll make it six.'

Harrop and Damodar sportingly slowed down, possibly feeling that it would be improper and most un-British for us to straggle into Dhuli. That three-plus miles took me three hours to cover, because it contained the usual downhill, and then accursed uphill sections. For what seemed an age, we expected every rise to be the last one, and the next corner would bring Dhuli into view. But no, the track seemed to stretch ahead interminably. But now, we could see signs of man's handiwork. Looking down the hillside towards the Seti river, we could see that it was terraced and cultivated.

There was one more steepish descent, and I swore out loud, for I knew that it had to be paid for later on. Then three women came round a corner of the track, each carrying a brass urn. They were on their way to a nearby spring, and they gathered around me like a trio of hens, fussing and tut-tutting. I could not converse with them and, begging to be excused, left them talking to Damodar. One more corner, no more uphill sections, and we would be there.

A couple of houses came into sight, and a small child, seeing me, ran yelling indoors. In a matter of seconds I was surrounded by the sympathetic populace and escorted to a piece of flat ground in front of the headman's house. I looked around for Harrop and Damodar, but they were obviously still gossiping to the women at the edge of the village.

The headman appeared bearing a large hubble-bubble pipe and I was invited to help myself. I declined signifying that all I wanted was food. We had not eaten for nearly two days, and God knew when we had last eaten a real cooked meal. A straw mat, of the type on which vegetables and tobacco leaves are dried in the sun, was produced, and I was invited to sit down. Nearby a young man, whom I recognised as one of our original expedition porters, was weaving baskets, and he offered me a home-made cigarette, which I had to decline. A pan was brought, and I drank deep draughts of sweet-tasting mountain water.

The headman's wife went off to find some aloo (potatoes), the mere thought of which made my mouth water. A few moment later Harrop and Damodar arrived and we were able to converse with the villagers again, thanks to Damodar interpreting. While we sat in the sun, food was prepared, and soon we were enjoying a meal of potatoes boiled in their jackets, chapatis, wild honey and boiled eggs. It was the most enjoyable meal of my life. The honey was to be our dessert, and I noticed items in suspension in the honey bowl. There were all kinds of crawly things including one huge centipede. When I fished it out of the honey to cast aside, Harrop took it from my fingers, swallowed it, and said, 'You don't throw protein away. Not after the diet we lived on in Tibet.' Later we discovered that in this meal we had consumed all the potatoes in the village of Dhuli.

The headman informed us that shortly after our returning expedition members had passed through, a checkpoint had been set up, staffed by Indian Army officers and Gurkhas. It looked as though Cricket Wallah's prediction had come to pass. The Indian intelligence unit was camped about a mile to the south of Dhuli on the track to Chainpur, and the Indians had rented several houses. Furthermore, they possessed a radio transmitter/receiver. Perhaps we could now send out a message telling our families that we were safe. The headman sent his son to the Indian post to advise the officers.

'This is one for the book,' Harrop commented. 'Who'd have thought that the Indian Army would be here in Nepal? Maybe they've seen the light with regard to the Chinese build-up?'

Meanwhile we were shown to an upstairs room in the headman's house and told that we could stay as long as we wished, and we would not be charged rent. Like most top storeys in west Nepal houses, this one had a completely open side, providing a fine view of the village and mountains to the north. Harrop sat watching the headman's wife spin wool, and I photographed the scene.

About an hour later, our expected visitor appeared, clad in sports coat and grey flannel trousers, but carrying a .455 Webley & Scott revolver in a shoulder holster. He advised us in English that he was second in command of an Indian Army intelligence-gathering unit, and that his co would be along presently. He was greatly surprised to see us in Dhuli. Like everyone else, he thought that on our release we would be able to choose our return route and that we would naturally elect to cross the easier and lower Lipu Lekh pass into India.

Shortly afterwards, the unit's commanding officer arrived, also in mufti. A most charming man, Major R. M. Dass, he first questioned us about alleged improvements made by the Chinese at Taklakot, with particular reference to agriculture and tractors. Harrop informed him that there were no such improvements. To our surprise, we learned that Koila had been spreading these false stories on his return. We told Dass that Koila only did this because he was terrified of the Chinese and what they might do to him when he traded with Tibet the following year.

I decided that I would reveal my intelligence data to R. M. Dass, but I would not confide to him my true role in what had taken place over recent months. The opportunity was offered when Dass invited the three of us to dine at his HQ that afternoon. He apologised for the fact that his table would not be as well endowed with food as would be the case if he had invited us into his regimental mess in India.

Dass and his second-in-command departed, and we asked for and obtained hot water, thus allowing us to have a sponge bath in that upstairs room. The water was dark grey when I had completed my ablutions.

We dressed for dinner, and set off for Dass's HQ wearing what the well-dressed Himalayan explorer was throwing away that year. I wore my old cord trousers and blue sweater, the one with the big rat hole in the chest. On nearing Dass's camp, I reversed my sweater so that the rat hole was at the back. When we were close to the Indian Army post we could smell wood smoke, and Damodar said, 'Look. There's my country's flag.'

Fifty yards or so ahead, we could see a crude flagpole, from which flew the Nepalese flag at the top, with the Indian flag just beneath it. When we were closer, I suggested that we march three abreast and in step. (It's the form that counts.)

The Indian post was set in a small clearing and there were two Nepalese houses on the western edge. Dass stood on the verandah. His second-in-command stood on the 'parade ground', and as we marched in step up to the flag, a detachment of Indian Army Gurkhas emerged from one of the houses, and forming up, presented arms as we went by. That was a very proud moment for me. Harrop, Damodar and I came to attention, heels stamped down on the turf, to give a military-style salute to the flags of our host nation, and her new protector. I turned to Dass. He was beaming. The Gurkhas, clad in jungle-green fatigues, all grinned, and on the command dismissed. Dass invited us indoors, offering profuse apologies for the sparseness of the repast we were about to enjoy. 'Only chicken, I'm afraid, gentlemen. And some potatoes, eggs and chapatis, some Indian sweetmeats, and some native rice wine.'

The thought of boiled chicken made our mouths water. As we dined, seated cross-legged around a low table, Dass filled us in on the state of play.

'The British government has been raising merry hell about your imprisonment by the Chinese, and my government has also played its part. Nehru and Krishna Menon have been pressing hard for a seat in the United Nations for communist China, and India has put it to China that arresting and imprisoning Himalayan mountaineers who are on their lawful occasions does not help India in its task of obtaining UN recognition and a seat for China. The Americans are totally opposed, and they support Formosa as representing the interests of the Chinese people.'

His second-in-command cut in. 'Our radio transmitter went on the blink yesterday. Right now we should be advising Delhi that you are out and safe.'

'The Chinese have not yet announced your release. I wonder why?' Dass said. 'If we had known of your release, we would have made some effort to reach you and give you a hand.'

'Wouldn't have advised it,' Harrop commented. 'The Seti Gorge this time of the year is strictly technical-mountaineering terrain. A bad place in summer, a bloody awful place in winter.'

Eventually Dass enquired about the Chinese at Taklakot, and I gave him some essential data about troop strength, claims to Indian territory, and finally the completion date for the Strategic Military Highway to west Tibet. This latter information took both Dass and his second-in-command by surprise.

'You actually learned the completion date?' He asked incredulously.

'Straight from the horse's mouth, the most trustworthy Chinese I ever had the good fortune to meet. One who will be driving a military truck into Taklakot by sometime in 1957 at the latest.'

'Look,' Dass said. 'I'm going to have to reappraise my situation here. Damn nuisance our transmitter packing up. I have to get out to Delhi pretty quick, with this information. You've saved me an awful lot of leg-work. I'm going to get on the road within forty-eight hours, just as soon as I've set up procedure for my period out of station here at Dhuli.'

We finished off the bottles of local wine, and Damador soon became his usual giggly self. Dass and his second-in-command walked us back to Dhuli village in the dark, with Dass carrying a paraffin pressure-lamp. As we parted company, he said, 'Come in and have a drink of tea on your way through to Chainpur in the morning.'

Harrop and Damodar went indoors and Dass, shaking hands with me, said, 'You've done jolly well for an amateur.'

Those few words, spoken out of the hearing of Harrop and Damodar, served to inform me that Dass had not been brought into the small group of officers in Delhi who had been responsible for my recruitment. One thing was certain, Dass was a patriot, who loved his country, and held communist China in both contempt and distrust. My intelligence would be going to Delhi via two channels now, Dass and myself, straight to Cricket Wallah and his compatriots.

The following morning, after the usual haggling over hiring two porters, who would carry our tent, air beds and sleeping bags, leaving us nothing to carry, we were on our way. So lazy had we become, now that the pressure was off, we did not get under way until 2 p.m.

We called in at the Indian Army checkpoint, to find Dass packing his gear. He was not taking any Indian Army personnel with him, and had hired two porters, one to carry his personal gear, and the other to carry the defunct radio-transmitter. He asked Damodar to write out a report for onward transmission to the Nepalese Embassy in Delhi. While Damodar complied, Dass and I talked further about the Chinese and the undemarcated border. Dass possessed the same Survey of India map as we had taken into Tibet with us.

On it I plotted a circle with a twenty-three-mile-wide radius with Jitkot at its centre.

'There it is,' I said. 'That places the Chinese HQ at Kardung, at the western foot of the Gurla Mandhata. It is on the track that connects Taklakot with the Lhasa-Ladakh trade route. And that's why the Chinese are now stopping Indians and Nepalese visiting Kailas on pilgrimage, because they would have to pass through Kardung to get to Kailas. It's also out of sight of Indian traders at Taklakot.'

I showed Dass as closely as I could, the place where we had been kidnapped by the PLA. 'This map is hopelessly inaccurate, you will understand,' I said, 'but the approximate place is here.'

'The Chinese had no right to arrest you in that area,' Dass said. 'I have my written orders here, and in the spring of next year, I am to send a patrol into the Jung Jung Khola.'

'Then watch out,' I said. 'Be on your toes.'

I shook hands with Dass and his second-in-command and, following our two porters, I overtook them and caught up with Harrop and Damodar. We were on our way home, and one thing was quite certain. We would be celebrating both Christmas and New Year not with our families, but somewhere in the foothills of the west Nepal Himalaya.

Two days' march took us to the village of Dhalaun. On the morning of 23 December we set off for the village of Lokondo.

We had to climb something like 1,000 feet to gain the top of a ridge, and were rewarded with a splendid view of the 23,000-foot mountain Saipal, which our porters called Zema. In the centre of a great rock amphitheatre was a small green meadow, Pherali-Ket, which one of our porters, Arunya, said was the abode of spirits, demons and many wild creatures. Harrop and I looked at that small, well watered, lush oasis, which lay in the centre of a ten-mile rock barrier, through my binoculars. Arunya remarked that the locals, when snaring animals and hunting with their muzzle-loading shotguns, never entered the Pherali-Ket. They avoided it like the plague, not because of the Himalayan bear and snow leopard which lived there, but because of the wild creatures of the snows. Arunya had never heard the word Yeti, but his 'wild creatures of the snows' seemed to fill the bill.

Seated at the top of the next rise was a shepherd with his flocks of sheep carrying loads in saddle bags, bound for trade at Chainpur. On and off we enjoyed his company for the rest of the trip. He was accompanied by a cheerful young fellow whose right leg was set in a permanently rigid position, due, he said, to poisoning by a thorn some years earlier. He was on his way to see a herb doctor at Chainpur, who would, for a fee of ten rupees, ease the pain a little. At that time, the services of a properly qualified medical practitioner were not available anywhere in north-west Nepal. This cheerful lad would probably have his affliction until the day he died, but he regarded life with the buoyant philosophy of Voltaire's Dr Pangloss, who believed that 'all is for the best, and everything as it should be, in the best of all possible worlds'.

We were soon to be joined by three more pilgrims, a man ravaged by untreated syphilis with both his legs seized at the knee joints, followed by two men whose 'lion faces' denoted them as lepers whose disease was so far gone they were beyond both treatment and hope. One of the men had no fingers on his right hand, and only two on his left. They, like the lad with the stiff leg, were on their way to see the itinerant herbal doctor at Chainpur.

After reaching the top of the ridge the track zig-zagged steeply down the other side for about 1,500 feet. Looking across the valley I could see that we faced another uphill trek of at least a couple of thousand feet before we reached our destination. 'I'd really like mountaineering,' I commented to Harrop, 'if it wasn't for all this bloody uphill going.'

Another herd of goats approached us from below and the two men in charge introduced themselves as natives of Dhuli. They were returning home from a successful trading trip to Chainpur and the saddle bags of their sheep and goats were empty. The men carried the now familiar wicker basket supported by a head-band and these contained the bargains they had bought at Chainpur. One carried two new hubble-bubble pipes and a dozen spare bamboo stems. The other was loaded with an assortment of brass cooking pots and a few rolls of brightly coloured Indian cotton cloth.

They were joined by a companion leading a tiny white pony by a halter. In answer to our question about the practicability of using a horse in such mountainous country, we were told that the horse was not for riding, but had been purchased for the very large sum of 250 rupees as an offering to the gods. The pony would be tied to a stake in the middle of Dhuli village and fed by the villagers. This would placate the gods and ensure that last year's poor crops would not recur and the tiger that had eaten six buffalo would go away. (Some months later I received a letter from the headmaster of Chainpur school, telling me, amongst other snippets of local news, that the effort to placate the gods had not been entirely successful. The tiger ate the horse.)

When our two porters caught up with Harrop and me, Arunya introduced the man with the hubble-bubble pipes as his father. This was followed by a family get-together and we were made the handsome offer of a goat to eat, and at a very reasonable price. Pleased at the old man's generosity we asked which goat it would be.

'It isn't one of these, Sahib. It's back down the track, from where they came. It's sick. It's dying. It's eaten a poisoned plant.'

Having thanked the old boy for his dubious offer, we went to inspect the goat. A descent down the track in the direction of Chainpur for about three hundred feet brought us to the poor creature.

Arunya's father drew a large kukri and with one deft swing severed the head from its body. He skinned the carcass and cleaned out the offal. The young lad with the stiff leg viewed the stomach and intestines with obvious longing, and was delighted when I said that he could have them. We added the heart, liver and kidneys and he was completely overwhelmed. I enquired if there was any risk to health in eating the meat and Arunya assured me that there was not. At the worst, we might get stomach cramps and be ill for two or three days, but it would not amount to anything serious. I had the old man carve off some tender pieces for the limping lad, the syphilitic man and the two lepers.

At the next village, Lokondo, we made a fire and cooked a billy can full of goat meat. It was tough, but it was protein. We were replete after our meal, and I actually felt guilty at having eaten so much food. I felt then, that in civilised (so called) society we eat too much. Forty years later my views are unchanged.

It took some time to find our two porters the next day. It appeared that they were sleeping in, having been up half the night, skinning goats and sheep to sell to villagers. The goats had presumably been left in the village by Arunya's father, for collection at a later date, or so I thought. It eventually transpired that our 3-rupee goat had not been the only one to eat the poisonous plant. Half a dozen of Arunya's father's goats had died while we were dining.

We eventually located our porters and, accompanied by the goatherd and his flock, the boy with the limp, the syphilitic man, and the two lepers, we set off for Chainpur, the home of the young Rajah Oom Jung.

'Is this not a Christian holiday, Syd Sahib?' Damodar enquired.

I was trying to puzzle out dates when Harrop said, 'Good God. It's Christmas Eve.'

I asked Harrop what he wanted in his Christmas stocking, and he replied, 'A grand piano. Anything smaller would fall through the holes in my socks.'

'Just one more village to get to, before Chainpur, and that's Talkot,' Damodar said.

The day's march to Talkot was long and tiring, but thankfully most of it was downhill. It appeared that the headman of Talkot and his family were in the middle of a dispute with Oom Jung, Rajah of Bajang. The local Nepalese and the Taklakot Tibetans regarded the Rajahs of Bajang as their hereditary kings and paid annual tribute, in the form of about 2,400 pounds of rock salt every year.

The salt is transported over the Urai Lekh every summer on sheep and yaks. For the past two years, the headman of Talkot had seized Rajah Oom Jung's Tibetan salt without explanation. Oom Jung, who was only twenty-four years of age, possessed the legal right to try the case himself and pass judgement. He waived this right in order to illustrate to the people of Talkot that judgement would not be biased against them. He had transferred the case to the state capital, Siligari-Dhoti, where it would be tried by the local governor. We quickly learned that friends of Oom Jung were not highly regarded by the Talkot headman.

23

On Christmas Day we set out on the sixteen-mile walk to Chainpur. My reader might envisage a town like Chainpur, boasting as it did a rajah, would be large in size, with streets running every which way. Not so. There are no streets in Chainpur, and the town is really a scattered hamlet, with houses and the occasional shop dotting the terraced fields. The Chainpur houses, those of better quality, were built of fired clay and not unfired mud bricks, and the brick courses were arranged in intricate and attractive patterns.

The largest building of all was the old palace. It was a crumbling affair of stucco-fronted brick, with broken or collapsed statuary littering its terraces. It was like something out of a Somerset Maugham story. The young rajah, being something of an ascetic, declined to reside amongst its run-down splendour, and preferred his small, sparsely furnished room over Chainpur school, which was the second largest building in Chainpur.

The entrance to the school was decorated with flags and bunting, and the entire population appeared to be there. In the centre of the front compound a platform had been erected, and on this sat the headmaster, Mr Ram Watt Awhasti, and the young rajah, Oom Jung, who was wearing a smart brown suit. We had arrived on prize day and had made our appearance in the middle of the prize-giving ceremony. One of the teachers, Mr Mohan Chandra Pant, spoke the most perfect flawless English, and he took us in hand and we were found seats on the verandah overlooking the proceedings.

The majority of the prizes consisted of reams of blotting-paper given to our expedition by the British Museum and intended for the botanical collection Harrop was to have made. I was pleased that the returning members of our expedition had put the blotting paper to good use, instead of packing it back to England.

When the prize-giving ceremony was over, we were surrounded by small boys, all of whom spoke very good English, some pressing on me samples of the art work that had won them prizes that day. They were also curious about Taklakot and how the Chinese had treated us.

Rajah Oom Jung told us what had happened when Koila and our other three porters had returned to Saipal after their release. Berkeley had already reached Chainpur alone and, after engaging twenty porters to carry the expedition loads out of Saipal, had carried on to Pithoragarh to arrange for Indian customs to meet our expedition when it left Nepal. When we did not return to base camp, Roberts and the twenty porters went through the Seti Gorge to Chainpur. Our two professional mountaineering guides, Scotty Dwyer and Jack Henson, waited at Saipal for our return. Two days later, Koila and the other three porters staggered into camp after making that exhausting journey back over the Urai Lekh, bearing the news of our arrest. Koila handed Henson my brief note and the news of our capture by the Chinese communists was soon on its way out of Nepal. A runner was sent ahead to Roberts to tell him what had happened. Henson told Rajah Oom Jung that he expected that the Chinese would eventually release us, and when they did, we would in all probability return to India over the Lipu Lekh.

We sat on the school verandah and drank tea with Oom Jung. The headmaster brought a brazier of charcoal from indoors, and we had blankets around our shoulders to keep out the evening cold. Both Oom Jung and the headmaster took the view that the Chinese had no territorial rights in the Jung Jung Khola, or the Khatang valley. Oom Jung knew old one-eyed Phrupa, whom he described as one of his subjects, who paid taxes to him every year. The money helped pay for the restoration of the track through the Seti Gorge every spring, after the ravages of winter.

'The track should not have been in the sad state you encountered on your way back here,' Oom Jung commented. 'It's all down to that headman at Talkot seizing the taxes, in the form of salt and borax, which the Tibetans pay to me as annual tribute. As you see from our surroundings, I have no great need for money as a commodity. It's what one does with money that counts. Most of my local taxes in the Chainpur area are spent on educating the children. There was no English spoken here until my father left. Technically he is still rajah, but he has renounced both title and responsibility, and I have it all in my lap. So a few years ago, I converted this house into a school and recruited teachers from India. I am very proud of the children in my school. They speak good English. The headmaster and I both have a radio, and the children listen daily to the BBC World Service. That is why when the children were crowding around you, one of them asked if you supported Sheffield Wednesday football team. Actually, we are all cricket fanatics here, but we have no gear and no pitch. We are flattening out a pitch, and just as soon as I win my law case against the people at Talkot, and get my taxes back, I'll send someone down into India to buy a complete set of cricket gear.'

That evening an arrangement was made whereby we would be able to borrow sufficient money from Oom Jung's treasury to buy food and hire porters for our onward journey. The Chainpur treasury consisted of a tin trunk, kept under the headmaster's bed. He told us that his duties also included that of Chancellor of the Chainpur Exchequer.

The young rajah's total annual income was about £3,000 sterling, out of which he paid his taxes to Kathmandu, the central government. He was also obliged by custom to support all his relatives, and there must have been scores of them living in the lower Seti valley. The residue, some £1,800, was his own. Unlike the rajahs of international fame, who grace race courses and gambling houses, Oom Jung allowed himself about £6 per week for living expenses, spending the rest on education. The Chainpur school received the greater part of his income.

Refused government aid, Chainpur school in 1955 boasted the most comprehensive curriculum in Siligari Dhoti state. Oom Jung's education at the University of Benares in India must have led him to think that the future of his people rested with the younger generation. In addition to mathematics, geography and social sciences, the pupils were taught Nepali, Urdu, English and Sanskrit. Compulsory education was forbidden, the hill people little realising the benefits education could bring to their children. The rajah called in the Chainpur police force, which consisted of two men. They wore a uniform jacket and Dhoti skirt, and sported a World War Two Sten gun apiece. Their prime task, as crime was completely unknown in the Chainpur area, was to kidnap children from outlying hill villages and bring them into Chainpur for education. When the parents marched in to object, Oom Jung offered a complete remission of taxes, if the children were left in his care, to have an education, the standard of which was the envy of the state.

Long into the night we talked, dining off boiled chicken legs and trays of assorted and very tasty imported Indian sweetmeats. Harrop and Damodar turned in. I sat up, by the light of a small hurricane lamp, and wrote up my journal. I packed it in when I became beset with dizzy spells, curled up in my bag, and went to sleep.

I woke up on Boxing Day running a temperature, and was in a feverish condition. It was dysentery again. This was as bad a dose as I had experienced since I first contracted it in Iran five months earlier. There was no Western medication to be had, but a local herbalist prescribed a foul tasting mixture which he said would end my incontinence and passing of blood, but it would not cure my dysentery completely, leaving me a continuous feeling of lassitude, and the wish to lie down whenever I stood on my feet.

It was on 27 December that the Chinese authorities in Peking announced that we had been released from imprisonment at Taklakot seventeen days earlier. The brief announcement stated that we had been released 'close to the Nepalese pass of the Tinkar Lipu'. This was of course a lie. The Tinkar pass is not manned by the Nepalese, and nobody would know if we lived or died up in that area. The Indians, with their border checkpoint at the town of Garbyang, sent troops to meet us. As we had been released seventeen days earlier, and it is only seventeen miles from the summit of the Tinkar Lipu to Garbyang, the Indians reported to Delhi that we could be deemed 'missing presumed dead'.

Harrop, Damodar and I, totally unaware that our people at home were the recipients of news of a most unwelcome nature, continued to plod our weary way across the grain of the country, towards the India–Nepal frontier. Our journey back to India, via the Urai Lekh, was to take us twenty-seven days. We arrived in India on 6 January 1956.

Deciding that I was now fit enough to travel, we made plans to get under way. Back at the school, the headmaster hired two porters for us. We would have liked Koila to be with us, but he was out of station, taking some of his sheep to market. At 9 a.m. we were on our way, cheered by the entire complement of teachers and pupils. The first lap ended at a shop where miraculously we were able to purchase a 2-ounce packet of tea.

Our two new porters were very good value at 4 rupees a day. They sped like the wind, and I had my work cut out to keep up with them. They made it plain that they would be upset if we called off the day's march before 5 p.m. Our route took us along the north bank of the Seti river and the going was pleasantly flat. Our high speed and good fortune were not to last. By midday I began to feel ill, by 2.30 I was staggering all over the track, and at 3 p.m. I collapsed.

Harrop decreed that we stop just where we were, and our two conscientious porters complained that we had only covered eight miles. They went off to find wood for our fire and returned to tell us that the village of Sungala lay only a few hundred yards ahead, round a bend in the track. I got to my feet and assisted by Harrop and Damodar I staggered into the village.

The next morning we set off along a good, reasonably flat track, and ended the day's march at 3 p.m. just as my legs were beginning to buckle. This time we felt in need of a little solitude, not wanting villagers and children crawling all over us, so we camped by the edge of the Seti river, hard by the village of Suni-Khola. A small boy joined us, bearing a basket of tiny tomatoes, each one no bigger than a grape. We purchased the entire basketful.

He also had something wrapped up in a palm leaf, and it turned out to be three cauliflowers, the heads of which were no bigger than a golf ball. We purchased those also. The boy departed, to return shortly afterwards with a present of nine potatoes, for which he refused to take any money. We cooked and ate our tiny but very enjoyable vegetarian meal, and watched while our porters Moti and Nori went through a very strange ceremony. While Moti boiled water in a brass vessel, Nori disrobed until he was stark naked. It was a chilly evening, but the correct form had to be observed. Our two porters were of the Chetri caste, and their religious beliefs dictated that they must be completely naked when they cooked rice.

Nori, shivering in his birthday suit, squatted by the fire, and started to steam the rice, while Moti stripped off his own clothing. By the time the rice was cooked, both men were blue with cold, for after all, it was

late December, and we were at an altitude of about five thousand feet. I
started to laugh, as did Harrop and Damodar. Moti gave us a hurt look
and told Damodar that the Sahibs should appreciate that cooking rice
was a very serious and holy matter.

I felt much better in the morning, and thoroughly enjoyed our leisurely
progress along the banks of the Seti. All day long we encountered scores
of people carrying loads of cloth and tins of ghee from Pithoragarh or
Tanakpur in India, all bound for Chainpur. At midday, we went down
to the banks of the Seti, stripped off, and washed, using a bar of soap
Harrop had bought in Chainpur. Much scrubbing was needed to wash
away the layers of dirt. With our ablutions completed we felt much
happier. At 5 p.m. we camped on the banks of the Kali Ghad river
and dined off tsampa-porridge and chapatis. I sighed for a nice thick
juicy steak. It was New Year's Eve 1955. Tomorrow we would become
the 1956 Welsh Himalayan Expedition. Harrop and I were both quiet
and pensive: our thoughts turned to our families at home. Moti and Nori
livened the proceedings by cooking rice again.

'Can you imagine this at the Savoy?' Harrop said, grinning all over his
face. 'A load of stuffed shirts, stripping down to their socks to eat a bowl
of rice pudding.'

On 4 January, in the late afternoon, we reached Baitadi to the accompaniment of cheers from the villagers who had seen us pass through four
and a half months earlier. We went to the governor's residence and the
new governor, Mr Kirti Bahadur Bhista, came to the door to welcome us.
Seated in comfortable upholstered chairs, we gave him a full account of
our experiences and he promised to radio the news to Kathmandu the
following morning. He also promised that a separate message would be
transmitted on behalf of Harrop and me to Colonel Proud at the British
Embassy in Kathmandu.

His Excellency the Governor was greatly disturbed at the treatment
Indian and Nepalese traders were receiving at the hands of the Chinese
at Taklakot, and he described an incident he had investigated. A group
of traders had agreed to supply a large quantity of Indian cloth to the
Chinese authorities at Taklakot against a firm written contract. The order
was so big that about a dozen traders had to participate to finance the
deal. The cloth, made in the mills at Kanpur, was sent by rail and bus
to Pithoragarh, from where it was transported over the Lipu Lekh to
Taklakot by pony. When it was delivered, the Chinese refused to recognise
the contract price, offering an alternative that left no margin of profit. The
traders replied that they would rather take the cloth back to India than
sell it at a loss. The Chinese then informed the traders that as the cloth
was now in Tibet, and it was illegal to export cloth without authority
from Lhasa, the cloth would stay at Taklakot until the matter had been
dealt with by the appropriate Communist Party committee in Lhasa. The
export permit was applied for, and after a delay of several weeks, was of

course refused. The matter ended with the traders selling the cloth to the Chinese for half the original purchase cost at Kanpur.

The governor had kept Indian press cuttings concerning our arrest and the efforts made by the Indian, Nepalese and British governments to secure our release. High-level representations in Peking at regular intervals during our captivity must have convinced Peking that it was not in their interest to hold us any longer. Peking announced that the two foreign climbers had been released after admitting their guilt. That was a good one.

The fact that the Chinese had not informed the British government of our release until 27 December was not lost on the Governor of Baitadi. 'They sent you the long way round, via the impossible winter route, to ensure that you died in the process, and by waiting all that time before announcing your release, they ensured that you could not be rescued. They evidently did not want you to bear testimony to their outrageous claims to Indian and Nepalese territory.'

Early on 6 January we bade farewell to the Governor of Baitadi and ambled down the steep hillside track to the banks of the Kali, 2,700 feet below. At the bridge we paused to look back at the ancient Kingdom of Nepal. A few more strides would take us into India. In the middle of the suspension bridge lay that log of wood which delineated the frontier. I stepped over it, my right foot in India and my left foot still in Nepal.

At the far side of the bridge we were met by two officials, one representing Indian customs and the other the Department of Immigration. They knew who we were and, after examining and stamping our passports, one of them, with a fine lack of tact, stared at me and said, 'I am sorry, sir, to witness your miserable condition.'

We wandered through the village of Julaghat in search of a tea shop. Damodar located a stall selling sweets and we purchased a large quantity of sticky caramels. We sat on a low wall, chewing our sweets, when two Tibetans passed by, one about thirty years old and the other a lad of about fifteen. Their shubas were very ragged and their feet showed through their worn-out felt boots. I spoke to them and asked what they were doing in India. The older one said that they were from the Taklakot area, and that the Chinese had taken all their yaks, sheep and goats, leaving them to starve to death. He said that many Tibetans from Taklakot were now fleeing over the border into India to escape the brutal oppression of the Chinese. His younger brother, the young boy, was designated by the Chinese to be transported to Chamdo for 'political education'. That was the last straw. They headed over off over the Lipu Lekh into India the day before the young boy was to present himself to the Chinese.

I gave the poor Tibetan pair a few annas in coin, and Harrop offered them a cigarette. The older Tibetan said that he would rather have another anna. He received both, plus a few paper rupees.

The next day we moved on to Pithoragarh, arriving in the afternoon, and were directed to a small hotel. There was a simple shower stall, equipped with a suspended four-gallon ghee-can, the bottom of which was perforated. One of the staff stood by with urns of warm water, ready to pour them over us. It was sheer delight.

My next move was to find the post office, in order to send a telegram to Alex Campbell of *Life* magazine in New Delhi. Harrop and I turned off the main street towards the post office when a voice said, 'Gentlemen, I thought that you were dead.'

A man wearing a very smart suit and carrying a silver-knobbed cane introduced himself as Mr Ghanshyam Pande, assistant magistrate for that part of Kumaon. In a matter of minutes, arrangements were made to advance us any sum of money we cared to name. I was taken to the local medical dispensary for treatment for my chronic dysentery, and meals were ordered to be delivered to a Dak bungalow (government owned, and usually reserved for governmental employees). Our belongings were immediately moved from the hotel.

Mr Pande informed us that when the Chinese announced our release on 27 December, the Indian government sent word to him from Delhi that he was to render whatever aid we needed the moment he learned that we had crossed from Tibet into India. On hearing of our supposed release over the Tinkar Lipu pass, he had sent agents to Garbyang, the nearest Indian town to the Tinkar Khola, with instructions to provide clothing, food and money, and anything else we might need. Pande's representatives waited in vain, and Pande, on learning that we had been released nearly a month before his men had reached the Tinkar Khola, presumed us dead, as did the Chinese, no doubt.

We commented on the number of impoverished Tibetans we had seen, remarking that there appeared to be no restrictions on their movements, such as the ones China imposed on travellers in Tibet. We learned that the Indian government, being sympathetic to the plight of the Tibetan people, allowed them to travel wherever they wanted, without let or hindrance, provided they returned to Tibet within six months. The Tibetans, on crossing into India, were given a chitty stating that they must recross into Tibet by a certain date. When the six months was up, the Tibetans walked back over the border, stayed one day in Tibet, and then crossed back into India, hand outstretched for another six-month chitty. Aid was eventually sent to Uttar Pradesh in India from overseas, for the starving Tibetans.

Leaving Mr Pande, bearing the 'chitty' he had given us, which instructed the Treasury in Pithoragarh to let us have as much money as we required, we duly collected a loan of some £50, and then made our way to the telegraph office. I sent a short wire to Alex Campbell of *Life* magazine in Delhi, stating that we were alive and well, and had a tale to tell, and would he please drive up to Tanakpur, negotiate the 'gate' road system to Pithoragarh and pick us up.

Campbell arrived the following evening bringing with him all kinds of goodies from his wife Sheena, including a bottle of port (which we sampled, but found too rich for our delicate stomachs after the diet we had existed on for the past three months), a tin of genuine Scots shortcake, and a few bars of chocolate. We devoured the shortcake and the chocolate on the bus down to the river crossing at Julaghat, where we met Campbell's chauffeur, Singh.

From there we drove back to Delhi at a leisurely pace, stopping for the night at a hotel. Dinner was steak. It was a wonderful meal. But within half an hour I was in the bathroom throwing it all up. It would take some time for my digestion to return to normal. I went to bed feeling that I had left the real world, that of ice and snow and hill people, and was about to re-enter an unreal world, one called civilisation. I was not looking forward to it.

Alone for the first time in months, certainly since my solitary confinement cell in Tibet, I was able to reflect on what we had come through. I have since been asked if I would make that journey again, to which I replied in all honesty, not for all the brick-tea in China, or even a million pounds. On the other hand if you asked if I would have traded the experience for anything, the answer must be, 'Not for all the gold in Fort Knox, multiplied a dozen times.'

24

The following day saw us in Delhi, and divesting myself of my torn, indescribably filthy Himalayan apparel, I donned a blue blazer and flannels, and wore my Himalayan Club tie, with Tibetan chorten motif. Alex Campbell wanted me to go through my prison diary and write an article for *Life* magazine, but first there were certain formalities to be observed. It would have been most discourteous not to call on the British High Commission, the Nepalese Embassy and the Indian Ministry of External Affairs. Our first call was the embassy of the Kingdom of Nepal, where I gave a brief verbal report, with the undertaking that a full written version would be forwarded to the Nepalese Embassy in London on my return home. Here we had to say goodbye to our dear friend and cell mate Damodar Narayan Suwal, still only eighteen years of age, but now a very seasoned campaigner.

'My ice axe, Damodar. Swiss make. Mischabel. Present from my wife. You must have it. Look after it.' It was a sad parting.

Our next stop was the British High Commission where Harrop and I expressed our gratitude for all that had been done to secure our release. We returned to the Time-Life office for a bite of lunch, and while Harrop wrote letters, I went off to see the Indian External Affairs people.

I was shown into a high-ceilinged office with rotating fans overhead and, unlike at the Nepalese Embassy, the man I was to meet did not offer to shake my hand. He sat behind a desk, and half rose in a perfunctory manner as I was shown in. I expressed my thanks to Prime Minister Nehru and his government for their efforts to ensure our release from imprisonment in Tibet. He heard me out with a face as impassioned as a lump of Welsh slate.

'You have caused the Indian government considerable embarrassment,' he said. 'India and China enjoy excellent relations. We would not like to have those harmonious relations disturbed by itinerant explorers blundering their way around the Himalaya.'

I felt like saying, 'The Chinese are going to tear up your precious treaty, you pompous idiot.'

He went on, 'The Chinese have already complained to us that they have proof that you are an agent of the American Central Intelligence Agency. We are making our own enquiries. There are certain aspects of your presence in the area where you were apprehended by the Chinese which require clarification.'

We discussed, and then we argued, and finally I said, 'They are building up their army. They are preventing your religious pilgrims from visiting the holy mountain Kailas, because the route to Kailas passes a secret PLA base, and also the route to be taken by their Strategic Military Highway to west Tibet.'

'That is palpable nonsense,' he said. 'No restrictions are being placed on the passage of Indian nationals to Kailas.'

I got out of my chair, and heading for the door, I called out over my shoulder, 'I insist that what I have told you about the Chinese be written into the records of this meeting.'

Late that afternoon an Indian appeared. He was on his way to Pithoragarh and someone coming out had asked him to take back the money we had borrowed from the Indian Treasury there. Time-Life footed the bill. They also repaid our loan from Oom Jung's treasury. Then another Indian appeared. He had a note for me. It was from Cricket Wallah. Would I meet him in Connaught Place. I scribbled an affirmative response.

The following day I departed for Connaught Place for the second and final meeting with my friend Cricket Wallah.

'Bit of a sticky wicket, what?' he said as we shook hands.

'Like the Duke of Wellington said after Waterloo, a damn close run thing,' I replied.

We walked around Connaught Place, it was a beautiful clear January day and the sun shone in a cloudless sky.

'You got my material, some but not all of it, from R.M. Dass?' I enquired.

'If you mean the chap up in west Nepal, then the answer is no. He is operating on a different level. What did you glean from those blighters the Chinese?'

I told Cricket Wallah everything. His eyes lit up and he let out a low whistle. 'Good man. You know if they had never captured you, and allowed you to wander around the Taklakot-Manasorawar area at will, you would never have been able to obtain intelligence of this quality. The Chinese governor and his colleagues must have been very incompetent.'

'That sums it up,' I said. 'They are almost totally ignorant of the outside world, and victims of their own propaganda.'

'That Chinese governor must have thought that you would be going to Peking for a life-stretch, otherwise he would not have been so forthcoming about their claims to Indian territory. Did you keep notes? Have you anything in writing?' Cricket Wallah enquired.

I pulled an envelope out of my blazer pocket. 'This is my prison diary. Mostly daily events, and a study of the bestiality of the Chinese communists. I have it all summed up, however, here on this single piece of Chinese cigarette packet, bearing the emblem of a flying horse. I wrote this when I thought that I might not make it through the Seti Gorge and I planted it in John Harrop's rucksack. I addressed it to your chap Timmy.'

'Can I have it please?' Cricket Wallah asked, after reading through it. 'This cigs packet is a bit of history, you know.'

'Sorry, but no,' I said. 'I intend keeping this as a souvenir. But I have written it all out for you on this sheet of "Time-Life" notepaper.'

'Good enough,' he said. 'This will confirm all that my army colleagues and I have suspected, and it will raise eyebrows at the highest military level. It will be the veritable cat amongst the pigeons for our Prime Minister Nehru. There is still time for us to reinforce our positions in the north, most of which are completely undefended, thanks to Nehru and Menon. We must switch the emphasis away from Pakistan and towards China.'

'OK, I'll be off then,' I said.

'No, wait,' Cricket Wallah responded. 'I had a feeling that you might bring something of value out of Tibet, and I persuaded a senior officer, who is part of our military intelligence-gathering organisation, to come to this meeting. He is over there in that car. I can't reveal his identity to you. Please tell him what you have just told me.'

We walked over to the parked car. It had a Sikh driver and a man dressed in a dark suit, white shirt, and regimental tie sat in the back. He was tall and distinguished-looking, and had 'General Staff' written all over him. As I entered the car, I looked into a shrewd face, with dark piercing eyes. Cricket Wallah entered from the other side of the car. At a word from the dark-suited man, the Sikh driver took the car on a slow tour of New Delhi.

'Sir, this is Mr Sydney Wignall, code name Conway. He learned some remarkable and very valuable things while he was in the hands of the Chinese in Tibet. Wignall, I cannot reveal to you the name of the gentleman we have just joined, I can only tell you that he is a senior officer.'

It was almost like my first meeting with the Boys from Gartok. The senior officer put me right through the mill: my identity, my background, who financed my expedition, which academic bodies supported it, etc. After about ten minutes' grilling, Cricket Wallah put in his two annas' worth. 'His old headmaster, when a boy, bowled out the great W.G. Grace in one, sir.'

The senior officer looked surprised. 'Is that right, Wignall?'

'It is, sir,' I confirmed. He nodded his head, and I could imagine him, like Cricket Wallah, saying, 'Any chap whose headmaster bowled out W.G. Grace for a duck has to be all right.'

I then went into my spiel, going into great detail with regard to the Chinese claims to Indian and other national territories. The senior officer was impressed by Chungnya's story about the Strategic Military Highway to west Tibet being completed in no more than two years. 'They will be able to place a large army within two hundred and fifty miles of where we are now,' he said. 'It is all very disturbing.' He shook his head. 'Sadly we have a problem, Wignall. If someone could just sit down and discuss this information of yours in a calm dispassionate manner with our Prime Minister, I think that we could convince him that all is not what it seems with regard to that treaty we signed less than two years ago. Our problem is Krishna Menon. He is not only very self-opinionated and stubborn, he is also a malicious vindictive person. If he knew of this meeting, and the activities of our friend here and the other officers involved, Menon would hound us out of the army and destroy our careers. Just here discussing the matter with you in a clandestine manner could make me a marked man. I intend to raise the matter through certain channels, in the hope that our Prime Minister will see the truth while there is still time.'

The vehicle pulled over to the pavement, precisely where we had met half an hour earlier.

'You will appreciate, Wignall, that what you have been involved in must remain secret for the time being,' the senior officer said. 'We in the army had to do something to get through this intelligence fog that our Prime Minister has created with regard to communist China. Your contact in London came up with a brainwave which placed you in Chinese hands. Thankfully it worked. Neither Timmy nor I knew of that rather bold plan. If we had, we would have put a stopper on it right away as too risky. If you had lost your life, we would have had Baij here's guts for garters, and his chum in London. Now that I have met you, I know that their plan was the right one. Politicians come and go, Wignall, they are transient beings. But the Indian Army remains, and we must do what we believe is right for India.'

The senior officer turned to Cricket Wallah and said, 'I'll see to it that Timmy gets sight of this information. If anyone can alert our Prime Minister to the danger posed by China it has to be Timmy, and this data might do the trick.'

We shook hands, and Cricket Wallah and I stepped out of the car onto the pavement. 'Thank you for what you have done for India. In a theatre of war this information would be equal to a division in the field,' the senior officer said. 'The Indian Army will always be grateful to you.'

Cricket Wallah and I were left standing in Connaught Place.

'Just who is Timmy?' I asked Cricket Wallah.

'Better for all concerned that you do not know,' Cricket Wallah responded. 'He's the man who can knock sense into Nehru. But he won't have any luck with that fellow Menon. Menon adores China, Mao Tse-tung and Chou En-lai. We will probably never meet again. Great to have met a chap whose head bowled out the great W.G. Grace for a "Duck".'

We shook hands and he was turning to go when I said, 'You're not getting off that lightly. You don't think I did this for nothing, do you?'

Cricket Wallah looked at me with an expression of absolute horror. I could hear the cogs clicking in his brain. He was thinking, 'And I thought that this chap was a gentleman. He's just a mercenary.'

He frowned. 'I don't carry cash on me. How much do you want?'

'Have you got a piece of paper?' I asked. Cricket Wallah shook his head, and then with a shrug, shot his cuffs. Taking a ballpoint pen from his inside pocket he held it at the ready. 'All right. What do you want?'

'Two cricket bats, two sets of bails and stumps, two sets of cricket pads, two cricket balls, one cricket bag. Doesn't have to be new. Used and second-hand would be very welcome.'

Cricket Wallah scribbled away on his shirt cuff, and lookd up. 'Am I to get all this ready for you to take back to the UK?'

'No,' I said. 'I want it all packed up and sent to the Rajah of Bajang, at Chainpur.'

'A rajah,' exclaimed Cricket Wallah. 'I thought that they were all rich. Can't he afford some new cricket gear?'

'I'm afraid not,' I said. 'You see he's had a spot of bad luck lately. Some people at a place called Talkot have grabbed all his assets, and it's now a legal matter, and for the time being, this very nice 24-year-old rajah is skint, as they say, on his ruddy uppers. It's for the school. Chainpur school. They are levelling a cricket pitch and have no gear and are contemplating making their own bats, bails and stumps, and God knows what they will use for a cricket ball.'

'For a school. For the boys up in Nepal? What a jolly good idea,' Cricket Wallah enthused. 'Four sets of pads, not two. Remember, the wicket keepers need a set. What about cricket gloves?'

'The boys will be too small to wear adult gloves, and even the pads will come up to their chests,' I said.

'I'll see what I can do about small size cricket gloves. But what about cricket balls? Will two be enough? Could they not lose them?'

'Well,' I responded, 'I suppose that a really good batsman, hitting a six, might put a ball into the Seti river.'

'Then let's make it six balls,' Cricket Wallah said. 'I'll get on with this right away. Any message? I can't say courtesy of the Indian Army, it might prompt people to ask too many questions.'

'Just enclose a thank-you note, from one who received help when passing through.'

That really was it. Cricket Wallah was smiling all over his very pleasant countenance. He was a thoroughly likeable chap.

'You'll have to keep a very straight bat, up there in the Himalaya, if the Chinese do invade,' I suggested.

'Let us pray that your information is believed by Nehru,' C.W.

responded, 'otherwise we may not be in a position to hold our ground. We might even have to draw-stumps, and leave the pitch.'

'That senior officer called you Baij,' I commented. 'Is that your name?'

Cricket Wallah, over his shoulder, with a wide grin said, 'Everybody in my regiment calls me Baij. I'm Baij to everyone. Better for me that you do not know my real name. Unless of course we get exposed, and I am court martialled. Goodbye, old chap.' He vanished into the crowd in Connaught Place.

I returned to the Time-Life office and Harrop and I packed our gear for the flight home. It was the first time I had flown and I found it a frightening experience. Our plane was struck by lightning and it limped into Cairo on three engines. Harrop and I were agreed that the safest way to travel at high altitude was on foot. My wife and I were reunited at a hotel in Windsor, and life slowly returned to normal.

Harrop and I were called to the Foreign Office in Whitehall shortly after our return. We sat facing a long table behind which were arrayed unidentified persons in dark suits and school and regimental ties. We were fully aware that we were being interviewed not only by the FO, but also by MI6. I provided the same data as that I had given to my Indian principals in New Delhi. No eyebrows were raised when I gave them the approximate completion date for the highway to west Tibet, but it was the very first question they put to me. At that time, there were no satellites, nor were there any aerial reconnaissance flights over China by the CIA, of that I was aware. The US U2 spy plane was still some years into the future.

I presumed that the Foreign Office would communicate my information to the Indian government. It would add weight to what I had already told the Indians. Or would it damn me on the basis that any such data from 'British Imperialist sources' would be viewed by Nehru and Menon as evidence of a British effort to drive a wedge between India and her friendly northern neighbour China?

Time-Life in Delhi sent me a copy of *Blitz*, a left-wing radical Indian weekly newspaper. It ran a banner headline, 'Spies Masquerade as Mountaineers'. There was a picture of Harrop and me, followed by a florid description of how we had been refused permission to enter Tibet legally and had gone in to spy on China. There was even a sneering remark about us intending to write about 'Tibet groaning under Peking tyranny'. The word tyranny was in italics suggesting that *Blitz* was of the opinion that the Tibetans were having a lovely time under Chinese communist rule.

The *Liverpool Daily Post* wanted their money's worth and I spent the next five weeks writing about our experiences in Chinese-occupied Tibet. My articles, in serial form, ran for twenty-nine consecutive days. In deference to my Indian military contacts I made no mention of my undercover espionage role, nor did I reveal that I had been carrying a loaded automatic pistol when the Chinese arrested me in the Jung Jung Khola. I found myself unable to write about Chinese Roulette. It was to give me nightmares for years to come. I was suffering from what today is termed 'Post-traumatic Stress'. For all I knew it could have been 'Pre-menstrual Tension'. Telling the story of my Chinese Roulette sessions in print has cleansed my subconscious. I am now able to sleep the sleep of the just, with no clacking of PPSh breech bolts disturbing my slumbers. While typing my articles for the *Liverpool Daily Post* I received a bill from Cogswell and Harrison of London for the sum of seven pounds ten shillings for one second-hand Browning pistol, supplied on loan but not returned.

Weeks later, I received a note from Singh. Would I meet him at the usual place three days hence?

'Our chap in Delhi sent your cricket gear up to Chainpur. He really was tickled pink to have been able to do that for you.'

I broke in. 'They don't believe me, do they?'

Singh shook his head sadly. 'Our illustrious Prime Minister Nehru, who is so busy on the world stage telling the rest of mankind how to live, has too little time to attend to the security of his own country. Your material was shown to Nehru by one of our senior officers, who plugged hard. He was criticised by Khrishna Menon in Nehru's presence for "lapping up American CIA agent-provocateur propaganda". Menon has completely suppressed your information.'

'So it was all for nothing?' I said.

'Perhaps not,' Singh responded. 'We will keep working away at Nehru. Some day he must see the light, and realise the threat communist Chinese occupation of Tibet poses for India.'

'Your man in Delhi. He called himself Baij, and the higher-ranking officer he introduced me to stated that my intelligence would be placed before Timmy. What is Baij's real identity and who is Timmy?'

Singh shook his head. 'Timmy holds a very high rank in the Indian Army, and if his participation in all this were to come out, he could be forced to resign his commission.'

'But he is the man behind all this, is he not?' I further enquired.

'Yes, he is,' Singh confirmed. 'He is a true patriot and a very fine soldier. He commanded a brigade under you British in Burma in World War Two. I cannot reveal his identity to you. As for dear old Baij, he's also an officer in the Indian Army. He would get the chop and lose his career if the facts were known.'

'I don't suppose we will meet again?' I said.

'I doubt it,' Singh responded. 'But as things develop I'll let you have briefings in the post. You've earned the right to be kept informed.' I showed my Chinese 'Flying Horse' cigarette packet to Singh. He asked me to erase the name 'Timmy' at the top. I did so. 'It will all be explained, some day,' Singh said.

'One final question,' I said. 'Colonel Harry Tobin. Is he part of your intelligence network?'

'Truthfully, the answer is no,' Singh replied. 'Colonel Tobin is well liked and highly respected in the Indian Army. He won his DSO in the Great War in the Indian Army. It was just that his contacts in the Himalayan climbing fraternity are so extensive, I referred to him for a possible introduction to any British climbers who might be travelling close to the Tibetan border. It was solely my idea to send you into Tibet. Timmy was far from pleased that I had persuaded you to risk your life the way you did. Baij thought it a great lark. Baij is that sort of chap.'

On my train journey back to North Wales I reflected on the time I met Krishna Menon during World World Two. It was in 1940, during the so-called 'Phoney War'. All three major political parties in the UK, Conservative, Labour and Liberal, had joined forces in a National Government. The left political spectrum decided to form a new political party. It was called 'The People's Convention'. It was designed to give a voice to those who thought a coalition government, in a democracy, should face a loyal (I thought) opposition.

A close friend had joined the party, and invited me, an eighteen-year-old political virgin who held left-wing views (I have since moved very much to the right) to a meeting in London. I was to meet a veritable quintessence of what today is referred to as 'the chattering classes'. Menon made a short speech about the need for Indian independence. I warmly applauded that. Then people mingled, talked and drank tea. Amongst those present in star roles were Professor J. B. S. Haldane, actress Beatrix Lehmann, journalist D. N. Pritt, Arthur Horner (President of the South Wales Miners' Union), journalist Claud Cockburn, a scientist by the name of Nunn May and a young and very attractive Indian lady whom they called 'Indira'.

Unaware of the fact that I was sharing a teaspoon with Nehru's daughter, I was disturbed by the suggested programme . . . 'Peace with Nazi Germany; Britain out of the war' etc. When I whispered (at question time), 'What will happen to the Polish people?' (whose country at that time was occupied by both Nazi Germany and the Soviet Union), my question was ignored. Later, during more 'chattering time', I once again raised the Polish question. Trade Union leader Arthur Horner took me to one side. 'Of course we must not forget the Polish people,' he said. 'Ah,' I said to myself, 'they are not going to forget the Polish people, so that's all right then.' Menon looked down condescendingly at this spotty-faced English youth and said, 'You are impertinent.' I formed the impression that Menon was vain, arrogant and conceited. A thoroughly detestable man. I turned to my friend and whispered, 'This is not for me, let's get out of here before the pubs close.'

In 1941 Nazi Germany invaded the Soviet Union. 'The People's Convention' switched roles overnight, and after declaring 'Support for a People's War', the 'People's Convention' dissolved itself. I was to learn later that Haldane, Lehmann, Horner, Pritt and Cockburn were all members of the Communist Party of Great Britain. Nunn May went to Canada where he betrayed the secrets of the atom bomb to the Soviet KGB. After the Berlin Wall fell, Claud Cockburn was exposed as a long-term Soviet KGB 'Agent of Influence'.

In 1945, with war still waging, a general election was held, and socialist Clement Attlee's Labour Party was swept to power in a landslide victory. Krishna Menon had approached Attlee about the possibility of standing for parliament as a Labour candidate – a request Attlee viewed with favour, that is until the security services revealed to him Menon's close association with leading members of the Communist Party of Great Britain. Less than sixteen years after that London meeting, Menon suggested I was a CIA agent – turning a blind eye to the Chinese military build-up in Tibet. It would result in the ruination of his political career.

In 1957 I learned of the identity of Timmy, from a cutting from the *Times of India*, sent to me by Singh, and it stated that General K.S. Thimayya had been promoted to Indian Army Chief of Staff: 'A thrill has just passed through the army. The signal has gone out: "TIMMY IS ON".' The man responsible for the clandestine intelligence operations targeted against the People's Liberation Army in Tibet was now the top-ranking officer in the Indian Army. I read up on General 'Timmy' Thimayya. He had, as Singh had said, commanded a brigade under General 'Bill' Slim in Burma in World War Two. Timmy was in fact *the only* Indian officer to command a brigade in the Indian Army under the Raj.

Sadly for the Indian army Timmy was retired in 1961, a year before the Chinese attacked India. In his valedictory address to the Indian Army officer corps, he said, 'I hope that I am not leaving you as cannon fodder for the Chinese communists.' A profoundly prophetic statement.

Years were to pass before I learned the true identity of my cricket-loving friend Baij and that was not until after he met his death, gun in hand, facing the Chinese communist invaders of India in 1962.

The Mountaineering Club of North Wales wanted to know why I never turned up for climbing meets. They didn't know it, but for me, the fire had gone out, doused on the Urai Lekh and in the Seti Gorge. I did turn up for an annual dinner, simply because Tilman was to be one of the two guests of honour. Tilman agreed to attend, on the understanding that he would not be asked to make a speech. After the meal, and the usual speeches, I had a few words alone with Tilman.

'I'm glad to see that you got through safely. Did you obtain anything of value for the Indians?' he enquired.

'Everything they needed, and considerably more. The problem is that

Nehru does not believe it, and thinks that the sun shines out of communist China,' I replied.

'Never had any time for politicians,' Tilman offered. 'Politics and journalism are two trades for which no qualifications are required.'

I was approached by one of the Mountaineering Club of North Wales' old guard. 'Eric is here. Have you seen him? He got the old heave-ho from his Anglo-Chinese Friendship Society. He told me that they and he think that when he and his communist friends in London made that approach for you, to Peking, for that proposed climb on Gosainthan, you were in fact a British Secret Service agent, using them as the legal means to get inside Tibet, so that you could emerge with a false story. He and his Anglo-Chinese Friendship Society comrades actually believe that the Chinese have freed the Tibetans from a form of medieval serfdom, under the rule of the lamas. He believes that your story about the Chinese treating the Tibetans as near slaves and second-class citizens is a complete falsification of the facts.'

'None so blind as those who cannot see,' I suggested. 'I'll go over and try to break the ice.'

Eric saw me coming and, turning his back, cut me dead. In his view I had ruined an essential part of his life, and made him suspect in the eyes of his fellow Marxist followers of the personality cult of Chairman Mao Tse-tung.

My wife and I drove back to Colwyn Bay in silence. She and I had both regarded Eric and his wife as friends, and it hurt her to see me shunned by Eric. To please me, Jean said, 'That ice axe I bought for you. The one you gave to Damodar. I'll buy you another one for Christmas.' I did not reply. I had climbed my last mountain.

Within weeks of my return to the UK I received a letter from Damodar in Kathmandu, which read: 'Syd Sahib. After my adventures in Tibet my parents decided that I must give up expeditions. Last Saturday I was married to my sixteen-year-old cousin. I have written also to John Sahib. Please treat this letter as your invitation to my wedding. P.S. I have been told that Life magazine paid you $30,000 for your story. Is there any left over for me?'

Life magazine in fact paid the Mountaineering Club of North Wales £650 for our story, and that small sum was swallowed up by expedition debts.

John Harrop never got the travel bug out of his system. He joined the United Nations as a roving agricultural scientist and spent many years in former British colonies in Africa, where he met and married an English nurse whom he called 'Buzz'. My last communication from him came in the form of a postcard from the Philippines where he was a university professor. Attempts to contact him in later years failed.

In 1957 I received two letters from India. One was from Singh, to advise me that the Indian Army's latest intelligence information was that the Chinese Strategic Highway was completed, and PLA trucks were now rolling into Taklakot. The other was from one of the Indian teachers at Chainpur school. He had asked me if I would write out a reference for him, to assist him when his contract with Rajah Oom Jung ended, and he needed to seek a teaching job at his home town of Pithoragarh, just over the frontier in India. He told me that when the summer trading season commenced at Saipal campsite in 1956, the red-coated Tibetan agent of the Chinese had re-appeared, accompanied by two Chinese nationals, disguised in Tibetan garb. The Chinese were now infiltrating their agents to the Saipal hotbed of Western Running Dog Spies. The latter part of the letter gave me a sinking feeling in my stomach. The Chinese had warned the Nepalese traders at Saipal not to have any dealings with Westerners. To emphasise his warning he stated that a young Chinese soldier, who had 'assisted Western Imperialists' the previous year had been tried by the military court martial and executed in front of the Taklakot garrison a month after my release. The means of execution was the standard Chinese one of a bullet in the back of the head.

There was no doubt in my mind who that poor unfortunate PLA infantryman was. It had to be Chungnya. The friendship he so obviously displayed towards me, and his final act of forcing up Runty's assault rifle and threatening to shoot Runty, was sufficient proof that Sun Tian-sun, to give Chungnya his real name, could no longer be relied on to touch his forelock to 'the Leading Role of the Party' and, horror upon horrors, had the effrontery to think for himself. I grieved for the loss of that fine young man, to whom I am quite certain I owe my life.

Some months after General Thimayya was made Chief of Staff of the Indian Army, I received a further letter from Singh, telling me that great efforts had been made to persuade Nehru to allow the Indian Army to send patrols up onto the Aksai Chin plateau to ascertain if the Chinese had built their military highway across Indian territory. The answer was a flat refusal, prompted by Krishna Menon, who could always be seen whispering in Nehru's ear. I found it unbelievable that the Indian Army had been denied permission to patrol what Nehru claimed was Indian territory, and this nearly two years after I had brought that vital information out of Tibet.

We now know that when the Chinese communists captured us in October 1955, they had not only completed their survey of the Aksai Chin plateau, but were actually building their road across it. Before that highway was completed, it took the lives of more than 20,000 Tibetan slave labourers, not to mention a further 10,000 of diverse nationalities in its progress across Sinkiang.

In 1959 the Tibetans in Lhasa revolted against Chinese rule. The Dalai Lama, about to be arrested by the Chinese, fled to India. Nehru, deeply embarrassed by this episode, declined to comment. He did not want to criticise China. The *Observer* newspaper summed the matter up with a cartoon which is now a collector's item for Tibet watchers. It depicted three Nehrus, squatting side by side, each with a portrayal of Mao Tse-tung behind him. Each of the three Nehrus has closed his ears, his eyes or his mouth, with the caption, 'Hear no Tibet, see no Tibet, speak no Tibet'. The Chinese, who had a trade agency at Kalimpong in north-east India, infiltrated spies to track down the Dalai Lama. A letter from Singh advised me that the Indian civilian secret service was now at last in action, not investigating the Chinese in Kalimpong, but investigating Western journalists in the foothills of the Himalayas in Assam, denying them an interview with the Dalai Lama, bugging their telephones, and in some instances physically impeding their investigations. Nehru wanted to ensure that nothing was published which in any way threw doubt on his 'Hindee Cheenee Bhai Bhai' policy and that infamous 1954 treaty with China in which Nehru accepted Chinese sovereignty over Tibet.

When Nehru did speak, it was to announce that the Dalai Lama could enjoy sanctuary on Indian soil, on the understanding that he did not make any political statements, i.e. no criticism of China's role in Tibet. Nehru got no thanks from his Chinese friends, who now openly accused India of being party to Western Imperialist interference in free Tibet. Worse was to come. General Thimayya finally persuaded Nehru to allow the Indian Army to send a patrol of infantry up through Ladakh and onto the Aksai Chin plateau. The Indians were captured by the PLA. When members of the Lok Sabha, India's lower house, questioned Nehru about relations with China, Nehru deceived parliament and kept the border incident secret. The cat was let out of the bag when the Indian prisoners were released, in a half starved condition, after being beaten and ill-treated by the Chinese.

And so India's relations with China deteriorated. Nehru demanded that the Chinese withdraw from the Aksai Chin, and to reinforce his demands sent a further patrol into the area. They were fired on by the Chinese PLA, several were killed, and the rest captured. Nehru bleated that he had been deceived by communist China.

In late summer 1959, the Indian Himalayan Institute announced that they were going to make an attempt on Everest, and their expedition would include all branches of the Indian armed forces, led by Brigadier Gyan Singh. Listed amongst expedition personnel was a civilian mountaineer, Keki Bunshah, a Bombay lawyer who was to have joined my expedition, and whom the Chinese, at Taklakot, regarded as an Indian spy. Unknown not only to India, but to the world at large, the Chinese were getting into mountaineering, with the sole purpose of placing a few party members on the summit of Everest. 'Why? What was the political motive?' as my old sparring partners Smoothy and the Pheasant Plucker would have enquired.

The Chinese brought forward their plans by a year, and did their best to get to the top of Everest before the Indian expedition, which was planned for pre-monsoon 1960. The Chinese effort was no orthodox climbing expedition. It was a full-blown PLA military operation, with a PLA general in command. More than 200 of what the Chinese called 'Masters of Sport' (none of them mountaineers) and supporting athletes were to do the climbing, backed up by two battalions of the PLA (1,500 men) with 400 trucks. A special road was built to the Rongbuk lamasery at the foot of Everest on the Tibetan side.

The Indians on the Nepal side of Everest, who were totally unaware of the Chinese presence on the mountain, were initially a month behind them, but actually caught up with the Chinese by the time the PLA expedition was set to go for the summit. The two expeditions were separated by only a few hundred yards of mountain. In Delhi, Chou En-lai arrived and proceeded to tell Nehru in no uncertain terms that China would not vacate the Askai Chin plateau, and further claimed more than 25,000 square miles of Indian territory in NEFA. Comrade Chou then flew to Kathmandu and, at the precise moment when the Chinese and Indian teams were on the mountain, tried to persuade the Nepalese government to transfer sovereignty of the Khumbu Valley (i.e. Nepal side of Everest) to China. It is my considered opinion that if the Nepal government had acquiesced to this demand, China would have declared the Indian expedition (which in Chinese eyes was a military operation) illegal and would have forced it to withdraw from the mountain.

The government of Nepal was made of sterner stuff (at that time – they weakened in their dealings with China at a later date) and refused to hand over their side of Everest to the Chinese. In due course, the Indian party of experienced mountaineers, only a few hundred feet short of the summit, admitted defeat due to bad weather. The Chinese claimed in 1961 to have conquered Everest at precisely that same time. (Thanks to the Leading Role of the Party, yes, that is how they announced it.) According to the Chinese, they had been organising their expedition for two years. The three who reached the summit had never climbed a mountain when the project was mooted two years earlier. If you believe that, then you will believe anything.

It is interesting to note that the Chinese stated that for their training, they made ascents of both Minya Konka and Mustagh Ata. I recalled that during my interrogations I had told the Chinese that the CIA had intended dropping nuclear powered surveillance devices on both Minya Konka and Mustagh Ata. Why were the Chinese on Everest, when they told me only three years before they started their Everest preparations that they did not believe in Himalayan climbing expeditions? Could they, perhaps, have been trying to locate and retrieve the CIA surveillance apparatus I had told them Hillary and Tenzing had placed on the summit of Everest, aimed in the direction of Lop Nor?

I can, with due lack of modesty, formally claim that when subjected to interrogation by the Chinese in south-west Tibet in 1955, I placed in their minds the seeds for what was to become the largest, most expensive and most incompetent attempt on Mount Everest ever made. This was confirmed by a Kuomintang agent I met in 1976, who said that the assault on Everest was cover for a huge military exercise designed to locate and destroy American surveillance equipment. 'It failed on all accounts,' he said. 'They didn't even get to the top of the mountain.'

By 1962, American spy planes were flying over China with Taiwanese pilots. The Chinese shot down at least four of them. Peking forgot Everest for another fifteen years. There was no need to collect that CIA spy machine of the summit of Chomolungma. It was obsolete, the U2s had seen to that. In the meantime there were border clashes between Chinese and Indian troops, and in October 1962 the conflict erupted into open warfare. The Chinese, claiming they were responding to Indian aggression, invaded both the Askai Chin plateau and NEFA. Nehru announced that the Indian Army was going to evict the Chinese invaders from Indian territory. He even announced the date; a faux pas which must have pleased the PLA military planners in Peking enormously.

The Indian Army in Ladakh and in NEFA was under-strength, under-equipped and furnished with obsolescent weapons, as the Chinese well knew. Indian lack of artillery in NEFA gave the Chinese an enormous advantage when the fighting commenced. The Chinese learned that the Indian Army in NEFA possessed only two small lightweight pieces of artillery, and a handful of mortars, and about an hour's supply of ammunition for both types of weapon, if used in a sustained action. Thanks to this information, when the Chinese opened up their artillery bombardment from the top of the Thagla Ridge, looking down on the 'penny packet' Indian Army pockets of resistance, they brought into play 150 pieces of artillery and heavy mortars.

Brigadier John Dalvi, a close friend of Cricket Wallah, in command of the 7th Infantry Brigade, of the 4th Division of the Indian Army, facing the Chinese under the Thagla Ridge in NEFA, estimated that a full Chinese division of about 12,000 men swept down on his three under-strength battalions, which boasted less than 2,700 effectives. The Chinese also had a further full division in reserve. Dalvi had no reserves. According to Dalvi, the 7th Infantry Brigade suffered in excess of 90 per cent casualties. The two small artillery pieces were defended by a company of Gurkhas, who soon ran out of ammunition, and faced the advancing Chinese troops with the bayonet. There were no Gurkha survivors. The wounded froze to death in the night, Nehru having failed to supply the majority of his troops fighting at 16,000 feet in the Himalaya with tents, sleeping bags or warm winter clothing. They had just one blanket per man, for night temperatures well below freezing. For every Gurkha who died, at least three Chinese lay dead in front of the Indian positions. Brigadier John Dalvi, one of General Thimayya's protégés, whose warnings and pleas prior to battle had been ignored by Nehru, was captured by the Chinese and spent several months in prison in both Tibet and China.

My friend Cricket Wallah, Lieutenant-Colonel B.N. (Baij) Mehta, commanded the 1st Sikh Regiment in the 1962 battle for NEFA. He died facing the Chinese at Se-ha, to the south of the Thagla Ridge. Cricket Wallah (that's how I prefer to remember him) died a hero, a wasted life, a sacrifice on the altar of Nehru's blindness.

The Indian 4th Division was routed and forced back onto the plains at Tezpur. The Chinese invasion of NEFA was no hurried response to Indian border aggression as the Chinese alleged. The invasion was long-planned and well-planned, as the road they built through Tibet to the Thagla Ridge on the NEFA/Tibet border will testify. The Indians had no army in the field when the Chinese problem began on the NEFA border. When India did move, its army was handicapped by lack of roads for most of the way up to the frontier, and man-packing was the order of the day for the later stages of a journey which took three weeks.

The Chinese also struck simultaneously, hundreds of miles to the west on the Aksai Chin plateau, pushing the Indian Army back into Ladakh. Then quite remarkably the Chinese pulled back out of NEFA (but not off the Aksai Chin). Sophists say, 'China withdrew because she only wanted to teach India a lesson.' This is hogwash. The Chinese got out of NEFA because a new player had entered the game: John F. Kennedy. On the orders of President Kennedy, the CIA flew large air-drops of weapons and ammunition to the eastern provinces of Tibet, where the Khampa guerillas were interdicting the Chinese supply lines headed for the Thagla Ridge and NEFA. Dozens of air-drops of weapons were made into Tibet at that time. Good Old Charlie Brown's Company came up trumps for India in late 1962. The Chinese spearhead troops, by now almost on the Indian plain close to Tezpur, found that their victuals and ammunition supply was running low and very little was getting through. And there was another reason for the Chinese withdrawal.

Nehru, that self-appointed leader of the non-aligned states, committed an act which he kept secret to his grave. He wrote a memorandum to President Kennedy, asking the USA to go to war with China. What brought about Nehru's change of heart towards the so-called imperialist America? The non-aligned Third World nations had a great deal to do with Nehru's decision. In the United Nations nearly all of Nehru's non-aligned buddies sided with China. Nehru was bereft. As Machiavelli so wisely said, 'There is a need for nations to have allies and strong armies.' India had no allies and stood alone, and Nehru had shamefully run down and weakened the Indian Army since independence.

President Kennedy immediately ordered several squadrons of C130 transport aircraft, with American air crews, to be placed at the disposal of the Indian government. They were used to fly Indian reinforcements up to Tezpur in the east, and Leh and Ladakh in the west. Arms in abundance were flown to India from the USA. If that was not enough to persuade the Chinese communists that the USA would not countenance India falling into the Chinese sphere of influence, President Kennedy ordered a carrier task force up into the Bay of Bengal, within striking distance of the Chinese advance units. China took note and pulled out of NEFA. But to this day, the Chinese still occupy 15,000 square miles of Indian territory, an area twice the size of Wales. They never withdrew from the Aksai Chin Plateau, across which the Strategic Highway to west Tibet runs.

General Thimayya was recalled from premature retirement. He had the pleasure of seeing Nehru reluctantly dismiss Defence Minister Krishna Menon. Nehru's role as self-elected leader of the non-aligned states evaporated. He lost his charisma. He was a broken man. It was at this time that India began to enjoy real cabinet government. Nehru was dead within two years, laid low by the failure of his Hindee Cheenee Bhai Bhai policy, and his loss of face on the world stage. On October 16th 1964, my birthday, the Chinese detonated their first atomic bomb at Lop Nor. After his return to duty as Chief of General Staff of the Indian Army, General Thimayya set in motion the re-training and re-equipment of the Indian Army. That re-organisation revitalised India's armed forces. 'Timmy' was never to return to retirement. He died in harness (as I am sure he would have wished) on December 18th 1965, commanding the United Nations Peace Force in Cyprus.

In 1966 Mao Tse-tung embarked on the 'Cultural Revolution'. For the Chinese people it was a case of 'The World Turned Upside Down'. The Young Red Guards not only destroyed heritage and culture in China proper, and brought formal education to a standstill, they invaded Tibet and proceeded to tear down all the gompas and lamaseries. The full total of destructive sacrilege will never be truly known, but the figure the Chinese admit to of 2,400 destroyed monasteries including those at Taklakot and Jitkot, has been superseded by a figure from the Tibetan Government in Exile of 6,000.

When the Young Red Guards arrived in Lhasa, they accused the 'Pheasant Plucker' of failing to adopt politically correct revolutionary procedures against feudalist Tibet. Petitioning Mao's wife Chiang Ching (the main instigator and monitor of the Cultural Revolution), the Young Red Guards succeeded in having Comrade Mao demote General Chang. But such was the influence of the PLA, that Marshal Lin Piao, described as 'Comrade Mao's closest comrade in arms' had Chang restored to power in Tibet. The Young Red Guards responded by assassinating General Chang's PLA bodyguard, taking Chang captive. The PLA countered by massacring Young Red Guards, freeing General Chang in the process. Intent on vengeance, 'Pheasant Plucker' oversaw the slaughter of more than a thousand Young Red Guards. Their bodies, left to rot outside Lhasa, provided a 'Sky Burial' of all 'Sky Burials'. Vultures feasted and fattened themselves on the largest 'Chinese Take-away' in Tibetan gastronomic history.

In January 1993, official records smuggled to Hong Kong from the

Chinese province of Guangxi revealed that during the Cultural Revolution, Young Red Guard university students indulged in the ritual killing of college professors, their cadavers being hung on meat hooks in cafeterias. Flesh was sliced from the bodies of the allegedly anti-party 'politically incorrect' faculty members, cooked and eaten either on the premises, or sold 'To Go' on a take-away basis. 'Capitalist Roader Curry' and 'Counter-Revolutionary Ravioli' were presumably top of the menu.

More than a million Tibetan people have died since the Chinese invaded Tibet in 1950. The eastern provinces of Tibet, which are rich in forests and minerals, are being stripped by the Chinese of raw materials at a rate of twenty billion dollars' worth a year. Peking refers to Tibet as 'the Great Western Treasure House'.

In 1976, both Mao Tse-tung and Chou En-lai died. Mao's widow Chiang Ching tried to usurp power, with a handful of her cronies, known as 'The Gang of Four'. They were overthrown, arrested, tried, found guilty of crimes against the state and sentenced to life imprisonment.

1979 saw Deng Xiaoping's ascendance. He loosened the economic reins, allowed foreign investment and a modicum of free expression by the Chinese people. In 1987–8 there was open rioting in Lhasa against Chinese rule in Tibet. In 1989 the Panchen Lama, long suspected of being a Chinese stooge, died at Shigatse. He had just made the first anti-Chinese speech of his life. Within forty-eight hours he was dead, due to a heart condition, according to the Chinese. The shrewdest and most knowledgeable Tibet watchers believe that the Panchen Lama was poisoned. With the Dalai Lama in exile in India, refusing Chinese overtures for him to return to Tibet, the Chinese could not afford to have a dissident Panchen Lama spreading liberal anti-Chinese ideas. Panchen Lamas have been poisoned in the past. It's an occupational hazard.

The call for greater democracy in China proper proved too strong for Comrade Deng to tolerate. Unable to force the PLA to open fire on the hundred thousand or so students, workers and intellectuals assembled in Tiananmen Square, he handed control into the hands of one of the PLA's most rabid butchers, retired Marshal Yang Shangkun. Yang ordered the immediate arrest and execution of at least forty middle-ranking army officers, who had refused to open fire on the Chinese people. Yang had evidently read the history of the Royal Navy, and how for alleged cowardice in the face of the enemy at the Battle of Minorca, Admiral Bing was executed by firing squad. Voltaire commented, succinctly, 'The English now and again shoot an admiral, to encourage the others.' The PLA officer cadres were presumably so encouraged. Yang sent in a close relative, a PLA general, on 4 June 1989 with an army ordered to shoot on sight. The number killed in Tiananmen Square and surrounding streets certainly exceeds two thousand. A massive clamp-down took place, and the Chinese pro-democracy movement went underground. It is estimated that at least a thousand people were executed in the following months.

After the Tiananmen Square massacre, the civilian censor on the editorial board of the *Peking Daily News* was replaced not by a party political commissar, but by three officers of the PLA. Look to education. For the new influx of students to Peking University, there is an unexpected and unwelcome hurdle to cross. They must now be inducted for a year's service and 'correction of political attitudes' in the PLA. This has never before occurred in the history of communist China. Thus the Central Committee has bowed the knee to the PLA. No major decision can now be made in Peking without the say so of the PLA. Reduced in size and to some extent ridiculed as inefficient and under-educated during the late 1980s, the PLA is I believe in the process of taking over the reins of power in communist China. All party cadres graduating out of Peking University will in future be loyal not to the Central Committee, but to the PLA. In February 1990 the PLA's *Liberation Daily* ran the banner headline, 'The Future Belongs to Us'.

How does all this affect India and Nepal? Very ominous writing is on the wall. A long-term trade treaty between Nepal and India has recently expired. One of the provisos of the treaty was that India would be the sole supplier of arms and ammunition to the Nepalese forces. The King of Nepal secretly abrogated the treaty by purchasing anti-aircraft guns from China. India retaliated by sealing off Nepal's borders when their trade treaty expired. Fortunately for both Nepal and India, King Bihendra's rule as an autocrat (all political parties being banned) came to an end in 1990 when crowds of protesters filled the streets. King Bihendra bowed to popular will and ordered free elections. The largest political party in Nepal is now the Communist Party.

India lifted the trade embargo and signed a new trade treaty. In 1995 the Nepalese Communist Party's 'Youth Section' proclaimed solidarity with Peru's 'Shining Path' Marxist revolutionary guerillas. The Chinese already have a road across the Himalaya to Nepal's capital Kathmandu. Three years ago, King Bihendra acquiesced to a Chinese suggestion that a new road be built, joining east and west Nepal along a 500-mile stretch of foothill territory on the south side of the Himalaya, connected to the Lhasa-Kathmandu road.

Nepal applied for and obtained a promise of billions of dollars from the World Bank for this highly suspect project. India's then Prime Minister Rajiv Gandhi lobbied hard against the proposal, and the World Bank backed down. India's unease about this proposed lateral road is understandable when one remembers the outcome of the Chinese Strategic Highway to west Tibet. The proposed new road would offer an aggressive China the means to invade Nepal, and then, south of Kathmandu, spread east and west over a 500-mile front, facing the Indian Gangetic plain.

When the World Bank withdrew its financial support for the project, China, its economy in a mess and short of foreign hard currency, promptly offered to build that strategic road, using PLA engineers and Chinese labour 'Free, Gratis And For Nothing'. What is the purpose? What is the political motive?, as my old sparring partner the Pheasant Plucking General Chang Kuo-hua would have asked. Work it out for yourself. The Nepal 'East to West Highway' is now under construction, much to the discomfort of both the Indian government and the Indian Army.

Would India be able to defend herself against further Chinese territorial aggression in the future? The Indian Army of today is a different kettle of fish from that of the years 1947 to 1962. It is more than a million-strong, well-trained and well-equipped. The Indian Army officer corps of today, trained at Wellington Military College, can be described in one word, and that word is 'Superlative'. It is the finest and most professional fighting force in Asia. If the Chinese PLA decided to lock horns with today's Indian Army, the PLA would in my opinion receive a very bloody nose.

China's intention would probably be not to invade India, but to establish a threat, a destabilising factor, just over the border with India. At the present time there are ethnic riots in the Punjab, Jammu and Kashmir, and tension between India and Pakistan. There is a large and ever increasing Communist Party in India, and a burgeoning Communist Party in Nepal. For India the outlook looks unsettled for the near future. China can be expected to take advantage of India's predicament if such intervention coincides with China's aims, or helps divert Chinese public attention away from China's internal political problems, as did the 1950 invasion of Tibet.

And so I come to the end of my story about espionage in communist-occupied Tibet. It might puzzle my reader, as it has puzzled me, as to why I, a rank amateur, should have prevailed over the Chinese communists in Tibet. Might I offer as an explanation my equivalent of Parkinson's Law and the Peter Principle? It is Wignall's First Law of Adversarial Conflict, and it states, 'VICTORY GOES TO THE SIDE THAT DISPLAYS THE LESSER DEGREE OF INCOMPETENCE'.

Epilogue – The Sleeping Giant Awakes

The growing strength of China's military might arouse fear amongst her neighbours. Political figures may be removed from office, or convicted of corruption and imprisoned, but the widespread influence and corruption of China's top generals does not only go unpunished, it is ignored, due to the immense powers these new warlords possess. Sun Yat-sen promised an end to the warlords. They haven't come back; they never went away.

The most open and blatant of the warlords are those in command of the PLA in Sinkiang, Tibet, and the maritime provinces to the south of Hong Kong. Each general regards the province under his command as a personal fiefdom, from which tribute is exacted.

The warlords in command of the PLA and the Chinese Navy in the south-eastern coastal provinces of China are accused of turning a blind eye to open piracy committed by armed Chinese vessels which intercept ships sailing south from Japan via Hong Kong, heading for ports in Vietnam, Malaysia and Singapore. The Chinese pirates know which ships carry valuable cargoes such as automobiles and sophisticated electronic merchandise, via their undercover agents in Hong Kong who gain access to cargo manifests of all ships sailing into Hong Kong to discharge part of their cargo on their voyage south.

The pirate ships are fast and well-armed, with ostensibly civilian crews. They put out of South China ports to intercept these rich vessels at gunpoint. The pirated ships are taken into Chinese ports and stripped of their cargoes. Some crews are released and some just vanish. Once ashore, the pirate crews divest themselves of their civilian clothes and put on their PLA or Chinese Navy uniforms. The captured vessels are repainted, their names changed and they are issued with official Chinese registration papers. Thereafter they ply trade along Chinese coastal waters.

Calls from the international community for China to take action against this flagrant piracy are countered by indignant denials. Piracy on the high seas is not something the Central Committee of the People's Republic of China would openly espouse. The truth is that the Chinese authorities in Peking have only limited control over the actions of their provincial warlords. The generals and admirals are in it up to their necks.

One Chinese general has used his share of ill-gotten gains from piracy to set up factories in the free trade zone adjacent to Hong Kong. He has built himself a villa which looks more like a palace, and all his commercial operations are overseen by hand-picked PLA officers. The Central Committee needed the PLA to carry out the massacre in Tiananmen Square and crush the pro-democracy movement. The PLA is exacting its price. Cuts in the military budget were reversed after Tiananmen Square. No major policy decisions can be made by Peking's Central Committee without deferring to the warlords. Prophetically, after Tiananmen Square the PLA's own newspaper, *The Liberation Daily*, ran a banner headline, 'The Future Belongs to Us'. In October 1995 the Institute for Strategic Studies announced that Chinese published expenditure on its military was understated. China is spending four times her quoted figures on her armed forces.

There is an age-old maxim: 'Create a political or military vacuum and someone will fill it'. The wisdom of that saying was confirmed after the Americans vacated their huge naval base at Subic Bay in the Philippines and the Russians departed from their naval base at Camrahn Bay in Vietnam. Communist China wasted no time in filling the vacuum. The Chinese Navy, acting under Central Committee orders, is dispatching naval frigates and submarines far from her shores into what is recognised by international law as the waters of her neighbours, laying claim to the whole of the Spratly group of islands. In 1995 the Philippine Navy arrested Chinese officials in occupation of a coral atoll 18 miles inside the Philippines' 200-mile territorial waters, a clear 800 miles from China's shores.

The Spratlys, believed to be rich in oil-bearing strata, are claimed not only by the Philippines and China, but also by Vietnam, Malaysia, Singapore and Brunei. China has threatened to go to war to wrest the Spratlys from 'the threat of foreign domination'.

To emphasise her growing military power China now issues threats against the US Navy. In 1995 an American carrier group headed by the carrier USS *Kitty Hawk*, operating in international waters, detected a submarine. Aircraft were launched when the submarine entered an area in which the *Kitty Hawk* was deemed to be under threat. Sonar buoys were dropped into the sea and technical data returned from the sonar buoys confirmed that the *Kitty Hawk* was being closely shadowed by a Chinese nuclear submarine. The submarine, aware from the sonar buoy 'pings' that she was under surveillance, turned away and headed into China's territorial waters. China launched aircraft which flew within sight of the *Kitty Hawk*, until they were warned off by USN F14 fighter aircraft. China later issued a threat to use force if such an incident recurred.

When the President of the Chinese Republic of Taiwan was warmly welcomed as an official visitor to the US, China responded with angry denunciations of the US and with test-firing long-range ballistic missiles which passed close to the coast of Taiwan. China is developing a ballistic missile which is believed to be capable of targeting Europe or the US.

India and China occasionally hold meetings to try to demarcate a

Himalayan border acceptable to both parties, but failure is always ensured by China's refusal to return to India the strategic Aksai Chin plateau which China occupied during her border war with India. Human rights issues dog relations with China. Dissidents are imprisoned and tortured on mainland China. Women are forced to undergo forced abortions. Chinese doctors performing the operations have admitted that they sell the aborted foetuses in packs of ten, to be cooked and eaten. One doctor when questioned by a western journalist not only admitted to the practice, but added that human placenta made a very good base for noodle soup.

In Tibet the six million Tibetan population is outnumbered by seven million Chinese. China is demanding that all Tibetan children living in exile in India be returned to Tibet for a 'proper' education, in which they would be taught to speak Chinese and punished if they spoke their own language. The world is witnessing genocide in Tibet; a two thousand-year-old culture is being destroyed. The West does nothing. Why? The answer is commerce. If a profit can be made, some people will trade with Satan himself.

The future leadership of China is a constant issue of conjecture. The next leader of communist China might be a member of the Central Committee. The next leader but one could be a high-ranking general in the PLA. An economically strong military dictatorship is on the cards. It could happen. A strong China has always been an expansionist China.

My story was about to go into print when I received the following information from the Tibet Support Group UK and *World Tibet Network News* Dharamsala, India. The district administration and the Tibetan government in exile have chalked out a 4 million rupee security plan to deal with the possibility of a threat to the Dalai Lama's life. The plan comes in the wake of the arrest of three Chinese spies. Two of the spies, Tibetan by birth, were former soldiers in China's People's Liberation Army in Tibet. The security plan agreed upon at a high-level meeting envisages a bulletproof Mercedes car for the Dalai Lama. The Indian government will bear the expense.

Further security measures will include X-ray baggage scanners, metal detectors on door-frames, a more secure boundary wall, and arrangements for adequately illuminating the entire palace complex of the Tibetan religious and temporal authorities. Dharamsala Superintendent of Police, Mr R. K. Singh, declined to comment on details of the meeting, but reliable sources said that all Tibetans who entered India after 1975 will not be allowed to work in the palace. Special passes will be issued to palace staff, and extra police forces will be deployed in the area.

The personal drivers of the Dalai Lama have already been sent on an intensive course in defensive driving at the National Security training camp at Maneswar in Haryana. The alleged Chinese spies were observed stalking the movements of the Dalai Lama. They had been illegally infiltrated into India the previous December. Taking the espionage case seriously, the authorities have decided to upgrade intelligence networks in the district, and Establishment 22, a special frontier force of Tibetans, has been placed on alert. The three Tibetans, including a girl, were arrested under the Foreigner Act of 21 November, on charges of spying for China. Though the Indian police and Tibetan officials are tight-lipped after China's protest to New Delhi for reporting the incident in the media, interrogation reports have confirmed that Tsering Samten, aged twenty-five, and Phuntsok, aged twenty-six, were indeed involved in espionage. Copies of the interrogation reports have been sent to the Indian Cabinet Secretariat. These state that of the three, Samten was being groomed by Chinese authorities for 'bigger assignments'. Samten confessed that he was sent to India by a PLA army official of high rank. It was confirmed that Samten and Phuntsok had been trained in the use of weapons. Samten also stated that the senior PLA officer who briefed him in China had told him that the Dalai Lama's Establishment 22 Defence Force had already been infiltrated by Chinese PLA spies.

Why should the Chinese consider assassinating His Holiness the Dalai Lama? The answer is easy. The Dalai Lama recently initiated the new Panchen Lama, a six-year-old boy, as reincarnation of the Panchen Lama who died in 1989 (believed by many, including me, to have been poisoned by the Chinese due to his anti-Chinese statements). Peking retaliated by seizing the new Panchen Lama and his entourage in Tibet. This was followed by Peking's announcement that China had selected a new Panchen Lama, and that he was in Chinese custody, surrounded by pro-Chinese lamas.

The Fifth Dalai Lama instituted the religious position of the first Panchen Lama as a means of preventing in-fighting between religious factions, which might attempt to control his own reincarnation as the next Dalai Lama. The system has worked well for several centuries. An adult Dalai Lama initiates a child Panchen Lama. On the death of the Dalai Lama, the Panchen Lama initiates the next Dalai Lama. This procedure is necessary because the group of high-ranking lamas searching for a reincarnated Dalai Lama or Panchen Lama, on occasion come up with three choices. Hence the need for a higher authority to make the final decision.

With a phoney Panchen Lama in their control, when the Dalai Lama dies, his successor would be chosen by pro-Chinese stooge lamas, and the final initiation would be proclaimed by the stooge Panchen Lama. This would enable China to take complete control of the Tibetan Lamaistic Branch of the Buddhist faith. The true religion would be re-written in a 'Politically Correct' form, favourable to the perpetuation of Chinese communist occupation of Tibet. Political correctness is toxic waste of the mind, a form of 'book burning without the matches'. The Chinese communists are expert at it. Political correctness was in fact invented by Chairman Mao Tse-tung.

The Chinese would have to make the death of the Dalai Lama appear to be by natural causes; nothing so crude as the knife, the gun or the bomb. They are pastmasters at poisoning, and particularly expert in the use of ricin, a white powder derived from castor-oil beans. Ricin is 6,000 time more poisonous than cyanide. A prick from a needle coated in ricin would result in death. There is no known antidote.

The chinese communists have presumably arrived at 'The Final Solution to the Dalai Lama Problem'.

ASSASSINATION

Readers wishing to learn more about current affairs relating to His Holiness the Dalai Lama, and to the plight of the Tibetan people can obtain an information pack from:

The Tibet Support Group UK
9 Islington Green
London
N1 2XH